Praise for *Archie and Amélie*

"As compelling as a smoldering historical novel . . . Passion, marriage, and scandal . . . all against a glittery backdrop of New York mansions, Boston town houses, and Parisian hotels."

—*Boston Globe*

"Thanks to the vividness of its subject matter and the lucidity of its style, [*Archie and Amélie*] engages its readers in the initially charming and ultimately harrowing tale of the marriage between two self-willed and self-absorbed thoroughbreds."

—Francine Prose, *Washington Post*

"Sex, scandal and mental illness in the Gilded Age . . . Amélie comes across as the female version of F. Scott Fitzgerald with a touch of Madonna."

—*USA Today*

"Wonderfully entertaining . . . This is an absorbing book, never betraying the sweat of research. The romance and excess of the Gilded Age is deftly drawn and the characters are vividly profiled. Hollywood should grab the story at once, but Hollywood would probably ruin it."

—*Washington Times*

"Compulsively readable . . . turn-of-the-century New York meets post-antebellum South and fireworks do ensue."

—*Virginia Living*

"Enchanting . . . An engrossing story told vividly and accurately. Lucey has given us an artistically composed and exhaustively researched story of the tragic marriage of two brilliant and spirited denizens of the Gilded Age whose lives, despite every gift the gods could shower upon them in fortune and talent, were reduced to ashes by drugs and madness."

—Louis Auchincloss

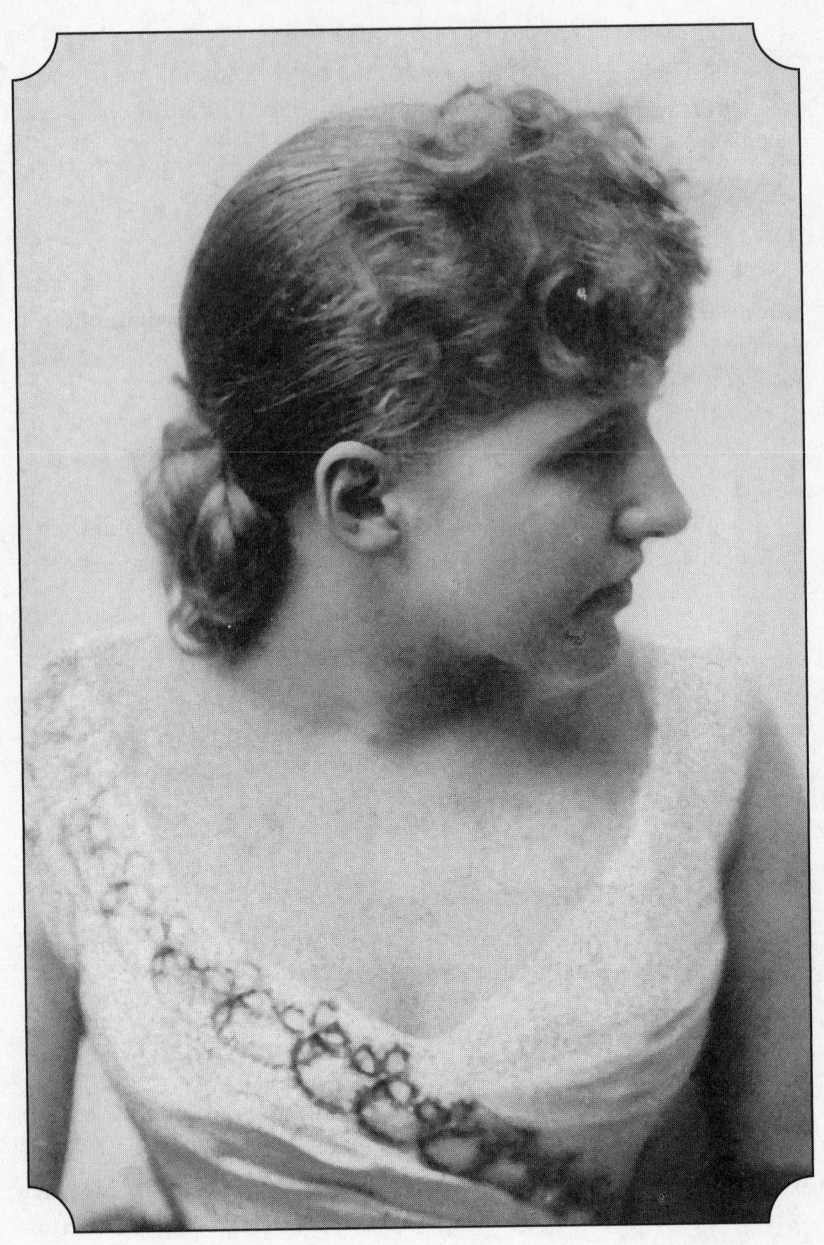

Archie

AND

Amélie

Love and Madness in the Gilded Age

Donna M. Lucey

THREE RIVERS PRESS • NEW YORK

Published in the United States by Three Rivers Press, an imprint of the Crown Publishing Group, a division of Random House, Inc., New York.
www.crownpublishing.com

Three Rivers Press and the Tugboat design are registered trademarks of Random House, Inc.

Originally published in hardcover in the United States by Harmony Books, an imprint of the Crown Publishing Group, a division of Random House, Inc., New York, in 2006.

Library of Congress Cataloging-in-Publication Data
Lucey, Donna M., 1951–
Archie and Amélie : love and madness in the Gilded Age / Donna M. Lucey. — 1st ed.
p. cm.
Includes bibliographical references.
1. Rives, Amélie, 1863–1945. 2. Novelists, American—19th century—Biography.
3. Chaloner, John Armstrong, 1862–1935. I. Title.
PS3093.A5L83 2006
818'.409—dc22
[B]

ISBN 978-0-307-35145-6

Frontispiece: Amélie Rives (UVA Library)

Printed in the United States of America

10 9 8 7 6 5 4 3 2 1

First Paperback Edition

For Henry, with love

CONTENTS

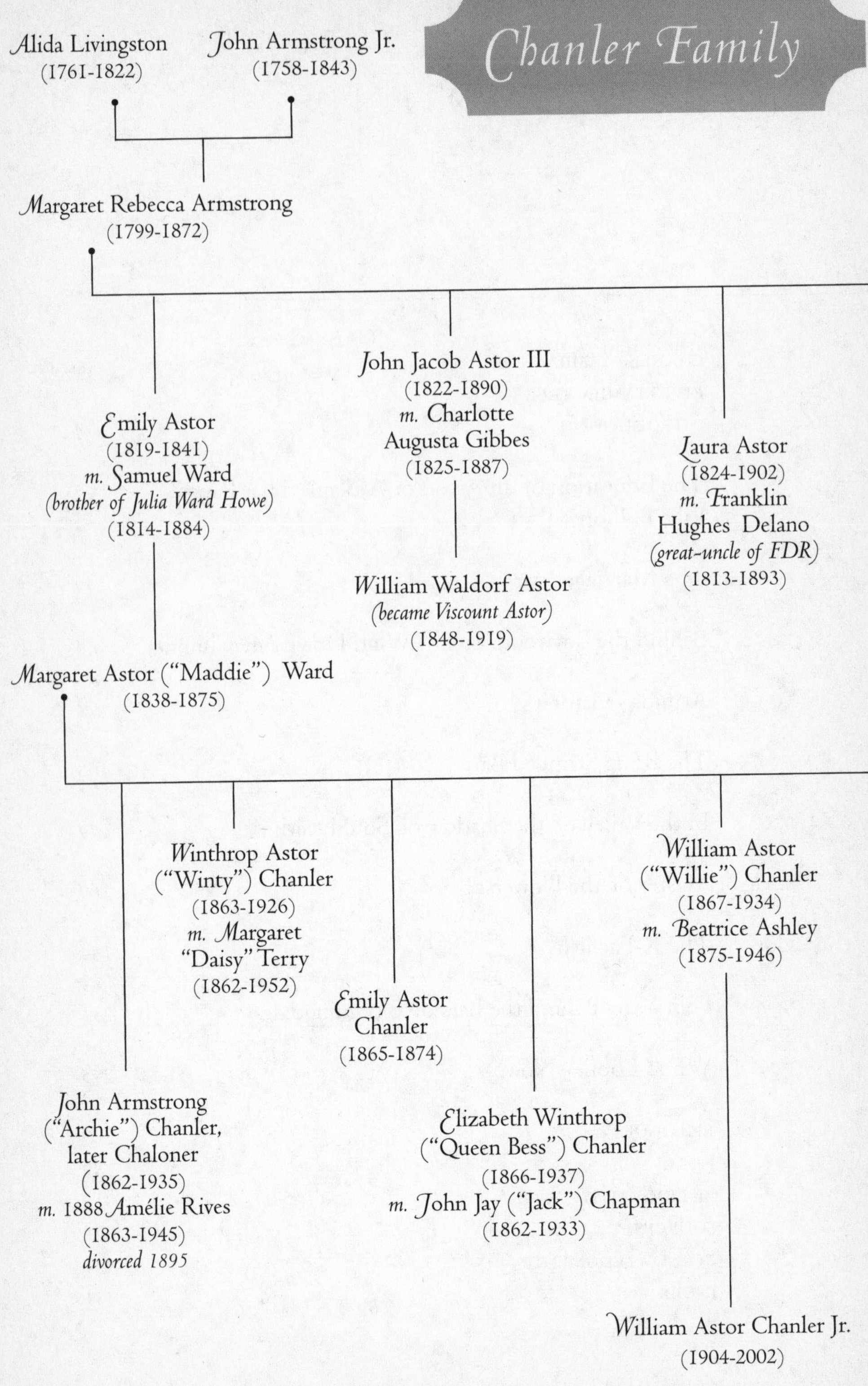

Chanler Family
Alida Livingston
(1761-1822)
John Armstrong Jr.
(1758-1843)
Margaret Rebecca Armstrong
(1799-1872)
Emily Astor
(1819-1841)
m. Samuel Ward
(brother of Julia Ward Howe)
(1814-1884)
John Jacob Astor III
(1822-1890)
m. Charlotte
Augusta Gibbes
(1825-1887)
William Waldorf Astor
(became Viscount Astor)
(1848-1919)
Laura Astor
(1824-1902)
m. Franklin
Hughes Delano
(great-uncle of FDR)
(1813-1893)
Margaret Astor ("Maddie") Ward
(1838-1875)
John Armstrong
("Archie") Chanler,
later Chaloner
(1862-1935)
m. 1888 Amélie Rives
(1863-1945)
divorced 1895
Winthrop Astor
("Winty") Chanler
(1863-1926)
m. Margaret
"Daisy" Terry
(1862-1952)
Emily Astor
Chanler
(1865-1874)
Elizabeth Winthrop
("Queen Bess") Chanler
(1866-1937)
m. John Jay ("Jack") Chapman
(1862-1933)
William Astor
("Willie") Chanler
(1867-1934)
m. Beatrice Ashley
(1875-1946)
William Astor Chanler Jr.
(1904-2002)

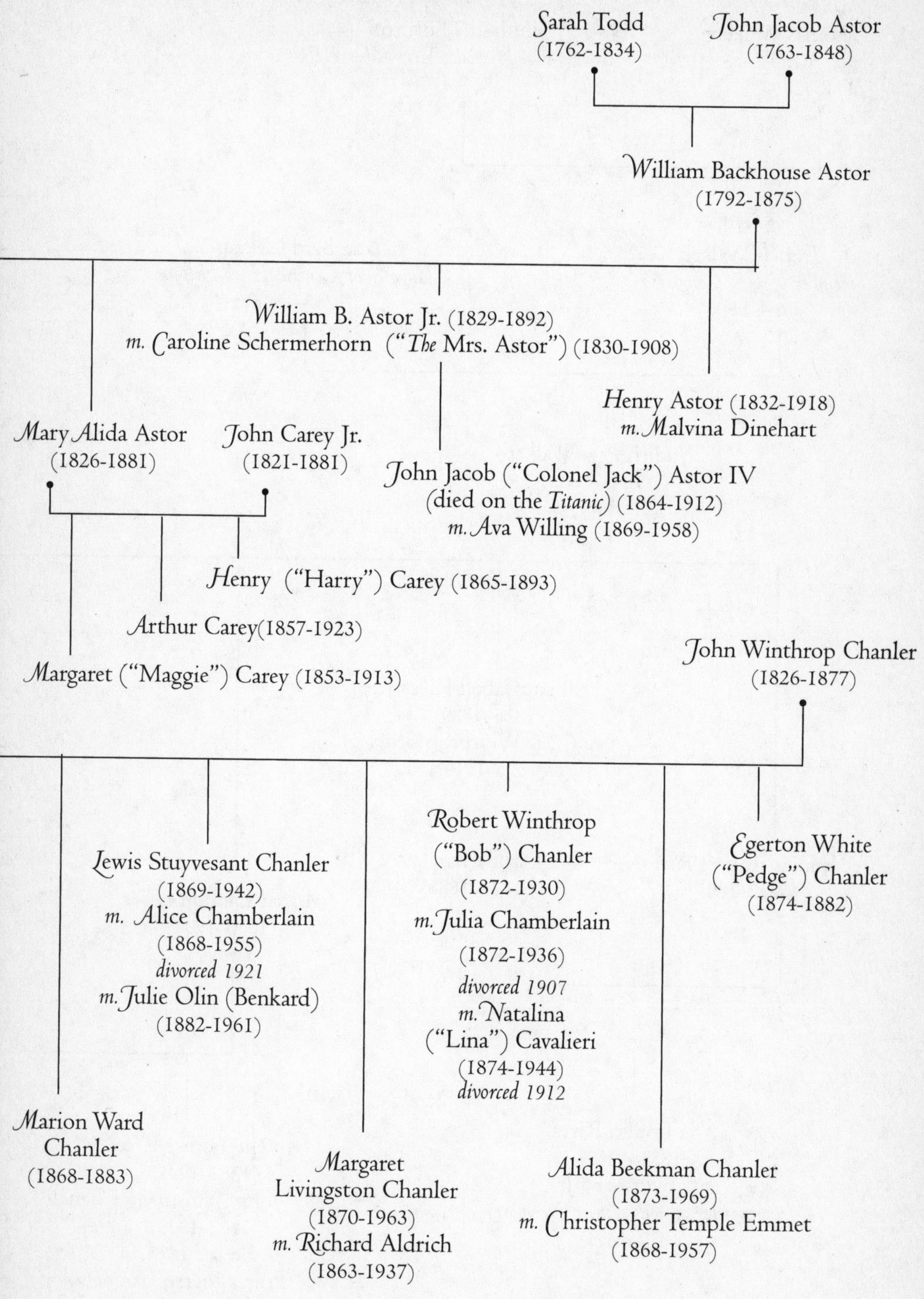

Sarah Todd
(1762-1834)
John Jacob Astor
(1763-1848)
William Backhouse Astor
(1792-1875)
William B. Astor Jr. (1829-1892)
m. Caroline Schermerhorn ("The Mrs. Astor") (1830-1908)
Henry Astor (1832-1918)
m. Malvina Dinehart
Mary Alida Astor
(1826-1881)
John Carey Jr.
(1821-1881)
John Jacob ("Colonel Jack") Astor IV
(died on the Titanic) (1864-1912)
m. Ava Willing (1869-1958)
Henry ("Harry") Carey (1865-1893)
Arthur Carey(1857-1923)
John Winthrop Chanler
(1826-1877)
Margaret ("Maggie") Carey (1853-1913)
Robert Winthrop
("Bob") Chanler
(1872-1930)
m. Julia Chamberlain
(1872-1936)
divorced 1907
m. Natalina
("Lina") Cavalieri
(1874-1944)
divorced 1912
Lewis Stuyvesant Chanler
(1869-1942)
m. Alice Chamberlain
(1868-1955)
divorced 1921
m. Julie Olin (Benkard)
(1882-1961)
Egerton White
("Pedge") Chanler
(1874-1882)
Marion Ward
Chanler
(1868-1883)
Margaret
Livingston Chanler
(1870-1963)
m. Richard Aldrich
(1863-1937)
Alida Beekman Chanler
(1873-1969)
m. Christopher Temple Emmet
(1868-1957)

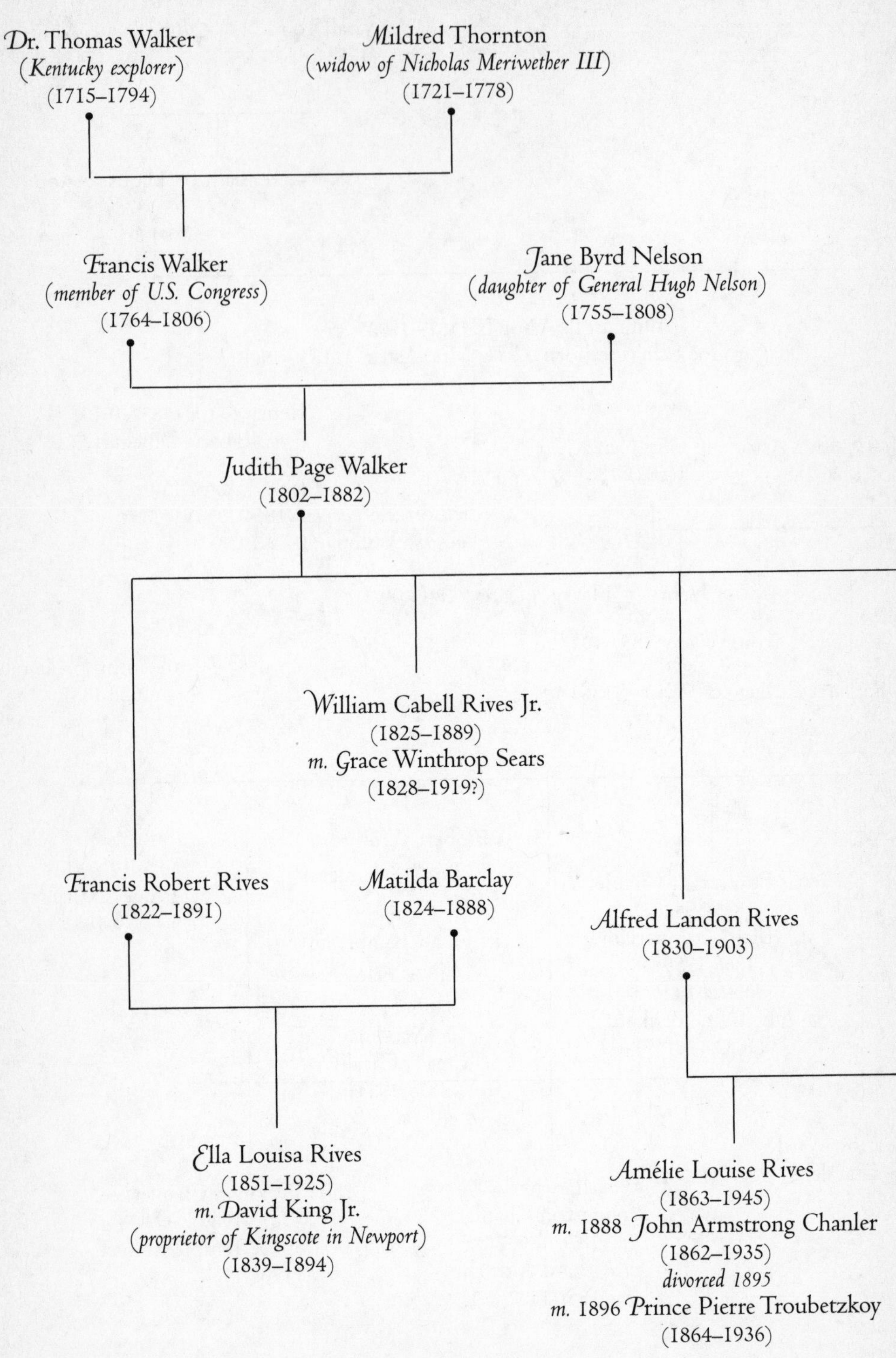
Dr. Thomas Walker
(Kentucky explorer)
(1715–1794)
Mildred Thornton
(widow of Nicholas Meriwether III)
(1721–1778)
Francis Walker
(member of U.S. Congress)
(1764–1806)
Jane Byrd Nelson
(daughter of General Hugh Nelson)
(1755–1808)
Judith Page Walker
(1802–1882)
William Cabell Rives Jr.
(1825–1889)
m. Grace Winthrop Sears
(1828–1919?)
Francis Robert Rives
(1822–1891)
Matilda Barclay
(1824–1888)
Alfred Landon Rives
(1830–1903)
Ella Louisa Rives
(1851–1925)
m. David King Jr.
(proprietor of Kingscote in Newport)
(1839–1894)
Amélie Louise Rives
(1863–1945)
m. 1888 John Armstrong Chanler
(1862–1935)
divorced 1895
m. 1896 Prince Pierre Troubetzkoy
(1864–1936)

Rives Family

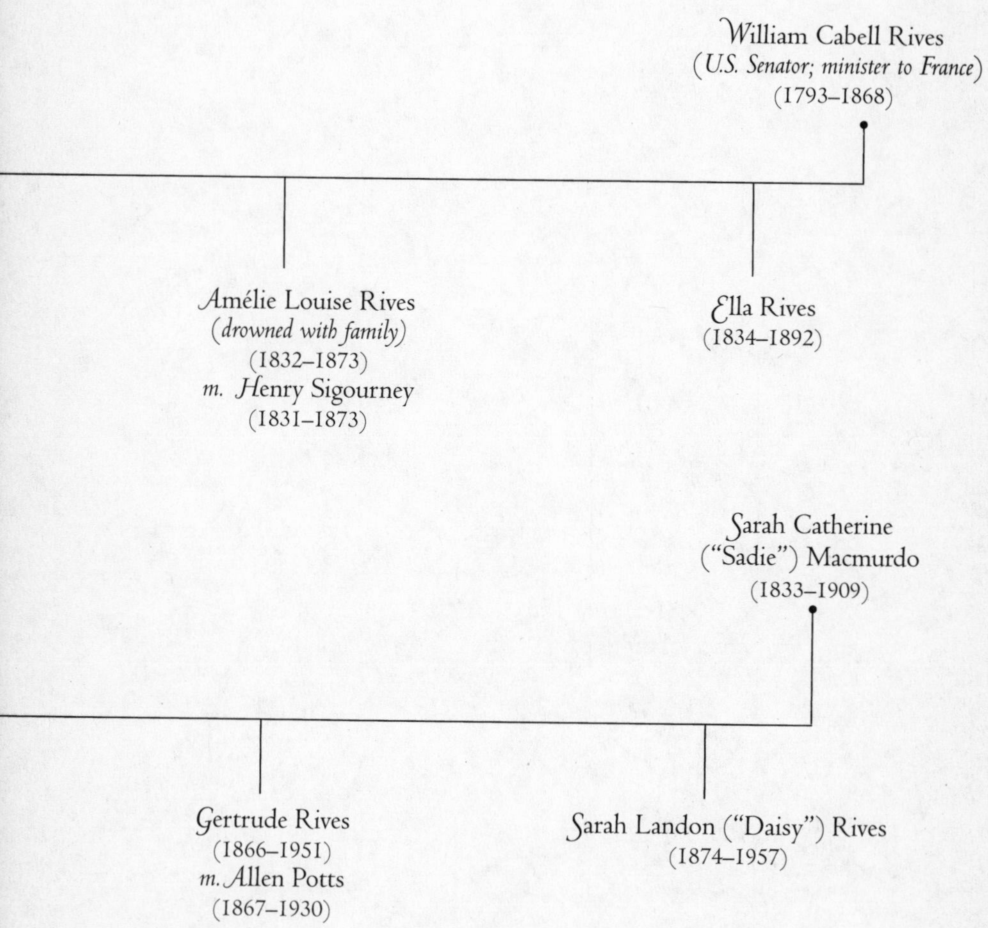

INTRODUCTION

On the eve of Thanksgiving in 1900, a distinguished figure walked out of the gates of Bloomingdale Asylum, the madhouse for the rich just outside of New York City. The thirty-eight-year-old man, smartly dressed in a black fedora, a navy blue melton overcoat, and a dark satin four-in-hand tie, could easily have been mistaken for a doctor who had just completed his rounds. Carrying a cane, he walked purposefully down the street and disappeared from sight. By train he made his way into the city, hailed a hansom cab, and asked to be taken to the Jersey City ferry. He held a handkerchief to his face for the entire ride across town, as if he were ill—in fact, he feared being recognized. He was, after all, a prominent lawyer, industrialist, patron of the arts, and esteemed former member of the Union, Century, Knickerbocker, Racquet & Tennis, and Players clubs. His bloodlines couldn't have been bluer. He was an Astor—the great-great-grandson of John Jacob Astor and an heir to his millions. To the city's newspaper readers he was the man who had stunned the haute monde of the Gilded Age by marrying the scandalous (and gorgeous) bestselling author Amélie Rives of Virginia.

He was also a madman. Within days, newspapers all over the country trumpeted the news that, after nearly four years of forced incarceration, the high-society lunatic John Armstrong Chanler—"Archie" to his family and friends—had escaped from Bloomingdale Asylum and vanished into thin air. A manhunt failed to find any trace of Archie, and as his trail went cold, his friends could only assume that this hopeless paranoid, as he had been diagnosed, had taken his own life.

◆◆◆

I heard of Archie and Amélie while tramping across the Virginia countryside just down the road from where the couple lived in the 1880s and 1890s, in the horse country outside Charlottesville. I had been invited for an autumn afternoon of "beagling"—following a pack of hounds as they unsuccessfully tried to sniff out a rabbit. The point of beagling is not the hunt, but the walk through the enchanting landscape, amid the rolling hills of genteel historic estates, each of which contains a story. The most astonishing stories were attached to Archie and Amélie. There were tales of séances and ghosts, a murder, the mysterious burning of a church, a sensational lunacy trial, and a hauntingly beautiful, barely clad young woman prowling her gardens at night as if she were searching for something—or someone—or trying to walk off the effects of the morphine that was deranging her.

I was inclined to dismiss all this as the tall tales Virginians love to spin; but when I looked into these yarns, I found the proof that they were true in yellowing front pages with banner headlines, along with the letters, court papers, books, and manuscripts this extraordinary pair left behind. One of my informants on that autumn afternoon in the hills was a Rives herself, the wife of Amélie's distant cousin Barclay Rives, a horseman, raconteur, author, and enthusiastic collector of the odds and ends of local lore. Barclay later took me to see Castle Hill, the eighteenth-century Rives mansion where the couple was married in 1888. With Barclay as my guide, I was able to call on the now elderly folks who had known Archie and Amélie, and I visited the house where Archie supposedly killed a man with a single pistol shot to protect the life of a woman. The details of the story were vague, but there was nothing vague about the bizarre, six-pointed metal star that Archie ordered set in the floor on the spot where the victim fell. The current owner of the house dramatically pulled back the carpet to show me this outlandish monument to Astor nerve and marksmanship.

Barclay also recounted how, after Amélie's death, when new owners were clearing the outbuildings of Castle Hill, they came across a truly extraordinary work of art—a voluptuous nude portrait of

Amélie. What makes this charcoal drawing extraordinary is not that it is a nude, but that *it is a self-portrait.* Amélie signed and dated the drawing, and kept it long after she had burned other personal items of her tempestuous past. At the very least, we know that Amélie took seriously the notion of mapping the self. Perhaps she forgot this sketch when she consigned other items to the flames; but it is just as likely that she deliberately left it, so that future generations would know exactly why so many men came to grief—to heartbreak and madness and suicide—having fallen under the spell of the woman who wrote, "Passion is perfume and flame and is its own excuse and *raison d'être.*"

Archie and Amélie were young at the height of the Gilded Age. They were, perhaps, the most glamorous couple of that most glamorous age—the Scott and Zelda of the 1880s and 1890s, with the genders reversed. Amélie broke new literary ground with a series of bestselling novels that won the esteem of Henry James, Thomas Hardy, and Oscar Wilde, but scandalized polite society with her provocative evocations of feminine passion. In turn, Archie exuded a devil-may-care eccentricity, a trait that was both cherished and reviled in the upper reaches of Gilded Age society, where the code of social propriety was rigid, ruthless, and appallingly destructive.

As a child, Archie had grown up in New York and at Rokeby, the family's four-hundred-acre Hudson River estate. He and his siblings—a wild and willful bunch—were left in the care of nannies, tutors, and distant guardians. The scene at Rokeby was one of frenzied, nonstop activity (to an outsider it seemed more like chaos). Packs of hounds, ponies, cats, chickens, rabbits, and all manner of other pets accompanied the competitive and argumentative children. The house rules were simple: no hitting, no "showing off," and, as a precaution against long-windedness, "a bore must shut up."

Amélie was the offspring of an old-line Virginia family. Her godfather was Robert E. Lee. From a young age, she was both a fearless horsewoman and a natural writer. When she was around ten years old, her grandmother limited the amount of paper she could use; undeterred, Amélie took to writing on the five-inch hem of her starched petticoat. She had a flair for melodrama. She once frightened a playmate by asking, "Do you think if I drank a whole cupful of warm, bubbly blood, I would see a real fairy?" When, at twenty-four, Amélie met Archie, she was already an up-and-coming literary figure, with a story published in *The Atlantic Monthly* and a novel in progress. In the grip of both passion and creativity, Amélie recast the male character of her novel to resemble Archie. Published in April 1888, *The Quick or the Dead?* caused a scandal with its depiction of a woman's sexual desire for a man who was not her husband. The clergy denounced its "pantherish" carnality, the Astors cringed at the instantly recognizable portrait of one of their own in this work of "sensual rot," the public bought 300,000 copies, and a literary celebrity was born. With her violet eyes and ash-blond hair, Amélie was called, among other things, "a sizzling vessel of molten lava."

Their love story was front-page news, and this golden couple appeared to live in a cocoon of success and celebrity—until the inevitable, spectacular fall. On the surface, the lives of Archie and Amélie played out like a bad Hollywood melodrama, with retribution dutifully arriving in the wake of fame, fortune, and vanity. At least that is the version of their tale that made it into the headlines. Their private papers revealed a deeper story—gripping, poignant, and terribly tragic—of the cruelty of money and class, the destructive power of passion, and the dangers of snubbing one's nose at a prominent family who could, with casual ease, bend the law enough to put a man behind the bars of an asylum and keep him there.

But for a time their lives had the shape of a fairy tale, beginning, as a fairy tale might, at a lavish Newport ball for the richest young people on the continent, in whose well-ordered universe every inhabitant had an ordained place, where marriage was a transaction between clans as in feudal kingdoms of old, until Fate spoke in the alluring form of a lost red satin slipper skidding improbably across a crowded dance floor. It belonged to the fairest.

ONE

The Education of an Astor,

or

A Name That Rings Like Bullion

The irony of Archie—man on the run, hiding his face as he crossed the familiar Manhattan precincts of his youth—was not lost on the Astor heir himself. He had been, and still considered himself, one of the princes of the city. In fact, much of the real estate he traversed during that hansom cab ride in 1900 was owned by his family.

The story of the Astor wealth was legend, and Archie could recite it chapter and verse. He had been schooled in the family history and in the expectations that it created. Archie understood only too well the burden involved. As the eldest son in his huge family (he had seven surviving brothers and sisters), he carried a particularly heavy load. All of the Chanler siblings prided themselves on their individuality, on their strong-willed and often eccentric ways. They all professed an indifference to money. Why not? They had plenty of it. Piles of it had been amassed by their forebears, and none of the current generation—least of all Archie—wanted to spend their lives the way their great-grandfather William Backhouse Astor had.

Nicknamed "Landlord of New York," William Backhouse Astor was both reviled and envied in his lifetime. He was a "hard dreary looking old man and the richest in the world," in the estimation of Lord Rosebery, the future prime minister of England. Six feet tall but stoop-shouldered, William B. Astor spent his life hunched over his contracts and leases. He had inherited from his father, John Jacob Astor, vast stretches of Manhattan real estate, and as the population boomed in nineteenth-century New York, the value of the land rose exponentially. By 1860 tenement slums with a population density of 290,000 per square mile became William B. Astor's specialty. The arithmetic was simple: one block filled with tenements could generate at least twice the revenue of a similar block with more-spacious middle-class housing. As immigrants poured into the city, the Astor name became synonymous with misery. When one newcomer proudly announced to a Board of Health inspector that his house was owned by Astor, the official shot back, "More's the pity."

William B. was the caretaker for the vast empire his father had acquired; he had little interest in building or transforming the landscape. He would just as soon let others erect housing for the poor on his land; he would merely collect the rents. Being a pious man, he could then blame others for—or claim ignorance of—the inhumane conditions that prevailed on his property. But of course his ignorance of conditions only went so far. Eager to maintain the status quo and keep his coffers full, he did his best to defy all attempts at tenement reform and for years succeeded in delaying the construction of subways that would allow immigrants to live in more distant parts of the city. Besides, in his view, it was laziness that kept a man in a miserable tenement with no ventilation, plumbing, or light. It was not William B.'s problem. One had only to look at his father's example to see the opportunity available to any man willing to work hard—a belief commonly held by William B. and other plutocrats who had inherited vast fortunes without lifting a finger.

Archie knew as well of the more colorful saga of his great-great-grandfather, who had amassed the original fortune. The family patriarch's saga was indeed impressive. As legend has it, John Jacob Astor, twenty-year-old son of a poor butcher in Waldorf, Germany, arrived in Baltimore in 1784 with seven flutes and about five pounds sterling, and parlayed it into a fortune conservatively estimated at $20 million, a sum that staggered the imagination of his contemporaries. In 1848, the year Astor died, the richest man in Boston left behind only $2 million. John Jacob's winter passage to America was in steerage, and he subsisted on salt beef, biscuits, and dreams of what lay ahead. Just short of Baltimore the ship became trapped in ice, and there it remained stranded for two months—enough time for Astor to hatch a plan. One of his fellow German passengers was in the fur trade, and he passed the time by telling stories of the fortunes that could be made by buying American furs for next to nothing and selling them in England for exorbitant prices.

Astor's course was set. Arriving in New York, he went to work for a furrier, and spent the following summer beating pelts to keep moths out of them. Astor became a keen student of the fur business, and within several years had set up his own shop. Shouldering a backpack stuffed with at least sixty pounds of trade items, he tramped hundreds of miles through the wilderness, struck tough bargains with the trappers, and then brought the pelts to London, where he sold them at great profit. One beaver pelt in London might bring the equivalent of three dollars—the same price as a musket, which Astor could then trade with an Indian for ten more beaver skins.

While in London, Astor cemented a deal with the firm of Astor and Broadwood (his older brother was a partner in the company), manufacturers of musical instruments. He served as New York agent for their pianos, flutes, and violins—valued and scarce commodities in New York—and, in the process, helped finance his burgeoning fur business. He opened a small shop in Manhattan that bore the unusual sign FURS AND PIANOS. One of John Jacob's original pianos remains at Rokeby, a reminder of the Astor patriarch's early strivings in commerce.

As his business grew, so did John Jacob's ambition. He leaped into the China trade, eventually sending his own fleet of ships to Canton, where furs could be bartered for tea, silk, and porcelain. With a ruthlessness and cunning that would be admired—and copied—by later robber barons, Astor turned his American Fur Company into the country's first great monopoly. Other successful merchants and financiers would hang paintings in their offices to display their refined taste; Astor preferred to hang a fine fur in his counting room, which he would stroke and boast of its worth in China.

As he piled up more and more money, John Jacob turned his eye toward investing it. All he had to do was look around and see the changes that had transformed Manhattan. When he had arrived in New York in 1784, the city's 23,000 residents lived largely below Cortlandt Street, at the southern tip of the island. By 1800 the population had more than doubled, and buildings had sprouted nearly a mile farther north. Betting that the city would continue that constant move northward, Astor began buying up property just beyond the built-up sections of the city. It was the future he was buying. In around 1810, John Jacob sold a lot near Wall Street for $8,000. The purchaser was certain that he had just fleeced Astor. Gloating, the new owner said, "Why, Mr. Astor, in a few years this lot will be worth twelve thousand dollars." "Very true," Astor replied, "but now you shall see what I will do with this money. With eight thousand dollars I buy eighty lots above Canal Street. By the time your lot is worth twelve thousand dollars my eighty lots will be worth eighty thousand dollars." And he was right.

Astor's real estate holdings made him as rich as Croesus, his very name conjuring up lucre. "John Jacob Astor," the narrator of Herman Melville's "Bartleby the Scrivener" opined, "[is] a name which, I admit, I love to repeat, for it hath a rounded and orbicular sound to it, and rings like unto bullion." The newly minted millionaire was disdained for his peasant aura, his heavily accented and grammatically fractured English, and his alarming table manners. In 1815, James Gallatin noted in his diary that the fur peddler had dined at their home and "ate his ice-cream and peas with a knife"—reason enough for his father, the patrician Jeffersonian statesman, Albert Gallatin, to decline Astor's offer of a partnership in the American Fur Company. Five years later, John Jacob once more discomfited the Gallatins, by dining at their home and wiping his dirty fingers on their daughter's white sleeve.

Like a character out of Dickens, the richer Astor grew, the more miserly he became. "I used to know him, when an ignoble dealer in Musk Rat skins," James Kirke Paulding, novelist of old Knickerbocker society, wrote contemptuously, "but cut his acquaintance when he became a Millionaire, for found he grew mean faster than he grew rich, and that his avarice increased with his means of being generous. He lived miserably and died miserably." Stories of his mean-spiritedness were legion. This "monarch of the counting-room" was tarnished by his greed, according to a scathing biographical sketch of the millionaire in the February 1865 edition of *Harper's New Monthly Magazine:* "The roll-book of his possessions was his Bible. He scanned it fondly and saw with quiet but deep delight the catalogue of his property lengthening from month to month. The love of accumulation grew with his years until it ruled him like a tyrant. If at fifty he possessed his millions, at sixty-five his millions possessed him."

Though he was reputed to "now and then, bestow small sums in charity," the magazine claimed that "we have failed to get trustworthy evidence of a single instance of his doing so." In his final years, however, he was talked into leaving behind a gift to the city that had made him rich: a library open to the public. Though the nuances of the English language eluded him, Astor was particularly fascinated by literary men, and in his semi-retirement years he frequently entertained writers and poets in his home. He befriended Washington Irving and chose him as one of the executors of his estate; he also employed the poet Fitz-Greene Halleck as his personal secretary for sixteen years. (The poet once made the mistake of telling his employer in jest that he had no need of millions, that he could live happily on several hundred dollars a year—as a cruel joke, that is exactly what Astor left Halleck as an annuity.) The Astor Library, John Jacob hoped, would serve as a permanent monument to him and to his fortune—and perhaps counter his infamous reputation as a tightwad.

Not everyone was convinced. The press, led by the irascible James Gordon Bennett, publisher of the mass-circulation *New York*

Herald, howled. Calling John Jacob "a self-invented money-making machine," he declared that by rights Astor should bestow half his fortune on the people of New York—after all, it was they who had created his wealth. In fact, Astor left about two and a half percent of his estate, a little over half a million dollars, for benevolent purposes. The largest chunk, $400,000, was allotted to fund the library, the rest given to a small assortment of charities: the German Society of New York, the German Reformed Congregation, the Association for the Relief of Respectable Aged Indigent Females, the Institution for the Blind, the Society for the Relief of Half Orphans and Destitute Children, and the New York Lying-In Asylum. Astor had a perfect horror of beggars, but obviously made an exception when it came to the poor in his native village of Waldorf, to whose care he pledged $50,000. The rest of his $20 million went to his family.

The reformer Horace Mann denounced Astor's parsimony as nothing short of "insanity," depicting him as "hoarding wealth for the base love of wealth, hugging to his breast, in his dying hour, the memory of his gold and not of his Redeemer; gripping his riches till the scythe of death cut off his hands and he was changed, in the twinkling of an eye, from being one of the richest men that ever lived in this world to being one of the poorest souls who ever went out of it." In Astor's defense, public philanthropy—with some notable exceptions—was not commonplace in the mid-nineteenth century; but the immense scale of his wealth in an era before the personal income tax, combined with the fact that he himself had come from poverty, made his gifts—with the exception of the library—appear paltry and, in fact, reinforced the stereotype of him as a mean-spirited old miser.

Archie was well aware of the contempt the populist press had for his forebear, and was determined that his life would be different. As heir to a fortune, Archie felt a keen sense of responsibility toward others; it was part of his patrician notion of noblesse oblige. Nonetheless, the sheer drama of John Jacob's life—from poor immigrant to fur peddler traipsing through the wilderness to merchant prince whose empire stretched from China to the streets of Manhattan—had a swashbuckling style that Archie and his siblings couldn't help but admire. John Jacob's energy and dash, and even his touch of eccentricity (attributes that could also be ascribed to Archie and his siblings), somehow managed to elude entirely his son and principal heir, William Backhouse Astor. Even the patriarch's uncouth manners lent him a comic edge—a humanity—that his somber son could never attain. At John Jacob's funeral, James Gallatin—who had once sneered at the senior Astor's boorish manners—was among his pallbearers. In a fitting touch, the family waiters marched with napkins pinned to their sleeves at the rear of the funeral procession.

Of course, by the time of John Jacob's death in 1848, he had long since been accepted—however grudgingly—into the fabric of the old Knickerbocker society that ruled New York. Having enough money will do that in New York. Besides, in 1818 his son, William Backhouse, had made a most propitious marriage to Margaret Armstrong, a woman with impeccable social credentials who helped raise the standing of the Astors. Margaret Armstrong was the daughter of General John Armstrong Jr. and Alida Livingston, one of the heirs to the vast Livingston lands—nearly a million acres—in the Hudson Valley and Catskill Mountains. The Livingstons were among the great landed aristocratic families in New York dating back to the seventeenth century, and they ruled the Hudson Valley like lords of a feudal empire. After serving as minister to France, General Armstrong built a country house on Livingston land overlooking the Hudson and christened it La Bergerie, "the sheep pen," in reference to the merino sheep he imported at the suggestion of Napoleon.

The Astor name rose immeasurably in social importance, tied as it was to the Livingston-Armstrong blue bloods. John Jacob was delighted at his family's enhanced status—but also crafty enough to dictate a marriage settlement that would ensure that the Astor fortune never passed out of family hands. To prevent that possibility, John Jacob paid the bride a lump sum (though large, it paled in comparison to the ever-growing Astor fortune); in return she gave up her dower rights. Thus a precedent was set for future Astor marriages.

The marriage between William B. and Margaret Armstrong took place in the dining room at La Bergerie in 1818; the following year, Margaret gave birth to their first child in the Rosewood Room and named her Emily, after the heroine of a popular Gothic romance. Over the years, seven more children were born to them (two died in infancy), and the growing brood wintered in Manhattan and summered along the Hudson. Eager to become part of the landed gentry and to have his own country seat—to say nothing of pleasing his wife—William B. Astor purchased La Bergerie from the general in 1836 for $50,000. Margaret renamed the estate Rokeby, as the landscape reminded her of the scenery evoked by Sir Walter Scott in his romantic poem of the same name. Though he might own the place, and even allow his wife to rename it, William B. still had not won absolute sovereignty over the estate. General Armstrong was not about to cede his primacy, and when he arrived at Rokeby every summer, he took his place at the head of the dining room table until his death in 1843. During his final summer in the house, General Armstrong, unable to negotiate the staircase, lived downstairs and set the tone of the household. He exhibited uncharacteristic kindness, dispensing small cakes that he kept in his wardrobe to the children at Rokeby, including Archie's mother Maddie, William B.'s granddaughter, who was then not quite five years old.

At Rokeby, William B. also had to contend with his bachelor brother-in-law Kosciusko Armstrong (so named by his father in honor of the Polish hero of the American Revolution), who refused to move out of the house altogether. He was deeply attached to the place and was outraged over its sale. "Uncle Koosey," as he was called by the children, kept his original room, and spurned any attempt to improve it. Not for him the fancy new marble mantelpieces being installed throughout the house by the Astors. The wallpaper in his room and the original wooden fireplace remained unchanged as symbols of his obstinacy. During the cold months, when the unheated Rokeby was closed up, he lived at the Union Club in Manhattan, but he would make the occasional winter foray to Rokeby. If he forgot the key to his room, he would use a ladder and crawl through his second-floor window. He dressed as he pleased, offending the sensibilities of the new Astor regime. Uncle Koosey once came down to breakfast decked out in bright green. "He should never be allowed to dress himself," gasped one straight-backed relative. Uncle Koosey's unconventional ways were a welcome bit of comic relief from the dour William B., and that eccentric tone would permeate Rokeby and continue to flourish from one generation to the next.

Until his mid-fifties, William B. Astor remained under the thumb of two demanding tyrants: his father in Manhattan, and his father-in-law at his country estate (to say nothing of Uncle Koosey's relentless presence). No wonder he became stoop-shouldered and grim. From the outset, William's life was shaped by duty. He had to take on the onerous responsibilities of being the firstborn son of the richest man in the country, even though he was not in fact the eldest son. His brother John Jacob II was a year older than he; but as the heir apparent grew older, it became clear that there was something wrong with him. He suffered from wild mood swings, ranging from violent episodes to catatonic spells. Try as he might, the senior John Jacob could find no cure for his son. Time spent in an asylum did not seem to help; so, resigned to his son's condition, the elder John Jacob built a comfortable home for him that he staffed with a doctor and servants. John Jacob II—referred to as an "imbecile" by the newspapers of the day—spent the rest of his days in seclusion, lost in his illness, though he had brief periods of lucidity when he would write poetry. (This strain of madness and poetry would also run through the generations.)

The paterfamilias turned his attention to young William; like a proper rich German, he sent his son abroad to study at the universities in Heidelberg and Göttingen. A serious student, William immersed himself in the study of ancient civilizations. Among his classmates at Göttingen was the moody philosopher Arthur Schopenhauer. A life of scholarship and travel appealed to William; but while in Europe in 1816, planning an elaborate tour of the Near East with his tutor, he was summoned home by his father. At twenty-three years old, the time had come for him to begin his apprenticeship in the family business. "He was practically taught the art of making money," the *New York Herald* noted in an article about William B., adding poignantly, "The youth studied his father's methods and began to live his father's life."

The young Astor dutifully took on the world of leases and rents and made it his own; it was said that he could recite the rent rolls by heart—and there were thousands of buildings under his purview. And yet he was basically a glorified accountant for his father, "a very good and trusted one—but an underling, nevertheless," a friend said of him. He was prudent and careful—and boring; by comparison, his father seemed almost lighthearted and gay. John Jacob loved theater and music and was particularly charmed to hear his granddaughter Emily sing old German songs in her clear soprano voice; her gloomy father preferred that she stick to hymns.

After William's death in 1875, *Harper's Weekly* described this colorless man as follows: "Of the late William B. Astor it is said that he used no tobacco and little wine. . . . He seldom was out late, did not attend theatres, did not get excited, nor indulge in profane adjectives, sported not with dogs and guns . . . never kept a fast horse, never gambled. His whole life was simple and orderly." And then, as a final indictment: "He minded his own business." His attention to detail paid off. By the end of William B.'s life, he had doubled or even tripled the value of the family fortune, leaving behind at least $40 or $50 million. Some estimates were even higher. Fluctuations in the real estate market in New York made it hard to pinpoint the exact worth of William B. Astor's estate. The *New York Times* estimated that his estate equaled "one hundred millions of dollars, even at present reduced value of real property on this island." A contemporary, industrialist and inventor Peter Cooper, put the figure closer to $200 million.

Whatever the final tally, William B. Astor's wealth was staggering. But it seemed to bring him little pleasure. His household, both in the city and the country, was somber and exuded an air of eighteenth-century formality. Strict rules dictated his children's behavior: they could neither wear bright clothing nor laugh out loud. After bidding their parents good night, the children were not permitted to turn their backs to them; they had to step backward out of the room.

Silence prevailed at the dinner table as no conversation was allowed. William B. himself was a man of few words. His friend Philip Hone, the mid-nineteenth-century diarist who chronicled New York society, wrote that Astor "thinks twice before he speaks once."

The gloom of the Astor household was dispelled by the arrival of Samuel Ward Jr., who courted and married William B.'s eldest child, Emily. These were Archie's grandparents, and their ill-fated story made clear to all the power of the Astor family—and the danger of transgressing against its rules of behavior. Sam boasted a distinguished lineage: his forebears included two governors, and his father was the most prominent banker in the city, whose clients numbered old John Jacob Astor. But Sam had little interest in the "clink of gold and the clamor of commerce," as he referred dismissively to business.

He was cosmopolitan and charming, a bon vivant who loved good food and wine, an intellectual with an interest in languages, science, mathematics, and music. He spent nearly four years abroad in Paris—the "city of Sin and Science," in his words—and Germany, studying and absorbing Old World culture. This sojourn transformed his life. Thereafter, Sam's tastes were decidedly European. His niece recalled that he seemed more French than American and "wore handsome rings and scarfpins, checked trousers, superb waistcoats, an overcoat of pale gray box cloth with large white pearl buttons, unmistakably from London." In Paris, Sam studied music and became a regular at informal gatherings at Franz Liszt's *pension,* where the composer gave electrifying impromptu performances. In Heidelberg he met Henry Wadsworth Longfellow, and they became lifelong friends and correspondents.

Sam fell in love with the world of books and ideas, and he returned very reluctantly to New York to take on the family business. Sam found life as a New York banker distressingly crass: "Everything here is greed," he wrote to a friend in 1837, "everything is arid, like the great desert of Africa for me, poor Sybarite, accustomed to tread with light and care free step the paths of soft indulgence." To a confidant in Europe, Sam wrote enviously of the intellectual life the German student still enjoyed, where "your mind is expanding and ripening under the rays of science." In contrast he found his own life constricted and empty. "In the office of an American banker one can feel that every day is a lost day," he wrote plaintively.

Unhappy as Sam might have been, his position as an Astor banker brought him into the orbit of the spirited—and very rich—Emily Astor, whom he began to court. He won over Emily's grandfather, John Jacob Astor, with his jokes and pranks, once bringing a ventriloquist to the family patriarch's estate. He would arrive at Rokeby singing—the only person who dared do such a thing—and would entertain Emily's sisters with German student songs. One family member referred to Ward as a "magician," for the happy spell that he cast over the entire household.

Sam married Emily in January 1838. A miniature wedding portrait still remains at Rokeby—Sam sweetly holding orange blossoms over his new wife's brow. The charmed pair appears blessed with love. The wedding, attended by family members and a few choice guests including Washington Irving, was "the most cheerful . . . I ever saw," according to his sister Julia. The wedding supper was sumptuous and "resembled the entertainments in the Arabian Nights." The nineteen-year-old bride wore a diamond star on her forehead, a gift from the family patriarch, John Jacob Astor. Sam was entranced. "I love and adore my dear Emily," he wrote to a friend, noting that love had overtaken him "like scarlet fever."

Within a year, Emily gave birth to Archie's mother, Margaret Astor Ward, whom they nicknamed "Maddie." Life was idyllic until tragedy struck a few years later. On February 18, 1841, Emily died from complications after childbirth. In a letter to Longfellow several days later, Sam poured forth his sorrow: "Death robbed my house of its gentle mistress, my heart of its dearest treasure . . . I have been shattered root and branch." His only consolation, he wrote that evening, was that "my little Babe is doing well. . . . Heaven grant we may rear him to do honor to his angelic mother and cherish her memory which is the only green spot left us in life." The next morning he took up pen once more: "I was too exhausted last night to continue, and grieve to say that my little boy exhibits this morning symptoms of languor and drowsiness which disturb me." The postscript to the letter, written in a faint hand, as if Sam could barely bring himself to write the words: "I fear we shall not be permitted to raise the little boy." His infant son was dead.

Sam was devastated, as were the Astors. Mrs. Astor never recovered from the loss of her favorite daughter. After staying homebound for a time, her doctor urged her to get out. She began taking daily walks with her two remaining daughters, seventeen-year-old Laura and fifteen-year-old Alida. In accordance with mourning custom, all three wore black crepe veils that covered their faces and stretched to the ground. At the grieving trio's approach, acquaintances would move to the side, pause, and—in deference to the family's sorrow—bow and sigh audibly. One of the daughters later recalled that the daily walk was a "torture . . . I woke up every morning dreading the ordeal." The already somber tone of the Astor household became even more funereal. William B.'s natural reticence was henceforth matched by his wife's sorrowful silence. It was said that she never spoke Emily's name again. The surviving granddaughter, Maddie, became the central focus of her grandparents; and she would soon be permanently folded into that dour household.

The wrath of the Astor family came crashing down on Sam when he dared to marry again in the fall of 1843. Two and a half years had passed since his wife's death, a proper interval in an era when two years of mourning was considered appropriate (society dictated that a year of deep mourning would be followed by a half-year of "black and white" mourning, and then another six months of quiet socializing before being able to resume a regular schedule); nonetheless, William B. and Margaret were enraged at his marrying so soon, and perceived it as a slight on their daughter's memory. To make matters worse, Sam had the temerity to give Emily's house to his new bride. Sam was perfectly free to do so, as the house had passed to him upon the death of his wife; in fact, the house had originally been given to Emily as a wedding present from Sam's father. But the Astors took matters of property extremely seriously, and they considered this an unpardonable breach, "a sort of outwitting & overreaching in the art of bargaining," in the words of an Astor cousin.

The Astors had never quite trusted the free-spirited Sam, and now their worst fears were confirmed. Sam's choice of wife further compounded his sin. Medora Grymes was a Creole beauty of dubious background. Among other things, her parents had divorced, grounds enough for the Astors to ban her from ever being received socially. Medora had also cut a swath through Manhattan's eligible bachelors; in fact, she was affianced to another man when she dumped him in order to marry Sam. The jilted man gallantly offered to sell Sam the trousseau he had ordered from Paris for his bride-to-be. Sam accepted the trousseau and married Medora. The union turned out to be a disastrous one. Commenting at the time of the marriage, one relative wrote that "Sam . . . has probably made a silly match—but the resentment of the Astors is, I think, carried beyond all just bounds."

Knowing the power and the moral rigidity of his in-laws, Sam was undoubtedly reluctant to tell the Astors of his plan to remarry. He decided to take a summer tour of New York State to the falls of the Genesee and Niagara Rivers in preparation for his announcement (or perhaps just to put it off a little longer). Sam placed Maddie under his sister Louisa's care. Twenty-year-old Louisa had been left behind when her other siblings had gone abroad for the season. At loose ends, Louisa took Maddie with her to Rokeby for an extended visit. Louisa knew of her brother's engagement to Medora, but did not dare mention it. One day, when returning from a walk to the Hudson River at the edge of the property, Louisa found the entire family—William B. and Margaret, along with their children—assembled in the library. Word had reached Rokeby of the impending marriage, and the news struck like a hurricane. Louisa was banished on the spot from the household. A carriage was summoned to take her away from Rokeby, presumably forever.

Thus began the dubious tradition at Rokeby of banishing relatives—even brothers and sisters—for decades at a time over what were considered social improprieties. (Archie felt that sting of exile in a profound way when his family had him incarcerated in the asylum.) The insult to Louisa Ward would still be remembered over forty years later, during Archie's generation. As fate would have it, Louisa's daughter Daisy married Archie's brother Winty. Winty and Daisy, first cousins once removed, wed despite being related, a not-uncommon practice in that tight-knit social world. (Sam Ward Jr. was both Winty's grandfather and Daisy's uncle.) The newlywed cousins came to Rokeby in 1887 and had their first child there. The irony was not lost on the Astor family that Daisy—whose mother had been banished from Rokeby—immediately became a force to be reckoned with on the estate. Daisy had the temerity to rearrange the furniture when the Chanlers went away that summer, an act that Archie's sister Margaret found so repugnant that she subsequently refused to sit in the parlor with her sister-in-law. After Daisy gave birth to a daughter, her mother's sister Julia (the redoubtable Julia Ward Howe, who wrote "The Battle Hymn of the Republic") agreed to come to Rokeby to tend to her niece and newborn. En route, Howe had the misfortune to run into John Jacob Astor III at the train station—the same man who had shown the door to her sister Louisa decades earlier. Julia had not spoken to John Jacob since that unpleasant event; but as she was unsure which train to take to Rokeby, she approached him for help. Once she announced her destination, he let her know in no uncertain terms that he could not help her, as he had no reason anymore to go to Rokeby. Nearly half a century had not diluted the Astor bitterness.

In the immediate aftermath of his remarriage, Sam discovered just how ruthless the Astors could be. Five-year-old Maddie became a pawn in a tug-of-war between Sam and his former in-laws. William Backhouse Astor basically resorted to blackmail: he threatened legal action that would jeopardize Maddie's inheritance as well as the property that Sam had inherited from his late wife, unless Sam agreed to give up his daughter. Sam felt he had no choice, and acceded to the Astor wishes. Maddie was brought up by her grandparents and rarely saw her father; when she did, it had to be in the presence of her stern nanny, Nancy Richards (the same nursemaid who had tended to Maddie's mother). And Maddie, who had absorbed the opinion of her grandparents, was cold and distant with her father. Sam effectively lost his daughter; soon after, he lost his family fortune and banking business as well.

Leaving his second wife behind, Ward headed off to the California Gold Rush in 1849. He promptly made a killing and grandly sent gold dust and nuggets to his sister Julia in Boston, to fashion brooches, combs, and rings for the family. Sam was a man of great imagination—especially when it came to spending money. (Archie and his siblings shared that exuberant trait.) While out West, he organized a gala ball to welcome an incoming ship. The city streets were not yet lit, so Sam hired a number of muscled seamen, bronzed their bodies, dressed them in flowing robes, and gave them flaming torches to hold aloft. Thus they stood like classical statues lining the route to the party. It did not take Sam long to lose another fortune.

Ward's apparent disdain for money, his flamboyant manner, and his spendthrift habits all rankled William B. And the thought that Ward had inherited Astor land from his first wife, Emily—in fact, still controlled thirty-two lots on West 14th Street that had been given to Emily as part of her marriage settlement and inherited by Sam—was too much for the vindictive William B. Astor to stomach. A lawsuit was filed by the trustees for Maddie in order to divest Ward of these lots. Though the property itself was merely a drop in the bucket in the vast Astor holdings, William B. was merciless about such matters.

Sam Ward's peripatetic career eventually led him to South America, Europe, and Washington, D.C., where he established himself as a fabulously successful lobbyist, earning himself the title "King of the Lobby." He was a famous host, and a dealmaker who could wheedle compromises from the staunchest enemies by seducing them with his charm and sumptuous dinners. It was said about him that "Sam Ward could strut even when sitting down." Yet tragedy stalked him. Both of the sons he had with Medora died young; she followed them in death shortly thereafter.

The whiff of Bohemia certainly stuck to Sam Ward. A poet, an adventurer, a lover of art and the subject of artists in Rome, Sam Ward was considered one of the romantic, colorful characters of his era. That unconventionality did not sit well with William B. Astor, whose early suspicions about Ward were confirmed by Sam's nomadic lifestyle and artistic temperament. (Astor's distaste for such outré behavior was shared by Joseph H. Choate, the conservative attorney who later represented the Astor interests against Archie. In May 1898, Choate wrote from his Wall Street office to Augustus Saint-Gaudens, the famous Gilded Age sculptor and friend of Archie's. The lawyer was checking up on an acquaintance of Saint-Gaudens, an artist in the city about whom "the means of information . . . seem singularly scanty." Choate asked Saint-Gaudens bluntly if this fellow was marriage material: "Tell me . . . about his family, his connexions, his character, his means of support, his professional study and chances. . . . How has he lived for the last ten years? And is there the making of a domestic man out of him; or," in Choate's—and Astor's—estimation, the worst sort of verdict: "Is he too far gone in Bohemianism for that?")

Sam yearned for a connection with his daughter Maddie, but, in his words, "[she] had been taught to eye me askance as a disreputable old Bohemian Paternal." Maddie found a husband more in the mold of her Astor forebears. John Winthrop Chanler, an aspiring politician, descended from the city's Dutch founder, Governor Peter Stuyvesant, and thus claimed membership in the old Knickerbocker society, the ultimate status in Manhattan. While courting Maddie in the early 1860s, J. W. Chanler lived with his widowed mother at 214 Second Avenue, in the city's most rarefied enclave. His mother, a Stuyvesant, had inherited a share of Governor Stuyvesant's 550-acre, seventeenth-century plantation, or *bouwerie* in Dutch. The famously named Bowery served as the southwest boundary of the governor's estate, and his land stretched all the way up to 23rd Street. Stuyvesant's original manor house was sited near the present-day intersection of Tenth Street and Second Avenue. For generation after generation his descendants clustered in that area—and were eventually buried alongside the one-legged Dutch governor in the family vaults located in the churchyard of St. Mark's-in-the-Bowery (the site of an earlier private chapel built by their petulant but devout ancestor). Echoes of the family still resound in the area, with a street and square and park—and even a housing project—named after the founding family. The Stuyvesants intermarried with some of the fine old New York families: the Hamilton Fish family, the Rutherfurds, and the Winthrops. The "Second Avenue set," as they were known, represented the purest pedigree in New York high society. To boot, Chanler was also related to the aristocratic Livingston and Beekman families.

John Winthrop Chanler was thirty-five and Maddie twenty-three when they became engaged. They married in January 1862 at William B. Astor's mansion on Lafayette Place; less than a year later Archie was born there. Though J. W. Chanler was a New Yorker by birth, he had grown up amid his father's family in South Carolina, where they had deep roots. (For that reason, Archie felt he enjoyed a kind of dual citizenship in Yankeedom and Dixie.) A month after Archie's birth, Chanler was elected a U.S. congressman under the banner of the Tammany Hall Democratic machine, which had distinctly Confederate political leanings. J. W. Chanler's duties brought the family to Washington, D.C.; Archie was there when Lincoln was assassinated.

The Chanlers shuttled back and forth from the capital to New York. Until Archie was eight years old, his family's official address was 218 Second Avenue, between 13th and 14th Streets, in the heart of the Stuyvesant preserve. Archie's grandmother, Elizabeth Winthrop Chanler, lived at number 214; his aunt Margaret and her husband, the famous astronomer Lewis Morris Rutherfurd, were just down the street at number 175. In this exclusive enclave of the supremely fortunate there also dwelled Archie's aunt Sarah, J.W.'s sister, who was demented and was kept locked away upstairs in a family house on Second Avenue. Archie and his siblings knew all about her. His sister later referred to their aunt as an "unremitting shadow," a dark angel hovering over all of them.

The Chanler children paid frequent visits to the Lafayette Place mansion of their dour great-grandfather William B. Astor, a forbidding but central presence in Archie's life. (It was William B. who nicknamed his first great-grandchild "Archie.") When Archie was a small child, William B. was hanging on at Lafayette Place, even though change was sweeping the neighborhood. The street was originally conceived in 1826 as an aristocratic, leafy preserve practically dedicated to the Astor family, a cul-de-sac closed to through traffic, carved out of Vauxhall Gardens. Though just a block from Broadway, Lafayette Place was insulated from its noise and bustle. On the east side of the street, William B. built his mansion and stables, and old John Jacob Astor moved across the street into one of nine new town houses designed by Alexander Jackson Davis in the early 1830s. An elegant nod to upper-crust housing in London and Paris, the separate residences were all united by a row of Corinthian columns made from marble quarried by convicts at Sing Sing Prison. Named La Grange Terrace after the Marquis de Lafayette's country estate, this grand edifice was commonly referred to by New Yorkers as "Colonnade Row." Next to William B.'s stables the family built New York's first free library, a Romanesque Revival palace (the current home of the Public Theater) that boasted the largest collection of books in the country—100,000 volumes, twice the holdings of the Library of Congress at the time. But not long after the Astor Library opened with great fanfare, in 1854, William B.'s children began to flee the family crisis. Trade was encroaching on the genteel street, and worse: immigrants who lived on the Bowery were pressing in on the elite enclave.

The Astor Place riot of May 10, 1849, had already fractured the peace of Lafayette Place. That night a mob of some ten thousand poor and working-class New Yorkers stormed the adjacent Astor Place Opera House—the very symbol of the upper class—to protest the "silk-stockinged" English actor performing there in *Macbeth*. The crowd had been whipped into a frenzy by an ongoing feud between the Briton William C. Macready and his rival, the "true-blue" American actor Edwin Forrest. Simmering class resentments boiled over that night as rioters wielding clubs and hurling paving stones attacked the "den of the Aristocracy" in an attempt to drive the hated English actor from the stage. Police and militia fought back, firing point-blank into the crowd and killing as many as thirty-one and wounding many more. The carnage could be clearly seen from one Astor residence; a gravely wounded man carried to the door in search of help was forcibly turned away. The aristocratic bubble of Lafayette Place had been burst.

By the mid-1850s the Astors, one by one, began to decamp for the open spaces of the old Thompson farm—a twenty-acre tract in an undeveloped section of Manhattan known as Murray Hill. Cannily, William B. had purchased a half-interest in that farm nearly thirty years earlier. The purchase included the stretch of Fifth Avenue and its surrounding side streets from Thirty-second to Thirty-fifth streets. Astor mansions rose and became a magnet for high society, which avidly paid Astor prices for Astor-owned tracts in a section once known for shanties and empty, garbage-strewn lots.

Archie recalled the family's move uptown in 1870 to a handsome brick house, one of a trio of residences William B. built for the families of his daughters Alida and Laura, and his granddaughter Maddie. They were all in a row on Madison Avenue between 34th and 35th Streets (eventually the site of B. Altman's department store). The Chanlers moved into their new house at 192 Madison Avenue in the fall, at roughly the same time that Maddie gave birth to her eighth child, a daughter named Margaret Livingston. Though new, the interior of the house was rather funereal—dark, cavernous rooms with heavy woodwork, in keeping with the Victorian tastes of the time. The place was full of mystery. Archie and his siblings raced past the inlaid cabinets, believing that bears lived inside them and would burst out at any moment.

Whenever Archie left the house, he would inevitably run into his cousins or great-aunts and -uncles. His mother had been raised with her aunts, Alida and Laura, and they were really more like sisters to her; on Madison Avenue all three lived next to one another as neighbors. Alida and her English-born husband, John Carey Jr., had lost a child—a ten-year-old daughter—the year that Archie and his siblings moved in. The Careys had three surviving children: a daughter, Maggie, and two sons, Arthur and Henry ("Harry"). Arthur was the level-headed brother; Harry loved a good wager, enjoyed the gaming tables at Monte Carlo, and famously drove a team of zebras down Brattle Street in Cambridge, Massachusetts. Harry, Archie, and Winty all went to St. John's School, a military academy in Sing Sing (now Ossining), New York. The three boys, along with their siblings, were all doted on by Laura and her husband, Franklin Hughes Delano, who had no children. Around the corner were other great-uncles and -aunts (including Mrs. Caroline Astor, stuffy "Aunt Lina," who would disapprove of any untoward behavior) and assorted cousins.

New horizons opened up for Archie. With a nanny or his parents, he could take the horse-drawn stage, its floor covered in straw, that lumbered up Madison Avenue to get to the "Central Park," still under construction. An old woman lived in a cabin at the 59th Street entrance, and the Chanler children bought violets and geraniums from her for five cents. On other occasions they would take a carriage as far north as the new Riverside Park, along the banks of the Hudson River, which was being created in the 1870s by landscape architect Frederick Law Olmsted (who co-designed Central Park with Calvert Vaux). There the children gathered daisies from a field. This was considered the far edge of civilization—the West Side then still being an undeveloped area of dirt roads and squalid shanties, stinking of slaughterhouses. Between this far outpost and the return to his Murray Hill mansion, Archie could watch from his carriage window and see the city as it rapidly transformed itself. Vacant lots with stray animals and squatters' shacks gave way to construction sites where millionaires' mansions were rising. The noise and energy were electrifying, and Archie was on the crest of the wave—an heir to the Astor fortune that was getting bigger every day. He could practically see it growing, for much of the booming midtown real estate belonged to his family.

Within several years, the aged William B. left his mansion on Lafayette Place and joined his family, moving to Fifth Avenue at 35th Street, a block north of his sons and just around the corner from Archie and his siblings. William B. turned his back on his beloved Lafayette Place reluctantly. But the death of his wife in 1872 left him lonely, and the world around him was changing rapidly. The city, over

William B.'s protests, had the temerity to open the southern end of the cul-de-sac to through traffic, further intruding upon the once-cloistered tranquility of the old street. So he headed north to join the clannish Astor brood in their new Murray Hill neighborhood.

Archie's mother provided an antidote to all of the Astor rigidity and formality. Archie adored her. She was a warm, loving mother who doted on her children. "God's brightest inspiration," she called them. She once announced to a gathering of society women that she had begun her pre-winter chore of knitting seventy-two pairs of stockings. She was vigilant about her children's health, keeping on hand a clinical thermometer—a highly unusual household item at the time—that she lent freely to friends. Despite her attentiveness, Maddie was unable to save Archie's sister, eight-year-old Emily, who died of scarlet fever in March 1874.

Maddie was also devoted to her grandfather. Every morning she would go to William B.'s Fifth Avenue mansion and read the Bible to him. One day in November 1875, Maddie brought along Archie's five-year-old sister, Margaret, to entertain the aging Astor patriarch. Margaret offered to dance a jig to the tune of "St. Patrick's Day in the Morning," something she had picked up from the Irish servants, if he would only whistle it for her. William B., sitting in a chair in front of the fire, did not know the song, and probably disapproved of it anyway. An utterly serious—some would say humorless—man, he did not enjoy such lighthearted fare. Margaret danced for him anyway.

A few days later the elderly Astor insisted upon going to his dingy office on Prince Street to get some work done, despite having a cold. By the time he reached home that afternoon his cold had worsened. Pneumonia set in, and he died four days later, on the day before Thanksgiving, with his family around him.

Archie and his brother Winty had been away at school in Westchester County during Astor's sudden last illness, but they returned for his funeral. The scene outside Archie's great-grandfather's Fifth Avenue mansion unfolded with the greatest solemnity and pomp. Cool and clear, it was a perfect autumn day. Thirteen-year-old Archie watched as an enormous mahogany casket with silver handles was carried down the front steps to a waiting horse-drawn hearse. Eight honorary pallbearers, including an ex-governor, lined the steps. They stood bare-headed, white silk scarves draped across their shoulders and fastened with rosettes of black and white ribbon. An attendant kept the two white horses still as the casket was carefully placed upon the plain hearse. The coffin plate read simply:

WILLIAM B. ASTOR.
Born September 19, 1792.
Died November 24, 1875.

Aged 83 years, 2 months, and 5 days.

The lead-lined coffin had been closed and hermetically sealed in accordance with city law the night before, relatives gathering in the parlor at Astor's Fifth Avenue residence to view the corpse and bid a final farewell. Archie and his siblings looked onto the lifeless face of their great-grandfather. Even five-year-old Margaret later recalled being lifted up "to see how very quietly the dead sleep."

Not all of the Chanler children attended the funeral, however. Maddie opposed "parading her children," but it was deemed necessary that the three oldest boys—thirteen-year-old Archie, twelve-year-old Winty, and eight-year-old Willie—attend. Particularly for Archie, as the eldest son, it would be a lesson in familial duty and protocol. William B.'s death had been announced in an article that took up two full columns on the front page of the *New York Times* under the headline DEATH OF A NOTED CITIZEN. In the rarefied social world he belonged to, funerals served as a kind of royal event, every detail calibrated to denote social rank—of both the deceased and the mourners.

The majordomo overseeing every last one of those details was Isaac Hull Brown, a renowned expert on the nuances of etiquette and protocol. He undoubtedly relished orchestrating the final obsequies for William B. Astor, a man whose very name "is as familiar as . . . the history of Manhattan island," according to Astor's obituary in the *New York Herald*. Brown's stock-in-trade was ministering to the city's elite and keeping out the riffraff. He was a vigilant and intimidating watchdog for the upper crust; yet he was not really part of that world. From a working-class family, he became a skilled carpenter and rose to the rank of sexton at Grace Church, "the most fashionable and exclusive of our metropolitan Courts of Heaven," according to a contemporary. His job consisted of maintaining the church, keeping it clean and well heated; he also had to collect pew-rents from its rich and powerful parishioners, among them William B. Astor. An ambitious man who knew how to play the obsequious courtier, Brown managed to expand his role in society significantly. His reputation soared after the reception and ball he organized in honor of the Prince of Wales in 1860; when part of the floor collapsed under the crush of guests anticipating the royal entrance, the ex-carpenter shed his jacket and directed his workmen in making an instant repair. The prince, engaged as he was in charming conversation with the daughter of New York City's mayor in an anteroom, never noticed the confusion and the evening proceeded elegantly. By 1875, Brown was not only the unofficial undertaker for wealthy Episcopalians throughout the city, but was also a trusted and invaluable consultant for high-society hostesses.

For a hefty fee and control of the invitation list, Brown arranged private dinners and balls for the old Knickerbocker society, and eventually for the nouveau riche engulfing the city in the post–Civil War boom. Nonetheless, he did his best to protect the Old Guard. If he saw someone from a fine old family about to set foot inside the precincts of the newly rich, he would take them aside and warn them sternly, "This is mixed, very!" For the arriviste with a thin invitation list or the dowager or debutante in need of an escort, Brown had on hand a list of eligible, well-mannered, and tailored young men, skilled at dancing and small talk. These "extra men" became known as "Brown's Brigade."

Isaac Brown had no need, of course, to paper the crowd for William B. Astor's funeral. The problem instead was to make sure that only those with the right pedigree be admitted into Trinity Chapel, where the service was to take place. And perhaps of even greater import was adjudicating who would follow behind the hearse in the official funeral cortege—and in what order. Archie undoubtedly saw the "beadle-faced" sexton at his great-grandfather's doorstep (after all, it was hard to miss him, as he weighed in at over three hundred pounds), directing mourners into the appropriate carriages. Archie was separated from his grieving mother and father, and placed in the eighth carriage in the procession along with his two brothers Willie and Winty (misspelled as "Winter" Chanler in the newspaper accounts the next day).

There were fifteen official carriages in all, not counting the four used to transport the pallbearers. As the funeral procession proceeded, Archie witnessed the family hierarchy on display. It was instructive. His two great-uncles William Backhouse Jr. and John Jacob Astor III led the way; his great-aunt Alida and her husband, John Carey Jr., followed in the second carriage; his great-aunt Laura and her husband, Franklin Hughes Delano (great-uncle of FDR), rode in the third; his parents came next; followed by his great-aunt by marriage, the socialite Charlotte Augusta Gibbes (wife of John Jacob Astor III), and her son William Waldorf Astor (who would eventually become a viscount); various Armstrong and Astor relatives filled the next two carriages. As the great-grandchildren of the deceased, Archie and his brothers took up the last family carriage. Behind them, in the next two carriages, were the favored family servants, followed by the family physicians. In the next three carriages Archie could see his great-grandfather's stern business associates, the men who had devoted their lives to following William B. Astor's wishes. The final carriage conveyed the trustees of the Astor Library. Thus was the Astor world order reflected in microcosm. Family always came first—a dictate preached by both John Jacob and his son William B.—and rank within that group was clearly ordered by gender and birth order. Following closely behind at a discreet distance were the hired help, who took care of all the mundane details. In fact, the devoted family servants outranked the business associates who trailed the procession.

Noticeably absent from the proceedings was the black sheep of the family, William B.'s son Henry, who had dared to defy his father and was paying the ultimate price—banishment. Henry was no longer considered part of the family, and his name was rarely uttered. So complete was his ostracism that, decades later, Archie's sister simply left him out when she drew up an Astor genealogy. For the Chanler children, "Uncle Henry" served as a cautionary tale about the Astor rules of conduct and the consequences of flouting them.

Neither business nor fashionable society interested Henry, and he made no effort to conform to either world. Boisterous and argumentative, prone to towering rages, Henry preferred the company of servants and farmhands to that of his own kin. An undistinguished stab at Columbia and a gentleman's tour of Europe with a tutor did little to smooth his rough edges. The barrel-chested, red-bearded Henry was all rough edges. He lived apart from his family in a gardener's cottage at Rokeby, staying even during the winter months when the big house was generally not in use. He loved country life and sport of all kinds—boxing, wrestling, horse racing—as well as drinking and cavorting with the local women. He was a favorite in the taverns near Rokeby, and a soft touch for a loan. In the feudal society that existed around the Hudson River estates, Henry overstepped the acceptable boundaries. His "going native" and mixing with the locals was considered an unseemly act of rebellion. But things got worse.

In 1871 forty-year-old Henry abruptly married Malvina Dinehart, the daughter (one account says she was fifteen, another that she was twenty-seven) of poor German farmers from across the river. Malvina had none of the proper breeding expected of an Astor spouse, but she did manage to pull off a spectacular coup. She and Henry married in such haste that she was not forced to sign the family's standard prenuptial agreement in which the bride agrees to waive her dower rights to the Astor fortune in exchange for a sum of money. This custom had the force of law within the Astor family. The reason for it was simple: by following this practice religiously, control of the Astor estate would never slip out of Astor hands. To the family's horror, Malvina retained her dower rights, the first woman in the direct Astor line to do so. When news of Henry's wedding plans reached New York, a meeting was convened at the family's Prince Street office, and William B. Astor Jr. was hastily dispatched to Dutchess County to stop the proceedings. He was too late; Henry had already married.

Consequences ensued. Henry's father, William B., all but wrote him out of his will. "My son Henry, having recently formed a matrimonial connexion under peculiar circumstances without my knowledge," the irate father wrote, referring to his son as if he were an adolescent boy rather than a middle-aged man, "I think it proper to revoke and annul to the extent hereinafter specified the disposition in his favor or for his benefit or for the benefit of his issue." The original bequest to Henry, worth hundreds of thousands of dollars, was summarily reduced to thirty thousand dollars. William B. ceased writing letters to his son.

Henry expressed indifference about this reduced patrimony. "Money counts for little in this world compared with love and life," he liked to say—perhaps an easy statement for a millionaire to make, for Henry had no money problems whatsoever. His grandfather, John Jacob Astor, had left him a lifetime quarter-interest in a prime stretch of Manhattan real estate from 42nd Street to 51st Street between Broadway and the Hudson—the original Eden Farm. The shrewd paterfamilias had picked up the farm for $25,000; in Henry's lifetime the land would be valued at $20 million.

William B. wavered at taking full financial vengeance on his youngest son. John Jacob's will gave William B. the power to strip heirs of Eden's income if they should "become unworthy of this devise." But William B. held back, either taking pity on his son—perhaps believing that Henry's volatile and obstreperous personality left him incapable of making his way in the world without assistance—or perhaps fearing the public ridicule that would ensue if he allowed a son to sink into penury. For whatever reason, William B. did not take away Henry's meal ticket. Henry continued to receive income from his quarter-share of Eden Farm, though his personal control of the property had long since been taken away from him. The Astor estate office sent Henry quarterly checks, which he would merely squirrel away, uncashed for long periods, until he needed money. This habit drove the estate managers to distraction—and may have brought Henry some perverse pleasure—as they were forever unable to balance their books.

The year before his estranged father died, Henry and Malvina moved northeast of Rokeby to a farm in Columbia County, on the Massachusetts border. Henry built a racetrack on the two-hundred-acre property, and paved one room of the house with silver dollars. When he heard that hotel bars and lobbies had picked up on the coin idea, he ripped out his own floor in disgust, feeling that his inspiration had been cheapened. He took to giving sermons in his parlor, wearing a surplice and banging on a bell with a crowbar to punctuate his remarks. He did this with or without benefit of an audience. These eccentric details became public fodder in a court case heard in Poughkeepsie, after a local farmer related to Malvina's family, a man whom many suspected of coveting a chunk of the Astor fortune, alleged that a drunken Henry had attacked his four-year-old daughter and permanently injured her. The Astors tried to look the other way, but the allegations—and the portrait painted of Henry—were humiliating to the family. The plaintiff's lawyer hammered him for drunkenness, claiming that Malvina had once stated that "the red-eyed hound ought to be hung"—a claim she later denied during her testimony. But the damage to his reputation was done, and the jury awarded the plaintiff $20,000.

Henry's name was invoked with horror whenever a family member exhibited outlandish behavior, or dared to enter an inappropriate marriage; but the renegade Astor left a more tangible and profitable legacy to his grandnieces and -nephews. When Henry's estate property was sold in 1920, several years after his death, the Chanler siblings all received their piece of his Eden—roughly $200,000 each, or, as Archie's brother Winty called it, "the last cookie in the jar."

With the prodigal son banished, William B. Astor's cortege moved slowly down Fifth Avenue amid the clatter of horses and carriages, its dignity intact. As the procession turned onto West 25th Street just before 10:00 a.m., Archie could see a crush of spectators gathered in front of Trinity Chapel, the handsome brownstone church designed by Richard Upjohn twenty years earlier as an uptown branch for Wall Street's Trinity Church. (In death, William B. preferred to be buried from his neighborhood chapel rather than from fashionable Grace Church on 10th Street, to which he also belonged.) A phalanx of police was on hand to open a path amid the curiosity seekers so that the mourners—the city's most august citizens—could make their way into the church. The *New York Times* reported that among those assembled were "representatives of all the oldest and wealthiest families of New York"—the Beekmans and Stuyvesants, the Rhinelanders and Brevoorts. Also in attendance were John Schermerhorn, Peter Cooper, John Jay, and Peter Goelet.

As Archie and his relatives made their way up the aisle at Trinity Chapel, the eyes of old- and new-money New York were upon them. Expectations were high for the heirs to the great William B. Astor. Bishop Potter, assisted by four other ministers, officiated at the Episcopal service for the dead. Thirty male choir members chanted the funeral psalm "Lord, Let Me Know Mine End" and sang a number of hymns. At the conclusion of the service, the procession re-formed, but this time only family members made the long, sad trip up Broadway and Bloomingdale Road to Trinity Cemetery at 153rd Street, the rural burying ground for Wall Street's Trinity Church and its uptown branch. William B. Astor's body was placed in the family vault there.

The service itself went seamlessly; but the *New York Herald*'s account of the funeral ends with the image of the three-hundred-pound Isaac Brown protesting the insinuation that William B. Astor was—to put it mildly—less than generous to those in need. Brown begged to differ. Having just successfully put the multimillionaire to rest in grand style, he was not about to denigrate Astor's character. Brown claimed that Astor had given freely to the fire department and the Masons—as if that were enough.

◆◆◆

After this melancholy break, Archie and Winty returned to their boarding school, St. John's Military Academy in Sing Sing. A much greater shock than the death of their great-grandfather awaited them. They received a letter from Maddie, giving her "dearest boys" an update on the comings and goings of the household. Despite the black band of mourning around the edge of the stationery, the letter had a cheery tone: brothers Willie and Marion had attended the first day of school at Mr. MacMullen's and it was a big success—"they came home charmed with it." Afterward they went off to riding school, and Maddie was happy to report that their equestrian skills had vastly improved from the previous winter. "We are all well," she writes, though admitting, "I miss Grandpa very much." She ends with "Goodnight dear boys—Your most devoted Mother," and then adds a final practical note as a P.S.: "If Winty's new drawers are too long he must turn up the leg a little way." This was probably her last communication with her boys. Twelve days later she was dead. There was no mention of any illness, but it was later said that Maddie had caught a cold at William B.'s funeral and it developed into pneumonia. She was thirty-seven.

Once more, Maddie's ten surviving sons and daughters, ranging in age from Archie at thirteen to Egerton, who had just turned one, endured the rituals of death. Once more, the smallest Chanlers had to be lifted up to peer into the casket to look upon the dead—but this time it was their mother laid out in the front hall of their own home at 192 Madison Avenue. Another funeral procession was organized; this time Archie and his siblings would be in the lead carriages. Hundreds of mourners packed St. Mark's-in-the-Bowery, and the neighboring streets were blocked with "private equipages." Nearly all the Astor family members turned out for the sad occasion.

"The great chancel was nearly covered in flowers," the *New York Herald* reported on December 17, 1875, "all of them being of the most exquisite design, while the casket, which was covered with purple velvet and lined with lead, could hardly be seen for the wreaths, crowns, and crosses of flowers heaped upon it." Eight ministers officiated, three of whom had just helped lay William B. Astor to rest, including the rector of Christ Church, the Episcopal church near Rokeby that had been built by the Astors. Once more, the long drive to the Astor burial grounds at Trinity Cemetery in the far reaches of upper Manhattan. The cemetery spread over a hillside rising above the Hudson River; it was a bucolic spot, once farmland owned by the famous bird artist John James Audubon. (He was also buried there.) Archie was immune to the view—after all, he had just been there for his great-grandfather, and he was still in shock over his mother's death. It had all happened so unexpectedly, so suddenly. Archie was bereft without her. His mother had been so generally beloved that the *New York Times* even printed an editorial about her stellar qualities:

> Yesterday morning the funeral services of a woman of the brightest excellence of character and life took place at the old Church of St. Mark's in the bowery, beneath which . . . the remains of Petrus Stuyvesant, the last Dutch Captain General of New-Amsterdam, are laid. This church has seen the weddings, the christenings, and the funerals of many persons distinguished in New-York society and in the annals of the country. . . . But the last rites were never paid within its walls to one who deserved more honor, or who will be more sincerely mourned, than the lady to whom we have alluded.

The writer went on to extol her "all-embracing love, good-will, charity and tenderness . . . [and her] air of sweet serenity which comes of self-restraint."

Though their mother had just died, Archie and Winty were sent back to school in Sing Sing. Before he left home, Archie received a legal notice, signed by his father as executor of his mother's estate, informing the oldest son that there was to be an official inventory and appraisal of all Maddie's "goods, chattels, and credits." Thus another critical element of the boys' education began: learning the legal intricacies, and the responsibilities, of inherited wealth. Their father would offer them some pointed instruction in a letter to Winty at school several months later: "Tell Archie to bring down the law paper served on him and on you by the young man from Mr. Van Winkles office. You must be very careful to keep all such papers. When you reach here I will explain the object of serving those papers on you both." Edgar Van Winkle had been appointed as "Special Guardian" to take care of the children's interests regarding William B. Astor's will since their mother Maddie had died before her grandfather's will had been settled. In short order William B. Astor's will became a public record—and the subject of much unpleasant discussion in the press, which decried his "modest" beneficence. Archie, of course, read all about this in the newspapers as did his classmates. (Archie subscribed to the Democratic-leaning *New York World* rather than the *Times,* which catered to the patrician interests in the city, so he would have seen the sharp barbs directed at his great-grandfather.) Archie's father offered a warning about the need for reticence: "In the mean time I think you should avoid talking or writing to any one about the [legal] papers; you may be misled or misunderstand the subject, & mistate the case." And then, as a final word of caution: "It is always best to keep family matters to ourselves—then no one can gossip about your affairs." This last bit of advice would be flagrantly ignored by his children in the years to come.

Emotional solace was in shorter supply than legal counsel. Their father was certainly concerned about them—in his first letter to Archie, just back to school after his mother's death, J.W. urged his son to write often—whenever you have leisure or feel like chatting with me." He went on to announce that the family had collected a box full of "Dear Mama's hair" and that lockets containing a miniature portrait of their mother were being made up at Kurtz's photo studio in New York. (The siblings had similar lockets for their dead sister, Emily.) Both boys would receive the mementos of their mother as soon as they were finished. But then the letter moved onto more comfortable ground—sports.

> Tell Wintie that I will have to refuse to let him box with his friends, unless he uses more judgment. He can never box well if he tires himself out in boxing with any one who happens to be in a humor to try on the gloves. He should pick out one worthy antagonist a little more skillful than himself and then try to come off best. By that he may learn something new each time. Wintie wrote us a very flattering account of your bout with young Hopkins. By this [time] you have your skates and I hope good smooth ice to skate on. Do be careful about the air-holes & thin ice.

J. W. Chanler and his sons could somehow never find a way or even the language to confront their shared grief. "I received your letter, and I am so glad that you want me to tell you all my troubles, and all my wants," Archie wrote to his father on January 10, 1877. But he failed to share his troubles, following instead with the pro forma, "We are both very well and we are enjoying ourselves very much, as the coasting is splendid, and as we can skate in the play ground." It was an era when feelings were rarely discussed openly, and upper-class children were kept at a discreet distance from their parents. Yet J.W. himself—though trained as a lawyer and experienced in rough political infighting—had the soul of a poet, and indulged his own feelings of loss in verse. Handwritten pages survive of his poems in progress—with lines edited, words slashed, and syllables carefully counted. He was putting his grief into sonnet form, and a series of these poems, written while he was in Newport during the fall of 1877, speak to his heartrending sorrow.

King Death

Death has been crowned our King today:
He bore my Love in triumph away,
With him to his realms beyond the grave.
I am left Oh! God! bereft to grieve

Alone, upon this blighted height,
Where she went from me. Around me all is night.
With pomp and pageantry did he come
To take my Love to her unknown home.
Decked with flowers and a velvet pall,
My love silently passed the portal
Of Death's Kingdom, where stands her tomb.
Here I am left in agony and gloom
To guard, the sweet flowers she hath left
As tokens of herself, my Loves gift.

The flowers Maddie left behind were their children, and J.W. had his hands full trying to tend to the eight little ones left at home—the youngest scarcely a toddler—while managing his dead wife's estate. He called upon an unmarried cousin from South Carolina, the dutiful and sternly Calvinist Mary Marshall, to come north and tend to his children. She devoted the rest of her life to that rambunctious brood. The children also needed a reliable tutor, so once more J.W. turned to a relative for advice. His cousin, Reverend Gibson, headmaster at St. John's, recommended a Mr. Bostwick as a live-in tutor for the younger boys. Bostwick, too, would become a long-term fixture and beloved member of the Chanler circle. In his letters home, Archie's interest in his other siblings was matched only by his inquiries after Mr. Bostwick—and his horses.

J.W. gave up his political life. The schoolboy letters addressed to and from "Papa" show him in a state of motion between the various family properties he now controlled—from the Manhattan town house at 192 Madison Avenue, to Cliff Lawn in Newport, to Brookdale Farm in Delaware County, New York, to Rokeby, the riverfront country estate in Dutchess County. Little more than a month after his spouse's death he went up to the Hudson Valley with his wife's uncle Franklin Delano. They stayed at Delano's estate, Steen Valetje, which was adjacent to Rokeby, so Chanler was able to check on the condition of the house that his wife had inherited. She had loved Rokeby deeply but had not had time to take over its care before her premature death. It seemed the proper place to bring up his motherless brood, but the house was not suitable for winter; there was no heat. Chanler recalled another January at Rokeby almost fourteen years earlier, when he and his bride had gone there for their honeymoon but found the place so drafty and cold that they picked up and left for Cuba.

The new widower checked in with the farmer working at Rokeby, and took a long Sunday-afternoon stroll with Franklin Delano. The two men walked through paths and fields covered in fresh snow. It was a moody day—clouds skittered across the sky, leaving the landscape "checkered with light & shadows." The mountains to the west across the Hudson varied in tone from white, snow-covered peaks to misty purple and gray ones. The foreground looked "very bleak" to Chanler, with the weight of his sorrow bearing down on him. J.W. went on in this pensive vein in a letter to his son Winty at St. John's, and spoke of the sad plight of an unattached squirrel, feeling an obvious kinship with this lonely creature:

> One little squirrel played about on the snow at the foot of the hill in the rear of Uncle Frank's house. I saw him running races with himself from the tree in which he lives, to a little clump of shrubs, where I think he must have buried some food. He cocked up his tail & skipt along as lively as if he had his mate with him. But I could not see any other squirrel or any other living thing within eyeshot. What a brave little chap he must be to fight it out all alone through the dismal winter.

J.W., caught in his own "black despair," left Archie and Winty pretty much on their own. He apparently never visited them at school, though they were but a short distance away; in fact, he would take the train from New York to Rokeby and pass right through Sing Sing without stopping. He probably figured they were not lonely; after all, they had each other—though that was a decidedly mixed blessing, given how competitive they were. Yet the boys' letters home were upbeat:

"We like our room in the Tower very much indeed," Archie reported on their shared quarters, a plum room assignment arranged by the headmaster at their father's request. "Besides having a beautiful view of the river it has a chimney & register & a ventillater." When the cold weather descended, however, it was a different story. A pitcher full of water froze in their room that winter, and when it rained in January, "our room leaked like a sieve."

In the winter of 1877, J.W. had a brief reunion with his two boys at West Point. Archie and Winty had gone there on a school outing, but the pageantry of the day was outshone by the sheer pleasure of seeing their father. J.W. left before the cadets had completed their maneuvers, and the Chanler boys could scarcely wait for the formal dress parade to be finished before dashing to the dock to try to catch one last glimpse of their father on a departing boat. Archie and Winty waved their handkerchiefs frantically. "Did you see us?" Winty later wrote plaintively to his father.

J.W. made preparations to move his children to Rokeby, where he hoped the clean country air would revitalize them; besides, this move would have pleased his wife. She had been delighted and surprised to have been left the house by her grandfather; she had already begun ordering wallpaper for the bedrooms in the few short weeks between his death and hers. Chanler set out to make the place habitable year-round. He put in a hot-air furnace to heat the place, though the house was so vast—full of huge, high-ceilinged rooms, enormous French windows, and long, drafty hallways—that the furnace would always be overmatched. The rooms on the east side of the house on the first two floors could get warm enough; but the rest of the house remained frigid during cold weather. He improved the indoor plumbing, though the entire household had to share one bathroom. (Prior to that, there had been a large, separate privy, a stuccoed structure with its own cornice and separate entrances for the family and the servants. The gentry's side of the privy was paneled in walnut, the servant's portion in pine.) Chanler updated the farm buildings. He built a new stable and barn, a new corn crib and chicken coop. Archie followed news of the renovations eagerly.

In May of 1876 the children—minus Archie and Winty—arrived by horse-drawn carriage to the front door at Rokeby. This would be their new home. Margaret raced to the lawn to pick a flower that had caught her eye, but her sister Bessie tried to prevent her from plucking it. An old gardener, a man who had worked at Rokeby since the days of General Armstrong, admonished the older sister. "Don't stop her," he said. "She owns it as much as you do." And indeed the house now belonged to all the children to "share and share alike" according to the terms of their mother's will. Rokeby, once the province of silent dinners and rigid decorum, rang with the shrieks and laughter of children. J. W. Chanler, a brilliant talker himself, encouraged the art of conversation around the dinner table. In letters to his sons at St. John's, Chanler described the mayhem at Rokeby—the children's riding accidents and tussles with one another. On one occasion he feared that Robert had dislocated his hip in a fight with his sister Margaret. A surgeon was summoned, but the injury proved minor. Nine-year-old Willie took on the personas of heroes he admired: after reading *Ivanhoe,* he "went forth . . . with a rush & is scalping the crowd with savage ferocity," according to his father. The younger Marion followed suit—he "borrowed the tales of the crusaders from Willie & is riding rough shod through Palestine." For their boisterous antics, the middle boys—Willie, Marion, and Lewis—came to be called "the three Pirates." Exiled at St. John's, Archie could not wait to get home to join his siblings in this country paradise. It meant horseback riding and goat carts, swims in the Hudson and long walks in the woods, and contemplative solitude afforded by climbing up the spiral staircase in the "wasp-haunted" attic to the observation deck atop William B. Astor's four-story tower. All was peaceful here. Archie could look out upon the sheep grazing on the lawn, the hired hands working in the fields, and the Hudson River and Catskill Mountains in the distance beyond. He could survey the domain passed down through generations of Livingstons, Armstrongs, Astors, and Chanlers. This was his patrimony; as firstborn son, he was expected to take all of this under his wing. But first Archie would be sent into further exile.

In the spring of 1877, John Winthrop Chanler abruptly removed his two sons from St. John's before the end of the term. He wanted them educated as gentlemen, and in that gilded era there was no better—or more prestigious—way of gaining a high social polish than by rubbing shoulders with the sons of British aristocrats. An English public school, heavy on the classics and rich with tradition, would be the answer. In addition, J.W. decided that poor, nervous Bessie—who had taken on the burden of being the surrogate mother to her younger siblings—could also benefit by making a fresh start abroad and entering an English finishing school for girls. Winty was deposited with a tutor to prepare him for Eton; Archie was left at Hillbrow, a preparatory school for Rugby; and Bessie was delivered to Miss Sewell's school on the Isle of Wight. Archie was terribly homesick and begged his father to let him come home, but to no avail.

Archie survived Hillbrow and then Rugby; that is, until he flunked out—or, in official parlance, was "superannuated." Though an indifferent student, Archie was drilled in the classics and in the brutal social order of the English public schools. Canings were administered by the masters as well as by the "swells"—the best students, the star athletes who were given free rein to do pretty much as they pleased. (The masters chose to look the other way.) The "swells" preyed on the younger, weaker students who became their "fags." It was an entrenched system of power, a kind of legalized slavery that Archie did his best to avoid. There were endless rules of etiquette, and if a student breached any of them it was considered "swagger," and there was hell to pay. Archie later wrote in depth about the "mysteries of swagger."

> What was swagger for one was not swagger for all, for what was swagger for a new boy was not swagger for a boy who had been there a term and what was swagger in one boy was not nearly so much so in another boy who had been there the same length of time but who was better than he in games, and so on a regular gradation, based upon the length of time a boy had been there, how good he was at games and where he stood in school. . . . Among the numerous things which were considered swagger & which . . . [a fellow student] warned me against were the following. Never to whistle, shout, or talk

> loud about the house, the only place I could do that being in my study, & there not loud enough to be heard next door, for if the fellows next door . . . [were] at all swell they were liable to come in & see who it was, and tell me to "shut up and stop swaggering" which would at once give me a bad name in the house, as the swells next door would report it to the rest of the house. . . . Another, and a very important thing was never, under any considerations to have both hands in your pocket when walking or standing by yourself, a breach of this was tremendous swagger as only swells of the 1st water could do this. If it was a very cold day and you had your books in one hand you could put the other in your pocket but not if you had both hands empty, then you must walk with both hands at your side. When two fellows were walking together they must always "hook on" [arm in arm], and then the one who is hooked onto can have both hands in his pockets while the one that hooks on can only have one in. Two fellows in different houses can never under any circumstances walk together, but if by accident they are both going the same way and one happens to catch up with him they must not "hook on" as that is not only the topmost pinnacle of swagger but "awfully bad form." A fellow must never unless way out in the country out of sight of everybody turn his trousers up no matter how rainy the day or how dirty the streets, and if coming in from a long walk he forgets to turn them down but goes into tea with them turned up he is "spotted" immediately and must be very circumspect in his conduct for a week or so in order to escape a "journey to the North." [What horror that involved, Archie does not say.] In short a new boy has got to be on the lookout the whole time in order to avoid committing some breach of etiquette. For a School Swell no such thing as swagger exists, so he can go about with both hands in his pockets, hook onto a swell in another house, or do whatever he pleases.

Another unwritten rule of the English public schools was that one must never speak of mothers and homes. This indicated weakness and violated the culture of "manliness." In fact, photos of mothers or sisters were considered taboo items, never to be displayed in a student's room. In the first letter Archie wrote to his father giving a lengthy account—it ran to twenty handwritten pages—of his new life at Hillbrow, he mentions that he entrusted the locket with a photo of his mother to Mrs. Elsee, the wife of a Rugby master. Archie visited Mrs. Elsee frequently to view his mother's portrait and to pour out his sorrow. "I saw dear Mamma's portrait & had a nice quiet talk with Mrs. Elsee. I really love Mrs. Elsee she is just like a mother to me. She told me to tell her everything & that whatever I told her [she] should never tell to anyone." Archie later brought the kindly Mrs. Elsee another locket for safekeeping, this one containing the miniature photo of his dead sister, Emily. Mrs. Elsee kept the lockets of his dead mother and sister side by side in the same box. When Archie came to visit, he would look upon them as precious relics. He did not dare keep such treasured items in his room and risk the mocking insults of his schoolmates. Order, rank, discipline—and the cruelty that resulted if those tenets were violated—these were the lessons absorbed by Archie at Rugby.

In the fall of 1877, Archie received an unexpected telegram from his cousin Bob Winthrop in Paris, saying that Bob would be arriving that day to see him. Archie must have been pleasantly surprised. He had not seen his cousin since the previous spring—in London, when his father had been in town. While eating his midday dinner, Archie was summoned to the headmaster's study by a servant. Cousin Bob stood there, looking pale and nervous. He made a few polite inquiries—How was Archie getting on? Had he finished his midday dinner yet?—and then blurted out that "dear Papa was dead."

J. W. Chanler had died at fifty-one, at Rokeby, from an excess of chivalry. He contracted a cold, which quickly developed into pneumonia, after playing croquet on wet grass. His female opponent wanted to continue to play despite the conditions; John Winthrop, being a gentleman, deferred to her wishes.

"I was nearly knocked off my feet by the blow," Archie wrote to his siblings. "But Cousin Bob comforted me and told me that I must be the strongest as I was the oldest and bear up against it." Archie had just turned fifteen. He had to act bravely—even if he did not feel that way. He asked the headmaster, Mr. Vecqueray, to join them in the study. Cousin Bob repeated the tragic news for Vecqueray. What should Archie do? The three of them decided that he should stay put, continue on at school, and focus on his work. In short order, Cousin Bob was gone, off to deliver the stunning news to Winty and Bessie. He would be too late; telegrams had already arrived at their schools announcing the death.

Astors, Stuyvesants, and Winthrops crowded once more into St. Mark's-in-the-Bowery. The mayor of New York served as one of the pallbearers. No funeral oration was delivered; there were no flowers. Perhaps this had been John Winthrop's request; or perhaps the death was just so sudden and incomprehensible and sad, that neither words nor flowers could console the orphans left behind. The funeral cortege moved slowly up Broadway to Trinity Cemetery at 153rd Street. The silver casket was placed in the family vault; John Winthrop was laid beside his wife.

Archie did not even hear about his father's death until the day of the funeral. That day he took up pen and, in his new role as the eldest in the family, wrote in stoic fashion to his siblings at Rokeby:

> *To Willie, Marion, Lewis, Margaret, Robert, Alida and Pedge—*
>
> *My dear brothers and sisters, I am very well and I am trying to bear up under this great affliction, which God has seen fit to send us, as well as I can. . . . I have just got a letter from Wintie yesterday. Wintie is bearing up very well, and so is Bessie as I got a letter from her a day or two ago. We are all in perfect health, and are in as good spirits as we can afford. . . . Write to me soon. How are you all.*
>
> *Keep cheerful as possible. From your loving Archie.*

Despite Archie's stoic tone, the moorings of his world had come undone.

Marooned in England, Archie received a notice to appear at Surrogate's Court in New York for a proceeding about his father's estate, though it was all but impossible for him to attend. He wrote to his cousin Mary Marshall, who was watching over his siblings, asking for "a copy of Dear Papa's will." As the eldest son Archie received the lion's share of the property and responsibility. He would become the master of Rokeby, the heart and soul of the Chanler empire. Although all ten surviving children shared equally in the estate by the terms of their mother's will, J.W.'s will made it clear that Archie should eventually become the sole proprietor. This would help ensure that the Chanler name would continue on the Hudson. When he turned twenty-one, Archie would receive $100,000 as an "unconditional gift" bestowed "with the hope and wish" that he would use the money to maintain Rokeby. Archie received the ancestral Armstrong silver, woods and farmland south of Rokeby, and, ironically, an orphanage—St. Margaret's Home for Orphan Children, a charitable institution near Rokeby, founded by his great-grandmother. Archie was charged with "keeping up and supporting the said St. Margaret's Home as a memorial" to his mother and great-grandmother. To that end, he was bequeathed a $50,000 fund, the income from which would maintain the institution.

Perhaps the most important clause in the will was the nineteenth and final one, in which J.W. named the guardians who would look after his children if he should die, an event he assumed lay in the distant future—but just six months after writing his will, J.W. was dead. The majority of the eight guardians, all relatives, were childless and had not a clue as to how to raise children. At first the guardians considered breaking up the family, but the children begged not to be separated. Their Southern cousin Mary Marshall rallied to their cause, agreeing to stay on at Rokeby and bring up the orphans under the legal and financial oversight of the guardians. Archie would become a guardian when he reached his twenty-first birthday.

Archie remained in England and gained admission, after several tries, to the elite Rugby School. He lasted little more than a year before flunking out in 1878. A report card in the papers at Rokeby portrays a less-than-sparkling performance by a boy who was undoubtedly weighed down by the crushing losses he had borne: "Gives a great deal of trouble by talking & fidgetting. . . . Is always in a hurry

& so blunders a great deal . . . rather disobedient & grumbling at times."

Archie returned to the States in the spring of 1878 for a reunion with brothers and sisters he had not seen in two years. Everyone had changed, especially Archie: during his public-school life he had gained the polish of a young British aristocrat, with the wardrobe, manners, and accent of the English upper crust. His academic failure at Rugby did not derail his education. The guardians engaged a tutor to prepare Archie for Columbia College, a school favored by his social set and by the Chanler family in particular. The onetime slacker remade himself into an excellent student, taking two degrees at Columbia, his B.A. in 1883 and a master's in 1884, studying philosophy and psychology. He took a break with a trip to the Southwest, where he mingled with cowboys, marveled at the tobacco-spitting prowess of ranch women, and returned east with a six-shooter—a memento, he claimed, of time he spent with Indian fighters in Apache territory. He went back to Columbia and studied the law long enough to pass the bar exam, but did not linger to get the degree. He had had enough of classrooms.

Archie capped off his studies with the Grand Tour, the conventional rite of polish for young gentlemen of his class. Nine days after his law exam, he boarded a ship bound for England with his brother Winty and a farmhand from Rokeby, Charles Hartnett, pressed into service as a valet. Well-connected cousins and letters of introduction opened doors at the highest rungs of society in London, Paris, and Italy. The brothers were entertained by "titled swells," and enjoyed a Foreign Office reception with the Prince and Princess of Wales. But then Archie led his traveling companions off the traditional path to more exotic locales—Havana, Vera Cruz, and Mexico City—and to farther outposts in the West Indies and Central and South America, places where the accommodations were not so "swell." They tramped across mountains and through dusty, insect-ridden backwater towns. One winter night they slept in a mountain hut, wrapped only in Mexican serapes to protect themselves from the cold (the shawls did nothing to deter the ravenous fleas that feasted on them). Along the way the party was joined by the Gilded Age bon vivant Oliver Hazard Perry Belmont and several others; but as time went on and the dirt and fleas and bad food continued, the boon companions peeled off one by one. Accompanied only by a local guide, Archie journeyed on alone.

It was Archie's nature, perhaps abetted by his studies in philosophy and psychology, to be introspective, a trait that set him apart from many of his roistering Gilded Age peers, whose interests ran to attending balls, hunting, building a more extravagant mansion than the pals at the club, and not much deeper. Around this time Archie made an oath to himself, a vow that he would strive to "know his own mind." He was a seeker, restless and driven, and the landscape he most yearned to know was the one within himself.

TWO

The Marriage Mart

Twenty-four. Unattached. Handsome. And very rich. In his stocking feet he stood five feet ten and a half inches, and moved with the grace of an athlete. He had taken up amateur boxing—a gentleman's sport at the time—and proved to be an apt pupil. His brown, wavy hair was parted in the middle; he sported a rakish mustache and a beard in the current French fashion. There was a sweetness about him, a sincerity and seriousness in his eyes, and a guarded, mysterious look as well. That was Archie in the summer of 1887 when he arrived in Newport for the social season, one of the most eligible young bachelors in town.

Newport was "the very Holy of Holies, the playground of the great ones of the earth from which all intruders were ruthlessly excluded by a set of cast-iron rules," according to one dowager. In some ways it was an odd choice for the Gilded Age rich. The "season" was short, its high point stretching only from the Fourth of July to September. There were only a handful of beaches, and there was no broad promenade where strollers could be seen and admired; instead there was a narrow, winding "Cliff Walk" along the bluffs overlooking the water. Fog blew in often, and the wet sea air kept everyone and everything damp. Yet the place gained fame for a healthful climate, a *New York Times* reporter pronouncing that its atmosphere offered "a kind of elixir vitae." Invalids were immersed in the water and seaweed as therapy. Even the fog got a boost from a local clergyman: "The fogs are proverbially a good cosmetic and there is a tradition that the fair daughters of Newport owed their lustrous complexions to sleeping with their heads out the window when the mists of the sea prevailed."

Founded in 1639 as a refuge for religious dissenters from Massachusetts, Newport became a haven for Quakers who flocked to the town and built a simple, unadorned meeting house and school. In the eighteenth century, the West Indian slave trade turned Newport into a booming commercial harbor and a popular summer resort for planters from the Caribbean and the South. So many Southerners, particularly from Charleston, began to congregate in Newport that the town became known as "the hospital of the Carolinas."

Archie had a connection to almost every aspect of Newport's history (save the Quakers). The litany of his Newport relatives included colonial governors, wealthy Southern planters, intellectual trendsetters, and millionaire potentates. Courtesy of his grandfather, Sam Ward, Archie could boast roots back to the very earliest days of Newport. The first Ward who came to America settled in Newport in the seventeenth century. During the colonial era, two different Wards—father and son—served as governors of Rhode Island. "Aunt Julia," Sam's sister Julia Ward Howe (she had married Samuel Gridley Howe of Boston in 1843), presided over Newport's literary and intellectual circle and served as the resort's unofficial, and largely ignored, social and political conscience. She had been a precocious thinker. As a young girl Julia discussed predestination with the Astors on the piazza at Rokeby; undoubtedly the Astors were pleased to learn from their young relative that their fortune might have come to them as part of a divine, unalterable plan. A tireless reformer, ardent abolitionist, woman suffragist, writer, and lecturer, Aunt Julia crisscrossed the country giving speeches, mesmerizing her overflow audiences. Her appearances would inevitably be capped by her stirring recitation of "The Battle Hymn of the Republic," the poem she had written in 1861 after watching Union soldiers march into battle.

For Julia, Newport had always been part pastoral refuge, part intellectual hothouse. There she was surrounded by great writers and thinkers. Henry James Sr., one of the titans of intellectual thought in the mid-nineteenth century, came by often for spirited discourse—as did William Wadsworth Longfellow, Dr. Oliver Wendell Holmes, and Bret Harte. Oscar Wilde stayed with the Howes in 1882, and caused a sensation in Newport with his shoulder-length hair, slouch hat, salmon-colored scarf, and a flower in his hand. In 1871, Julia helped create the Town and Country Club, an organization devoted to pursuing intellectual subjects lest, in her words, "the Newport season should entirely evaporate into the shallow pursuit of amusement." The club lasted for some thirty years, and its list of members was formidable, including the Harvard naturalist Alexander Agassiz, the artist John LaFarge, the neurologist Silas Weir Mitchell (who would loom large in Archie's life), the architect Richard Morris Hunt, and the poet Emma Lazarus, who penned the famous lines on the Statue of Liberty ("Give me your tired, your poor, your huddled masses," hardly the constituency of the Town and Country Club). Scientists and poets—and, of course, Julia Ward Howe herself—lectured the group; on one occasion Mark Twain "furnished the champagne with his witticisms."

The intellectual ferment surrounding Julia helped shape Archie's development. He shared a deep love of literature with his great-aunt. He also shared her belief that the old-timers in Newport were a cut above the nouveau riche descending upon Newport in greater and greater numbers in the waning years of the nineteenth century. Fortunes had been made in the post–Civil War industrial boom, and a garish competition in excess took hold of Newport by the 1880s. The fastest yacht, the largest "cottage," the most sumptuous party—these became the yardsticks by which newcomers measured one another. The Chanlers, like their great-aunt Julia, looked askance at that kind of conspicuous consumption. Archie's sister later wrote that their father laughed "at the social pretenders and their vulgarities [which] taught us to resent some of the resort's grandness."

Archie's father had built their house in Newport in the early 1870s, just before the high tide of money and ego. The January 4, 1873, edition of the *Newport Mercury* described the Chanlers' "handsome two story house" then being erected on the cliffs overlooking Easton's Beach. "The location is one of the finest on the island," the newspaper opined, "and the home is being built in an expensive manner." (Of course, the $30,000 price tag would pale next to the reported $11 million that the William K. Vanderbilts spent to build and furnish their marble "cottage" about twenty years later.)

Chanler named his new summer home "Cliff Lawn," and a contemporary book about Newport described its picturesque setting, the house sitting "almost on the extreme verge of the cliff," commanding "an uninterrupted view of all that is going on at the beach."* It was one of the first great houses in Newport to be built on the bluff. The rocky "Cliff Walk" footpath passed by the Chanler property, but below the level of the lawn, so that anyone strolling by would remain unseen. The house was charming, with a mansard roof punctuated by several pyramidal towers, and a spacious wraparound piazza that allowed one to enjoy the spectacular views and the cool sea breezes. Julia Ward Howe's daughter recalled the gracious cotillion ball given as a housewarming for the Chanlers' new home, during which bouquets of white camellias were given out as favors.

For Archie and his siblings, Cliff Lawn evoked happy memories of sailing and picnics and sport. From every perch in the house, Archie could hear the foghorns and look out to sea. Newport was full of stories about the island's pirates—even Captain Kidd had lived

---

*The building still sits on its perch above the water, but has been remodeled over the years and is now barely recognizable. It has undergone a series of incarnations—all-girls country day school, summer residence for a bishop, museum for the paintings of a local eccentric, and finally a hotel. The house earned a measure of fame in 1960 when the great jazz bassist Charles Mingus held a music festival there as an alternative to the official Newport Jazz Festival.

there. The beach just below Cliff Lawn had its own curious history. A crewless brig had landed there over a century earlier. The ship had been discovered stuck in the sand with her sails set, an uneaten breakfast laid out for the crew, a fire burning in the galley, and not a living soul on board except a dog and a cat. The crew had vanished, and Newporters still puzzled over the mystery.

A sepia photograph shows the Chanler family at Cliff Lawn in the summer of 1875, just months before the death of Archie's mother. The photo was taken from a distance to get a full view of the large but cozy wooden villa with its gingerbread touches. It sits alone in the landscape and overlooks the sea. The family is strung out along the verandah. Mother and father are seated flanking the open front door, holding their youngest children in their laps—one-year-old Egerton and two-year-old Alida. The other eight children are in various poses, along with what appear to be several members of the household staff. A horse and carriage stand waiting in front of the house. It is a mysterious, evocative photograph. All the figures are dwarfed by the size of the verandah and house; the distant camera cannot capture any of their expressions. It's a rather lonesome image, as if the house and large family were a world unto themselves, dropped into the middle of nowhere.

The old-money ethos gave way before a tidal wave of cash that washed over Newport. Archie's friend and traveling pal Oliver H. P. Belmont built Belcourt Castle, the incarnation of the nobody-can-top-this mentality of the Gilded Age, with sixty rooms and a staff of thirty. Part medieval fantasy, part Louis XIII hunting lodge, Belcourt (now open as a museum) distinguished itself from other palaces in that it housed Belmont's horses as sumptuously as the human occupants. Julia Ward Howe described the mansion with mixed bafflement and outrage: "It is a most singular house. The first floor is all stable, with stalls for some thirteen or more horses, all filled, and everything elaborate and elegant." The horses were not only comfortably quartered but fashionably clad, sporting different garments for morning, afternoon, and evening wear. They had elaborate coverings made of crisp white linen on which was embroidered the Belmont crest—a helmet along with the motto *Sans Crainte* ("Without Fear"). Julia was disgusted that horses should be housed so lavishly while the poor lived so wretchedly: "But Oh! To lodge horses so, and be content that men and women should lodge in sheds and cellars!" she wrote. Above the stable was a grand salon. Two stuffed horses—Belmont's particular favorites during their lifetimes—stood like sentries at either end of the magnificent room. Atop them were figures in medieval armor. (Oliver, who was small in stature, decided to wear one of those coats of mail to an 1897 costume ball in New York, and collapsed under the weight.) Julia, invited to lunch, described the service: "The table servants wore red plush breeches and silk stockings, and had powdered heads! The coffee, *café Turque,* was served by a black in Oriental costume." Afterward Belmont brought his guests downstairs to the stable, so that he could show off his prized horseflesh.

In a town richly blessed with egomania, no one strutted with more hauteur than James Gordon Bennett Jr., heir to the *New York Herald,* consummate sportsman, and one of high society's most notorious boors. "He never stifled an impulse," one of his friends admitted. (Enemies said much worse.) Bennett had an unrivaled flair for publicity: it was he who sent Stanley in search of Livingstone in Africa, and introduced polo to America in 1876. The events of New Year's Day, 1877, earned him an even more outrageous reputation. According to an old Knickerbocker tradition, members of New York society made the rounds on that day, visiting from house to house, sipping punch and eggnog while offering each other felicitations for the new year. Bennett indulged freely in the libations and was well soused by the time he reached his fiancée's house, where he reportedly—in public view—unbuttoned his trousers and urinated in the drawing-room fireplace (others say that the grand piano was his target). In a scene out of a Victorian melodrama, Bennett's fiancée promptly fainted, and he was thrown out of the house. Several days later the young woman's brother took a horsewhip to Bennett outside the Union Club in New York. Needless to say, the engagement was off.

At Newport, Bennett managed to stir up another storm the following year. On a dare, Bennett's polo comrade and guest, an English colonel, rode a horse up the steps and into the hushed precincts of the all-male Newport Reading Room, the fanciest club in town, and one in which Bennett was a member. The colonel and his horse woke up a roomful of elderly, napping members, irritating them enough that the guest privileges the Englishman enjoyed under Bennett's aegis were summarily revoked. It was really a rather mild penalty, but more than enough to rile Bennett. He vowed that he'd build his own club. Thus was born the Newport Casino, the fabled shingle-style club designed by McKim, Mead & White, which opened in 1880 with a theater, restaurant, lawn tennis, and entertainments. Despite the dubious reputation of the club's founder, the Chanlers could not avoid joining the Casino, as it instantly became the most popular spot for high society's younger set.

Every day there was a grand spectacle on Bellevue Avenue when fashionable open carriages drawn by high-stepping horses promenaded up and down the leafy avenue so that their beautifully clad occupants could see and be seen, with the Astors taking a prominent place in the pageant. Archie's great-aunt Caroline, *the* Mrs. Astor, joined in the daily parade, her carriage immediately recognizable by the distinctive blue livery her coachmen and footmen wore. "Aunt Lina," as Archie called her, was the most feared social titan in both New York, where she designated the "Four Hundred" members of society—the number that could fit cozily in her ballroom—and in Newport, where it was "as imperative for a social aspirant's claims to be passed upon by Mrs. Astor as it was for a potentate of the era of Charlemagne to go to St. Peter's, Rome, for coronation."

The borders of the social kingdom had to be guarded ferociously because an invitation to one of Mrs. Astor's parties, or a choice spot in Newport's daily parade of coaches, could yield enormous dividends. Newport was one of the places where high society's young men and women displayed themselves in a high-class marriage mart. In Archie's lofty stratum of society, marriages were still being "arranged," brokered by parents eager for dynastic and financial consolidation, and indifferent to any human feeling. Alva Vanderbilt (second only to

Caroline Astor as a social potentate) virtually imprisoned her daughter Consuelo until the young woman agreed to break off with the man she loved and marry a British nobleman hand-picked by Alva. The drama played out at Marble House, Alva's Newport cottage of half a million cubic feet of marble—a pile as icy as Alva's heart. The love of Consuelo's life was Archie's cousin Winthrop Rutherfurd, who of course boasted an impeccable patrician lineage, but it was an American lineage. Alva desperately coveted a European title for her daughter. She kept Consuelo at Marble House, prevented her from communicating with Rutherfurd, and bombarded her daughter with complaints about her suitor, even citing the taint of madness in the Chanler family (the mad aunt kept hidden away from view). Worn down by her mother, Consuelo finally agreed to marry the Duke of Marlborough. She was betrothed in the seaside mansion's gloomy Gothic Room, a "melancholy" place "propitious to sacrifice," in Consuelo's words.

Perhaps the depth of psychological cruelty was reached by the Astors themselves with the marriage Aunt Lina arranged for her only son, John Jacob Astor IV, to Ava Willing of Philadelphia. Despite his millions, Jack Astor was so socially inept and such a ridiculous figure that he "had not a friend in the wide world"; but the Willings, desperate for a connection with the Astors, forced Ava into the marriage bed of a man as reptilian as he was rich. Archie's brother Winty wrote an account of the wedding and Ava's travail:

> *It is amusing to see how Aunt Caroline has managed the whole affair. . . . A day or two before the wedding [Jack] is to give a farewell (it is his first as well as his last) bachelor supper to his* friends *at the Knickerbocker. Delicious, isn't it? Not one of the men would cross the street to shake hands with him for his own sake. But the mother is such a social power & has done so much for them that they are only too glad of the chance. [As for the bride, Ava Willing] Poor girl! They tell me in Philadelphia that she has been perfectly desperate about the whole business. Has left a puddle of tears on every parlour floor in the town. Her family which is very rich & quite the* fine fleur *of Phil, has forced her into it. Up to the last*

moment her friends feared that she would rebel & break loose—but she did not. They seldom do! [As she came up the aisle on her father's arm] she looked like death, trembling & in a state of seemingly hopeless despair. . . . The girl whispered her responses below her breath. She trembled & cried a little, so that I felt as if I were attending a sale in a slave market.

Archie and his siblings had no parents around to "suggest" a marriage match. The first to take the matrimonial plunge was Winty, who married a cousin, Margaret "Daisy" Terry. Daisy was not the typical Gilded Age ornament: she possessed a formidable intellect and wrote two impressive memoirs, *Roman Spring* and *Autumn in the Valley*. Edith Wharton sought out Daisy's opinions, and Henry James pronounced her the most intellectual woman in America. Winty spent most of his time hunting, traveling, entertaining pals like Theodore Roosevelt, and spending money. Work was beneath him. He once said that he wanted his epitaph to read, "Here Lies One Who Laughed in Many Lands." Daisy was far more serious than Winty, but their marriage proved to be lasting and close, despite adamant opposition to Daisy from some of the siblings.

Daisy was *Catholic*—a perfectly fine religion for the family's Irish servants, but certainly not for a Chanler. Worse, she had converted, "gone over" to the Roman Church, turning her back on the Protestantism of her parents—an unpardonable breach and a cause for fear. What if her religion spread like a disease to other family members? Before the wedding Winty journeyed to Rokeby by himself to try to soften the blow; but his siblings—Margaret, in particular—could not be mollified. They sent him back to Italy for the wedding by himself, tucking into his bags a number of anti-Catholic books and pamphlets, including one titled *Plain Reasons Against Joining the Church of Rome*. In June 1887 the newlyweds arrived at Rokeby to a frosty reception. Feelings ran so high against Daisy, the carrier of Catholic contagion, that the governess, cousin Mary Marshall, issued an edict: the children were not allowed even to mention Daisy's name lest they speak uncharitably.

For her part, Daisy found life at Rokeby appalling. The boys, then aged fifteen, eighteen, and twenty, were ill-mannered and rude. Screeching and fighting at the dinner table were the norm. One evening at dinner, Robert howled that hairs from his governess's wig had fallen into his soup. "The brothers quarreled like angry dogs and were the next moment the best of friends," Daisy wrote. She was totally baffled by their mercurial behavior. Daisy had grown up in Italy amid Roman aristocrats and artists; her refined European sensibility was offended by what she considered to be the country-bumpkin atmosphere at Rokeby. She judged the girls dowdy in their dress and provincial in their musical taste; and as for the house itself—old-fashioned, frumpy, and, worst of all, cheap. In *Roman Spring,* Daisy grumped that the woodwork, painted to look as if it were golden oak, remained unchanged from the time William B. Astor had remodeled the house decades earlier. She conceded that fake woodgrain had once been a fashion, but she thought it also appealed to Astor's "thrifty German taste for *Ersatz.*"

In Daisy's view, Rokeby needed to be shaken up. The drawing room boasted a spectacular view of the grounds, but was furnished as if for a wake, with chairs lined up drearily along the walls—in fact, for some time the room had only been used for that purpose. The decor remained exactly the way Archie's mother had left it, and nothing could be changed because Rokeby had become a kind of shrine to the orphans' deceased parents. The mausoleum atmosphere drove Daisy to distraction, so when the family decamped for Lake George a few weeks after the newlyweds' arrival, Daisy rearranged the furniture. She added a piano, flowers, and book stands, so the elegant room could be used for music and conversation in the evening.

Margaret was apoplectic upon her return to Rokeby. Though only seventeen years old at the time, she took seriously her role as unofficial mistress of the family's manners, morals, and the ancestral ways of doing everything. Her siblings gradually grew accustomed to Daisy's changes, but Margaret kept up a stony resistance. While the others gathered in the redecorated drawing room for an evening of cards and music, Margaret maintained a silent, seething vigil in the room they had formerly used, a "dreadful little 'home parlour' " where, in Daisy's words, "the family would gather around a very bad square piano." Margaret would sit alone in the "dreadful" room until one of the other children would take pity on her and visit with her for a time. Margaret refused to set foot into the desecrated drawing room.

The stakes grew even higher after Daisy gave birth to a baby girl at Rokeby and, naturally, had the infant baptized in a Roman Catholic ceremony. (The child, Laura Astor Chanler, would eventually marry Stanford White's only son.) Margaret was beside herself that a Chanler would be sprinkled in a Roman rite, and she asserted to her brother Lewis that it would have been kinder to have "smothered the little creature in its innocence at birth." Thereafter, whenever the baby was brought into the family circle, Margaret would get up and leave. Daisy recalled one occasion when the nanny brought baby Laura to the tennis court where the family was watching a match and having tea. Margaret "rose and fled, as at the approach of a leper." Yet even Margaret's heart eventually melted. She confessed to her sister Elizabeth that she adored the baby and stole into the nursery at night to give her a secret kiss; but in public, Margaret stuck to her role and shunned the child.

For Archie there was a sharp irony in the tempest Daisy touched off in the Chanler family: he, rather than Winty, could have been the one suffering Margaret's stony stares and icy disapproval, for he also had pursued Daisy. On their Grand Tour of Europe, both Archie and Winty had courted Daisy in Italy; but Winty won that contest and married Daisy in 1886. Archie was approaching his twenty-fifth birthday—about the right time, he believed, for a man to be considering marriage. His younger brother had reached the goal first, and had snared a woman both attractive and smart. Marriage was much on Archie's mind when the annual migration of the social set brought him to Newport for the summer season of 1887. He had his eyes open.

There was a new face at Newport in the summer of 1887, a young Southern woman, an author by the name of Amélie Rives, who had caused something of a stir with a story that she had recently published in *The Atlantic Monthly.* Though she had relatives in New York and Newport, Amélie herself was unknown on the social circuit, and she took a decided risk by showing up at the resort, a lamb strolling among lionesses. "Avoid Newport like the plague until you are certain that you will be acceptable there," one battle-tested veteran of the place warned—"it will be your Waterloo." But Amélie came from one of Virginia's finest old families. She was brilliant and gorgeous and shockingly daring—it was perfectly, gloriously apparent that Amélie dispensed with wearing a corset. With her deepset violet eyes, halo of ash-blond hair, and voluptuous figure, she was called—among other things—"a sizzling vessel of molten lava." Half the men in Newport fell instantly in love with her.

Amélie was dazzled by the scale of wealth on display at Newport. She and her family led a rather simple life in the countryside of Virginia. Though they resided in the Rives's grand ancestral home, Castle Hill, they were like British aristocrats with august titles and little cash: the family correspondence of the time indicates that Amélie's father, Alfred Landon Rives, was hanging on by his fingertips financially. A talented engineer who had been trained in Paris and had worked on the renovation of the United States Capitol in the 1850s, Alfred found it difficult to earn a decent living in the post–Civil War South. He moved from job to job, leaving his wife and children with his mother at Castle Hill for long stretches. Castle Hill itself was teetering on the edge of financial ruin.

Alfred's two older brothers had no money worries whatsoever; both had moved north before the war and married extremely well-connected, rich women. William Cabell Rives Jr. was a fixture in Newport society. He had married Grace Winthrop Sears, a Boston Brahmin who could trace her ancestry back to both an early Pilgrim colonist, Richard Sears, and the Puritan governor of Massachusetts, John Winthrop. (The Chanlers shared a connection to Winthrop.) The Sears family was so hidebound that well into the twentieth century they still looked down upon the Rockefellers as merchants and unworthy of inclusion in the *Social Register*—that, at least, according to one ex-wife. Alfred's oldest brother, Francis R. Rives, achieved an even higher standing on the social scale. A lawyer who practiced with Alexander Hamilton's grandson, Rives married the New York socialite Matilda Barclay. During the Civil War, Rives felt distinctly ill at ease in the North and largely withdrew from socializing and from practicing law; but in the postwar years his wife inherited a huge fortune and he reached the pinnacle of New York society, being selected in 1872 to join the "Patriarchs," the twenty-five men deemed *the* most important members of society. Among the Patriarchs were a number of Archie's relatives, including his great-uncles John Jacob Astor III and William B. Astor Jr., his uncle Lewis Rutherfurd, one of the Wards, and several Livingstons. Thus Amélie's uncle Francis was well entrenched in Archie's world. In addition, Rives enjoyed life as a country gentlemen in a Hudson Valley estate called Carnwath, not far from the Chanlers' Rokeby, that had been inherited by his wife in 1869.

Francis's wife, Matilda, often wrote to her Rives relations at Castle Hill, giving accounts of gala social events at Carnwath and in Newport. Thus young Amélie learned of a glittering society up North, quite different from her own slow-paced country life. Amélie generally spent her summers at home in Virginia, riding, and daydreaming, and writing, while her cousins went to glamorous Newport every year: "The girls left us . . . for their annual visit to Newport," Amélie's aunt wrote one August. "They are already plunged into a sea of invitations; dinners and sailing parties seem to be the favorite entertainments now." Amélie's cousin Ella married one of the pillars of Newport—David King Jr., a merchant who had made his fortune in the China trade, and who spent his summers at Kingscote, among the oldest and most revered of the town's summer cottages, a Gothic Revival marvel full of gables, dormers, and latticework, a charming and quirky wooden house built on an intimate scale. Designed by Richard Upjohn and completed in 1841, Kingscote was later expanded by Stanford White, who artfully maintained the house's unique personality. While at Kingscote in the fall of 1880, visiting her daughter and two young grandchildren (and tended by a staff of ten servants ranging from butler to nursemaid), Amélie's aunt Matilda sent a dispatch to Castle Hill describing a seaside Eden of "large costly houses & elegant grounds" where "the luxury of living is daily on the increase." She went into raptures over the new Casino club, the epicenter of "the beauty and gayety of Newport" with its tennis courts, fountain, flower gardens, and the gallery "where the *beau monde* sit,—the ladies beautifully dressed, listening to music, flirting."

In the summer of 1887, Amélie would finally get a good look at the flirtatious and romantic world her Northern cousins enjoyed. One evening in late August she attended a ball at the Casino club. Everything about the evening was intoxicating: the sea breezes, the artfully arranged hydrangeas, the women dripping with jewels, and the millionaire gentlemen, including Archie. The long, open piazzas at the Casino had been swathed in luminous white cloth to shield the three hundred revelers from ocean gusts, and to create a sensuous backdrop for dancing. A fashionably late supper was served at 1:00 a.m. Japanese lanterns swayed gently and cast a seductive light on the elegantly clad men and bejeweled women. "The display of diamonds was an exceptionally grand one, some of the ladies being adorned with fortunes in this way," a newspaper reported. The club was awash in flowers and plants—white and pink hydrangeas, palm trees, and ferns throughout.

In this impossibly romantic tableau, "akin to fairy land," a petite red satin slipper flew off the foot of a dancer and went skimming across the parquet floor. For a moment the room froze, then at once the young men made a mad dash for the shoe. The winner, Donald Swan, gallantly presented the shoe to its owner, the Cinderella-like Amélie. Resplendent in a crimson gown, she dramatically lifted her leg while Swan dropped to his knees and placed the slipper on her foot. He then stood and bowed deeply before her. The dancers on the floor and the gallery of onlookers in the balcony burst into applause. Watching from a doorway of the ballroom, Archie turned to a friend and asked who that creature was. As he later recalled, that was the instant he fell in love with Amélie Rives. That night he asked if he might pay her a call. The next day he appeared at her doorstep. Before leaving Newport, Amélie invited Archie down to her Virginia estate for the quail-hunting season that fall.

Archie's head was spinning. He took up pen and addressed a note to his teenaged sister Margaret: "Dined out seven out of the eight nights I was at Newport, went to four or five balls, I forget which, & a reception at Mrs. Paran Stevens, so you see I was pretty well in the whirl. . . . Enjoyed this taste of fashionable Lotos eating immensely, had just enough of it, much more I would have found too sweet." Archie did not mention Amélie's name to his sister.

In the following weeks he had meetings in New York to manage family affairs with the Chanler attorneys and guardians. But for the last conference, Archie was uncharacteristically absent. He had decamped for the South, for a bit of quail hunting at a place called Castle Hill.

THREE

Behind the Boxwood,

or

The Wind Down My Chimney

Archie had never met anyone quite like Amélie—so charming and brilliant, with a passion and ambition that rivaled his own. But America was not ready for Amélie Rives. Her writing created a social and literary tempest that seemed to catch even the author herself by surprise. Clinging to a slender raft of Southern female innocence, Amélie rode out the gigantic waves of controversy and condemnation—or so it seemed. Part of her appeal was her naïveté, her apparent victimization by the grim forces of polite society for doing nothing more than giving voice to suppressed feminine truths. But in the staid precincts of a university archive, in the forgotten papers of the staidest of old-line Virginia gentlemen, a different Amélie emerges—a female Prospero—not the victim of the storm, but its creator and its mistress.

From early on, Amélie understood that she had two unmistakable gifts—a knack for writing and a mesmerizing appeal. Men could not resist her, and she was ruthless in wielding her charm. She seemed to bewitch her suitors. Men became powerless in her presence, particularly on her home turf at Castle Hill. One contemporary described arriving with a party of sophisticated Northern Brahmins—Archie's brother Winty among them—young, world-weary types who had seen it all and were immune to easy charm. They came to Castle Hill curious and cynical—how could anyone measure up to the advance billing Amélie had received? But they left gasping for air. As their carriage made its way out of the estate, one of the men nearly fell out of it, he was so overcome by "his ardors."

Amélie was totally aware of the effect that she had on men. She counted on it and she used it to her advantage. While in her early twenties Amélie wrote a series of love letters in which she rather shamelessly pursued her very upright Virginia cousin, the soon-to-be-famous writer Thomas Nelson Page. Stretching over a period of two years, the letters present a kind of blueprint of the way she drew men into her net and then had her way with them. Thomas Nelson Page was the ultimate stuffed shirt, the last person to fall into a lovesick craze; and yet as the letters progress, one can see the prim author being reeled deeper and deeper into Amélie's lair. The ulterior motive that drove Amélie on becomes clear as well. Desperate to become a published writer—she slyly admits as much in her letters—she thought her cousin could be useful in that regard.

Though Page was a practicing lawyer in an old-line Richmond firm, he also moonlighted as a writer. He wrote verses and stories set in the antebellum South that reeked of plantation glory. It was a land where the darkies were happy and loyal, and the masters were a race of noble men and women; a place where an ancient code of chivalry thrived. Page specialized in Negro dialect and the romance of the "Lost Cause," in which Southerners sacrificed themselves heroically for the old order. This, of course, had a seductive appeal in the beaten-down South. And by the 1880s, Page's work even spurred the interest of Northern editors. There was a taste for that kind of nostalgic regional writing at the time—a response, perhaps, to the postwar commercialism and greed that consumed the country. Readers yearned for a simpler time, a bygone era soaked in honor and heroism. Some Northerners were also interested in reconciling with their past foes, which entailed minimizing the horrors of the plantation system and maximizing its nobility and graciousness. Page's writing captured that idyllic tone perfectly, and before long he was recognized as the voice of the Old South.

In the spring of 1884, Page first achieved national attention with the publication of his story "Marse Chan" in New York's popular *Century Magazine.* This was a great professional breakthrough for him, and an opening for Amélie as well. She did not miss a beat. It was at that precise moment that she took up her sultry letter-writing campaign to win over the heart of her fellow Virginia aristocrat and cousin. (His relation to her made him all the more appealing, as, in her view, he had the correct bloodlines.) In letter after letter, she gushes over his promise and talent. "I am as sure that you will be one of the famous writers as I am of the moan of the wind down my chimney." Amélie specialized in such sexually charged language while posing as an innocent. Ludicrous stuff, for sure—but cousin Tom was soon hooked. (In short order, the salutations of her letters change from "O cousin-cousin-cousin" to "Dearest Tom.")

Between the great gobs of praise she heaps upon Tom (telling him, among other things, that his work is superior to that of Henry James and "quite as perfect" as that of Shakespeare), she ladles on the drama of her own precarious health. "I have been very near to death since last you wrote to me. There was a night and a day in which they thought there would never be day or night for me anymore forever this side the stars." Amélie was like the heroine of a Victorian melodrama who suffered from the vapors and whose swoons stirred the hearts of her suitors. Over the years, Amélie referred to her "neuralgia of the brain," a nonspecific malady that seemed to afflict her. Perhaps it was migraines (her grandmother suffered terribly from them), or just overwrought nerves. Her doctor blamed it on the fact that Amélie spent too much time writing—a woman's brain could not bear such stress. The doctor confined her to her bedroom and the only consolation for Amélie was that she could sit center stage. "At present I am 'maladive'—and that is very charming," she writes to

Page. "Every one comes to see me—my room is a little court, and a big, gilded-wicker chair, run-about with blue ribbons, is my throne."

Amélie wins her cousin's undying sympathy for her travail, but is also careful to remind him periodically of her magnetic—and powerful—sex appeal. "Don't think I neglect this strong, young body of mine—Today I rode the wildest mare I fancy in all Virginia land—When you come you shall see me do it," she writes provocatively to her prim cousin. And, in even bolder fashion: "Tom—take my face between your two hands and kiss me on my eyes which are full of big tears ready to fall. . . ." She ends her passionate entreaties with "You are my own, dear, good, true, loyal, unselfish, brave, sympathetic cousin, and I am your wild, wayward, savage, untamed. . . . Amélie." Cheap histrionics, but highly effective. Page accuses her of being a flirt—and she admits to as much, admits that she can't help herself—but hastens to add that she has been studiously avoiding another man who is smitten with her, a man she can tell is "susceptible" to her fatal allure.

She convinces cousin Tom that she is saving herself for him, loves only him—and then entreats him to read her latest verses. She is churning out a constant stream of poems, stories, plays, and songs—material steeped in Elizabethan idioms and medieval tales, and larded with classical references and Scottish dialect. She admits that she is even working on a novel, though not "what one would look for from the pen of a girl,—being meat of so muscular an order that even men would have to chew right manfully to digest it." (But she is careful to assure her uptight cousin that while her fiction might be "muscular," it is certainly not immoral: "God being my witness, I would not shake such golden apples as He has let grow on the tree of my knowledge, into the pig-stye of vulgarity.") She needs his advice and help as an editor, so she resorts to Elizabethan coquetry: "Methinks an author is something like a maid without a looking glass:— it doth take others to tell her wherein she is most pleasing. So from time to time I will send you a jingle,—and you shall pull it to pieces, and commend it, and revise it at your pleasure—"

He visits her at Castle Hill, and becomes more deeply enmeshed in her world. She understands only too well his rigid morality and conservative worldview—particularly when it comes to the role of a woman. She downplays her own ambition—("To be called a good, true woman—'A maiden, most excellent, shining white and clear'—this is what I would rather have, even than fame, even than honour")—and thereby wins him over completely. How could he not show the work of such a "good true woman"—a naïf with no real ambition—to his editor in New York? Before long her pieces are being published by *Century.*

And then Page gets wind that another suitor—a Rives family friend and distant relative by marriage, a Bostonian named William Sigourney Otis—is also visiting Castle Hill. "Will" is in love with Amélie as well. And he, too, is helping her professionally. In a bit of serendipity (so serendipitous, in fact, that it smacks of careful stage-managing by Amélie), Will comes upon one of Amélie's short stories that is conveniently mixed in with the sheet music in the drawing room. Naturally, he is swept away by the story and insists on bringing it back to Boston to see if he can get it published. Amélie reluctantly allows him to take it, as long as he promises not to reveal that she is the author. (More melodrama from the shy, retiring authoress in an Oscar-caliber performance.) Will gets the story into the hands of Thomas Bailey Aldrich, editor of *The Atlantic Monthly* and one of the great literary kingmakers of the day. Aldrich loves the manuscript and demands that Will produce the author at once; but Will demurs, saying that it would be quite impossible. The high-powered editor then blurts out that if the author is in jail he'll bail him out, he is so eager to meet this fresh talent.

Amélie is delighted at being mistaken for a male author, and even more delighted that Aldrich plans to publish her work—a love story titled "A Brother to Dragons," set in Elizabethan England—in the pages of *The Atlantic.* Amélie breathlessly tells Thomas Nelson Page of her latest triumph. She boasts that the famous Boston editor wants as much of her work as he can get, and even proclaimed that "if 'Lorna Doone' had never been written . . . he is sure I could have written it. Oh! Dear Tom—isn't it too good to be true? . . . I feel that you brought me luck, & love." She begs Tom to come back to visit her at Castle Hill, but not before asking him to forward her manuscripts (which he had been reading and editing) to her beau Will in Boston.

By this time the love-sick Tom has been brought to his senses. He announces his own engagement to another woman. Amélie, who has played both suitors simultaneously to her own advantage, acts like the aggrieved party:

TOM! You villain! You rogue!! You wretch!!!-

Whyever didn't you tell me you were engaged to be married?- "O these men- these men!-" . . . I am going to heap coals of fire on the tortoise-shell of your conscience- It is all off between Will and myself—and oh!—I feel as free as air- I do love Will- He is good, & dear, & sweet, & noble, but I don't want to be married and oh! dear- I didn't think you did either-. . . . You will never find anyone to love you any better than your crazy little cousin

Amélie

For all her flirtatiousness, the reality was that Amélie was ambivalent about marriage. In a moment of candor she admits as much to her cousin Tom.

Dear Cousin:-

here's for a long talk with you- You ask me to tell you of myself- I fear I know less of myself than I know of Greek,—and of that, I know only that there is a beginning and an end, which two are 'Alpha' and 'Omega'. . . . -They say that marriage is the end with women- I do not know —but I hope not. -I do not want to be married myself, and yet—and yet—how lonely are the old-maids! -My Aunt Ella Rives is a living warning to me- She is forty eight- She is very yellow- One of her front teeth is lacking- She wears pale brown stockings that wrinkle, and cloth slippers that are out at the toes- She is very good, very queer, and unbearably disagreeable- She feeds ducks and plays on a melodion for recreation- I do not want a husband, but I think a melodion equally undesirable-

Amélie was in her early twenties when she wrote this, an age when any self-respecting southern belle would be making wedding plans. Yet Amélie had larger ambitions. She admits, further on in the letter, that she wants to be an artist or a writer; that she wants to be famous and rich enough to dispense money generously to others. She realizes that a conventional marriage would be death for her, but the alternative seems even more frightening. Just the sight of her maiden aunt Ella, who lived with them for many years at Castle Hill, irritates Amélie. She certainly does not want to end up like her eccentric and unfashionable aunt, who was still wearing hoopskirts twenty years after they had fallen out of style.

Having successfully used both Tom and Will to introduce her to the literary world, Amélie then sets her sights on a new, even more powerful target—the eminent editor Thomas Bailey Aldrich himself. She attempts another seduction, and the twenty-two-year-old siren pulls out all the stops. She begins by flattering the middle-aged literary arbiter:

> *You must be sure to cut [my story] just as much as you think best. In fact, I would rather have these imaginative shrubs of mine straggle as they like at first, that so kind and judicious a gardener may trim them into shape. . . . You shall have the very firstlings of my brain and heart, & I will write for no one else in all the world if you want me to write for you.*

She claims that if there is anything at all objectionable in her stories—perhaps the way she deals directly with a woman and her passionate feelings about love (a taboo subject at the time)—it is done out of ignorance, not coarseness. "You know I have not been much in the world & have spent nearly all my life in an old Virginia Homestead among my books, horses, dogs, flowers." Once again she is the pure naïf. But then the tone abruptly turns conspiratorial as she implores Aldrich not to tell Will Otis that she has written. After all, she may still need Will as an intermediary and suitor.

Before long Amélie begs Aldrich to send a photograph of himself, and the married editor readily complies. In turn, Amélie claims that she has no photo of herself to send him, though her home is full of such images. Why not come to Castle Hill yourself to see me, she asks? Her come-hither invitation, written on New Year's Eve in 1885, is almost comical in its tone. It reads more like a Mae West come-on than professional correspondence between a fledgling author and editor.

New Year's Eve-

My dear Mr. Aldrich:-

I hope you will not think me a very wild and uncivilized being after you have read this letter-

I am going to ask you a very unorthodox question indeed . . . I would like so very much to have you come to our old Virginia home for a visit.-

I know how very busy you are, and tremble at my own temerity in asking you such a thing, but I would so like to know you and have you tell me the things I did wrong, and some things to do right-

It is very quiet here- I love the old place myself- It is one of the very few old Southern Homesteads which have remained in the same family for two hundred years- We will treat you with all ancient circumstance & pomp and put you in the Haunted-Chamber! with its moth-eaten, old green silk-tapestry-, and its mahogany wardrobe which resembles nothing so much as a Mausoleum. . . .

I hope I have not done anything too unconventional in asking you this— have I?- The truth is I am so full of gratitude, that I want to tell you of it, to look it, to shew it- -Oh! I think I want to wait on you a little, and fetch things for you,- and know you, and learn to do things you like, and to earn your approval and the right to your friendship. It isn't too much—is it?

Apparently not, for Aldrich accepts her invitation. She manages to use Castle Hill—the exoticism of a gracious old Southern plantation steeped in history and stocked with "fine horseflesh" and Amélie herself—as a potent lure for the New England editor. He cannot resist. Luckily for him, however, the visit never comes to pass. Perhaps his wife got wind of the siren call from Virginia and put an end to it. Soon enough, Amélie grows testy when Aldrich actually begins to criticize her work. (So much for her wanting her "gardener" to prune her "imaginative shrubs.") Her letters to him cool and stop abruptly not long after she is published in the March 1886 *Atlantic.* She then moves on to the editor of *Century Magazine* in New York, taking up a correspondence with him.

Caught between ambition and propriety, her own talent and the expected life of a conventional wife and mother, Amélie chose her own path. And like a good general, she used the arsenal at her disposal: her beauty and charm. She felt compelled to seduce almost every man she encountered—thus the daisy chain of her flirtations from cousin Tom to Will to editor Aldrich. She used each man to advance her position, to secure her foothold in the literary firmament. (With Archie she would have a different agenda.) She did as she pleased, with her eye always on the prize. The emotional carnage that she wreaked in the process was but the casualty of war. One contemporary compared Amélie to Helen of Troy, the face that launched a thousand ships and brought a city to its doom.

Her letters expose the gears at work—her thinly veiled machinations and her raw ambition. Amélie was amazingly shrewd and calculating. And yet that cold streak was tempered by her genuinely poetic and romantic nature. She was in love with being in love, had a fevered imagination and a propensity for theatrics. People were either terrified of her or intoxicated by her. There seemed to be no middle ground. She was like a great actress, forever in character, who played her part to the hilt. Even she did not know exactly where reality began and ended. And that unpredictability—that frisson she created at all times—was part of her immense appeal. She made every man—and even every passionate woman friend—feel as if he or she were the most important person in the world. She radiated electric charges that turned even the most straitlaced and phlegmatic personalities into lovesick creatures. Once she got her emotional claws into someone, they were almost always stricken for life. At least one man would commit suicide over her.

Archie had no idea what he was getting into when he came to Castle Hill. For all his aristocratic hauteur and polish, his world travels and Astor fortune, he was a babe in arms compared to Amélie. Upon his arrival, she proceeded to weave a spell over him that he could not resist. The performance began with Castle Hill itself. Amélie loved showing off the estate. She believed it was an enchanted place, set apart from the rest of the world, and that even the ancient boxwood that surrounded the house wielded extraordinary powers. She wrote a poem about the hedges, a kind of incantation:

Hedges of Box,
Magical, severe, serene,
Full of promises,
Promising strange fulfilments,
Welcoming their own,—
Swaying with somber witchery,
With threatening even
For intruders, for inquisitive strangers. . . .
Tirelessly watching,
Waiting,
Sentinels of centuries,
Content with the wisdom of root and leaf,
With the mystic bondage of earth,—
Themselves mystical, magical, secret,
Possessed of unknown powers and beatitudes. . . .

Further on in the verse, Amélie catches sight of herself, atop a unicorn, amid her beloved boxwood. Even the hedges at Castle Hill were bathed in romance for her.

Amélie introduced Archie to her magical world in the fall of 1887. One can imagine that the tour began, naturally, with the boxwood—perhaps the most extraordinary feature of the landscaping—which entirely enclosed the front of the house. She explained that the massive, impenetrable wall of hedges had been planted by a gardener who had worked for King George II in the eighteenth century, adding a regal pedigree to the Rives' shrubbery. This was in keeping with her own self-image. Amélie carried herself like a princess, and believed her family to be, if not royalty, then the next best thing.

She brought Archie through the immense shield of boxwood with its pungent aroma, and paused dramatically for effect. Before them lay a magnificent expanse of lawn in the shape of an hourglass—or a lady's slipper—that stretched for some eight hundred feet to a handsome brick manor house. The greenery was dappled with shade from walnut, maple, English elm, and tulip trees. Amélie stopped to point out the prickly nuts growing on a spreading chestnut tree. This was, she said, the "King's Chestnut," grown from seeds belonging to the king of France. Her grandmother, Judith Page Walker Rives, had brought the seeds back from Europe and planted them decades earlier. The tree was now beginning to take on the grandeur of its name.

Her grandmother Judith, the grande dame of Castle Hill, had died almost six years earlier, but her footprint remained. Gesturing around her, Amélie said that the design of the slipperlike sanctuary had been the creation of her grandmother, who had been inspired by landscaping ideas from France. Her husband, William Cabell Rives, had served as minister to France from 1829 to 1832 and again from 1849 to 1853; Judith had been a favorite at court.

As they approached the staircase to the house, Amélie mentioned that her grandmother had also been largely responsible for the design of the Federal-style mansion. There had been grumblings about this building when it was constructed in the 1820s. Not over the design, but over the fact that it had been built at all. Amélie explained that her grandmother Judith had been orphaned at a young age and sent away from her home. (This must have resonated with Archie and his own wandering life.) Upon marrying at seventeen, Judith was able to claim her share of the eight-thousand-acre estate, which she had inherited with her sister. The two young women drew lots, and Judith won the portion that included the original eighteenth-century colonial farmhouse where her grandfather and father had lived. Judith and her husband, William, decided that they wanted a grander place, more in keeping with the style of the day. Old-timers rolled their eyes. Wasn't the original homestead good enough for them? It had been built in 1764 by the family patriarch, Dr. Thomas Walker, one of the seminal figures in Virginia colonial life.

Amélie sketched for Archie the outlines of her great-great-grandfather's colorful and peripatetic career. Not content to live quietly on his tobacco plantation in the Virginia Piedmont, Walker had been by turns a land speculator and explorer (he was the first white man to enter present-day Kentucky, beating Daniel Boone by nearly two decades); a town father who had helped establish Charlottesville, some fifteen miles to the southwest of Castle Hill; an entrepreneur and merchant who had outfitted Virginia soldiers during the French and Indian Wars; a backwoodsman who had negotiated skillfully with Native American chiefs; a politician who had served as a member of the House of Burgesses; and a practicing physician, who had attended to his friend and neighbor Peter Jefferson. At the elder Jefferson's death, Walker became a guardian and mentor for the young Thomas Jefferson.

Walker's memory loomed large in the area, and his house was a piece of history, a connection to the early settling of Virginia. Best not to tamper with it, said the locals. Amélie's grandmother was immune to the grumbling over her remodeling of the house. She went ahead and devised an ingenious plan. The original clapboard homestead remained intact; and a new brick mansion, suiting her and her husband's tastes better (and making use of Jefferson's master brick masons), was built parallel to it. The two separate houses were connected by a central hallway that created an H-shaped configuration.

The houses faced out in opposite directions—the eighteenth-century farmhouse looking out upon the peak of Walnut Mountain, which rose up before it; and the classic brick planter's mansion looking out upon the grassy slipper. Amélie took pride in her grandmother's determination to create a world of her own design—regardless of public opinion. Amélie was determined to do the same. Stepping onto the columned front portico with Archie, she could savor once more the view that her grandmother had designed. Looking out from the house, one could not see beyond the cozy wall of green hedges—those "sentinels of centuries"—save through a narrow notch carved out at the very foot of the lawn, at the farthest distance from the house. The Rives family—Amélie included—would view the outside world on its own terms.

Inside, the house exuded a combination of rustic Virginia charm and European style. The older portion of the house breathed an eighteenth-century simplicity with its wood-paneled rooms. Here, Amélie told Archie, the young Jefferson played fiddle while James Madison danced a jig. George Washington visited as well, and a portrait of him by Gilbert Stuart hung in the colonial-era parlor. This connection with the Founding Fathers lent a noble air to the estate. Amélie pointed to a gash in the mahogany doorway in the center hall—a tangible reminder of the history that had played out in the house. On the morning of June 4, 1781, Amélie's great-great-grandparents managed to delay British troops planning to surprise and capture then-governor Thomas Jefferson and the members of the Virginia legislature who had taken refuge at Jefferson's nearby estate, Monticello. Alerted to the impending raid, Dr. Walker and his wife plied the British troops with a hearty plantation breakfast of mint juleps and Sally Lunns and waffles. After the leisurely repast, Dr. Walker measured a soldier who claimed to be the tallest man in the British army against a doorjamb. The orderly stood six feet nine and two-eights inches tall—an enormous man in any day—and a notch cut by a saber marked his height. The slash was still visible. The family's Southern hospitality succeeded in holding the soldiers long enough that Jefferson and the others could make their escape. This story, of course, had been told and retold at Castle Hill, and Amélie must have loved spinning it out for an eager Archie.

While the aura of the Founding Fathers and revolutionary heroism hung over the old section of the house, a European sensibility informed the nineteenth-century addition. Amélie showed Archie into the formal French drawing room that featured gold chairs, elaborate candelabras, and bric-a-brac from Paris. The graceful draperies were made of pure silk in a delicate shade of grass green. Amélie pointed out the family portraits lining the walls. Here above the mantel was a striking oil of her father, Alfred Landon Rives, and his two older brothers. Alfred had been born in Paris in 1830; Lafayette was his godfather. An itinerant American artist painted the three young sons of the U.S. minister to France in 1831. Baby Alfred is dressed in a gauzy gown, and his brothers in clothes suitable for presentation at the royal court; in the distance behind them are the Tuileries gardens and palace. It is the perfect evocation of young aristocrats, to the manor born.

The Riveses had known everyone of importance in Paris. The drawers at Castle Hill were filled with the calling cards and invitations the family had garnered in France. The names on the engraved cards were impressive indeed: assorted Turkish princes and European noblemen, Alexis de Tocqueville, Le Comte de Lesseps, Le Baron James de Rothschild, and the emperor himself, Napoleon III, who invited the Riveses to his marriage to the beautiful Eugenie at the cathedral of Notre-Dame. The Rives family's connection with a Napoleon doubtless struck a chord with Archie, for his great-great-grandfather, General Armstrong, had served as U.S. minister to the court of the original Napoleon—Napoleon Bonaparte—from 1804 until 1810. Archie felt a special kinship with the first emperor of France—a brilliant man of history who had been driven from his native land and forced into a lonely exile—so there was something comforting about the fact that the Rives family had a direct connection with Napoleon's nephew.

Amélie's aunt—her namesake—had been a glittering presence amid the court society surrounding Napoleon III in the early 1850s, and she continued to cast a ghostly presence at Castle Hill. A pastel portrait of Amélie Louise, wearing an off-the-shoulder gown and an enigmatic smile, gave the younger Amélie an opportunity to tell the story of her fabled relative. Her aunt had been born in France in 1832 during the reign of King Louis Philippe, and named after the queen herself. Her Majesty, Queen Marie-Amélie, served as godmother. Amélie Louise's life proceeded in fairy-tale fashion. A classic Southern belle, she became the stuff of legend as a teenager in Paris. A favorite at balls and diplomatic receptions, she attracted a long string of suitors. After a seventeenth-century Spanish painting was sold at auction to the Louvre for an astounding 580,000 francs, one beau said that if he had known it would go for such a "trifle," he would have sent it to the beautiful young Virginian with his compliments. She disappointed her legions of admirers in France when she announced her engagement to the rich and prominent Bostonian Henry Sigourney in 1853; she then set out to conquer Boston and Newport society. She lived grandly, and died in melodramatic fashion—drowning at forty-one with her husband and three children in the middle of the Atlantic when their ship sank en route to France.

Amélie recalled for Archie how devastated her grandmother Judith had been over the drownings. Her golden daughter and three grandchildren lost in an instant. It was incomprehensible to her. Less than a week before their deaths, her grandmother had been fretting over Amélie Louise and her little ones, fearing that they might be seasick en route.

Castle Hill, 16 November, 1873

. . . I cannot express to you, my precious child, the feelings with which I laid down on my ample and luxurious bed last night, and thought of you and your dear ones cramped up in little berths, and probably pitched and tossed about on the briny deep. I fervently trust that all of you will escape that fearful sickness so often ridiculed, but which I certainly found no joke, for I shudder when I remember the iron band around my aching head, the clutch at my sinking

heart. . . . You are so continually in my thoughts and prayers, my darling that I sleep very lightly, and dream constantly of you. . . . Adieu my dear dearest daughter, may good angels always guard you.

your ever loving and devoted Mother, JPR.

That they should be lost forever in the "briny deep" was almost more than the matriarch Judith could bear.

Castle Hill remained haunted by the tragic Amélie Louise. Some said it was she who appeared as a ghost in the colonial portion of the house, telling unwanted guests that they had to "Go! Go! Please *go!*" Amélie certainly told Archie of the ghostly apparition—after all, every self-respecting old Southern house had a ghost of some sort. It was part of the enchanting lore of such places. Though Amélie insisted that she herself had never seen what she referred to as the "very charming but very imperious lady" ghost, she did feel a special connection to her namesake. Amélie was ten when her aunt had drowned, and she had felt the crushing sense of tragedy and loss that had overtaken Castle Hill. The death of Aunt Amélie and her family had been the second great cloud to darken the estate.

The first one had been the Civil War. Archie was doubtless riveted by Amélie's narration of the war years and beyond at Castle Hill. It was the romance of the South—the noble cause, the tragic carnage, the loss of the old, aristocratic order. Twenty years after the end of the war, it was a powerful intoxicant. (It still is. One of the biggest problems for present-day Civil War reenactments is getting enough people to take on the roles of Northern soldiers; almost everybody wants to be the tragic Southerner.) Archie was susceptible to this sort of heart-tugging sentiment. He had a romantic and generous soul, and a natural sympathy for the underdog. He also had a deeply ingrained sense of noblesse oblige; it was part of his aristocratic duty to look after and protect the less fortunate around him. And certainly the South was suffering. All Archie had to do was look around to see what the war had wrought. Archie was accustomed to the pristine landscapes and interiors of Newport and the Hudson

Valley, where every glade was carefully manicured, every room burnished and buffed. By contrast, the Virginia countryside was tattered, the estates seedy and overgrown.

The antebellum Southern economy—based as it was on slave labor—had been destroyed. Many of the nearby plantations had been broken up into boardinghouses. The Rives family continued to hang on to Castle Hill, but just barely. The place had gleamed during its heyday, before the war. Up to a hundred slaves had worked the fields, tended the grounds and gardens, and maintained the house. After the war most of the slaves had dispersed, and many of those who did stay on were elderly and useless as laborers. An exception was Amélie's personal maid, Martha Jane, who worked tirelessly for her mistress, until Amélie abruptly fired her in the 1890s.

As charming as Castle Hill was—a contemporary described it as having "an air of civilized taste and ancient leisure"—the place was decidedly old-fashioned. It had not changed for decades. Many of the furnishings reflected the years in France, the height of the family glory; but at this point the upholstery was threadbare, and the draperies musty from years of Virginia humidity. But in the midst of the decay, the family dignity—and the ancient Southern courtesies—remained untouched. Archie could not help but be moved by the pathos of the situation.

The rootless Archie found something compelling about Virginia, and felt an undeniable kinship with the South. Through his mother he claimed descent from a sister of South Carolina's celebrated Revolutionary War hero, General Francis Marion, better known as the "Swamp Fox." His father had an even stronger link with Dixie: he had been raised in South Carolina, and perhaps had retained soft traces of a Southern accent. After Archie's parents' deaths, his saintly cousin Mary Marshall had come up from South Carolina to take care of the orphans. His Chanler forebears in South Carolina stretched back to the early eighteenth century, and Archie was proud of that fact. In later years, he circulated copies of a daguerreotype showing his paternal grandfather—a dyed-in-the-wool South Carolinian—next to a bust of John C. Calhoun, the ultimate Southern apologist. On the back of the image, Archie listed his South Carolinian ancestors, and made proud reference to the fact that his grandfather was a "bosom friend" of Calhoun. And so the South did not seem like a foreign land to Archie. In fact, in 1910 Archie would self-publish a newspaper titled *The Confederacy and Solid South,* in which he stated categorically, "We are a different race from those living north of Mason & Dixon's line."

Politically, Archie's father and Amélie's grandfather had shared some common ground leading up to the Civil War. They had both been opposed to the war and to Lincoln's abolitionist policies. Amélie's grandfather, William Cabell Rives, did all that he could to prevent the war. He begged his fellow Southerners not to desert the good ship of the Constitution for "the crazy raft of secession." He feared the Civil War with reason. He had witnessed revolution in France and knew what it meant: "I have seen the pavements of Paris covered, and her gutters running with fraternal blood: God forbid that I should see this horrid picture repeated in my own country." In trying to broker a compromise between North and South, Rives met with newly elected President Lincoln and found him hardly up to the task of rescuing the country from the precipice of war. "He seemed to be good-natured & well-intentioned, but utterly unimpressed with the gravity of the crisis & the magnitude of his duties," Rives wrote to his son.

The formidable Virginian—esteemed statesman, retired U.S. senator and minister to France, intimate of Jefferson and Madison, intellectual, writer (he authored a three-volume biography of Madison), and gentleman farmer—found Lincoln distressingly common. Rives was offended at the way the president greeted him in a jocular manner, joking that he had imagined the distinguished Virginia statesman would be taller—although he was surely a "giant in intellect." Rives was not amused by "this piece of Western free & easy compliment. . . . He seems to think of nothing but jokes & stories." Amélie's grandmother Judith was even harsher in her assessment of Lincoln. In her unpublished autobiography she looked back fondly on an earlier era, when landed Virginia aristocrats—including three presidents who lived within a short ride of Castle Hill—were at the center of power in the country; a time when "a rail splitter might have been deemed a useful citizen, but he could never have aspired to the Presidency." (Clearly, she had no tolerance for a democracy of the common man. She admitted as much in an 1867 letter to her son William Cabell Rives Jr.: "You know I never had any faith in the masses, being an aristocrat in the true sense of the word—i.e.—for the government of the best. The multitude have always been in the wrong, ever since the days of Barabbas—and before too, if we observe the difficulties the grand old aristocratic patriarchs had in keeping the people in order.") It has been said of the Rives family that they always believed they were better than anyone else—presidents included. That notion was heartily embraced by Amélie; and Archie could understand and appreciate that arrogant sensibility—after all, he was an Astor.

The two shared other similarities. Both were born during the Civil War and were at the respective nerve centers of the conflict. As an infant, Archie was brought to the nation's capital, where his father served in Congress. Amélie was born on the other side of the Mason-Dixon line—in Richmond, the capital of the Confederacy, on August 23, 1863. Both her grandfather and father were in Richmond for much of the war. The senior Rives served in the Confederate Congress. (Despite his early opposition to secession, he fell in loyally with the Southern cause once Virginia left the Union.) Amélie's father, Alfred, also threw in his lot with the Confederacy, giving up a promising career as an engineer in Washington, D.C. (He helped plan and personally supervised the construction of the impressive Cabin John Bridge, a single masonry arch that spanned 220 feet, the largest ever constructed up to that time.) Alfred eventually rose to the rank of colonel and served as acting chief of engineers for Robert E. Lee. Rebel officers crowded the streets of Richmond the summer Amélie was born, and the city's hospitals overflowed with wounded. Housing was so scarce that Amélie's mother, Sadie Macmurdo Rives, had taken up residence in the rectory of St. Paul's Episcopal Church, courtesy of her grandfather, the Episcopal Bishop of Richmond.

Thus Amélie was born in a rectory, and the irony would be thick years later, when she was denounced from pulpits across the land.

Grandmother Judith Rives wanted the child named Amélie after her own daughter and her dear friend, the former Queen of France. The infant was christened Amélie Louise in Richmond, with both godparents in absentia. Her godmother and namesake, Aunt Amélie Louise (who would meet her tragic end a decade later), was stranded in Boston, unable to visit or even communicate with Castle Hill during four long years of war. (She shared that plight with two of her brothers who had also married rich Northerners.) Infant Amélie's godfather—Robert E. Lee—also had a proxy. Amélie loved to boast about her illustrious godfather, and surely did so with Archie. She later claimed that if she ever wrote her memoirs, it would begin, "My family was happy in godparents: Lafayette was my father's; General Lee, mine."

Not long after Amélie's christening—and once it was safe to travel—mother and child moved to Castle Hill. Amélie became the treasured grandchild, doted on by her grandmother Judith and maiden aunt Ella. The child was made to feel as if she were the center of the universe—and indeed she was (until she later had to share the stage, uncomfortably, with two younger sisters). Squiring Archie about the estate in 1887, Amélie doubtless steered clear of her aunt Ella—Amélie being humiliated by the mere sight of her peculiar relative—preferring instead to accentuate the romance of her early days.

She waxed poetic about her childhood at Castle Hill, telling Archie of the happy times she spent on horseback. As a tiny child she was introduced to horses and would ride, like a princess, on a pillow in front of the family's black retainer, Henry. Riding lessons began at age four, and in short order she became a skilled and fearless equestrian. (This was the one and only arena where Amélie, skillful as she was, was outshone by her younger sister, Gertrude, who became one of the most famous horsewomen in America—both in competitions and in the hunting field. Gertrude eventually started up her own private pack of foxhounds—bringing back a tradition first started by Dr. Thomas Walker at Castle Hill in the pre-Revolutionary era—and earning herself the distinction of being the first woman in the country to serve as Master of Fox Hounds.)

Archie loved to ride, so he and Amélie doubtless spent many hours on horseback, cantering through the magnificent Virginia countryside. Whether they actually bagged any quail that season—the ostensible reason for his visit—one will never know. But his thoughts were more on Amélie, watching her as she rode sidesaddle, entranced by her athletic grace and energy. He was an athlete himself, and appreciated her love of the outdoors. She tramped for miles over the red-clay hills in a corduroy skirt, trim flannel shirt, tam-o'-shanter, stout walking boots and hiking stick, a pack of dogs by her side. Amélie was photographed wearing that tomboyish outfit in a series of portraits made that year in Richmond—a rather unlikely costume for a formal studio sitting. The photos were probably a conscious piece of self-promotion, for at that time she was finishing a novel, and in it the main character wore precisely the same kind of outfit. (However, when the novel appeared and caused a sensation, Amélie swore that the heroine bore no relation to herself—though the photos tell another story.)

Horses and books had been the great loves of Amélie's young life. As one magazine article later commented on her education: "She was never sent to school, but had governesses who were directed only to guide, never to govern her." The governesses gave her free rein in her grandfather's impressive library, amid works of history, literature, Elizabethan drama, and medieval and classical texts. There Amélie would open volume after volume, and get lost in imaginative worlds beyond the boxwood. By age six she preferred the real Shakespeare to Charles Lamb's bowdlerized version for children. Amélie read voraciously—and in eclectic fashion—following her own interests and picking freely among the several thousand volumes in the library. Her erudite grandmother was delighted at her granddaughter's bookish ways, but she did not necessarily approve of Amélie's reading *everything* in the library. When Judith discovered the nine-year-old nestled with a book that she considered inappropriate, she dramatically tossed the offending volume into the roaring fireplace. Archie must have laughed over the story. But he also understood completely what a refuge this library had been for Amélie. The smell of William Cabell Rives's musty old volumes must have brought Archie back to the octagonal library at Rokeby, where he, too, roamed freely, amid his great-grandfather Astor's leatherbound books. Amélie and Archie shared a love of literature, as well as dreams of great literary success. (Archie had already penned a memoir of life at Rugby, and he would make several attempts to write novels, none of which were successful.)

Perhaps Amélie admitted to Archie how deeply influenced she had been by her grandmother. Judith had been a woman of charm and grace and steel, of passionate beliefs and immense talent—and a role model for Amélie. Grandmother Judith wrote poetry in a tiny, meticulous hand, using a copper-colored ink that looked like liquid gold. She published several books, including a collection of European travel sketches and a novel set in a fictionalized Castle Hill (just as Amélie would do later). Upper-crust Southern women of that era did not ordinarily publish books—it was considered beyond the pale—so Judith did so anonymously. The books were credited to "A Lady of Virginia" or "A Mother." But of course everyone knew the books were by Judith.

From early childhood Amélie followed in her grandmother's footsteps. The young girl believed she *had* to write—that she would die otherwise. Almost as soon as she learned block lettering, she began to write short stories, poems, and other "childish effusions." (The *New York Times* reported that as a child Amélie "was fond of shutting herself up in her room for some days at a time, subsisting on strong tea and bread and writing epics on the deluge and kindred subjects.") By age ten she wrote and illustrated a weekly magazine for her family's edification. Amélie delighted in telling the story of how her frugal grandmother—horrified at how much foolscap the youngster was using—cut off her supply of paper. Undeterred, the young author used the five-inch hem of her starched petticoat. When

Amélie's father saw her scribbled-upon hem, he laughed uproariously and insisted that she have as much paper as she liked. When he was home, which was not often, he spoiled her shamelessly. He adored her precocious ways and encouraged her independence. At age twelve, presumably alluding to her parents, Amélie wrote, "Married love is like champagne with the sparkles out!" Her mother was shocked, but her father beamed with pride, instructing Sadie to "let her observe! . . . let her think!"

Headstrong, determined, and irritating, Amélie was nonetheless an acute observer of human behavior. Despite her tender age, she grasped the psychology of the household: poor Sadie lived in the shadow of her mother-in-law—whose dictates ruled at Castle Hill until her death in 1882—and of her cranky sister-in-law, who made life miserable for her. Amélie once recalled coming upon her mother sobbing over her "sad, unsatisfied life"; Amélie's dress became soaked with tears as she tried to comfort her mother.

Amélie lived amid a society of women at Castle Hill. During the war, the three generations of women largely survived on their own. After the war, the matriarchy continued. William Cabell Rives, in failing health, died in 1868. Desperate for work, Alfred became an itinerant engineer and architect. "Alfred's movements are so erratic that we do not know when to count on him," Amélie's grandmother wrote to a daughter-in-law in 1869.

> *His duties now call on him from various directions—to the Alleghanies to Richmond and Alexandria. . . . His account of the scene of his labors is very interesting—part of that region being so wild and strange. People meet with romantic adventures there. One of the engineers tells of his mother narrowly escaping the claws of a panther as large as a Bengal tiger—another of a boy of nine years old killing a lady bear and taking possession of her four baby bears—another of getting into a nest of rattlesnakes etc. His life is pretty hard. A few days ago he had to pass the day walking from point to point . . . in . . . [a] snow storm and the next day to ride*

twenty miles in the teeth of a roaring wind with the thermometer at eighteen. Still he is cheerful and bears it bravely.

Alfred had no choice but to be away from home. The South lay in ruins, the economy was a shambles. Money and jobs were scarce. The one thing the Rives family had left was their land. Land had always been the basis of wealth in the South; credit would be extended without question to a landed Virginia aristocrat. In turn, more land would be purchased. The Civil War ended all that. Overnight the property was worthless; squatters, and unpaid taxes, and conveniently lost land records swallowed up Rives land in distant counties. Large prewar debts from William Cabell Rives's brother overwhelmed Castle Hill. Much of the burden fell upon Amélie's father, Alfred.

Family papers reveal the increasing desperation over money at Castle Hill. By 1875 the handwritten accounts were telling:

> *There is nothing left to pay House servants. . . . The only economy possible, if the plantation is kept going, is to dismiss the house-servants, dispose of the carriages and horses, and dispence with the purchase and use of whatever cannot be had within the limit of ninety dollars per annum.*

Alfred was away working, so Amélie's aunt Ella was left in charge of the ruinous finances. She appealed to her rich brothers up North and got a sharply worded reply from her elder brother, William Cabell Junior, who took time out from his hectic social season at Newport to point a finger—perhaps at the absent Alfred—over the "great carelessness & waste & abuse—& in past times—dishonesty in the management" at Castle Hill. He gave Ella a list of practical rules to follow ("abstain from the use of guano & other expensive fertilizers" being one of his dictates); in addition, he gave her other tips for success:

> *Napoleon ascribes his success—while he was successful—to being always prepared for his emergencies 3 months in advance, & to*

> *always calculating on the worst. . . . The great weakness of Virginia farmers seems to be that they are perpetually indulging in illusions. Facts being facts, they ought to be recognized as such, & ought not to be blinked [at].*

And, as a final bit of financial advice: "If you get a little ahead—however slightly—lend your money—even if it be but twenty dollars—seeking no more than 6 per cent interest." (William's brother, Francis, was lending money to Castle Hill at a 7 percent clip.) William assured his sister that if she followed this simple formula, "You may yet live to become a millionaire."

Try as he might, Amélie's father, Alfred, would never be a millionaire. In fact, he had to go far afield to earn a decent income at all. He briefly considered a railroad post in Egypt—with a salary in gold—that was offered to him by the South's old foe, General Sherman; but decided instead to accept a position as chief engineer and general superintendent for the Mobile & Ohio Railroad. In order to keep the family together for at least part of the year, Alfred dragged his wife and children to semitropical Mobile, Alabama, for the winter. This went on for most of Amélie's childhood and teenage years. Amélie hated Mobile and resented being torn from her aristocratic enclave. "Every year the same parting—the same horrid journey to that horrider Mobile," she wrote at sixteen in her journal. "How I hate this southern town with its warm ennervating winds—its sickly scent of flowers—its lazy drones of citizens!" The dislocated family battled mosquitoes in midwinter and hung photos of Castle Hill in the parlor. Amélie counted the days until her return to Virginia. In her wake she left behind whispers about her peculiar behavior—and lovestruck teenage boys.

Returning to Castle Hill each spring, Amélie would be folded back into her magical world, back into the matriarchal society dominated by her grandmother. A photograph taken around 1880 at the estate captures the spirit of the place. It is summertime, and the place is lush with vegetation. Three generations of Rives women are portrayed in a parklike, sylvan corner at Castle Hill. Grandmother Judith, the elderly grande dame, is seated in a chair, her arms folded, with a look of determination and repose. She is dressed in dark colors—perhaps still in mourning for her husband and her drowned daughter; all the other women are wearing light-colored dresses. Amélie's mother, Sadie, petite and rigidly posed, sits on a bench—as far from her formidable mother-in-law as possible. Seated next to her is her daughter, fourteen-year-old Gertrude. Amélie, a young beauty at seventeen, stands behind and between the powerful figures in the photo—her grandmother and her granite-faced Aunt Ella—as if she were next in line in the dynasty. To the right of the grouping is a black servant, holding a cow. The iconography of the photograph is clear—the women at Castle Hill run the farm, and here is a prized animal to prove it. There is not a male Rives in sight, though there is perhaps one oblique reference to the absent Alfred. One of the conventions of nineteenth-century photography was to portray missing loved ones by including a picture of them, or a piece of their clothing, or some other physical representation. The photographer may have remembered Alfred by including the parrot, which sits in a circular birdcage behind Sadie and Gertrude. While residing in Mobile, the family sent back exotic items to Castle Hill—including mandarin oranges and a canary, which they dubbed "Colonel A. L. Rives" after Alfred. Perhaps this parrot had been a gift from Alfred while he was away on his exotic business travels. Though gone, Amélie's father was not completely forgotten; but it was the women who ruled at Castle Hill.

Alfred hated his nomadic existence, which kept him separated from his family. And Amélie—spoiled as she was—found it tiresome that her father could not restore the luster of the family's glorious past. Alfred's career seemed fraught with disaster. After more than a decade in Mobile, he accepted the post of vice-president and general manager of the Richmond & Danville Railroad, a Virginia line that would keep him closer to home, but he was forced to resign after two years. "I am so very tired of the wretched life I have been leading," he wrote to his wife. He warned that times would be tough, but he assured Sadie that "I will be with you to strengthen guide & defend . . . [I] hope to pick up some financial crumbs & yet live with my family." It was not to be. Alfred went to New York and enlisted the help of his well-connected brother Francis to line up some "New York magnates," including the Astors, to help him get a new job. But that attempt failed. Alfred ended up having to go all the way out to the West Coast, to the state of Washington, for work. While there, he managed to get mixed up in a bad investment that would haunt him for years.

Three months before Archie arrived at Castle Hill, Alfred accepted the position of general superintendent of the Panama Railroad. (He had declined the same position two years previously, but now he was desperate.) His Old World connections undoubtedly played a role in his being offered the job, as the railroad was then controlled by the French, who were building a canal across the swampy isthmus. Alfred had been trained as an engineer in France, at the government's official engineering school, the Ecole des Ponts et Chaussées. And upon graduation the young son of the American minister had been sent, by Emperor Napoleon III himself, on a surveying expedition to the coast of Algiers, along with Ferdinand de Lesseps and other engineers. De Lesseps went on to design and successfully complete the Suez Canal in 1869; he was now building a canal in Panama.

This all must have sounded rather grand to outsiders, but Archie had actually been to the Isthmus of Panama the year before, and he knew how truly grim it was. "This is the worst place I ever was in, unhealthy dirty & uninteresting," Archie had written to his brother Bob. "The ride across the Isthmus is not so pretty as I expected, or as the geographers make it. The work on the canal has destroyed most of the trees hung with vines & other tropical growth which used to line the track from Colon to Panama. . . . The roads are bad, dusty, & ugly, there are no sights to be seen, & the weather is so hot & muggy that one hasn't the energy to go down to the water & take a sail." Archie's traveling companion, Oliver Belmont, was so appalled by the place—its heat, mosquitoes, and bad food—that he left mid-trip and proceeded directly to San Francisco.

Alfred would stay on for a decade with the Panama Railroad,

surviving the purge of de Lesseps and his canal company when it went bankrupt, amid charges of corruption, in 1888. By all accounts, Panama remained a pesthole rife with disease, its jungles and swamps infested with alligators, snakes, and poisonous insects. But Alfred wrote back sunny letters to his youngest daughter Landon, asking how tall she was and describing his home at Colon and his brightly colored parrots, butterflies, and monkey. He almost never mentioned Amélie. Perhaps he understood how deeply he had disappointed his eldest daughter. She wanted Paris, not Colon. And Archie could give it to her.

Archie had sworn an oath to himself that he would never marry before the age of twenty-five, as he felt that he would not be able to fully understand his own mind before then. Archie turned twenty-five the fall he visited Castle Hill, and his mind was made up. Amélie was the woman he wanted. He believed that he and Amélie were fated to be with one another. He was enchanted with her, with Castle Hill, with the stories of her family and their glorious/tragic past. He proposed marriage on the spot. As rich and handsome as Archie was—and as tempting as his offer might have been—Amélie was not prepared to make a commitment. She turned him down flat. She was perhaps considering other suitors; she was also madly writing.

FOUR

Armida's Garden

In 1887, Amélie's career was slowly gathering steam. The year before—at the age of twenty-two—her literary debut in *The Atlantic Monthly* had caused a stir. Oddly enough, at Amélie's insistence, her first story, "A Brother to Dragons," had been published anonymously. Amélie was undoubtedly influenced by the memory of her grandmother, who had considered it the height of bad taste for a woman author to allow her name to be used. Amélie might also have been hedging her bets, just in case the story was a critical bust. To her relief, the *Atlantic* story was greeted warmly and the young author was hailed as a prodigy; thereafter all of her work was signed.

Editors snatched up Amélie's poems and stories, which began to appear regularly in the pages of *Century, Harper's,* and *Lippincott's Magazine.* As proof of how powerful a draw she quickly became, when *Harper's Magazine* produced an advertisement to boost subscriptions in November of 1887, Amélie Rives and Henry James were among the brand names touted. When Archie was unsuccessfully wooing Amélie at Castle Hill in September, the current issue of

Harper's carried one of her stories, and another story was scheduled to appear in the December issue. Perhaps counting on the holiday spirit to melt Amélie's resistance, Archie returned to Castle Hill at Christmas and pressed his romantic claims once again. For a second time he was turned down. Shortly thereafter, he sailed to Europe with his sister Elizabeth, to lick his wounds and take up residence in Paris, where he had been living before falling under Amélie's spell. It certainly seemed that their romance was over, but back in Virginia a strange alchemy was under way.

As midwinter settled over the countryside, Amélie withdrew to her sanctum to finish *The Quick or the Dead?*, a romance set at an old Virginia plantation not unlike Castle Hill. As she wrote, the male protagonist, Jock Dering, took on a physical appearance he had not had before: "Curling brown hair above a square, strongly-modelled forehead; eyes the color of autumn pools in sunlight; the determined yet delicate jut of the nose; the pleasing unevenness in the crowded white teeth, and the fine jaw which had that curve from ear to tip like the prow of a cutter. . . . In manner he was delightful—abrupt, frank, original, and a trifle egotistical." It was Archie.

The story was about a tempestuous, forbidden courtship: Two years after the sudden death of her husband, a young widow, Barbara Pomfret, falls desperately in love with her late husband's cousin, Jock, who bears a striking resemblance to the dead man. Torn by guilt, Barbara must choose between honoring her marriage vows by continuing her mourning (and chastity), or yielding to passion and the fervent embraces of the living, here-and-now cousin. Barbara's temptation is dramatized with episodes of heated lovemaking previously unknown in American fiction. In one scene, Jock kneels in front of Barbara and "kissed her dress, her knees, her waist, her arms" as Barbara "bent over him, panting, intoxicated." Amélie unmistakably suggests that Barbara and Jock are recklessly leading themselves to something forbidden.

The book apparently made its author nervous. Before submitting the manuscript, Amélie sent it to a cousin, a professor at the University of Virginia, and asked for his advice. He warned her not to publish it, or at least to obtain her father's permission first. She ignored his advice (her father was in Panama, after all), and sent it in.

The Quick or the Dead? appeared in the April 1888 issue of *Lippincott's Monthly Magazine,* and the whole country seemed to rise up against it. Libraries banned it from their shelves, preachers condemned the novel for its sordidness. Amélie was accused of being an atheist, and worse. Moralists across the land gasped at the very idea that a woman would disgrace her dead husband by expressing passionate sexual desire ("*Jock*! *kiss* me!") for another man—and worse yet, that this carnal fantasy could be written by a woman. America blushed, and ran out to buy it. A separate book edition came out in 1889. More than 300,000 copies of the novel were sold, an enormous sale at the time.

The 1889 edition afforded Amélie the opportunity to reply, in a preface, to "those who call me impure." First of all, she denied that Barbara Pomfret was "a representation of myself"; and she neatly turned the tables on her detractors by calling the book a mirror in which "the pure will see purity,—the foul-minded, foulness." The defensiveness was not a pose; Amélie was genuinely frightened by the anger that she had unleashed—she got so many vitriolic letters that she asked her publisher to screen her mail.

She became the pinup girl for a generation of college men. Princetonians snipped out the sensuous *Lippincott's* frontispiece engraving of Amélie, which displayed a sizable expanse of authorial bosom. Women secretly read the book and rejoiced at the sultry heroine. Though surreptitiously admired and viewed as a role model in some quarters, Amélie had to endure the venomous public denunciations that rained down upon her.

Lippincott's editors apparently realized that the novel would cause a sensation, and sent a reporter to Castle Hill to write a profile of the author for the same issue that carried the novel. The profile seems to have been calculated to simultaneously promote the author and defuse in advance any accusations of her personal depravity. The reporter took pains to depict the author as a genteel naïf, but Amélie defeated the purpose by brazenly inviting the interviewer into her boudoir for a tour. The poor fellow was bewitched, describing in hushed tones the "haunted chamber" where Amélie "dipped her pen in herself." The decor he described was part museum, part girlish refuge, part whorehouse. Amélie composed her poems and stories at a large oak table with legs carved in the shape of resting sphinxes. Books and manuscripts covered the desk. But the interviewer was much more taken with the "dainty toilet table, with linen cover sprinkled with blue forget-me-nots, its large mirror framed in carved white holly and china painted with peach-blossoms, its ivory-backed brushes, etc., etc." The mantel over the fireplace was draped with a "richly-wrought blue silk and cloth-of-gold 'Abba,' sent to Miss Rives direct from Persia." (Amélie perhaps failed to tell the interviewer that the sumptuous draping had been sent by one of her passionate suitors, a man Amélie had promised to marry once he got his diplomatic posting. He had recently been sent to Persia—and assumed that he had won the fair Amélie's hand.) The reporter was treated to a view of the greatest prize, Amélie's canopied brass bed, hung with embroidered muslin and India silk. After several pages of these intimate—and, at the time, shocking—details, the journalist then wondered aloud why such "an inoffensive creature" as Amélie Rives should be subjected to hate mail.

"Beastly . . . horrid . . . vulgar . . . a most sensual bit of rot." Thus did the Chanler family explode at *The Quick or the Dead?*. The Chanlers of course recognized Archie as the male character in Amélie's book. Archie's very public courtship of Amélie was identified by one journalist as the inspiration for the plot of *The Quick or the Dead?*. Indeed, Amélie wrote the novel while wrestling with her decision about Archie. She was faced with a choice between the "quick," persistent Astor descendant or the "dead"—the idealized version of what her lover should be—a man perhaps in the mold of her aristocratic Virginia cousin, Thomas Nelson Page, who had spurned her advances. The Chanlers were aghast. It was bad enough to have the family's intimate affairs broadcast to the public—but in a novel so vulgar! Archie's sister-in-law, Daisy Chanler, pronounced the bestselling novel "dreadful . . . one of the earthiest, most disagreeable pieces of literature it has ever been my misfortune to read." Daisy and her husband, Winty, were so disgusted, so perfectly revolted that they decided they had to meet the author. Putting aside the fact that Amélie had twice rejected Archie's proposals of marriage—thus the Chanlers had no social excuse to call on her—they wangled a letter of introduction to Amélie's mother from a mutual acquaintance and set out for Castle Hill.

Winty organized a riding party through Virginia with several friends, including William C. Endicott, whose father was then secretary of war, and a pair of English diplomats. After riding for nine days—during which time Winty was deemed "the life of the party"—the group headed for Castle Hill. Daisy joined them by train from Washington. Late on the morning of May 7, 1888, they arrived en masse with the expectation that they would find Amélie as vulgar as her novel. The redoubtable Daisy was charmed by the old-fashioned house and "pretty half-cultivated grounds about it," and she pronounced Amélie's mother "an exquisitely refined person." They were all invited to lunch.

Amélie did not appear at first. As was her custom, she preferred to make a delayed—and dramatic—entrance. Even Daisy had to admit that when Amélie did arrive, "the effect was dazzling, especially to the young men." She strode into the room and commanded it. Her two sisters were there—renowned beauties, both of them—but in Amélie's presence they paled, and "became part of the background." The newly famous author wore "a romantic white tea gown [that] draped and flowed from her shoulders in most becoming fashion"—and here Daisy gets rather catty—"all but concealing her want of stature." The effect on the men was astounding—by the time they left Castle Hill they were "heaving with excitement." Endicott was nearly beside himself, his "black eyes were rounder than ever; he kept exploding with enthusiasm, almost throwing himself out of the carriage in his ardors," as Daisy wrote in her memoir *Roman Spring*. She had to concede that the bestselling young author was "a siren, a goddess, perhaps a genius." Yet, in a letter to her mother, Daisy expressed her reservations about Amélie and how self-absorbed she was. Noting that "this . . . is strictly private; only for your discreet ears," Daisy wrote, "[Amélie] is certainly one of the cleverest women I have ever met—but she is in love with her own person & intoxicated with her own success. It is hard for people who are successful to live in such perfect isolation for they get to have an idea that the whole outside world is merely occupied with themselves."

In that spring of 1888, Amélie was besieged by a torrent of condemnation and ridicule, and by the relentless scrutiny of the press. Her novel had touched a nerve, had breached some wall of propriety. The notion that women had an erotic life of their own—and that a beautiful young female author would express such feelings—made the book supercharged.

Parodies sprouted like mushrooms. "The Quicker the Better" by O'Melia Overripe appeared in the scandal-rich society journal *Town Topics*. Poking fun at Amélie's overwrought heroine, Barbara, the spoof begins:

> She leaned against the mantelpiece, her glad red hair in its wanton waywardness blown branksomely about by the gusts of her long-drawn sighs. She stood crooning there, the firelight glowing on her full white bosom, which shone through the cambric of her robe, rising tempestuously with the sobs that choked her and shook her glorious body with tremors.

And ends with the widowed heroine entwined with her lover,

> the two swooning souls tortured with Love's frenzy. Bursting from his embrace, Barbara said, gasping: 'Oh! I am coarse. Let's go to church. . . .'

Another parody, "Be Quick and Be Dead" by "Ophelia Hives," even pokes fun at Amélie's portrait—a rather sensuous engraving showing the author in profile, wearing a low-cut dress with a heaving bosom partially in view—that appeared in the frontispiece of her novel. The send-up includes a portrait of an obese, middle-aged author who writes, "My purpose is simply to write a romance which shall sort of revolutionize things in a quiet, unostentatious sort of way, and make the reader wonder when he gets through why he was ever born, any way."

In the midst of this onslaught, Archie went to Castle Hill. He had just returned from Europe, had read *Lippincott's,* and had seen himself in Amélie's creation. Whether he wrote to Amélie or she wrote to him is not known, but he turned up at her door when she most needed a champion, the chivalrous white knight, rescuing a damsel in distress. He alone could shepherd Amélie through the attacks by mudslinging critics. His money and Astor connections could provide a protective shield. *The Quick or the Dead?* ends with Barbara rejecting Jock, but in writing that story Amélie may have written herself into a passionate frenzy even she could no longer resist. She had written herself into love. Archie proposed again, and Amélie said yes.

Archie was beside himself with joy. "He was the proudest and happiest man in America when he won her," one journalist wrote. His family was floored. His sister Elizabeth, still in Europe, received a telegram from Archie: "Just engaged Amélie Rives." Several months earlier the cousin responsible for the Astor orphans had died, leaving open the question of who would take charge of the sisters. The obvious choice seemed to be Archie—and his wife, if he had one. "At that moment," Elizabeth later wrote, "we were all looking for a Chaperone to succeed Cousin Mary Marshall, & my hair rather rose at the thought that my morals were to be cared for by the shadiest young authoress of the day."

Archie raced to New York to trumpet his engagement. In a whirlwind day, Archie made the insider's tour of Knickerbocker New York, calling on mansions and counting rooms and law offices, and setting those staid precincts aflame with the revelation that he had bagged Amélie Rives as his bride. "The news," Archie wrote, "burst like a thunderclap on society & the world." (Like his fiancée, Archie did not suffer from excessive modesty.) His great-uncle John Jacob Astor III was so delighted that he invited Archie for a drive to Riverside Park and a celebratory dinner in which the two men drank a toast to Amélie's health "in solemn state." One of Archie's aunts simply refused to believe him, "saying that a girl like Amélie wouldn't have me[,] that she knew of three men herself who were in love with her at that moment [&] that I made the fourth." The groom-to-be carried a photo of Amélie with him, and he pulled it out as proof; only then was his aunt convinced. Archie made his way to the Wall Street offices of Coleman Drayton, son-in-law of his great-uncle William B. Astor Jr. and Caroline Astor. Drayton was "rattled" by Archie's news, and wondered how another rival for Amélie's affections, "a prominent swell approaching middle age," would react. "Make the best of it I imagine," Archie crowed. Drayton was then delegated to make a formal announcement at the Knickerbocker Club.

Like a hunter who had scored a prize bit of game, Archie strutted about town, spreading word of his conquest. He ambled over to cousin Egerton Winthrop Jr.'s law office, knowing that Winthrop would welcome any distraction from the law. Winthrop was "literally speechless with astonishment. He opened & shut his mouth for several seconds without uttering a sound." Then Winthrop was off to a polo match on Long Island, and Archie instructed him to spread the good news out there.

Archie was bursting to return to his beloved Amélie, but before that he had to help settle some pressing family matters. First and foremost, he had to extricate himself from an upcoming trip to Europe. He had been scheduled to take the youngest girls, Margaret and Alida, to Europe for a summer of travel. Passage for the three of them had already been booked; they were set to sail the following Saturday. With his engagement, the trip would be quite out of the question. The Guardians, the committee charged with making decisions about the orphans, agreed that it would be best if brother Willie, then finishing up his sophomore year at Harvard and about to celebrate his twenty-first birthday, would shepherd the girls. Willie agreed to take on the task, and Archie was very grateful; but he was also concerned about his younger brother, who was making noises about dropping out of Harvard.

Archie went up to Rokeby to huddle with his younger brothers Willie and Lewis, both of whom were facing school decisions. In the wake of Mary Marshall's death, there was no parental figure left at Rokeby (save for the children's tutor, Mr. Bostwick); so Archie took on the role of surrogate father and sage counselor. He interrogated Willie as to his reasons for wanting to leave Harvard. Willie claimed that he hated the bitter Cambridge winters. In fact, he hated sitting still. The polo team and his membership in the Porcellian Club were about the extent of his interests at Harvard. He much preferred wrestling alligators in the Florida everglades, and rounding up wild mustangs in Arizona—and he had experience in both endeavors.

After hearing Willie out, Archie wisely concluded that there was no point in arguing with him further. "He has no interest whatever in getting a degree," Archie wrote to his sister Elizabeth in Paris, "& when a man is of age & feels that way & is his own master there is no use in trying to inspire an interest." And then—in something of an understatement when it came to the Chanler crew—Archie concluded, "We can't make characters to order, dear, we have to take things as they are." With Archie's blessings, Willie dropped out of Harvard and spent the rest of his life chasing adventure around the globe. Among other highlights: he fomented revolution in Africa, and took personal responsibility for blowing up the *Maine* and starting the Spanish-American War.

Eighteen-year-old Lewis was a much more sober sort (an anomaly among the Chanler brothers), and although he had already passed half of the entrance exams for Harvard, he had no interest in matriculating there. Nor did he have any interest in traveling. Archie questioned Lewis closely as to how he wanted to spend the next few years. Lewis was focused on a career in law—a real one, not like the gentleman's avocation that it was for Archie—and he was eager to leapfrog over college and work in a lawyer's office right away. He wanted to do that while studying at Columbia Law School. Archie embraced Lewis's program, and envisioned that his younger brother might also take a course or two in literature or history at the college on the side, just to round out his education. Having reached a consensus, the two brothers went to New York to face the assembled Guardians; and to their joint relief, the plan passed muster. It was arranged that Lewis would work during the school year in the offices of Henry Lewis Morris—the trusted family lawyer who managed all the financial details of the Chanler estate. (The firm, now Morris & McVeigh, still represents the Chanler interests.)

Archie felt quite pleased with himself that he had helped resolve these family issues. In writing to his sister Elizabeth, he fairly brimmed with pride over his parental role. But as time went on, his focus turned increasingly to Amélie, and he began to shirk his Chanler duties—an offense that became especially irksome to his brother Winty, who then had to take on the mantle and duties of the eldest sibling. A breach between Archie and his family was about to open.

After having made his joyous announcement in New York, Archie returned to Castle Hill with his sister Margaret in tow. The wedding was planned for the following autumn, and he wanted his sister to get to know Amélie. Margaret's opinion would be important. If Amélie could win her over, then Archie felt certain his beloved would be accepted at Rokeby unconditionally. (Daisy Chanler's rocky introduction at Rokeby—and Margaret's continued coolness toward her sister-in-law—were probably on Archie's mind.) The teenaged Margaret was delighted to be brought into her eldest brother's confidence, and to be ushered into the circle at Castle Hill. (This Southern interlude must also have been something of a relief for Margaret, for she was still in official mourning for cousin Mary Marshall, and her social activities in New York had been limited to churchgoing.) Using stationery edged with a thick black mourning band, Margaret wrote to her sister Elizabeth, in care of the Rothschild bank in London, giving all the details of life at Castle Hill. She reported that Archie was incredibly happy, and that he and Amélie would go out in the evening after dinner for long drives in the dark, "there being no malaria." She was pleased to note that everyone at Castle Hill doted on their brother.

Margaret found the Rives family "the most natural people in the world and while very southern not like southerners." (Obviously, Margaret did not share her brother's unbridled affinity for Southerners.) She thought some aspects of life in Virginia were rather picturesque. She found it charming that even though most everyone was "terribly reduced" financially, people held on to their dignity. Amélie's cousins were reading "translations of Plato's Republic and Greek poets and trying to learn German"—though of course they would never get to Germany to speak it. "It is delightful to find such cultivation," Margaret wrote, even if Southerners "talk queer English sometimes." She reported that Amélie's sister Landon says "I reckon" all the time but so languidly that it does not sound inelegant. Margaret also loved the little stone church, Grace Episcopal, which Amélie's grandmother had been instrumental in building. Half the congregation arrived for services on horseback, and the minister " 'raised' the hymns" as there was no choir. "It was so primitive and simple," she reported. Margaret found it comforting that Amélie's mother was much like dear departed cousin Mary Marshall, both being very religious—though Mrs. Rives was decidedly "more feminine."

To bed early and up in time for breakfast, Margaret spent her mornings knitting in the company of Amélie's mother and maiden aunt Ella. The two older women rolled their eyes over the headstrong Amélie and her sister Gertrude, muttering how they "are very unpunctual, do not dress as their grandmothers did and are otherwise incomprehensible to them."

The bestselling author kept odd hours. She did not emerge until one o'clock in the afternoon, "for she is not at all well and then her correspondence is so large." She received as many as thirty-five letters a day (and an untold number of vicious notes withheld by the publisher). She wrote letters to some of her fans, and acknowledged others with autographed calling cards or photographs; sometimes she had a friend answer on her behalf. (Among the fan letters was one from a country boy from Tennessee who invited Amélie to his home in the mountains: "I know if you come mother will give you white bread and take down the jam.") Margaret had to admit that she did not like Amélie's stories—and in fact had not dared read *The Quick or the Dead?*—and she hoped that Archie's bride-to-be would stop writing for a year or two in order to rest, "for her brain has been much excited and her general health affected by the criticism which you must have heard of."

Word of Amélie's engagement managed to create more unnerving publicity. Newspapers on the East Coast were buzzing with the announcement—but it came with inferences that were less than auspicious. The *New York Times* expressed surprise over the betrothal, and managed to misspell Chanler, adding an unnecessary *d* to the name. This rankled Archie's siblings, particularly Winty. A week later the *Times* spelled the family's name correctly, but attached a bit of scandal to the future bride:

> The engagement of Mr. Armstrong Chanler and Miss Amélie Rives has excited no end of gossip. The simultaneous announcement of Miss Rives's engagement to Mr. Coolidge of Boston was rather confusing, but those persons who know Miss Rives would not have been surprised at the announcement of her engagement to six men, for it has been hard to decide which of the small army with whose individual members the fair authoress, it is understood, has carried on a more or less desperate flirtation for some years she would finally choose.

The article then went on to mention a few specific members of that defeated army, including the jilted minister to Persia and a widower who had been devoted to Amélie at Newport the previous summer (and whose first wife had been a member of the Astor family). *Town*

Topics had a field day with the confusion. Referring sarcastically to Amélie as "the mistress of chaste and moral family fiction in America," the society rag noted:

> In Boston . . . they are now laying odds that Miss Rives will never be Mrs. Chanler. The facility of that gifted young woman for engaging and disengaging herself is pointed to in support of this prediction, but perhaps Boston's nose is slightly out of joint at the failure of its own . . . Archie Coolidge to capture the volatile genius of the Virginia lowlands.

And then with a kick—and a snicker—at the Astor family, the magazine opined that if indeed Amélie did wed Archie, then "the intellectually igneous but auriferous Astors will have at least one person of brains in their select family fold," and the bride will help rescue "the Astor name from intellectual nothingness."

Humiliated and angry over the sensational news reports, Archie decided that he and Amélie had to marry as quickly and quietly as possible. He wanted no one to know, least of all his family in New York. Archie slipped into Charlottesville to get a marriage license, and swore the clerk to secrecy, but word spread. Journalists descended on the pair. Not totally averse to publicity—as long as it could be controlled—Amélie met with a *New York Herald* reporter who was a friend of hers. That favored journalist was invited to the wedding, but others were turned away. The *Herald* got the scoop and ran an in-depth account of the proceedings.

On the afternoon of Thursday, June 14, 1888, a number of "Virginia cousins" arrived at Castle Hill and were ushered into the French drawing room and greeted by Amélie's Aunt Ella. The Rives women and their servants had created a glorious, fragrant confection for Amélie's wedding bower—honeysuckle trailed over the mirrors and doors, roses covered the mantels, a mass of white lilies adorned a small stand, and bowls of fresh flowers were artfully placed around the room. Anticipation rose among the tiny gathering when Amélie's sisters, Gertrude and Landon, entered the room, along with Archie's sister Margaret, and Amélie's two dearest friends and cousins, Leila Page and Louisa Pleasants. All of them were dressed in white. Next came the "fine, well knit figure" of Archie. He had no attendants. Outside the room, the black house servants and farm workers "appeared softly, one by one, and lined the long stretch of the hall," peering into the drawing room. The murmur of the servants heralded the arrival of the bride, who walked down the hallway leaning on the arm of her mother. The still-handsome Sadie looked striking in a black silk gown, "setting off admirably her snow white hair and delicate ivory complexion." Amélie appeared like an angel. Dressed in "a rich gown of corded white silk cut high, with half long sleeves," Amélie clutched a white prayer book ornamented with a gold cross and her monogram, and wore a corsage of Castle Hill roses. Her veil was fastened with two pins—lover's knots of diamonds, with a large ruby in the center of one, a sapphire in the other. These were wedding gifts from Archie.

Amélie's father, Alfred, was in Panama, unable to take part in the ceremony or even weigh in with his opinion. His brother, William Cabell Rives Jr. of Boston, stood in for the absent father, and officially gave the bride away, but it was mother and daughter who walked arm-in-arm across the room to the minister and Archie. As for the groom, he was "radiantly joyful," according to his sister. She reported that the brief Episcopal service "was the most solemn I have ever known—not a sound but the clergyman's voice and those of Amélie & Archie as they responded." Margaret cried quietly, the only guest to do so. They were bittersweet tears—of joy for Archie but heartache for her family who had been excluded. "It seemed so strange to be all alone at Archie's wedding," she wrote.

The guests then sat down to a "bounteous dinner, many of the dishes . . . prepared in the old ante-bellum Southern style now almost unknown." This final tidbit was supplied by the *New York Times,* though its reporter had been shut out from the proceedings and had only gotten his information secondhand. (That snubbing might account for why he referred to the bride—not very generously—as the "fair writer of weird stories.") *Town Topics* also added its own acerbic commentary, noting that during the ceremony Amélie had been "supported in her ordeal by her mother," and that after the ceremony, the first act was to "post a horseman off to the nearest telegraph office, to communicate the news of his daughter's change of condition to that redoubtable Brother of Dragons, Colonel Rives, at Panama."

Another telegram had to be sent to Rokeby—but Archie somehow didn't get around to it. All of New York society—and even the local yeomen farmers around Rokeby—had been curious about the rumors of Archie's imminent marriage to the scandalous and gorgeous Amélie. Brother Winty vociferously denied the possibility to everyone. Their famously proper great-aunt Lina had arrived at Rokeby the day of the wedding and had been nosing about for information. Winty assured her that his brother was not being married anytime soon; all the gossip about it was just that—gossip to sell newspapers. Imagine Winty's shock and embarrassment the next morning when he picked up the *Times* and *Herald* and read that Archie and Amélie had been married. Winty was absolutely furious, feeling that he had been made the fool by his older brother. Archie's youngest sister, Alida, was so wounded that at the dinner table "tears rolled down her cheeks into her strawberries."

It took four days before Archie contacted his family—an unpardonable sin to his siblings. Winty, in the meantime, was beside himself, so angry that he refused even to speak about the subject at Rokeby for several days. He did, however, write two scorching letters to his sister Margaret at Castle Hill. He made it plain that he considered her a turncoat for not having informed the family beforehand of the nuptials. "If ever two people deserved a good spanking, those two are Brog [Archie's nickname] and you," he wrote. "It is all over the country that not a single member of his family knew he was going to be married so soon. That don't look well does it?" Winty's wife, Daisy, tried to intercede and calm the waters, writing her congratulations to Archie, but even she could not help lecturing the newlywed:

> You do not seem to realize in the least how very keenly we all felt your treating us as if we were mere outsiders to be classed with reporters and other noxious and inquisitive bipeds. The news of your marriage was known to hundreds of people before it reached us . . . we had a stream of visitors who could none of them fail to be surprised at our being left so totally in the dark.

She urged Archie to come to Rokeby as quickly as possible—with his new wife—to avoid the appearance of a family feud. "You have got yourself into this false position," she wrote, "and you owe it to the family to get yourself out of it." Winty was less politic. Writing a note dripping with bitter sarcasm, Winty referred to Amélie as "Armida," the sorceress queen in Handel's medieval opera "Rinaldo":

> *Dear Brog:*
>
> *Just a line from an outsider to disturb the bliss of Armida's garden. Ask for and read the two letters I have written to Margaret in the name of the Rokebyites and use your own judgement about repeating the contents. Love to Armida. We don't want any cuttings from the Herald or any other of your friends the journalists.*
>
> *P.S.—The weather here is very warm, 93 in the shade today. I wonder if you wouldn't find it cool in spite of the thermometer.*

As far as Archie was concerned, a gauntlet had been thrown down. "I shall want an apology from you in writing before anything further can pass between us," he wrote to Winty. From then on, resentment and bitterness would mark the tone between the two brothers.

FIVE

The Bride Stripped Bare

The woman soul leads us upward and on.

Goethe, quoted by Amélie, 1892

Many years after Amélie's death, a rather shocking charcoal sketch was discovered in one of the outbuildings at Castle Hill. It is a self-portrait of Amélie, made in the summer of 1892, after four years of marriage to Archie. She is naked and lies provocatively on a divan. Calling her figure "shapely" hardly does justice to the sketch. Her breasts and hips are enormous, the curving contours of her body unbelievably sensuous. Her hair is undone and fans wildly around her head. She lies with eyes closed, looking as if she were enjoying a bit of postcoital bliss. You can practically hear her moaning softly. Here indeed is the Gilded Age queen of sex, the chronicler of female lust, the siren in full cry. But the reality of her married life bore no relation to that portrait.

Within weeks of the wedding, Amélie was writing plaintive letters to her new sister-in-law Margaret:

dear, dear Sister

Yesterday I was so tired and worn out body and soul, that I simply curled up in bed all day and my mother read to me. You will never know my Margaret, the comfort your little note brought me. It was like a kiss on a bare and aching heart, and the tears came into my eyes and stayed there as I read it. God has given you to me Margaret—has given us to each other, and you do not know how humbly thankful I feel to him, or how I think of you with almost every breath I draw. No matter what happens, no matter how life may widen or contract for us both, we have each other, and so much sweetest and best of all—love each other with all our hearts. God has let you save me from the very pit of gloom, and grief, and terror. . . .

"Gloom, and grief, and terror" after only two weeks of marriage. More followed. Amélie pulled out her newly acquired stationery from Tiffany's with its handsome red monogram (an intertwined *A* and *C*), and between acknowledging the wedding gifts that were pouring in, she continued a series of long and heartfelt missives to her ally Margaret. "My darling Sister of Charity—(which means 'Love,') . . . I have been fighting battles of such mortal anguish in my soul," she wrote dramatically on July 15. In another letter the newlywed referred to "that terrible feeling of foreboding [that] has not left me yet." She begged Margaret to pray for her: "Oh! Margaret, pray for me—pray for me all the time—I am trying to be brave. . . ." She was practically never out of the sight of her devoted followers and soul mates—cousins Leila Page and Lutie Pleasants, and her dear friend and fellow author Julia Magruder. At least one of that troika always seemed to be at Amélie's side, catering to her, ministering to the young author when she suffered from her headaches and dark moods.

Could it be that the love goddess herself (*"Jock! kiss* me!")—the woman who made men quiver with lust—was actually afraid of sex? Perhaps Amélie had been right when she confessed to her cousin Thomas Nelson Page that marriage was not for her. A Chanler family member later hinted that the marriage might not even have been consummated—and that might have been what drove Archie over the edge of sanity. Amélie thought she could detect something very wrong in Archie's demeanor, and wrote to her sister-in-law:

> *Margaret, tell me as though you were my own sister as well as Archies, have you ever thought in the bottom of your soul, that Archie's mind was not quite right?—He laughs at me in such a dreadful way sometimes, until I am crying & trembling with terror. And the more I cry & beg him to stop or to tell me what is the matter, the more he laughs—Oh! Margaret, Margaret write to me darling. Pray for me . . . what I have suffered no earthly power could describe.*

But the witnesses conflict. In later years, Archie's sister Elizabeth, the soul of kindness and a longtime confidante of Amélie's, wrote a scathing portrayal of her erstwhile friend. Writing in the 1920s, she warned her own son about the dangers of a siren like Amélie:

> *There is a type of cold blonde, who is fascinated, in a way, by men with a flame in them, & yet who can never fully respond to their love-making. Such was Amélie. . . . These blondes have an almost hypnotic charm for the fiery men who fall in love with them. But no happiness can ever come of that love. If the man finally browbeats & wheedles the girl into marrying him (as was the case with Archie, who wooed Amélie . . .) that coldness, which gave a sort of charm to the chase, becomes a red hot Hell after marriage. In all their marital relations, that type of woman looks upon a hot-blooded husband as an aggressor. And after a nightmare on both their parts, she throws him out.*

Elizabeth went on to describe Amélie as having a "strange mixture of coldness & warmth, advancing & retreating like a white cat . . . who rubs against your hand & seems to want a caress, but who walks off in a huff if you give it to her." Archie's sister concluded that a woman like that should only "marry a man as cold as herself"—not a soft-hearted sort like her brother, who would be "broken on the wheel" by her.

The metaphor of the cat who seeks but does not actually want a caress, who teases for affection and then angrily spurns it, was particularly apt. A reporter for the *Chicago Times-Herald* wrote tellingly about Amélie. In the wake of the scandal over the publication of *The Quick or the Dead?,* he had gone to Castle Hill and returned a man possessed. He wrote a spirited defense of Amélie and her work (while trying to resist the "impulse to break into raptures of admiration"), and, in a letter to Archie, referred to himself as "one of her knights" who "talked of little but the genius, beauty and sweetness of Mrs. Chanler." The journalist admitted: "My friends tell me my head has been turned, and I retort: 'So would yours be turned if you had seen what I have seen." Yet a few years later the same reporter saw a different side of Amélie. He recounted an evening in which he witnessed her startling "moods of genius." A Washington hostess asked Amélie to read some of her poems to another guest, an older man noted for his literary taste. Amélie was left alone with the man and practically cooed the verses to him. The literary arbiter was overwhelmed:

> I don't remember a word she read to me; all I can remember is the sweetness of her voice, the charm of her presence. She read poem after poem in a low, impassioned voice, standing with her face near to mine, her eyes ablaze with poetic fervor. To me she seemed unearthly, angelic. I had no power to concentrate my mind upon her words. I could see nothing, think of nothing, but the petite, radiant, soul-stirred woman by my side.

An hour later, a jolly dinner party ensued, with half a dozen guests. The alluring young author was the center of attention. All eyes were riveted on Amélie when the family kitten jumped into her lap and she began to fondle it seductively at the table. She fed the "little mewing mouth with dainty morsels," prompting more than one of the guests to wish they could have a photograph of the tender scene. Then, just as suddenly, Amélie grew angry with the little creature, picked it up by the nape of the neck, and hurled it against the wall. The guests were stunned into silence, the well-bred hostess improvised a new conversational gambit, "and in a short time the clouds left the face of the capricious Virginia girl, and radiant sunshine took their place."

If Archie had glooms and terrors in the first weeks of the marriage, he hid them well. Ten days after the wedding he sat down on a rainy, steamy day to write a long letter to his sister in France. He was settling into the ways of the South; he hired a four-year-old black girl to fan away the flies that swarmed around him as he wrote. A dime bought him a full afternoon's service as he scratched away at a twenty-page missive to his sister Elizabeth, detailing for her his whirlwind courtship and marriage. There was one issue that had to be explained away to his siblings: Amélie kept putting off the expected, much-awaited visit to Rokeby, claiming that she was too weak to travel, or too busy with her literary endeavors. For the next two months, Archie would write repeatedly to Winty and Daisy, promising that he and his bride would soon be up to the Hudson Valley to meet the family. Amélie, he said, was awaiting the publication of her new drama in blank verse, a Roman-era tragedy titled *Herod and Mariamne.* Winty shuddered in anticipation of his sister-in-law's latest work: "We are all waiting with the bedclothes over our ears for the storm to burst."

Meanwhile the Chanler brothers entertained themselves at Rokeby as best they could until the arrival of the famous Amélie. They spent their time furiously competing at lawn tennis on their two courts—playing "till we drop," according to Winty—and hunting rabbits with their pack of beagles, "much to our joy & the amusement of the rabbits." One day the Chanler gentlemen played a spirited game of baseball against a team composed of farmers' sons. The aristocrats won. "It was curious to see how infinitely better the better bred men moved and played and played together," Daisy Chanler wrote to her father. "Other things being equal I suppose the gentlemen would always win." Daisy shared that particular brand of arrogance with her class, but even among her peers she had a hauteur that was positively terrifying. She certainly cowed Amélie, who had already gotten a taste of Daisy's "treachery" when she had earlier visited Castle Hill to get a look at the scandalous author.

For all that Amélie wanted to be introduced to the aristocratic precincts that she felt were her birthright—the salons and drawing rooms of London, Paris, and New York—she hated leaving her beloved Castle Hill. This was the world where she ruled without a quiver of doubt. But the Astors/Chanlers were an entirely different species. They lived on a grander scale and consorted with the richest and most powerful people on earth. It was daunting even for Amélie. And, until she married Archie, she didn't quite understand how restless the Chanlers were. They moved around obsessively, perhaps in response to their having been unmoored as children. Letters among the siblings have the feel of a travelogue; they are constantly reporting on their peregrinations as they wander aimlessly from Europe to Asia to Africa. As Daisy Chanler wrote of her in-laws: "The Chanlers are like turkeys and must not be enclosed. They cannot thrive unless they be allowed to range." And indeed, like free-range turkeys they roamed.

Movement—or resistance to it—became a persistent theme and sticking point in Archie and Amélie's marriage. When Margaret had to be escorted back to Rokeby at the end of June, Amélie would not budge, citing the excessive heat. (Upon hearing that lame excuse, Daisy countered by saying that it had been so cool at Rokeby the week before, that they had to have fires going.) Archie went, sans spouse, to his ancestral home and arrived in time for the Fourth of July festivities. All the Chanler siblings, save Elizabeth, who was in Paris, gathered for a grand dinner at Rokeby. There were speeches by various siblings (*no one* suffered from shyness in that household), and toasts galore. Afterward there were fireworks on the lawn. And then, in an old-fashioned display of feudal country life, the farmers and servants on the estate, along with their children, all came into the house and drank a toast to Archie's health. "It was quite a Baronial scene," Winty later wrote. Archie beamed with pride and doubtless wished that his fair Amélie had been at his side to witness the show of affection. He couldn't wait to introduce her to this world.

Finally, at the end of August, Archie induced Amélie to proceed northward. The first stop on the marital tour was Newport and James J. Van Alen's cottage Wakehurst (dubbed the "granite palace" by *Town Topics*). This must have been a kind of dream come true for Amélie. The author of romantic Elizabethan stories was now the guest in an ersatz Elizabethan stone mansion, an exact replica of the sixteenth-century English manor house of the same name. The host might have been mistaken—at least he hoped so—for a Shakespearean hero, for his vocabulary was decidedly antiquated and very, very English. But also completely ridiculous. He liberally sprinkled his conversation with "egad" and "zounds" and "prithee." A contemporary noted acidly that "one almost needs a special old English dictionary to talk to him." With his monocle firmly in place, Van Alen, a notorious womanizer, must have adored getting a look at Amélie. He probably rendered his favorite compliment for a beautiful woman—"a most delectable wench, forsooth."

Van Alen was a widower and perhaps the most eligible and richest bachelor in Newport that summer. His first wife, Emily Astor (Archie's cousin, the eldest daughter of William and *the* Mrs. Astor), had died in childbirth. As a schoolboy, Archie had come down from his boarding school in Sing-Sing to attend the Van Alen/Astor nuptials at Grace Church in Manhattan. (Archie's great-aunt and -uncle hated Van Alen, and the couple's fathers nearly came to a duel over the marriage.) Van Alen inherited a vast amount of money, and spent it prodigiously. His summer "cottage" at Newport had taken some four years to construct. Several entire rooms had been built in England and imported to America. He ransacked antique stores and rural villages in England to fill Wakehurst with authentic period furnishings, ensuring that the walls of the damp seaside mansion would be covered with a formidable collection of moldering English tapestries. *Town Topics* had a field day describing the "cargo of sumptuous furnishings" that Van Alen had picked up abroad, saying that they were purchased "with a lavish disregard for cost, and, as some of his acquaintances assert, of even good taste." Archie disagreed, pronouncing Wakehurst "the handsomest house I ever was in."

Van Alen had an official housewarming party for his summer cottage the week before Archie and Amélie arrived, an event hailed by the local newspaper as "one of the grandest fêtes ever given in Newport"—an accolade of some weight, given the scale and lavishness of the entertainments in that resort. On the night of the party, Wakehurst shimmered in romantic candlelight—223 candles in the ballroom alone—as Van Alen preferred using the old English-style illumination to gaslights. Seen from the ocean, the diamond-paned bay windows glowed like beacons in the night.

Having just recovered from Van Alen's gala evening, Newport society now braced itself for Amélie's arrival. "The papers were full of Amélie & all complimentary," Archie wrote to his sister Margaret. "We went everywhere, to Casino dances, dinner & luncheons." Amélie was a huge success, and news of her triumph was carried to the remotest corners of the country. In distant Kansas a newspaper reported:

> Miss Amélie Rives Chanler was the centre of attraction at the last Casino hop at Newport, where she held quite a levee at the upper end of the hall. She was dressed in a rich red gown that showed off her peculiar style of beauty to great advantage.

But not everyone in Newport that season was a fan. When the local press discovered that the vacationing plutocrat Jay Gould was reading *The Quick or the Dead?*, they asked if he was enjoying it. "Tolerably," was his grumpy response. "It is a curious study of a morbid mental condition in a woman. The features which have popularized it are disagreeable." He had to admit that he could not even remember when he had last read a novel and he was doing so then only under duress: "My doctor told me to try fiction, and let thoughtful books alone. So I am obeying orders."

After two weeks in Newport, the bridal couple moved on to visit Archie's cousin Arthur Carey in New Hampshire. It was cold and wet, and Amélie was anxious to leave, so they departed after a few days. The bridal couple then progressed to New York City, where Amélie managed to court both the press and her husband's brothers. Some gentle seduction of the press was in order because Amélie's drama, *Herod and Mariamne,* had just been published in the September edition of *Lippincott's Monthly Magazine* to scathing reviews (and another misspelling of the Chanler name).

> Amélie Rives Chandler has written a tragedy called Herod and Mariamne. In it when Herod is not kissing the heroine he is dyeing his sword in blood. The tragedy is so exciting from start to finish that men cannot even wait for the fall of the curtain between acts to go out and see each other. And no doubt they will call for blood at the bar.

Like a celebrity author on a book tour, Amélie received a string of newspaper reporters at the dignified hotel where she and Archie were staying—the Brevoort House, on Fifth Avenue in Greenwich Village—to talk about her life and work. Looking fetching in a cream-colored silk tea gown, Amélie captivated her audience. Archie stood behind her chair in protective mode, seemingly content with "being known through life as 'Amélie Rives's husband,' " according to the journalist for the *New York World.* When asked where the couple would eventually settle, Archie was vague, saying that they might end up in New York, but that his main concern was for his wife's health. "That poor little girl . . . has been at high tension for a year and a half now and I am determined that she shall rest." But Amélie certainly did not wilt under the demands of the press. She loved the spotlight, and "chatted by the column." She also managed to draw even more attention to herself by going to the theater for three nights, sitting each time in a proscenium box filled with flowers. The floral displays were eye-catching and beautiful—and, as the press reported, were "not provided by the theatrical managers, as might be supposed, but were ordered by the eccentric bride" herself. This wonderful bit of self-promotion was so successful it started a fad. Amélie needed the publicity, for a dramatization of her scandalous *The Quick or the Dead?* was set to open in New York in several weeks. (The production was a disaster—"A Complete Failure" one headline read—and Amélie wisely steered clear of the theater.)

Having tended to her career, it was time to face the Chanlers. The introduction began in stages—a dinner at Delmonico's with Archie's brothers Lewis, Willie, and Winty helped break the ice. Winty had written sarcastically from Rokeby to an old Harvard pal:

> *My brother J. Armstrong Amélie Rives Chanler and his consort are expected up here for a few days, and I am reading "Titus Andronicus," "The Curse of Kehama," and "Ten Days in a Bar Room" so as to have a little ready conversation of a literary turn.*

But once in her presence, Winty's sarcasm stopped. Amélie's ascension to Rokeby followed smoothly. Everyone was bewitched by her (at least temporarily)—from cynical Winty and Daisy down to the youngest brother, sixteen-year-old Robert, who wrote:

> *Amélie has arrived . . . I know that I have not seen anybody that can hold a candell to her in the way of looks, & besides she being very religius, I do not know what more we can want in the way of a sister in law.*

The dark, hulking Robert—he would grow to be well over six feet tall—was the family enigma. From early on he preferred the company of children and farm animals to his studies. Robert caused no end of worry by his apparent inability to learn, as evidenced by his atrocious spelling. One day, as a punishment for not paying attention to his studies, he was given a number of lines to write on the blackboard in Rokeby's classroom. When the tutor, Mr. Bostwick, returned to the tower room where classes were held, he found a beautifully drawn horse on the blackboard instead of the lines. This was the first clue that Robert had an artistic gift, a gift that would be encouraged by Amélie, who also had a talent for drawing. Amélie became a muse for Robert; in turn, he became another ally in her camp.

At Rokeby, Amélie was introduced not only to the Chanler family, but to the larger Hudson River society. One entire afternoon she spent "receiving the 'county families,' " who were dying to get a peek at the celebrated addition to the Chanler family and to pay tribute to her as Rokeby's new queen. After all, her husband was the eldest heir to the ancestral home, and it was assumed that Archie and Amélie would take over Rokeby. It was both Archie's duty and his right. Amélie had other ideas.

Archie thought the family introduction had gone beautifully. "You don't know how delighted I am to be able to say that Amélie is a success with all here. It is the greatest relief to her & to me," Archie wrote on October 1, 1888, to his sister Margaret in Europe. But as soon as they left the Hudson Valley, Archie and Amélie began squabbling. The center of the storm concerned where they were to live. Archie assumed they would live in Paris (where he had an apartment and where Amélie could study painting), or Manhattan, with Rokeby as a country refuge. But Amélie, who had yearned for Paris her whole life, was suddenly gripped by a longing for hearth and home. She did not want to leave Castle Hill, and the matter became a larger issue of control—who exactly was to control the marriage, Archie or Amélie? Both had been the eldest child, and strong-willed to say the least. They were used to getting their way. Now it was a battle of wills between the newlyweds.

Having been turned into a literary character by his wife, Archie took up his pen and began writing his own fictionalized account of their marriage. Amid a huge trove of Archie's papers at Duke University is a box containing a novel that he was working on in October of 1888. The book was never finished, but the portion that remains—some thirty-five handwritten pages—is illuminating. Though supposedly fiction, the plot is lifted entirely from Archie's own life, and details the real-life struggle that was going on between the newlyweds. The book presents a kind of forum for Archie's confusion and anger over his independent wife and her manipulative behavior, as well as insight into his own complicated psychology. The story centers on love—what does it mean?—and marriage, and control. The husband and wife are fighting for happiness, "a drawing room their battleground[,] the bedroom their camp."

The story opens in a Fifth Avenue men's club, where the hero, named Stutfield (i.e., Archie), announces to a crusty old New England captain that he is engaged to be married. Horrified at the mention of marriage, the captain spears an oyster with a "viciousness that suggested a fugitive wish that the bivalve had been the heart of the lady." Over bottles of champagne and claret, the wise old captain tries to talk the young man out of marriage. Love, he tells Stutfield, is a "hydra-headed" monster that requires self-denial, self-effacement, and self-control. And it is even worse if the woman is of an artistic temperament. The hero admits that he has fallen for the "charm and fascination" of such a creature, and the older man warns him that "these charms have their price & it is heavy." He makes dire predictions if the younger man persists in taking on a wife, especially an artistic and moody one. "You are an ambitious man . . . a public man. And to a public man a wife is not only unnecessary but dangerous." Marriage will prevent Stutfield from making "a mark on his age & generation," which he otherwise surely would do. Love is like an "overgrown lusty parasite" that will destroy a man, the sage captain opines, and the "jarring jangling discord in his heart" will make it impossible to accomplish anything useful in life. At the end of his long, impassioned tirade, the old man tells the young groom-to-be that marriage is fine for a man interested only in breeding children, as then "no harm is done to the cause of science or art or politics." But it is a tragedy of the highest order—a loss to the entire world—if a "gifted man wrecks his life on the rocks of the syrens."

Fast-forward, then, to the newlyweds some months later at her family's ancestral estate, Vanderdeckenkill (the Knickerbocker version of Castle Hill), and the captain's warnings are being realized. The marriage appears doomed from the start—after all, the bride's surname is Vanderdecken—the same name as that of the legendary "Flying Dutchman," the captain of the spectral ship condemned to wander forever on the high seas, unable to make port or come to rest. In some versions of the legend, the only way that the Dutchman can break the curse upon him is to find the love of a faithful woman—but, alas, that search proves hopeless.

The deck appears stacked against the poor hero, Stutfield, who is not only battling a legend but also his wife, Ursula, and the bevy of women who rule her family's home. Like Castle Hill, this fictional household is the domain of women. The mother and her three daughters henpeck and dominate the father, an elusive character who is rarely home as he is usually away on business. "Vanderdecken [the father and stand-in for Colonel Alfred Rives] was one of those even tempered warm hearted characters who can rule men but are ruled by women," the author notes. Stutfield is determined not to fall into that trap, though he finds being one man arrayed against so many women "oppressive odds. . . . It required more diplomacy to live in the house with four women than to control the unbought votes of four hundred men." Mealtimes could be particularly painful. During one such dinner he cannot shake the idea that he is "sitting at a Tyrant's table in Ancient Greece. All the tyrants were dressed as women but under their long gowns had knives a foot long waiting for him." Keenly aware that he is being scrutinized, the hero loses control of his face. (In later years, Archie would become obsessed by his belief that he could control and transform his face at will.) His twitching face turns into a nervous smile. Despite himself, he cannot control this silly grin, which provokes Ursula, as he cannot tell her what it is that he is laughing at. He feels endangered and his imagination runs wild: "Whenever one of the ladies lowered her hand for a napkin he pictured the hand clasping the hilt of the twelve inch knife—each & every inch meant for him."

Skirmishing continues in the boudoir with his wife. Amélie's alter ego is alternately seductive and icy. She wants him to leave the estate and go to France—alone—for the winter. The groom is crushed at the notion of being separated from his wife "as though she were his sister or his cousin." He feels this is banishment, pure and simple. Ursula urges her husband to go live with his painter friend Robinson in the Latin Quarter in Paris—she is sure this will make him happy. (The expatriate impressionist painter Theodore Robinson was indeed a friend of Archie's; in fact, he painted in Archie's Parisian apartment—yet another realistic note in this work of "fiction.") Stutfield tells Ursula that happiness is not possible without her. "You've got my heart Darling[,] every atom of it. You own it." But Ursula confesses that she is afraid of her husband—afraid of his anger, and afraid to have to face him without her mother and family surrounding her. She calls him a Jekyll and Hyde, his moods and even his facial features apt to change so completely that it terrifies her. She brings up past indiscretions—the first night they were in New York, when he came home drunk; and the way he sometimes uses shocking language in front of women. He counters later by saying that he just loves her too much; that in fact *she* is the one who controls war or peace; that he has been "innocent of any warlike interactions," and that even an argument between them that ended violently was her fault. It was she who pushed him away so forcefully that he fell over and landed on her doll's house. Stutfield realizes that his every word and deed is being weighed by the women in the household. He is under constant surveillance, eyed suspiciously, his mental condition discussed openly in the household and gauged on a daily basis like the fluctuations of the stock market.

Stutfield becomes convinced of the Greek axiom that "no <u>man</u> can live with his mother in law," but he can see no enticement that will lure Ursula away from her home. "I might as well try to move a monument with a maul stick as budge Ursula from . . . the sacred ties of Vanderdeckenkill," he writes. In an era when married women had practically no legal rights, Stutfield is enraged by the lack of control that he has over his own bride and his inability even to persuade her to join him in Paris. "My authority over you is greater than that of your Father or your Mother," he argues, to no avail. "You recognized that when you married me & promised to obey me." He accuses her of only loving him "with a third rate love at best. . . . [coming] after Vanderdeckenkill & your mother." He is fighting for her affection and her loyalty and feels that this humdrum question of where they should spend the winter requires "as much discipline as much courage as much heroism . . . as was ever displayed in the bloodiest battles since the world began."

Ursula fights back with the same weapons that Amélie employs—her beauty and charm and seductive powers. Even Ursula's clothing seems designed to overpower her husband—"her blue [riding] habit sticking as close to her splendid figure as a wet bathing dress," and made even more revealing by her habit of not wearing a corset. "A straightened waist was a sign of a straightened intellect," according to Ursula. (Amélie shared the same unconventional distaste for corsets, eschewing the hourglass figure then in vogue for flowing gowns and a corset-free sensuality.)

Stutfield comes to realize that Ursula is an incredible tease, using her wiles to get what she wants. When she fails, she grows angry and vindictive, reminding him that *she* is the artist, not he, that *he* is at fault for their difficult marriage, and not she. Her wild mood swings make it hard for him to sort out the truth from her "humbuggery," and he grows disappointed in her lack of sincerity. The novel fragment ends with no resolution, husband and wife still locked in warfare over who holds the "reins of power."

Archie's fictional rendering was a mirror of the struggles he and Amélie were enduring. It seemed that in many ways they were too much alike—each totally self-absorbed and moody and controlling. Yet in another way they were polar opposites—Archie unable to restrain his passionate feelings for Amélie, while Amélie seemed able to turn her emotions on or off at will. She flirted with him and stroked him when she needed something; when she didn't, she retreated to her room—overcome by the vapors, or her work, and surrounded and supported by her female cohorts. This behavior had worked with other suitors, but with Archie it drove him crazy, perhaps literally. Whether Amélie was actually afraid of Archie, or just perplexed at how difficult he was to control, is hard to gauge. Many years later she told a friend that Archie had kept a gun under his pillow and threatened her, but her confidant admitted that he could never quite believe anything Amélie told him, as her life was cloaked in a kind of melodrama in which it was hard to separate fact from fiction.

One thing was certain: Archie's moods—or at least Amélie's perceptions and descriptions of them—could change frighteningly and drastically. Amélie's letters, and the fictional accounts of marriage that both she and Archie wrote separately, point to an elemental struggle over control of the marriage and over sex. The parallels between Archie's fictional view of the marriage and her own version are striking. In *Barbara Dering,* the 1892 sequel to *The Quick or the Dead?,* Amélie composed vivid scenes of the heroine, Barbara, toying with her husband, Jock, and of Jock's towering rages. Early in the book, Jock puts his hand on Barbara's chest, feels her heart race, and sees her skin flush; Barbara immediately seeks to deflate this moment of sexual expectation by speaking of chaste "sisterly" love—to Jock's frustrated fury. In one small but revealing passage in the novel, Amélie hints at a terror of losing her virginity, of being polluted by sex, but in the book it is a *male* who harbors this fear, a husband who despises his bride once her "maidenhood" is gone. Was Amélie writing of Archie's fears? Her own? The ambiguities multiply. In real life, Amélie wrote to Margaret during a calm stretch, pleased that the "old Archie I used to know" was back in residence. Before that, she confided, "he must have been possessed of the devil to behave as he did. . . . His face didn't look like his own. It was frightful. So malignant and half-smiling & half-scowling."

The strain became too much for the newlyweds. After five

months of marriage, they decided to separate, with Archie going to Paris by himself that winter. It seemed that Amélie had won round one, but in a letter to her sister-in-law Margaret she portrayed herself as the victim.

15th of November 1888

Dearest, sweet Margaret . . .

Archie agrees fully with me that for the present it is much best for him to go abroad without me. . . . Oh! Margaret, no one but Christ, Our blessed Saviour, knows the unutterable tortures that I have endured. . . . I cannot help being haunted by some words of that wonderful writer George Meredith when I think of my misery. He says in his book <u>The Egoist</u> Page III—

"What of wives miserably wedded?- What aim in view have these most woeful captives?- Horror shrouds it, and shame reddens through the folds to tell of innermost horror."- . . . You know of course that my life is ruined for me. My chains cut and gall me at every turn. I am to be a prisoner (God knows a willing one!) in my old home. I have promised Archie to sign a paper to the effect that I will not go away from Castle Hill for two years, also to sign one giving him permission to remain abroad two years. . . .

Oh! Margaret, Margaret—give me your strong love, and sympathy, and help. I am in such despair & anguish that I can write only of myself. I do not believe that things will ever come right between me & Archie. . . . Pray for me. Pray for poor

Amélie

The letter to Margaret was in strictest confidence. Amélie told her not to let on to Archie that she knew such intimate details of their married life. The cover story for the separation was that Amélie was staying behind at Castle Hill because she had been offered $25,000 to write a new novel. "It is true, but of course only part of the truth," Amélie confided to Margaret.

Archie wrote his side of the story in a calmly reasoned letter to Margaret two weeks later.

Saturday, Dec 1st/88

Dear Margaret

Thanks so much for your sweet letter. I feel that it is undoubtedly best for Amélie to stop here [at Castle Hill] this winter both on account of the rest it will be to her nerves, which have been on a tremendous strain for over twelve months, & for her writing. I ought to, & want to, see you all so I go abroad. The rest to my nerves will be most refreshing after the strain I have been on since I first set eyes on Amélie & tried to make her acquaintance. In the spring I come back & take her abroad. She is hard at work on her new novel, expects to finish two before spring. People will of course talk at my going away & say 'seperation' & prophesy trouble. What people say is a matter of infinite indifference to both of us. We understand one another, other people can misunderstand us until they tire of it or begin to get sense. There has been a great strain now & then between Amélie & me, or a loud discord, so to speak; it is & always must be the case when two strong natures come together for the first time. We had to strike discords in order to attain harmony. That we have reached. We are convinced of the advantage of our present course. Nobody but ourselves can understand the matter. It is an affair between us & no advice or talk can be of the least use. Time is the test of whether we are right & the world wrong or not. So cheer up. Everything is all right. . . .

Yr loving bro
J.A.C.

About a week later, Archie sailed with his brother Willie on the French ocean liner *Bretagne* for Havre. He spent Christmas in London with his sisters and Willie, all the while thinking of Amélie. After settling Margaret and Alida into English schools, Archie returned to

Castle Hill. According to Amélie, he was a changed man. She wrote to young Margaret in England:

> *O Margaret I can scarcely believe it all. I look at Archie and think that he must be part of a dream not the real Archie, not the man who has given me such unspeakable anguish during the last seven months. He is so gentle, so quiet, so considerate, so tender, so loving—I cannot write half my darling . . . I am so dazed by it all that I cannot quite recollect things in order. . . . We will now surely come Abroad in April. . . . All and more than my old trust in Archie has come back. . . . Your own devoted sister-*
>
> *Amélie*

Archie was beside himself with happiness. He wrote in rapturous tones to his sister Elizabeth:

> *March 4th/89*
>
> *Dearest Bess . . .*
>
> *Everything I ever wished for in my Ideal . . . I get in Amélie. You know that I am not prone to gush or to take an enthusiastic view of things . . . [though this] sounds like a young lady's novel! But all my happiness has been fought for & worked for & is founded on a rock foundation of Faith in God. . . . All I have time to say is that Amélie loves me as I love her & you know how that is. . . . I had not been with Amélie half an hour after my arrival from Europe before she blossomed in love for me like a flower before the sun. I just thawed & convinced her of my tenderness & love at the same moment. . . .*

Now reconciled, the couple went abroad in the spring of 1889 for a belated honeymoon trip. Amélie was ushered into the world that she longed for—the aristocratic precincts that she felt she, as a Rives, deserved. Spring in Paris was followed by the summer season in

London. Amélie was swept up in the romance and beauty of her surroundings. But it was more than a little daunting. The pampered and spoiled Virginian was thrust onto a stage unlike any she had ever experienced. London seemed like a John Singer Sargent portrait come to life. Amélie was greeted by the imperious Margaret ("Daisy") Stuyvesant Rutherfurd White, Archie's cousin and the woman whose portrait helped make Sargent famous. When Daisy chose Sargent to paint her portrait in 1883, he was an up-and-coming artist in Paris, but not yet the darling of the upper class. In her early sittings, Daisy had to climb five flights up a dark stairway to his studio in the Latin Quarter, which was notable both for its filth and its unusual furnishings—a suit of Japanese armor and a collection of butterflies that Sargent had carefully asphyxiated with his cigar smoke stood out amid the general disorder.

Sargent captured perfectly the stately and arrogant "Daisy." His canvas rose over seven feet in height, and Daisy is portrayed in all her glamour from head to toe in a couture gown of bone-white mousseline de soie with a billowing satin overskirt and train. She stands at a slight angle that accentuates her tiny waist. In one hand she holds a fan; in the other a pair of opera glasses. She has an icy, determined stare; this was a woman of ferocious ambition. A few years after the original painting had been made, Daisy insisted that Sargent alter the tilt of her head to give her a more formal and imposing appearance.

This towering portrait of Daisy looked down upon Amélie from the walls of the formal dining room at the Whites' Grosvenor Crescent house in London. In real life, Daisy loomed over the diminutive Amélie as well, being of regal height and carrying herself with rigid posture. It would be important for Amélie to win over Daisy in order to succeed in London. The Whites were at the center of English high society. As first secretary to the American Legation in London, Henry White was the epitome of the polished, upper-crust diplomat. His friend Theodore Roosevelt would later describe him as "the most useful man in the entire diplomatic service." Among other things, he helped negotiate the Treaty of Versailles at the end of World War I.

Daisy understood perfectly the intricacies of the English class system and assumed the privileges of high rank. To say that she treated people differently depending on their status is putting it mildly. A contemporary once said she greeted a duke so differently from the way she greeted a commoner that it was positively "awe-inspiring." Some months before Amélie's arrival in London, the Whites had arranged for Archie's sister Elizabeth to be presented at court to Queen Victoria, a rare honor for an American (and one that caused some consternation when Elizabeth forgot to curtsey at the appropriate moment). The Whites enjoyed theater evenings in the Royal Box, and they surrounded themselves with titled aristocrats, political chieftains, and literary lions. Daisy counted Edith Wharton and Henry James among her dear friends. In 1888, Henry James wrote of her:

> *The* happy American here, beyond all others, is Mrs. Henry White, wife of the First Secretary of the American Legation—who is very handsome, young, rich, splendid, admired and successful, to a degree which leaves all competitors behind. A lady said to me the other day (a certain queer Lady Lothian), "She is very high up, isn't she. . . . I mean tremendously well-read; all the new books and that sort of thing.

James had to admit that Daisy "has never read a book in her life; but she is 'high up' all the same."

Eight years older than her cousin Archie, Daisy acted like a bossy elder sister. She had been named by Archie's father to serve as one of the guardians for the Chanler children in the event of his death. When she first took up that duty, Archie was one of her charges; but since reaching his twenty-first birthday, he shared jointly in the duties. Daisy was not above lecturing Archie for what she perceived as lapses in his role as guardian, such as not apprising her of his younger brother Robert's movements. She was also eager to pass judgment on Archie's choice of wife.

The Quick or the Dead? had been published in London the previous fall, and had received much the same reaction in England as it had in America. "Wild and rank as the vegetation she so charmingly depicts," wrote one critic; another complained of the "monstrous deal of talk over the new American novel." Thus spake the critics, but the top shelf of the British literary establishment begged to differ; the leading writers in England fell over themselves to embrace Amélie. Oscar Wilde sent her a copy of his book *The Happy Prince and Other Fairy Tales* with the inscription: "For Amélie Rives, from her sincere admirer, Oscar Wilde. London—A rose-red July. '89." He also enclosed a magazine piece that he had published, one that, in his words, the general public would never comprehend, since it required the "artistic temperaments" that he shared with Amélie. Thomas Hardy sought out the young author to gush over her short novel, *Virginia of Virginia,* which had appeared on London's newsstands not long before her visit. Years later, Amélie recalled that Henry James had pleaded with her to make her home in England, where her work would be better appreciated. " 'It would mean a different future for you,' he said in his earnest, slightly stuttering way." (In retrospect she agreed that it would have.) Amélie's favored status among the British literati was helped, no doubt, by her magnetic appeal and sensuality. George Meredith, a cranky prima donna thirty-five years older than Amélie, was completely charmed by the beautiful author during one of her subsequent visits. Guests together at Lady Battersea's country estate in Norfolk, Meredith and Amélie got along famously. He was mesmerized by Amélie's deep-set eyes, which reminded him of Swinburne's as a young man. He called her affectionately "the poet's sister." He found the whiff of Amélie's Southern plantation life fascinating—down to her black mammy, brought from Castle Hill by Amélie to serve as her lady's maid. Meredith had a private tea with the servant, and Amélie returned to find him patting her maid's hand, asking if she didn't have "a sister or a niece who is like you," whom he might hire for his own estate. "I'll pay her passage and give her good wages and make her happy—I'll promise you that!"

Invitations piled up for the heralded Amélie—and Archie, who followed along. Ettie and Willy Grenfell, later Lord and Lady Desborough, welcomed the striking young couple to their manor house in Buckinghamshire for Ascot Week in June of 1889. Ettie was a young bride herself—in her early twenties, with a toddler—and already a famous hostess. Taplow Court, the Grenfells' enormous, fortress-like brick villa overlooking the Thames, became a kind of salon. Here the elite members of the "Souls" often gathered—that famous circle of high-born friends noted for their wit and intellectual curiosity and charm. Among them were the political titans A. J. Balfour, future prime minister, and George Curzon, the future viceroy of India, who eventually earned the title of marquess. Lords and ladies, dukes and duchesses, earls and countesses filled the ranks. They moved easily in royal circles. The only Americans included in this hushed preserve were Archie's cousin Daisy and her husband Henry ("Harry") White, for along with money and impeccable social credentials (for Americans anyway), they could boast Daisy's impeccable taste. The Souls prided themselves on their avant-garde preferences in art—John Singer Sargent became a favorite (thanks in part to Daisy) as did Burne-Jones and Whistler. And they shared a passion for literature and ideas. Oscar Wilde, Henry James, and Edith Wharton were "occasional Souls"—admired deeply for their work and on the fringes of the group, but not quite accepted as insiders.

The Souls loved word games and clever repartee, and invented their own inside language using code words and nicknames inscrutable to outsiders. They preferred cerebral gamesmanship over fox hunting and they looked down on baccarat and bridge and gambling. (Ettie Grenfell made an exception for the races at Ascot, which she adored.) The group was said to spend a great deal of time talking about one another's souls, which they considered a cut above the ordinary. Thus the name, the "Souls"—though the Countess of Warwick later wrote that the members were perhaps "more pagan than soulful." The women Souls were almost uniformly young and beautiful and clever and flirtatious, and love affairs between members—married though they were—were not uncommon. Outsiders looked upon the group as hopelessly snobbish. A British newspaper, *The World,* referred to them as a "most aristocratic cult . . . [in which] a limited acquaintance with Greek philosophy is a sine qua non." Another journalist noted sarcastically that the members of the Souls suffered from "the insidious dry rot of mutual admiration." Despite the critics, the group shared an intimacy and a youthful playfulness and a love of conversation that was exhilarating.

Amélie was folded into the group. By the end of the week at Taplow Court—where members of the Souls had gathered for the festivities—Amélie was embraced as one of their own, and eventually presented with the small red letter case that was the badge of entrance. She was now a "Soul."

At Taplow Court, Amélie witnessed the pageant of English country life—the three-thousand-acre estate staffed with some twenty servants; the four-story-high arcaded entrance hall in ecclesiastical Romanesque style, with stag heads on the walls and elephants' feet as vases; the ancient Anglo-Saxon burial mound adjacent to the house that had just been unearthed six years earlier and was still a great topic of conversation.

The host, Willy Grenfell, was like a Greek god. He was six feet five inches tall, handsome, a consummate athlete at the height of his powers. A fellow Soul, Margot Tennant (later Countess of Oxford and Asquith), described him as "a British gladiator capable of challenging the world in boating and boxing." He won the punting championship on the Thames for three years in a row, beginning in 1888. He swam across the base of Niagara Falls, the second time in the midst of a snowstorm, just to prove that it could be done. He climbed the Matterhorn three times, hunted big game from Africa to the Rockies, and eventually became an Olympic fencing champion. This was all very un-Soul-like, the group priding itself on intellectual virtuosity rather than athletic prowess. But Ettie was the prime hostess —the glue that held the Souls together—so that Willy was accepted as part of the package. Amélie grew very fond of him. But compared to the other members of the group, who prized witty bon mots above all else, Willy was rather quiet. When exhausted by the nonstop conversation, perhaps he retired to his smoking room and nipped at the bottle he kept behind the trapdoor near the hearth.

In the evenings, Ettie initiated Archie and Amélie into the "Games" that the Souls adored. Ettie was a master at charades. "I shall always remember with almost more pleasure than anything else you writhing and twisting on the parquet floor in red velvet, your conception of the serpent's tail being one of the greatest triumphs of modern art," wrote one of her admirers. And she invented a clever game in which one had to guess what a particular person might have left behind after a country weekend—an exercise that could lead to all kinds of fiendish innuendos.

George Curzon was among the guests at Taplow, soaking in Amélie's beauty and wit. The thirty-year-old Curzon was a rising star, a member of Parliament, and heir to Kedleston Hall, his family's monumental Palladian mansion in Derbyshire. He was perhaps the most sought-after bachelor in England. Brilliant and witty, he had "an expression of enamelled self-assurance," according to the Countess of Oxford and Asquith. Women adored him—and in turn, he adored them. He found Amélie irresistible. He invited her to a dinner party he was hosting for the Souls several weeks later at the Bachelors' Club in London. On the chair of each Soul, Curzon placed a printed copy of an ode he had composed for the occasion. Each Soul was honored with a few lines; for Amélie, Curzon wrote:

VIRGINIA'S marvellous daughter
Having conquered the States,
She's been blown by the Fates
To conquer us over the water.

Curzon's dinner was a farewell; he was setting off on an expedition to Persia. Every member of the Souls was "honourably and categorically mentioned" in Curzon's lighthearted ode, including Amélie; but there was no mention of Archie. Archie was surely at the dinner, so he could not help but feel superfluous. In fact, he had been overlooked and pushed to the background during their entire English sojourn. His own sense of grandeur and his notion that he was an important mover and shaker, a man who would make his mark on society, had been seriously bruised. As an Astor, he felt *he* should be the one garnering the attention. It was *he* who had introduced Amélie to this world; yet *he* was the one being ignored.

In London, Amélie attained the peak of celebrity. She was lionized by some of the greatest writers of the day—Wilde, Meredith, James—who greeted her as the rising literary star of the young generation. She traipsed like a queen through the most rarefied salons of the imperial city, while on her arm she had a husband, devoted to her, who was among the richest men in the United States. Ideas for new work floated in her imagination. Riding this surging wave of astonishing success, what did Amélie do? She began to take drugs.

Perhaps it was the headaches. Despite the adulation that poured down on her, pain relentlessly pounded in her head, and she frantically sought medical advice. A doctor, perhaps somewhere in England or France, prescribed a miracle drug that eased Amélie's mental and physical torment. She learned about morphine.

By the end of the London social season, Archie and Amélie began to quarrel; they were in need of diversion and relief. A pattern emerged: when things got testy, they packed up and moved on. It was the Chanler way. Archie thought that the thermal waters at Bad Kissingen—a resort in Bavaria—might soothe his jealous, tortured soul and Amelie's frightful headaches. It did little good, and the doctor there warned Amélie that Archie was "not always responsible for what he says & does." The pair studied German together, and attended Wagner's opera at Bayreuth. Wagner was a particular favorite among aesthetes at that time; but Archie had his doubts. He thought that Wagner's music rarely rose "above poetic prose," and his description of it sounded vaguely like his own marriage: Wagner's "three notes of melody turning at once to harmony & sometimes discord . . . was like a man starting to run in long graceful bounds &

suddenly squatting down. . . . He is always reaching toward something without reaching it."

The couple traveled across the Continent, tended to by their respective loyal retainers—Amélie by her mammy and ex-slave from Castle Hill, Martha Jane; Archie by his faithful valet, Charles Hartnett. They made their way to Algiers. Archie had determined that Amélie should focus on her painting rather than her writing, and he arranged for an art instructor to join them there. Amélie found the teacher an annoying egotist; nonetheless she continued to sketch. From their quarters at the Hôtel d'Orient, Amélie wrote to Margaret on December 1, 1889, about the local scene with its vivid Mediterranean colors, its graceful cactus and aloe plants, its distinctive Moorish architecture, and its exotic inhabitants. All of it was inspiring:

> The fluttering draperies of the Arabs and the bare brown legs of scampering children. Crowds of meek little furry donkeys go pattering through the streets loaded with dates, & straw and very often with great solemn Arabs draped and cowled elaborately & beating a tattoo on their sturdy beasts' sides to encourage them to trot! . . . I must stop now darling. The garçon is waiting to set the dinner-table . . . on which I am writing. Good-night dearest sweet Margaret.

But the scene grew less enchanting. Amélie got ill, and without family or friends the holiday season felt bleak. "I never never NEVER spent such a Christmas in my whole life," Amélie wrote in despair. "The only cheerful thing in it was the really lovely service in the little English church."

Archie was like a caged animal and his letters from that period pulse with anger. He lashed out at everyone. If he could not control Amélie, then he would order his siblings about. He wrote to Margaret and lectured her about her dreadful singing voice, telling her not to waste her time and money on lessons—a mistake that he had made some years earlier. ("Your voice has so little timbre—in fact hardly any—& such a decided absence of charm that your attempting to sing would be hopeless.") Archie began plotting a four-to-six-month safari to Africa, and sought out the company and the advice of his twenty-two-year-old brother, Willie, who had just returned from a lengthy hunting expedition there. Willie declined the invitation, as he was spent both physically and financially, but he offered some concrete bits of advice. Archie took this as the height of cheekiness, and went on a twenty-four-page tirade against his brother's "cold & patronizing tone." Archie's letter is an astonishing exhibition of his own sense of importance. Using the third person, he referred to himself as "an elder brother who has seen—a low estimate—four times as much of men & the world, & has travelled over miles where his younger brother has travelled yards." He called Willie "a virgin green regarding serious 'roughing it' " compared to his own experiences. Willie, of course, had just spent nine months in a remote region of Africa where no American had ever hunted. Steaming mad, Willie wrote back to Archie, disputing his assertions point by point, and saying sarcastically that he was now following his older brother's advice—this letter not being "flippant" but deadly earnest. Archie overlooked the sarcasm and took it as a sign that his brother was bending to his authority. Archie's need to be in charge—his need for others to be subservient to him—is evident in his letter back to Willie:

> *I was delighted with your letter, & with the tone of it. You're a dear Bunksie [Willie's nickname] & I love you more than ever—if that is possible—from the way in which you took what I had to say. . . . I'm more proud of you than ever, it's a comfort to have a brother like you. I feel sure that I shall never have to criticize you for being cold or off hand again. I feel most deeply, & appreciate it as the highest compliment, the way in which you all, boys & girls, listen whenever I have any suggestions to make. It's the greatest incentive to do my best to deserve your respect & confidence.*
>
> *Your loving brother*
> *John Armstrong Chanler*

The sun in Algiers did little to help their marriage, so in the new year the couple packed up again, this time for Paris. To Archie's delight, Amélie agreed to focus primarily on painting, where he believed her true talent lay. Or perhaps he was just sick of the endless controversy that swirled around her literary work, and jealous of the success she had already achieved in that field. Up by lamplight, Amélie set off each morning to study in the Montparnasse atelier of Charles ("Shorty") Lasar, a well-known expatriate artist who specialized in teaching young American women, most of them "half-financed and half-starved." Lasar paid particular attention to his rich and beautiful new student. Under his tutelage, she drew in the morning and painted in the afternoon. She would later recall it as a congenial time with fellow students: "At noon there was a recess for luncheon. We used to go to a little crémerie for milk and baked apples, or when we wanted a more substantial meal, to the nearby Café des Cochers." Amélie marveled at the world of the bohemian artist, and reported that Shorty's wife spoke freely of the "nuptial couch," telling frank stories of their marital relations. Amélie, who specialized in just that sort of thing in her fiction, expressed shock in a letter to her sister-in-law Elizabeth: "What a strange Country is Bohemia & how weird the inhabitants thereof!"

Indeed, Bohemia was not only a strange but a tragic country. A fellow student fell madly in love with Amélie, became obsessed with her, and finally committed suicide. The *New York Times* and other American newspapers reported the story in March 1890. According to one account, Amélie had "jilted" the artist; another journalist suggested that it was her stories and poems that had driven the lovesick young man to his death: "She probably now has a better idea of the effect of her writings." Withdrawing behind the veil of ill health, Amélie retreated to the country at the advice of her doctor and thereby gave herself a convenient excuse to leave Paris at the moment rumors were circulating about her. As a further prop, Amélie summoned from Virginia her old friend Julia Magruder.

◆◆◆

As with almost everything about Amélie, her discovery of a romantic country retreat—the ideal studio for a writer—was like something out of a storybook. On a spring day in 1890, Archie, Amélie, and Julia were taking a carriage ride through Fontainebleau, site of a royal palace southeast of Paris, surrounded by more than forty thousand acres of forest. This was the place where French kings hunted stags and stashed their mistresses. Napoleon loved the palace at Fontainebleau; he abdicated there in 1814, bidding farewell to his heartbroken followers before departing for his exile on the island of Elba. While riding through this enchanted forest, rich with romantic and tragic associations, Amélie and company came upon a large stone gateway with the gilded inscription "Hôtel de Pompadour." Told to stop, the carriage driver announced that this had been the home of Madame de Pompadour, Louis XV's mistress, but that the property was closed to all visitors (an *hôtel* being a private mansion in France). That, of course, piqued their interest all the more. They peered through the gate and saw a verdant oasis—"immense old trees with their trunks thickly matted with vines" and glints of a white mansion in the distance. The group approached the concierge hoping for a private tour, but were shooed away unceremoniously. At the clang of the gate behind them, Amélie sighed, "If a fairy gave me a wish at this moment I should ask that someone would offer me that house for the summer." Within days Archie had fulfilled her fantasy. He rented the villa from mid-May to mid-October. Anything to make his Amélie happy.

Having taken possession, Amélie was in heaven as she prowled about the charming mid-eighteenth-century hermitage, a classical gem of elegant proportions designed by the famous Ange-Jacques Gabriel, the court architect also responsible for Le Petit Trianon. This hideaway had been built within sight of the castle, so that King Louis XV could gaze out his window and look upon his beloved. (And for easy access, an underground passageway supposedly connected the two buildings.) How fitting that Amélie should escape rumors of an ill-fated love affair by going to a love nest from the previous century.

The thirty-room mansion was still filled with pieces of furniture belonging to the famous mistress. The room known as the "little salon" where Madame de Pompadour held court became Amélie's preserve; a portrait of the young author was even hung next to the fireplace, in "la place d'honneur." The original writing table remained, an exquisite piece "inlaid with porcelain, painted with roses and wreaths and loveknots of blue ribbon." Here Amélie wrote her fiction, amid a pile of books and papers.

Directly across from the gateway to the Hôtel de Pompadour lay the palace gardens, which provided romantic rambles—"never were there lovelier walks than under those great old trees with their screening vines; never sweeter trysting-places." Amélie spent her days with her "painting and book scribbling & French." She immersed herself in literature, reading Flaubert, Stendahl, Gautier. "O I do find the days about forty hours too short for all that I want to do." She urged Archie's brother Robert to join them at Fontainebleau: "Give dearest Bobbems my warm love & many hugs & kisses & tell him I must see him here— I have so many things to say to him." He could not resist her invitation. At Fontainebleau she fawned over her brother-in-law and whisked him away to the garden, where she painted an oil portrait of him "en pleine aire," dressed jauntily in straw hat and flannels. Robert, of course, was enchanted by the ethereal Amélie.

The household was enlarged by the arrival of Amélie's mother and then by the arrival of Archie's sister Elizabeth, an aspiring artist who announced that there, in that charmed circle, she was "in a state of dirt, paint and bliss." Despite the presence of her mother, Amélie rather daringly arranged for a nude model to pose for Elizabeth outside in a private nook. Julia Magruder later published an article in *Once a Week* magazine (a publication devoted to "fiction, fact, sensation, wit, humor, news") that described the daily artistic scene at the Hôtel de Pompadour:

> In a secluded corner of the grounds [Elizabeth] posed her model and worked for many hours a day. Here we had a rustic table, with books and writing materials and canvases and

> paints heaped up on it promiscuously; and sometimes one of us would read aloud while the model posed and the picture went forward; or, when the model rested, we had our afternoon tea brought out, and the gentlemen joined us with their cigars and newspapers.

Amélie felt very much at home in that lush landscape; it reminded her of Virginia. She and her entourage took daily jaunts atop liveried carriages through the densely shaded woods, and at night they had "coaching parties by moonlight, when our horn would wake the echoes through the vast still forest, and the French ears that listened were regaled for the first time, probably, with the sound of negro melodies, camp-meeting hymns, and corn-shucking songs." A series of photographs were taken that summer and fall at the Hôtel de Pompadour. The images reveal the rarefied country life Amélie enjoyed, surrounded by a protective circle of family and friends. Archie is never seen in the photos. But Amélie's mother is captured with her feet up and shoes off in her boudoir, with its rich draperies and bed coverings, obviously feeling very much at home amid the elegant surroundings.

Amélie, ever alert for publicity, sent these "private photographs" to *Once a Week* magazine to help illustrate her friend Julia's article—and to keep her own name and romantic reputation alive, lest her American audience had forgotten her. She penned a note to the publisher Peter Collier and offered him the opportunity to publish her latest work—a novel tentatively titled *A Flower of the Pavement* (the name was later changed to *According to Saint John*)—"the story of a young Virginian—a girl who comes to Paris to study the violin, and an account of her adventures & love story, which takes place in the Latin Quarter."

As usual, the people and places in the novel were torn directly from Amélie's own life with minor adjustments—from the faithful black servant brought from Virginia to the heroine's sojourn to Fontainebleau, where she and her beloved, Adrian, visit the royal château and look upon the bed of Napoleon and the table on which he signed his abdication and then proceed to the forest "with its violet gray mist, its moss-greened tree stems, its tender spray of young spring leaves." Here the heroine is sketched by Adrian, a moody, difficult artist who sometimes laughs at her in a strange way. The two of them marry—but, in a neat reversal of the real relationship between Archie and Amélie—it is Adrian who does not really love his new wife. His heart remains loyal to his first wife, and he treats the heroine like a beloved "sister, rather than a wife." It is a sham of a marriage. This must have hit very close to the bone for Archie. To add further insult, there is a cameo appearance made by Thomas Nelson Page, Amélie's early idealized love. In the novel Page turns up as an expatriate painter from Richmond, Virginia, a distant cousin named "Nelson." (In turn, he asks if her name is "Page.") Archie must have further gritted his teeth when Nelson is revealed as a heroic character, who rescues the couple financially and even paints a better portrait of the heroine than Adrian does. But whatever anger Archie might have felt toward Amélie was surely undone by the novel's ending. In a surprise twist, the heroine borrows a syringe from her bohemian neighbor and commits suicide by taking an overdose of morphine. She does this as a noble act of loyalty and love, to prevent her husband from having to live a life of hypocrisy.

The suicide scene is vivid, and captures the potent allure of drug use. Amélie's fictional description of the rush of morphine through the body seems to indicate a firsthand knowledge of its effect: "Next came a delicious languor; it was as though warm, rosy wine were streaming through her veins. Her mouth became slightly dry, and it was an effort for her to moisten her lips or move in the least; but this strange, thrilling heaviness of her body was in some way delicious. Life had never seemed half so full, so charming, so worth living. . . . Oh, how lovely this is—like floating on a magic carpet."

The ending of Amélie's novel offered a shocking peek into a shadowy corner of her own life. A sterling silver syringe—a haunting relic of Gilded Age addiction—remains at Rokeby. The Chanler heirs assume it belonged to Amélie. Similarly, a Rives descendant has a number of items rescued from Castle Hill, among them an ornate opium pipe presumed to be Amélie's. In her later years, Amélie spoke openly of her addiction.

In real life, Amélie's drug-induced reveries took her farther and farther away from Archie and from society in general. She had been introduced to the *haute monde* in Paris by another of Archie's cousins, his old neighbor, Maggie Carey, now married to a prominent Dutch diplomat posted in France. Whispers soon began to circulate about Amélie's erratic behavior. She accepted invitations and then failed to turn up. She refused to host her own entertainments. Eventually, Archie and Amélie began to fall off the invitation lists in Paris. Amélie withdrew more and more frequently into her darkened room, surrounded by her inner circle, a veritable tag team of attendants—Julia Magruder, followed by Lutie Pleasants and Leila Page. "It's such anguish overcoming people's doubts & distrust of me," Amélie wrote. Archie's sister Margaret, for one, had grown disenchanted with her sister-in-law. Years later, Margaret wrote of Archie's "unfortunate marriage with a woman who did not love him in the least." She recalled having been seduced by the "Rives charm" until she became "disillusioned" in Paris:

> I had not the slightest idea that with her opium habit Amélie could not help being no use as a housekeeper or hostess. I saw my brother living in extreme discomfort, adoring his wife and allowing her to reduce his life to complimentary interviews over her. They co-operated with nobody they knew. People passing through Paris would appear and praise the authoress, but all the people they met through the Dutch Legation were ignored.

Among those who wandered through Paris singing her praises was George Curzon, whose appearance occurred at about the same time that the lovesick French artist committed suicide over Amélie. Curzon took a decided interest in her work and did his best to help shape her career. He thought her paintings "showed character and originality" and her writing exhibited great talent, but was marred by an unfortunate tendency to sensuous phrases and a morbid sensibility—a tendency that he believed was entirely unconscious on her part, as she was purity itself. All she needed, in Curzon's estimation, was someone to censor her literary output—a role he took upon himself. He read through the poems she was considering publishing, and advised her to suppress them. Amélie appreciated Curzon's praise, but his criticism did not sit well. She later complained to Elizabeth about Curzon's effect on her poetry in surprisingly brutal terms: "[He] tried to drag out my wings with forceps" and succeeded in "maiming me for a time, but somehow the matrix of my brave pinions was not destroyed and behold me in full feather again & soaring away as obstinately as ever towards the sun!" Ever the romantic, Amélie enclosed with the letter, "the prettiest fairy-green candle moth in the world."

Despite Curzon's meddling, which grated on her, Amélie considered him a great friend for the rest of her life. Amid her personal possessions were an autographed portrait of the young, handsome Curzon and a copy of the odes that he had written for the second Souls dinner that he hosted at the Bachelors' Club in the summer of 1890. Archie and Amélie were at Fontainebleau, unable to attend (Amélie claiming illness), but Curzon paid tribute to the pair nonetheless, Archie even earning a glancing nod this time around, though only because of his brilliant wife:

No more bold ***Chanler*** *comes, upon*
Whose birth some star of blessing shone,
Since by its augury he won
The enchanting little ***Amélie;***
The glades of sumptuous Fontainebleau,
Where zephyrs murmur soft and low,
Or some rare work in embryo
Have torn her from our family.

This prize that the bold Chanler had won was proving onerous. He could not understand or accept that he would always be the forgotten man in the background. The limelight did not seem big enough for the two of them. Their marriage was an emotional rollercoaster, with Archie alternating between passionate love and anger. Calm periods were inevitably followed by unpleasant scenes. The more Archie raised his voice in anger, the more Amélie receded into her bedroom, finding solace in her coterie of protectors and her drugs. A poignant photo taken of Amélie in her Parisian boudoir shows her seated upon—in fact, practically swallowed up by—a white fur throw that covers a chair. She looks absolutely tiny (her feet can barely touch the floor, she is so small) and childlike and lost. There are dark circles around her eyes. This hardly seems the image of a siren; rather it hints of drugs and depression. It is the portrait of a haunted goddess.

SIX

In the Valley of the Shadow of Soul Death

The languid routine in Paris, where Amélie had managed to construct a household centered entirely upon herself, proved exasperating for a man of Archie's active, restless temperament. "You are an ambitious man . . . a public man," he had written two years earlier in his unfinished novel, and Archie had not laid aside his burning ambition to make "a mark on his age & generation." As he cooled his heels in the fall of 1890, Archie began to envision a way to make that mark.

Inspired by the struggling, half-starved expatriate artists in the ateliers of Paris, he came up with the idea of establishing an art prize to support Americans studying abroad. The plan reflected Archie's innate generosity (a trait not generally shared by the famously tightfisted Astors) and the aristocrat's notion that you should get something for your generosity: Archie would become known as a great and beloved patron in the manner of the merchant princes of the Renaissance. There was an added, immediate benefit: setting up the prize required him to decamp from Amélie's enervating circle of females and head back to the clubs of Manhattan and Boston, the manly precincts where large sums of cash were dispensed over brandy and cigars. By the end of 1890 he was back in the United States—without Amélie.

Archie took on the role of art impresario with gusto, and met with success as soon as he returned to the United States. His plan called for American artists to compete for a $900 annual stipend for five »years of study in Europe.* He contacted his Gilded Age acquaintances—George Vanderbilt, among others, politely declined to contribute—and his relatives. Not all of his cousins were in favor of a plan designed to "support some young riffraff in Paris for five years doing nothing." To show his personal commitment to the project, Archie reached into his own pocket and donated $13,500. His cousins Arthur and Harry Carey followed suit. Arthur threw in $2,000, and Harry made an initial donation of $5,000. But Archie also made a bet with his younger cousin Harry during a jolly dinner at the Somerset Club in Boston. Though both men were young and hale, they agreed that whoever died first would leave $25,000 to the fund. Some two years later a blood clot killed poor Harry, and the Paris Prize was $25,000 richer.

The East Coast press heaped praise on Archie's worthy project. Even William Sigourney Otis, Amélie's old Boston paramour, had congratulatory words for Archie: "As for your art scheme, that is a great work and one to be proud of. You have humbled the fault-finders and made a name for yourself." That was exactly Archie's intent—to make a name for himself. But, in his letter, Otis also could not resist the temptation to refer to Amélie's "genius," and to "what a delight it must be" for Archie to witness her success. His wife's celebrity continued to shadow him.

Archie threw himself into the art project partly as an antidote to his crumbling marriage. As much as he loved Amélie and wanted to be with her, it seemed they could not live together in peace. The

---

*Initially called the Paris Prize, Archie's funds continue to the present day to support budding art scholars under the auspices of the American Academy in Rome.

pattern was always the same—an optimistic return to his beloved would soon be followed by recriminations and anger. And scandal. So it went in the spring of 1891 when Archie, buoyed by the initial success of his art prize, returned to Paris to escort his wife back to the United States. But Amélie was too ill to travel. In addition, she was not in a great hurry, as her cousin and soul mate, Lutie Pleasants, was about to undergo a series of operations to correct the harelip from which she had suffered her whole life. This miracle treatment had long been a dream of hers and of Amélie's. So Archie had to wait patiently.

He busied himself with various matters, including the distant affairs at St. Margaret's Home, in the town of Red Hook, near Rokeby. In effect, St. Margaret's was Archie's personal charity. He had inherited it, along with a $50,000 endowment for its upkeep, from his father. It was his duty as eldest son to maintain and oversee the operation of this private family charity for orphaned girls, which had been founded by his Astor great-grandmother. The orphan girls—many of them not really orphans, but young farm girls abandoned by their destitute parents—were practically considered wards of the Chanler family. Supported by the Astor money, the girls were brought to Rokeby once a year, to be looked over at an annual Christmas party. They were educated in the domestic arts—sewing, cooking, cleaning—so that at age sixteen they could go into service as maids for the local gentry. Archie expressed concern for the welfare of his orphaned charges in the spring of 1891. He had heard of a local Red Hook scandal in which a young woman—from a fine family, no less—had been seduced by a rich and prominent citizen within a few feet of the church—in fact, on the rectory steps. The predator continued to strut about town, unscathed, as if he had "an added feather in his cap." Archie was enraged at the "immoral atmosphere of the village" and feared for his young charges. He wanted to hire a new matron at St. Margaret's—a no-nonsense, middle-aged woman with experience. (Amélie's friend Julia Magruder recommended to Archie a Southern woman who took over the post at St. Margaret's; less than a year later, that woman became embroiled in her own sexual scandal.)

Archie, however, did not have to look that far away to find scandal. There was one brewing right under his nose. His nineteen-year-old brother, Robert, had fallen hopelessly in love with Amélie. Like a lovesick puppy he had followed her between Paris and Fontainebleau. For years Robert had been a problem for the Guardians in New York. What were they to do with a teenaged boy who seemed incapable of learning and was apparently headed for nothing but trouble? College appeared out of the question. Throwing up their hands, in 1889 the Guardians had dispatched Robert to Europe for an extended stay. Accompanying him was Mr. Bostwick, the long-suffering family tutor who would continue giving lessons abroad. Teaching Robert at Rokeby had been a futile effort; but the Guardians hoped that the culture of the *ancien régime* would rub off on Robert, that he would at least acquire the aristocratic sheen worthy of an Astor. Because Robert was highly impressionable and unstable—and because the penny-pinching Guardians were ever mindful of saving money—they preferred that the young man steer clear of places like Paris and Fontainebleau. But Robert refused to leave once he was in Amélie's aura. The Guardians were not happy about it, but since Robert was in Paris amid family, his legal overseers let it slide. Little did they realize that Robert's own sister-in-law would turn out to be his greatest temptation.

Amélie and Robert formed an intense connection. She encouraged his art; he, in turn, looked upon her as his muse. She lavished attention upon him—he was her beloved pet—and she drew him into her inner world. Mr. Bostwick did not trust Amélie for a minute. He had formed an immediate dislike of her when she had first appeared at Rokeby with Archie. Mr. Bostwick felt an intense loyalty to the Chanler orphans, and was extraordinarily protective of them. He watched warily—and with disapproval—the growing intimacy between Robert and Amélie. Before long, Amélie was muttering about the tutor to Robert and the others gathered around her court. Robert hung on her every word and opinion, and soon he began spreading rumors that Bostwick had a drinking problem. In disgrace, Bostwick resigned as tutor and companion to his young charge in the summer of 1890. (Robert eventually admitted his treachery; in the fall of 1891 he confessed to his sister Elizabeth that the charges against Bostwick were totally false, but he had been inspired to spread such dreadful lies by his own adolescent rebelliousness—he was sick of being bossed about—and by Amélie's clear distaste for the tutor. "Like a cameo [I] changed colours with the strongest," he wrote with regret.)

Freed from Bostwick's steadying influence, Robert became even more besotted with Amélie—so besotted, in fact, that he suffered a mental breakdown over her in London in June of 1891. The family blamed Amélie. Daisy White, a member of the Guardians, wrote from England about the mess. The first order of business was to keep Robert away from Amélie. "He should not see Amélie[,] not for a year not for longer if possible." And, as far as Daisy was concerned, letters from Amélie should be stopped altogether; but if Robert insisted upon hearing from Amélie, then she must be careful about the substance and tone of her notes to the poor boy. Daisy directed that Amélie's "letters should be short, natural (what other people call natural[,] not what is natural to her) & all her ideas of special influence upon Bob or any excitement of this sort must be absolutely stopped. . . . The less he thinks about her the sooner he will get well." In retrospect, Daisy felt remiss for not having put an end to the "intimacy between Bob & Amélie" earlier. She knew that the relationship was dangerous and unhealthy for Robert. "I thought of it, felt that it was unwise[,] hinted at it to Archie, but did not act upon my fears—& in this I feel myself terribly to blame, for I am the boy's guardian[,] the only older one out here & I should have taken the whole matter in hand & not left it as I did to Archie," she reported to Elizabeth. Daisy—and doubtless other family members—felt that Archie was at least partially to blame; after all, it was *his* wife who had lured the innocent teenaged Robert with her charm and then driven him beyond the breaking point.

Archie was barely back from the United States when this new scandal involving his wife burst upon him. Daisy White wrote, sternly, no doubt, to Archie about his younger brother's pitiful mental condition. The overwrought Robert was exiled for the summer to a farm in Wales, a place as far away as possible from Amélie and from excitement of any kind. (The enforced quiet settled him down, but, being an artist with a discriminating eye, Robert found his host's eclectic furnishings not up to Parisian standards: "O dear me the pictures & the conflomerations of furniture of every age, Egyptian mummies down to New Town chairs," he complained.) Archie turned the whole sordid business over and over in his mind. It is hard to say by whom Archie felt more betrayed—his wife? his brother? his relatives who blamed him? or even himself, for his own inability to control Amélie? Within weeks, however, Archie had rationalized the whole affair. In a letter to his sister Elizabeth, he wrote that Robert had merely a "hallucination" over Amélie owing to the fact that she "was the first person he met who understood & fully sympathized with him." It was neither Amélie nor Robert's fault. His brother just fell victim to "inexorable nature." After all, how could he resist Amélie? No man could. As for Amélie, she "is as brave as a lion & stands cool & collected, the point of rest in the whirlpool."

Kept under wraps in his Welsh safe house, Robert was unable to speak in his own defense or Amélie's. But years later, after he had achieved considerable success as an artist, he said of Amélie: "She was the one who helped me to my freedom." In that summer of 1891, however, both Amélie and Robert's conduct was considered scandalous.

Archie was humiliated. He asked Elizabeth not to tell Winty's wife, and to break the news gently to Willie. As one of the legal Guardians and the eldest in the family, he had been derelict in his duty. He would make it up to his sisters. He intended to return to the United States with Amélie and go directly to Newport, where the couple would spend six weeks at the height of the social season with his three sisters. Archie took charge of the complicated logistics for the trip. In July he sent pages and pages of minute instructions to his sister Elizabeth and brother Willie. He seemed eager to prove that he would be the perfect host, and would consider every conceivable detail—though he was not shy about delegating much of the work to his brother.

Archie's long-winded list of concerns seems ludicrous today, but Gilded Age life was a complex affair. "Our passage to Newport [is] like Hannibal's passage of the Alps," he wrote solemnly. "Two coachmen, two pair of horses & two victorias & a landau" had been hired from a stable on 28th Street in Manhattan, between Fifth and Madison Avenues. Archie asked Willie to go in advance and check on the horses and coachmen to make sure they were both "stylish & safe." He worried whether the gold buttons on the servants' livery would clash with the silver harness. (He deferred to Elizabeth and Willie over whether the buttons should be silver instead.) He asked Willie to hire a third man to ride on the outside of the carriage—a necessity when the girls would be leaving their calling cards and visiting at Newport "cottages." Even Archie's devoted valet, the former farmhand Charles Hartnett, agreed to dress in green and gold livery, breeches, and top boots, to wait on their table in style. Archie had arranged for a butler from Newport to be hired, but worried about whether he was handsome and clean-shaven. Archie asked Willie to make the trek to Newport just to check that the butler had no mustache; if he did have one, then he should get rid of him and go to the Manhattan Club and ask the "tall light haired man behind the desk" to help get a suitably presentable servant.

The litany of instructions went on and on. He ordered his brother Willie to lay in a stock of cigars and cigarettes and wine—including good claret and dry champagne—and liqueurs. Archie was bringing his cook from Paris, a woman who spoke no English—an advantage, he thought, as she could not do the marketing and cheat them. Archie tried to entice Willie to join them at Newport, and give up a scheduled trip to Japan. His younger brother's presence could mean the difference between social success and failure for their unmarried sisters: "You are much more in touch with 'the boys' than I," he wrote to twenty-four-year-old Willie. "You are 'in it' with the Knickerbockerites while I'm rather side tracked from absence. . . .

Knowing the dancing men & dining men will make it easier to give a good time to the girls than I could, although I'll make it my business to go to the club & get in with the boys once more."

Archie anticipated the trip eagerly. This was his chance to make amends with his family, to prove his worth as eldest sibling. All was prepared, including plans for a family ball in Newport. And then, abruptly, Amélie announced that she would not go to the seaside resort. Her uncle from New York, Francis Robert Rives, died in mid-July, and she was wrestling with the decision over whether she should or should not go into a formal period of mourning for him. This was enough to cancel the trip to Newport. Archie's siblings were staggered —and Willie, particularly, was furious. He cabled Archie and implied that the mourning question was just a smoke screen, an easy excuse for them not to follow through on their plans. It did indeed seem like a transparently bogus excuse (despite the pages and pages that Archie wrote defending the decision); after all, Amélie's father and uncle had barely gotten along in life, and they rarely saw each other. In addition, Amélie's parents had never allowed her or her sisters to go into mourning for *any* relative; they did not believe in the custom, so they ignored it. And if further proof were needed, Amélie gave an interview in Paris that July, *before* the death of her uncle, in which she told the journalist that upon returning to the States, she planned to "go directly to Castle Hill, Virginia, where I expect to remain for the next few years." She made no mention of Newport. She clearly had no intention of going to Newport that summer, perhaps because she feared facing the Chanlers. She had good reason to be wary of them. There was that messy business with Robert, and she could sense the growing coolness of the sisters toward her (though Amélie continued to fawn over Elizabeth—the sympathetic sister, the forgiving sister—writing her letter after letter, presenting her side of every controversy, appealing to dear "Queen Bess's" good nature). And there was Amélie's drug addiction, a vice that she had to hide from her in-laws.

Archie tried to soothe his sisters. He promised that they would have a family ball in New York that winter. (They never did.) And he assured Elizabeth that the dresses that had been made for Newport would be fine the following year—the fashion would hold up, he had checked with the Parisian dressmaker on that score. All of this groveling and apologizing was a severe blow to Archie's dignity. Once more he had failed his siblings. Once more Amélie had won.

They returned to New York on the steamship *La Champagne,* but the fizz seemed to have gone out of their relationship forever. Thereafter they lived increasingly apart, leading parallel lives. The arrival of the "famous authoress" caused a stir in the press (though poor Archie was referred to as "Archibald" in the Richmond newspaper, another slight to his self-respect). Amelie's entourage also disembarked—her cousins Lutie Pleasants and Leila Page, and her maid Martha Jane, "the old colored woman . . . who is an ex-slave and the favorite domestic of the brilliant young writer." They all took the night train to Virginia, arrived in Richmond the following morning, and went directly to Lutie Pleasants's home. She had been transformed by the surgeries in Paris—her harelip repaired, her diction improved. Lutie had not told her family about the surgeries—it was all to be a surprise. There was an emotional reunion—Lutie entering with a veil covering her face and then dramatically raising it. Her mother screamed and burst into tears. Archie gave all the credit to Amélie; it was she who had conceived of the plan to bring Lutie to Europe and have her operated on. In typically self-aggrandizing fashion, Amélie hinted to a journalist in Paris that the money to help her friend had come from the sale of her latest novel; but it seems inconceivable that she didn't dip into Archie's ample pockets as well. At the very least, it was the cushion of his fortune that made the whole medical endeavor possible. Archie had long since grown accustomed to footing the bill for her family and friends in Europe—whatever their needs might be.

At Castle Hill, they were greeted by an arch emblazoned with "Welcome Home" in dark green letters, and by "a band of intoxicatedly (with joy) joyous negroes who cheered & threw up their caps on sight of us. It was," Archie wrote to his sister Elizabeth, "a real old time Virginny Welcome." Despite the boisterous homecoming, Archie gave hints that all was not rosy. He wrote that he was suffering terribly from insomnia and taking sleeping draughts. He was sure it would be just a matter of time before he got over it; but he never did. As the years progressed, he turned the clock upside down—up most of the night, brooding and writing, and sleeping a good part of the day.

The press inquired eagerly about Amélie's future. In addition to her writing, she announced loftily that she planned to study German, French, and English literature under the tutelage of her cousin Professor James Page of the University of Virginia. And she would paint. Her teacher in Paris, the artist "Shorty" Lasar, was to follow her to Virginia. She intended to build a large studio at Castle Hill where she would pursue her art.

Amélie's return to the United States in August 1891 coincided with the first installment of her drug-influenced Parisian novel, *According to Saint John,* in the pages of *Cosmopolitan* magazine. The reviews piled up, one more dreadful than the next. "It is fully as hysterical as 'The Quick or the Dead,' and even dismaler in its ending." "The volcanic sensuousness of her former efforts have lost their novelty, and . . . the result is a tiresome though gaudily garlanded insipidity." Her women characters particularly rankled the critics: "The young ladies of Virginia may be as wild and silly as Mrs. Chanler describes her heroines; she ought to know them, as she has lived her life among them; but, if so, they should all be sent to lunatic asylums and kept out of men's ways."

Perhaps the final critic had gotten a peek inside the grounds at Castle Hill, for Amélie's behavior became cause for concern. Besieged by the press, deranged by drugs, and fearful of her husband's temper, she withdrew further and further into her own interior world. At night she prowled the grounds dressed only in a gossamer nightgown. A servant nearly shot her one night, mistaking her for a ghost. She immersed herself in her artwork and, propped up with pillows in her bed, wrote morbid poems:

A Voice from the Night

Dost thou despair my Soul?
Looking through sorrow's glass upon the world
Say'st thou all promises are unfulfilled?
And melancholy sweet:—
Woulds't thou believe in perfect human love? . . .

She would fold that grim verse into a novel she was writing. Her heart was dark indeed.

Lutie Pleasants fended off Archie's sister Elizabeth, who wanted to visit: "Just now things are not at their best at Castle Hill," she wrote at the beginning of 1892. "Amélie [is] so sick and depressed . . . I feel sure that your first sweet impressions of Castle Hill would be much more happier in the spring than now." Elizabeth had hoped to take a trip out West with her sister-in-law, but that, too, had to be canceled owing to Amélie's health. She seemed to be forever down with the "grippe" or some other physical ailment—she was alternately described as delicate, sad, ill, feverish. Her drug use was never mentioned, though it was the dark unspoken truth. Archie, nearly beside himself, traveled frequently on his art business and other projects. He couldn't bear to stay at Castle Hill. By June of 1892 he and Amélie decided to separate for a time—what Archie referred to as a "gruesome, uncanny period of heart-string-tearing separation." Archie now wandered from place to place, unmoored. He was desolate. His near-hysteria was captured in an astonishing letter that turned up amid his papers at Duke University. In all the thousands upon thousands of pages that Archie would write in his life—and, as it turned out, Archie spent most of the rest of his life writing endlessly about himself and his travails—this letter is perhaps the greatest key to his psychology, to his inner torment as well as to his delusions of grandeur. It is also a testament to his undying devotion to Amélie. Alone in a hotel room in Cincinnati, a distant, friendless city to him, Archie picked up pen in June of 1892 and wrote a sixty-page letter to Amélie's dear friend and protector, Julia Magruder. Archie bared his soul and hoped that Julia—the intermediary between the two of them—would share it with his estranged wife. And that Amélie would recognize his suffering and welcome him back.

Fearing that the letter might fall into other hands—and also to cloak himself in a mantle of grandeur—Archie took on pseudonyms for himself and Amélie. Archie became "Ulysses," the classic Greek hero who wandered for years after fighting the Trojan War, Archie equating that warfare with his own struggles in creating the Paris Prize. In the depths of his deepest misery, in his "Valley of the Shadow of Soul death," Archie still believed that he was a great man of history, a classic hero of Greek mythology, no less. A man of power, with deep reservoirs of valor. A kind of mythic superhero whose tale was steeped in tragedy and triumph. Amélie was, of course, Ulysses' devoted wife, "Penelope," who remained faithful to her beloved husband even though the palace was besieged with suitors.

And that indeed was Archie's greatest fear. For he got wind that an English rake—a married man who "has been living for years in the deadly shadow of . . . corruption and marital infidelity . . . [of] the Prince of Wales' set" and thus had no moral qualms—was already sniffing around after his beloved Amélie. Archie identified his rival only as "Mr. F.,"* the brother-in-law of "Lord R.C.," whose wife had made such a fool of him with her amorous affairs that he "carries horns on his head as long as an antediluvian monster's." Amélie had written to Archie and had made the mistake of mentioning casually that "I like Mr. F. very much." That sentence rattled around Archie's head like a poisonous mantra. "I like Mr. F. very much." Archie became unglued, knowing only too well how men became obsessed with Amélie. His own brother had fallen victim to her charms. Archie could only imagine what would happen with the Englishman.

"Penelope is unquestionably capable of creating a grande passion especially in a cultivated, blasé, experienced man of the world

---

*This was probably Moreton Frewen, who married one of the Jerome sisters; Lord Randolph Churchill married another.

like 'F'. His experience . . . of women will help him to appreciate the rarity and purity of Penelope though the shadow of the Upas [in Greek legend, the berries of the Upas, or mulberry tree, turned red when its roots were bathed in the blood of the ill-fated lovers Pyramus and Thisbe] may prevent his comprehending her purity, with its wild streak of freedom, frankness and lawlessness, which, like three Greek nymphs, go hand in hand." Archie was certain that this satyr would pursue his alluring—yet totally innocent and noble—wife. "No man who has known her has failed to fall desperately in love with her. It is this fact also which makes my anxiety about F. all the more poignant & fact-founded. . . . Why, in the name of all that's Diabolically Liable should he prove the first solitary, sole & only exception to this invariable Seemingly Fatal rule of her Omnipotent charm & fascination." There had been other suitors before the Englishman, and Archie knew of them. He admitted as much. But he had been able to keep them at bay. "F." seemed to present an especially dangerous threat, in part because he hid "behind that wretched, battered, tattered old charlatan and mountebank 'Platonic Love.' Pah!" Archie would not be taken in by such posturing, for in his words, "Running away with other men's wives is the usual denouement to Platonically Begun & Successful Friendships in England."

Archie ranted on and on about his rival. His very appearance was offensive to Archie—even his bad comb-over: "He drags those reluctant locks from one ear clear across the Saharan desert to the other ear, and holds them chained there by vaseline. . . . It shows the vanity, the silly vanity, and real helplessness in an emergency of the man." "F.'s" nose—a red "abortive radish" in Archie's phrase—further betrayed his decadence. Archie had seen "F." one night in Delmonico's in New York and was disgusted. There his rival stood, striking a pose in his voluminous yellow opera cloak.

Amélie's single reference to this grotesque Englishman had unleashed a torrent of emotions in Archie's frenzied brain. His sixty-page letter was equal parts fantasy, polemic, and heartrending baring of his soul. As disorderly and feverish as it was in its composition, it was also as controlled as a lawyer's brief. Under the headline "Last

Words," he summed up his fears about the future of their marriage: "Now she's opened . . . the door to suitors . . . unconsciously, but open it is, and the garden of my love is unguarded, and although Penelope won't allow anyone to pluck [her fruit,] the suitor can prowl in and out, at will." And, in a final desperate admission by Archie: "This makes me feel lonely, desolate, unprotected."

This was a bold statement from a man who took pains to hide his emotions, a man who prided himself on being as stoic as Hannibal, the leader so well prepared and self-contained that he had carried his own vial of poison. Archie believed that he, like Hannibal, would control his own destiny. Throughout his life, Archie had been trained to put on a mask of calm in the midst of tragedy. He had lots of practice, as early death had stalked his family. In addition to his parents and his sister Emily, Archie had also lost two brothers before he turned twenty-one: Egerton died of a brain tumor at Rokeby at the age of eight, and Marion succumbed to pneumonia at fourteen while a student at St. Paul's in New Hampshire. All of the deaths had taken their toll on Archie, none more so than that of his mother. At the center of this letter, this *cri de coeur,* was the admission that the loss of his mother had informed—and deformed—his psyche. "My internal life, since the death of my dear Mother has been so lonely, so absolutely soul-starved," he wrote—that is, "until my meeting with Penelope." His mother had been really the only warm, emotional presence in his childhood. She died when he was thirteen, and thereafter Archie had been more or less on his own, moving from school to school, from place to place, from one distant adventure to another, with no emotional ballast. He was looking for love, passion, understanding—and he thought he had found all those things in Amélie.

Amélie felt his neediness and seized upon it (while seizing control of his pocketbook). She professed to feel an almost mystical connection to Archie's mother. Like Archie, Amélie was interested in psychology and the mysteries of spiritualism (in later years, she held séances at Castle Hill). On one occasion she claimed that she could feel the presence of Archie's mother in a room; he could as well. This shared connection to his mother convinced Archie that he and

Amélie were fated to be together—that their love had a cosmic dimension. Even Archie's rather hard-hearted sister Margaret was impressed by Amélie's devotion to their dead mother. "One of the strangest things about Amélie," Margaret wrote to her sister from Castle Hill in 1888, "is her extraordinary feeling for Mamma." Archie talked endlessly to Amélie about his mother; and early on, Amélie kept a picture of her mother-in-law in her room. How much of this was genuine on Amélie's part is hard to decipher, since she would readily take on whatever part was necessary for her to get what she wanted. And what she wanted first and foremost was Archie's money and the life he could provide her.

In his letter, Archie blamed himself for his failure with Amélie. He believed that it was due to his emotional and psychological makeup. With all the tragedy he had endured, Archie had trained himself to mask his innermost feelings at all costs. *Control* became the absolute bedrock of his mental state. He wrote to Magruder that the only way that he could successfully navigate in the world was by becoming "Sphinx-like." Though prone to explosive outbursts of anger, he carefully guarded his tenderest, most vulnerable feelings. He refused to show weakness of any kind. He had carefully honed this defense mechanism since childhood, and found himself locked into that mode. His "Sphinx-faculty," as he called it in the letter, made him hide his own internal suffering from Amélie and prevented him from revealing the "throbs of my really soft, tender heart." He feared that this failure to show his true self had been his downfall. He was desolate and wailed that all he really wanted to do was "put my head into her lap like a little child and say: 'Mother, comfort me.' " And that was not about to happen. Amélie was not exactly the maternal sort, and might not appreciate Archie with his head on her lap. Archie, in exile, brooded.

Amélie was beset by her own demons—and at least one other suitor. In August 1892, George Curzon—charismatic and rich and godlike—invited himself to Castle Hill. En route to the Far East on his "Second Journey Round the World," Curzon managed to land at Amélie's doorstep. He was a hopeless romantic, reckless in his liaisons. And he could not get Amélie out of his mind.

Curzon kept a diary of his travels, and it reveals his passion for Amélie, as well as his immense sense of superiority. En route from England to New York, he and Harry White—the diplomat from London who was married to Archie's cousin Daisy—shared accommodations, a grand "saloon" consisting of two apartments. Curzon despaired over the "aesthetic distress" of being cooped up on board ship with a passenger list full of Germans ("What a people! How coarse! how hideous! how utterly wanting in the least external element of distinction!") and middle-class Americans ("the least attractive species of the human genus"). To add to the indignity, Curzon complained that the boat officials did not have a proper appreciation of who he was—and even misspelled his name on the table list. He swore he would never take a German steamer again.

In such thin company, Curzon spent the bulk of his time with the aristocratic Harry White, and inevitably the discussion must have come around to the rapturous Amélie and her separation from Archie. As soon as Curzon arrived in New York and discovered that the Japan-bound steamer he planned to take from Vancouver had been delayed three days, his very first thought was of Amélie. Indeed, he was seized by lust. He had no thought of spending a few days in the great metropolis of New York (he dismissed the place, anyway, as a "wholly unimpressive" city, filled with sweaty, straw-hatted men interested only in business). Nor did Curzon rush to Washington, D.C., to see his beloved, but straitlaced, Mary Leiter, to whom he would propose seven months later. No, he thought immediately of Amélie. And then he had the great good fortune to cross paths with Archie at the hotel where he was residing in exile. Chance probably played little part in the meeting—Curzon had breakfast and lunch that very day with Archie's cousin, and Daisy White's brother, Rutherford Stuyvesant, who would certainly have known where Archie was. Archie allowed that Amélie was at Castle Hill, and that was all Curzon needed to know. He raced to catch the next train south.

Curzon slipped quietly into Washington that same night, hoping to keep a low profile lest Mary Leiter get wind that he was in town. Within minutes of his arrival at the hotel, however, he was handed a card from a reporter from the *Washington Post*. Curzon pleaded fatigue and refused to be interviewed. The next morning—a sleepy Sunday morning in Washington—he took in the sights before boarding the train to Virginia. As with New York, he was not terribly impressed: "Magnificent public buildings emerge from surroundings that are altogether tenth rate; . . . elegance and outlay jostle up against the economy of wooden shanties and the repulsion of dust heaps." Curzon managed to charm the sergeant-at-arms of the Senate into giving him a guided tour of the Capitol, so that he was able to stride into the congressional chambers and compare them to the House of Commons, where he had recently served as a member of Parliament.

At some point Curzon sent Amélie a telegram announcing his romantic detour to her Virginia home. After a three-hour train trip he reached Cobham, and for the first time since his arrival in America, he waxed poetic about his surroundings. It was, he said, exactly the way Amélie had portrayed it in her books—the landscape was "wild unkempt, sparsely & irregularly cultivated . . . everything up & down & without system or order. The soil praeternaturally and sanguineously red." Amélie, with her sensual and unconventional nature, represented the same kind of freedom from restraint. Curzon loved it. He found himself the only male (save the fiancé of Amelie's sister Gertrude) amid a sea of women. He spent "40 hours of happiness" at Castle Hill, luxuriating "in the liberty of its country life existence"—and in the presence of Amélie. He was enchanted by the seductress as they wandered through the grounds of the estate. "Upon me Amy shone with the undivided insistence of her starlike eyes!" he gushed in his diary. "Oh God, the nights on the still lawn under the soft sky with my sweetheart!"

On the day that Curzon arrived at Castle Hill, Amélie drew her astoundingly voluptuous self-portrait. She carefully signed and dated the drawing—August 21, 1892. It was a Sunday. Was Amélie thinking of Curzon as she portrayed herself so provocatively? Or of Archie and the shambles of their marriage? Or of herself and her great alluring beauty? In order to execute the level of detail in the drawing, she probably had to study her nude body carefully in a mirror, like Narcissus admiring himself in the pool of water. One can imagine her alone in her studio, slowly taking off her clothes, loosening her hair, and luxuriating in the humid Virginia air. Perhaps she was in a druggy haze, though it seems hard to believe that she could execute such a drawing in an altered state. In an era when women were censured—Amélie included—for openly expressing the notion of female sexuality, this signed and dated self-portrait is astonishing. In fact, Amélie had the portrait copied by a photographer, something that she did with only a handful of her works, images that she sent to others. Perhaps she sent one of the photographic copies to Curzon as a memento of his visit. Years later, several photos of the original charcoal drawing were discovered in one of the outbuildings at Castle Hill. By that time the house had been lost to the family—the contents of Castle Hill sold at auction, scattered to the four winds. Local dowagers still turn up treasures from the estate in dusty attics. Perhaps one day the original drawing will surface—the famous siren in her Dionysian display. Yet for all of its voluptuousness, the image is also dark and forbidding. And tragic. One can imagine that poor Archie—separated from his beloved wife—would have been beside himself if he had seen this drawing. His own sexless marriage to Amélie stood in sharp contrast to her sensual self-portrait.

Archie learned firsthand about Curzon's whirlwind visit. The Englishman returned to New York before leaving for Canada, and had the audacity to lunch with Archie at his club on Gramercy Park, the jauntily named Players Club. Curzon found the club "tastefully & artistically furnished," but had no comment on poor cuckolded Archie.

Archie and Amélie's marriage limped along for three more years, but it was essentially over by the time Amélie drew herself. She was in a terrible bind. Officially breaking off her marriage was a complicated affair; after all, the fate of Castle Hill and the entire Rives family depended upon Archie and his bank account. For the next several years, Archie continued to send members of Amélie's family to Europe—Landon, for instance, who went to France to study art along with several other relatives. Jobs were also handed out freely. (One of Amélie's cousins was hired to collect rents in New York, and proved so incompetent that Archie's law partner complained bitterly.)

Thanks to Archie, prosperity had returned to Castle Hill and there was no more need to count pennies and lop off servants. The place gleamed as it had not since antebellum days. Even the snobbish Curzon, whose aristocratic tastes had been so offended by the reality of New York and Washington, was grateful to find Castle Hill an oasis of upper-class civilization. In a subsequent thank-you note to Amélie's mother, he enumerated the joys of her Virginia estate: "I think constantly of that charming family circle with the rows of good looking . . . young ladies, of the life of peaceful serenity in those most beautiful surroundings, of the mingled art, business & leisure of the household, of the grinning negro background. I should like to transport the entire mise-en-scène to England."

The pressure on Amélie was intense. If she ended her marriage to Archie, this existence could evaporate. The family's exile to Mobile during her childhood remained a bitter memory for Amélie. Without Archie's fortune, would the Rives family be able to maintain Castle Hill and the fantasy world in which Amélie ruled supreme? Not likely. Under emotional and physical duress from drugs and illness—and grappling with her impossible (but necessary) marriage—Amélie sought refuge in her art and in her fiction. With her self-portrait she bared herself literally; she did more or less the same with her fiction.

By the end of 1892 Amélie produced *Barbara Dering,* the sequel to her bestselling *The Quick or the Dead?*. The heroine, Barbara, who dumped "Jock" at the end of the previous novel, has finally agreed to marry him. The new book concerns their tumultuous marriage, which alternates between passionate love, and anger and recriminations. "Jock! *kiss* me!" scenes are followed by pitched battles. Jock to Barbara: "There's something monstrous about you! You're not like a woman. You are like some curious mythological creature." Barbara: "Men and women do not understand each other." She and Jock seem unable to live together in peace. Barbara bridles at her husband's attempt to control her: "I am certainly not going to run at your bidding like a good little girl." The heroine is an iconoclast who shocks conventional society. She is "too vivid, too daring, too brightly-colored," and she even smokes cigarettes! (Amélie was guilty of the same infractions.) Jock, infuriated at his wife, leaves for long stretches on business. Barbara remains behind at their Virginia estate. The only difference between Archie and Amélie's real-life marriage and the fictional one portrayed was the ending. In *Barbara Dering,* Jock returns after a long sojourn out West and to Japan, and announces that he is a changed man, and that he is going to devote his life to philanthropy. He plans to build "club-houses . . . [for] factory-girls . . . where they can find rest and recreation." (In fact, Archie would try to realize such a dream a few years later.) But the novel ends on an upbeat note, the couple discovering that "hope . . . has outlived despair." Not so with Archie and Amélie.

To underscore the bitterness and disillusionment that Amélie felt about her marriage, she wrote an essay that appeared in the September 1892 issue of *The North American Review.* Titled "Innocence Versus Ignorance," the essay makes a plea against the common practice of keeping young girls ignorant of intellectual and "moral matters"—such as the realities of men and marriage. She quotes from Browning that "ignorance is not innocence, but sin," and claims that a lack of knowledge of the world and of human relations (and of sex) can lead to both mental and physical harm. Rather than weakening marriage, the education of young girls would help solidify it and would "produce the comprehending companionship without which marriage is only a social compromise."

◆◆◆

Amélie endured her own "social compromise" with difficulty. The reality of her marriage—and her intense but tempestuous relationship with Archie—intruded upon her grandiose and romanticized vision of herself. Whenever fantasy and reality collided, Amélie sank into a profound depression. Her escape into morphine did not help. A January 24, 1893, letter to her sister-in-law Elizabeth reveals Amélie's deepening distress:

> *My Elizabeth, my treasure, the wings-of-my soul . . . At last I have laid down my armour dear—I am too sore wounded to fight more, & as I lie on this hard battle field waiting for the hoofs to crush out what life there is left to me . . . Oh! Christ knew how hard it was to say 'It is finished'—and I must say it. . . . It is over for me my darling— I have suffered too long. As I said once— Sorrow like poison is beneficial in small doses, it is a soul tonic— As for me I have sorrowed too long. And then my body has suffered so. If I were physically strong I could bear it—but not now. . . . I feel your blessed mother near me— I can almost see her, almost hear her. . . . I see why Archie must be triumphant, why I must lie down in meekness. He will help the world practically, materially, wonderfully— While I could only write —& paint and love— And how many have done all these things more marvelously & perfectly than I.*

Amélie was famous for her histrionic suffering, and her zeal for self-dramatization had long since become tiresome; but this time the suffering was real. Alarmed, Elizabeth went to Castle Hill and found the estate gripped in a death watch. Visitors and cousins swarmed in the house, while Amélie lay sequestered in her darkened room, attendants ministering to her. When Elizabeth was at last allowed in to see the patient, she found the twenty-nine-year-old siren "a shadow of her former self. Her hands have great hollows along their backs & her face is long and dragged."

Archie was heartbroken over his wife's pathetic condition, despite being shut out by her. Amélie remained the great love of his life. Concerned over her prolonged misery, he enlisted the help of Silas Weir Mitchell, the most famous neurologist of the day both in the United States and abroad. Archie was certain that the doctor would get to the bottom of Amélie's problem. Women were Dr. Mitchell's specialty—and women in that era were practically considered a different species from men, and thus had to be handled carefully. An encyclopedia from the 1890s put it succinctly:

> Woman is altogether, physically and mentally and in every respect, more delicately built than man, more sensitive to pain, more sensitive to public opinion, more dependent; less active, aggressive, originative; more passive, conciliatory, conservative.

In that gilded era, there was almost an epidemic of unexplained illnesses among women from the upper echelon of society—some with a gynecological or other physiological basis; some with a psychological or emotional foundation. Various names were given to the syndrome in which women failed to thrive and would take to their beds—"neuralgia of the brain" was one of the diagnoses pinned on Amélie over the years—but basically the doctors just lumped all these women together and considered them hysterical. Treating this syndrome was Silas Weir Mitchell's specialty.

Mitchell worked in Philadelphia, where he had progressed from treating hysterical soldiers during the Civil War to treating hysterical women—in his words, "nervous women, who as a rule are thin, and lack blood." In the late nineteenth century he developed his famous "rest cure" for such women, a mode of treatment best described in the title of his book, *Fat and Blood: And How to Make Them.* Women were separated from their families and all outside stimulation, put in bed for six weeks to two months (or more) and allowed to do nothing. "I do not permit the patient to sit up or sew or write or read," Mitchell wrote. "The only action allowed is that needed to clean the teeth. In some instances I have not permitted the patient to turn over without aid, and this I have done because sometimes I think no motion desirable, and because sometimes the moral influence of absolute repose is of use. In such cases I arrange to have the bowels and water passed while lying down, and the patient is lifted on to a lounge at bedtime and sponged, and then lifted back into the newly-made bed." Massage and electrical stimulation were used to prevent muscles from atrophying completely. The nearly immobile patients were fed by a nurse with a high-fat diet that consisted at first of only milk, and then eventually large meals with generous portions of meat. A soup made from raw beef was served with other high-fat foods. "I like to give butter largely," the doctor wrote. To whet the appetite, Mitchell sometimes ordered an aperitif of two or three glasses of dry champagne. The world-famous doctor boasted of the success of his regime:

> Miss L . . . [aged] 29, height five feet eight inches, weight one hundred and eighteen pounds, in four months became perfectly well, and rose in weight to one hundred and sixty-nine pounds. Two months were spent in bed.

Mitchell believed that a "hysterical girl is . . . a vampire who sucks the blood of the healthy people around her," so, if necessary, even more extreme methods might be needed. On at least one occasion he used a kind of shock therapy. He ordered all the attendants caring for a bedridden woman—a woman who believed she was dying—to leave the room. When Mitchell emerged from the room, he was asked whether there was any hope for her. "Yes, she will be coming out in a few minutes," he predicted. "I have set her sheets on fire."

According to Mitchell, the success of his treatment depended on a "childlike acquiescence" by the patient. The writer Charlotte Perkins Gilman underwent Mitchell's rest cure, was declared healthy, and was sent home with the command "never to touch pen, brush, or pencil again" as long as she lived. Gilman went nearly insane and wrote about it in her famous short story "The Yellow Wallpaper." (The writer later sent a copy to Mitchell, but he never acknowledged it.) Gilman believed that it was only her return to writing—against the express orders of Dr. Mitchell—that saved her from "utter mental ruin."

Despite the extreme nature of Mitchell's treatment, it became all the rage. Socialites flocked to Mitchell, and undergoing his "rest cure" turned into a kind of status symbol. It was like going to a famous spa. Mitchell became one of the central figures in Gilded Age life. Married to a rich heiress from Philadelphia, he moved in rarefied circles. He was a favorite among the old established patricians in Newport, and a member of the group founded by Archie's great-aunt Julia Ward Howe—the literary salon dubbed the Town and Country Club. (Like many of the old guard, Mitchell hated the invasion of the nouveau riche into Newport, and eventually moved on to Bar Harbor in Maine.)

Mitchell adored literature—discussing it and writing it. He became a poet and bestselling novelist. His own work has faded to a deserved obscurity, but he was not shy about ladling out literary criticism. As one scholar notes, there was "no top or bottom to his arrogance." Edith Wharton, the novelist who brilliantly captured the nuances of Gilded Age life, suffered from depression and underwent the famous rest cure in Philadelphia. Mitchell was free with advice—both medical and literary—to Wharton. He had the audacity to suggest adding different kinds of characters to *The House of Mirth;* Wharton wrote back diplomatically that the suggestion to "crowd my canvas a little more" was an interesting one, but "I am not sure that truth would have been served." She also took note of his advice not to begin writing again too soon. In another letter to Mitchell, she boasted that she had "added about 30 lbs to my bare bones!" The doctor of fat and blood must have been delighted.

Amélie was discreetly committed to Mitchell's Philadelphia clinic; it was kept a secret from all but the inner circle at Castle Hill and Archie's siblings. Winty was notably lacking in sympathy when writing about his brother's regular visits to Amélie:

> Archie arrives today from the Unknown. He disappears & goes to Phila. every few days. There all trace is lost & suddenly out of Space he bounds.

Amélie was under the direct care of Dr. J. Madison Taylor, Mitchell's top lieutenant. Mitchell was well aware, nonetheless, that the famous young author was at his clinic and paid particular attention to her. "Amélie is with Weir Mitchell in Philadelphia," Winty wrote to his sister Elizabeth on May 14, 1893. "They say he makes her get up at 7 a.m. & scrub the floor. I don't believe it, for they also say that he goes about attesting to her matchless charm. Rats! Doctors are all old women." Even the esteemed neurologist was not immune to Amélie's charms.

Poor Amélie endured the horrors of Mitchell's rest cure, surely without having to scrub the floor. The patient didn't mention how much weight she gained in the process; in fact, she never wrote specifically about her rest cure. (Years later, however, a legal document revealed that she had gone to an unnamed sanatorium in order to break her morphine habit.) Once released from the clinic, she was monitored for many months by Dr. Taylor, who made at least half a dozen house calls to Castle Hill, enjoying the hospitality of the estate while tending to his patient. On one occasion, Archie sent for Dr. Taylor to come to Castle Hill so that he might discuss his own "self-imposed rest cure" with the neurologist. Archie had given up wine and all red meat and wanted to chat up the doctor about his new regimen. Taylor predicted that Archie would probably experiment even further in his diet. Indeed, Archie began experimenting with all facets of his physical and mental health; and his acquaintance with Dr. Taylor would later prove pivotal.

SEVEN

Master of the Universe

After completing her rest cure in Philadelphia, Amélie went to the New Hampshire seashore—without Archie—to recuperate. She spent the entire summer there, before returning to Castle Hill in the fall. As always, Amélie was most loving and seductive toward her husband when he was at a safe distance. "My darling Archie," she began a letter from New Hampshire in late May of 1893. "Just a word to tell you how I love you and how your lovely lovely letter touched me. It is the only word I have been able to endure. . . . You understand so—" Archie had sent a dog to keep his wife and her companion, Julia Magruder, amused. Amélie gushed over his gift: "My dog is the loveliest I have ever seen— I have called him 'Leal' the Scotch for 'faithful, true, loyal.' . . . It is a word I love & use a great deal—" Amélie took the dog sailing with her. On his first voyage out, Leal fell overboard, "but now he loves it, & either stands by me with the wind in his ruff, or lies at my feet." The vision of such a scene—his beautiful wife on the rugged New England coast with a sweet dog at her feet—must have brought pleasure to the still-besotted Archie.

But she also managed to make Archie anxious about her mental and physical health, writing that although she was feeling better, she was still "very weak & [suffered from] lots of rheumatism." And then she invoked the death of the romantic poet Shelley, who believed his writing days were behind him and tragically drowned while yachting just before his thirtieth birthday—precisely Amélie's age. The very idea of the doomed poet lost at sea seemed to appeal to Amélie: "I read about Shelley's lovely boat made expressly for him & envy him— I should so love a white boat just that size. . . . Perhaps I can get one someday," she wrote. Archie obviously wrote back nervously, for several weeks later Amélie reassured him: "The Evelyn is one absolutely safe boat, lots of deck & air-compartments etc. I have her own Skipper with her." She ended the letter in loving fashion:

> *You don't say anything about wanting to see me etc—but I suppose I'm to take it for granted as the audience had to take the wall in the early English play of "Pyramus & Thisbe!"—*
>
> *Good bye & God bless you my dear mannikin—*
>
> *Your devoted wife—*
> *Amy*

She also reminded her "mannikin" not to pay too much attention to some romantic gossip being bandied about—"women (and men too) talk too much," she counseled him. There seemed to be some malicious talk about the exact nature of her relationship with her ever-faithful, doting Lutie Pleasants. Amélie dismissed the gossip, but Archie had yet another reason to fret.

Throughout his marriage, Archie had to endure more than his share of gossip about his wife. He was nearly consumed with jealousy over her—and with envy over her success and renown. He had his own grand ambitions. He did not want to be yet another Gilded Age millionaire who did nothing of value, and whose only aims in life were to entertain himself and impress others. Archie had little interest in "Society" and its suffocating demands. In a letter to his sister Elizabeth in November 1893, he congratulated her on her decision to focus on her own painting rather than her place in the *beau monde.* (Despite her rebellious intention, she would become, ironically, a kind of totem of society. The previous summer she had been painted in London by John Singer Sargent, an arresting portrait that hung for years at Rokeby in the summer and New York in the winter, and is now one of the treasures at the National Museum of American Art in Washington.) Upon returning to the States, Elizabeth had gone to visit Amélie in New Hampshire, and then on to Newport for the season. By late fall she had had her fill of social obligations, and Archie cheered her independence:

Nov 22nd /93

Dearest Elizabeth

Just a word of congratulation on your daring & excellently planned escape from the Society Galleys! You are at last emancipated & at liberty to follow your taste & cultivate your real talent for painting. You were perfectly right to try Society everybody should in order to ascertain how insipid & useless it is as an occupation. But now that you've freed yourself from its chain gang round of duties & time-destroying demands I actually rejoice!!! . . . I feel happy in the conviction that you want Art more than anything Society can hold out.

Archie had similar dreams of finding a place in the art world; thus the creation of his Paris Prize. Archie's scholarship idea was encouraged by the famous sculptor Augustus Saint-Gaudens and by Stanford White, the Gilded Age high priest of architecture. In 1890s New York, White was seemingly everywhere. "He swam on a wave of prestige that lifted him into view like a Titan," wrote critic John Jay Chapman. "Not a day passed without hearing something new about him. His flaming red hair could be seen a mile; and every night at the opera he would come in late, not purposely advertising himself, but intuitively knowing that every millionaire in town would see him, and that the galleries would whisper, and even the supers on the stage would mutter: *There's Stanford White."* White, like Archie, had endless energy and a restless need to find new projects. For Archie, it was a need to find some meaning and direction in his life; for White, it was to pay for his extravagant and reckless bacchanalian lifestyle.

Archie named White and Saint-Gaudens co-trustees of the art fund, and the three men enjoyed the high life of New York clubs, theater, prizefights, and horse shows. Archie, being something of a prude, probably took little part in the raucous stag parties that White threw, though it was said that he attended the infamous "Pie Girl Dinner" in the spring of 1895, during which a sixteen-year-old girl popped out of a huge pie wearing a stuffed blackbird on her head and little else. Archie later claimed he was elsewhere.

Amélie was delighted that Archie had thrown his energies into productive projects (which, conveniently, would keep them apart), and that he had allied himself with Stanford White. "Do take care of Archie," Amélie wrote to White. "He is so devoted to you, and I am anxious about all this excitement for him. He is happier in his friendship for you than I have ever seen him with anyone." White in turn—with his insatiable appetite for beautiful young women—urged Archie to bring Amélie to New York so that he could fête her properly in his infamous tower above Madison Square Garden, which he promised to have blazing with lights in her honor. He accused Archie of being overly protective and of trying to keep Amélie away from him: "You old rascal you—you ought to have been an Eyetalian in the 16th century."

Amélie rarely came to New York with Archie. When she did visit in the spring of 1892, Winty noted that his sister-in-law appeared drawn and anxious. The two brothers and their wives attended a rather risqué dance performance that was deemed "pure" in some quarters but "against the 10 Commandments" in others. Amélie and Daisy huddled in a corner and decreed that "Pan was not really dead after all." After her breakdown and treatment in Philadelphia, Amélie apparently avoided New York altogether. This was Archie's world, where he had established himself as an art patron, and she had little place in it.

In the 1890s Archie popped up on various art-related committees, often in the company of White or Saint-Gaudens. Archie and White went to Congress to lobby against the government's levying taxes on art brought into the country; and Archie and Saint-Gaudens served on the Executive Committee of the Municipal Art Society, which oversaw ornamentation and sculpture for public buildings and parks. All three men were involved in the celebrations planned for the four-hundred-year anniversary of Christopher Columbus's arrival in the New World. A parade took place in New York honoring the occasion, and Archie, White, and Saint-Gaudens helped oversee the decoration and illumination of the buildings along the line of march. The bigger celebration, however, took place in Chicago, where the World's Columbian Exposition opened in 1893. It was a spectacular display of art and architecture and scientific know-how. White helped design one of the major buildings in the fair's gleaming "White City," and Saint-Gaudens contributed sculpture. Joined at the hip as he was with White and Saint-Gaudens, Chanler also became interested in the possibilities surrounding this world's fair.

In raising money for his art scheme, Archie stalked the clubs and boardrooms in New York, and traveled to Boston, Philadelphia, Cleveland, Cincinnati, and other cities to meet with wealthy philanthropists. The talk of art and money led naturally to discussions about myriad investment possibilities. Archie was invariably presented with creative ways of investing his own Astor real estate money. For all the money he raised for his art scholarship (by 1892 he claimed to have attracted $60,000), Archie eventually poured even more of his own money into several promising inventions. One was a self-threading mechanism for sewing machines that Archie believed would revolutionize the industry and become a necessity in every household. The other was a new type of roadway for horse-drawn vehicles, an innovation that Archie designed and patented.

Both of the inventions were exhibited at the Columbian Exposition in Chicago. About one hundred feet of the patented roadway were laid at the entrance to the fair and "won the highest award," according to Archie. The self-threader also won a prize, and four thousand orders for the mechanism were received—an impressive accomplishment, especially in light of the fact that the threader had not yet been perfected for large-scale production. Nor had it been successfully modified to fit onto a Singer sewing machine—the machine of choice in most households, thus a necessity if the threader were to succeed. (At the exposition it had been attached to the lesser-known Wheeler & Wilson machine.) The impact that the threader had made at the Columbian Exposition—despite those drawbacks—was impressive indeed. Archie optimistically announced to his sister Elizabeth that "the future is golden with promise." Even Amélie's father in far-off Panama wrote optimistically about Archie's "brilliant hopes [for] . . . the famous 'self-threader'"—and envisioned more treats for Castle Hill, including a new horse for his daughter Landon. (Indeed, she got one from Archie.)

Archie never lacked imagination, and his dreams soared. Not content just to finance the threading invention, Archie envisioned an entire textile empire. He would build a New England–style mill town in the depressed South, where labor was cheap and real estate plentiful. While Amélie recuperated in New Hampshire in the summer of 1893, Archie reconnoitered a possible mill site in North Carolina—a wilderness along a stretch of rapids in the Roanoke River, where the water could be harnessed for electrical power. The South, desperate for investment, was eagerly advertising itself to Northern industrialists. This area along the Roanoke River was touted as a particularly prime and healthy location. (Advertisements failed to mention that Native Americans referred to the Roanoke as the "River of Death," and that malaria was endemic there.)

Meanwhile, Archie had started up his own law firm in New York in 1892—Chanler, Maxwell & Philip—not out of any particular interest in the law, but as a means of handling all of the legal matters stemming from his own private investments. His partners, Harry

Philip (a fellow product of the Columbia law school) and W. G. Maxwell, envisioned a gentlemen's firm with a distinguished roster of clients, thanks to Archie's connections. Instead, Philip and Maxwell eventually found themselves tangled up in malaria and madness. (As the firm began to sink, Maxwell begged Archie in 1896 to use his connections to get more clients—paying ones, this time. Archie was enraged and fired back an eleven-page typewritten letter saying that he found such "boot-licking . . . distinctly degrading"; that he knew of such a person who got references by supplying whores to a Supreme Court Justice, and that he would do no such thing.)

Maxwell accompanied Archie on exploratory expeditions to the investment site in North Carolina, where they were met by an ex-Confederate soldier, "Major" Thomas Emry, a local entrepreneur who had just completed a dam and canal to harness the water power. (Impressed by Emry's military title, Archie wanted one of his own; thus Maxwell began to refer to Archie as "the General.") Archie loved the idea of creating an entire town of his own, where he could be lord and master. Archie christened the site "Roanoke Rapids" (the name it has to this day), agreed to build a knitting mill by the river, and hired his friend Stanford White to design not just a mill but workers' houses, a hotel, a stable, and a Baptist church. Meanwhile, his brother Winthrop came on as a partner.

Winty had absolutely no interest in business. Once, while in Chicago, he wrote dismissively: "The air round me is full of the babble of money-grabbing apes. Real estate, stocks and bonds. And all so solemn and provincial and dirty." Dirty, perhaps, but Winty was running through his money at a great clip. Hunting mouflon in Sardinia and elk in Colorado, and hunting foxes in Ireland—this all grew very costly when one had no profession. Even the Astor money was not infinite. And so Winty, smelling an opportunity, jumped in with his brother as a partner in the business. Winty mortgaged "up to de limit" one of his last remaining "virginal" properties, and announced to Elizabeth that he and Archie were "busy laying the foundation stones of gigantic fortunes." Archie turned his sales pitch to his other siblings, and convinced Robert, as well as Elizabeth and Alida, to invest in his United Industrial Company, a holding company created to develop the Roanoke Rapids enterprise.

Archie, who envisioned a kind of utopian workers' paradise, wanted only the best in architectural design. Stanford White agreed to do the work at cost, and devised a handsome brick factory on the banks of the Roanoke that looked like a cross between a New England schoolhouse and a cotton mill. Topped with a cupola, the plans for the mill looked, in Winty's estimation, "first rate, very handsome & stately . . . prosperous & permanent." Archie concurred, and wrote to White's partner McKim in 1895, "It is the handsomest mill of this type I've ever seen, here or abroad, and excites admiration from the untutored natives." The "untutored natives" might not understand the glories of Beaux-Arts architecture, but they did understand what was needed inside the building to make it work. White knew everything about architecture for the rich, but he had barely a clue to the utilitarian needs of a functioning mill. So many changes were subsequently required that it led to escalating costs and frayed tempers.

With Archie and Winty's money as the prime engine, Roanoke Rapids slowly rose out of forest and cotton fields. Labor costs were incredibly low; the state arranged for convicts to build the mill and town at eighty cents per day. A camp for the prisoners was set up, and at least one of them fled successfully during the construction, though another was shot while attempting to escape. Archie, meanwhile, wandered amid the construction site in a long, flowing black cape, which set him off nicely from the prisoners in their striped uniforms. He kept a hammer at the ready to drive down any loose nails on the boardwalk through town, as he explained, he did not want any of the young ladies to catch and tear their dresses.

Archie took a particular interest in the houses being designed for the workers and their families, recommending that White include porches in deference to the Southern heat, ordering the architect to enlarge the original size of the rooms, and even insisting that he see the color samples being considered for the houses. White warned him that all this meddling was going to add to the cost of the design, but Archie was blithely unconcerned. White built scores of houses, the most distinctive being cozy, single-family dwellings referred to as "turtle-top" houses, so called because each one had a distinctive overhanging roof that resembled a turtle shell.

Roanoke Rapids became Archie's personal laboratory, and he took a paternalistic interest in every aspect of the workers' lives. He helped organize and build churches in the town, and he considered bringing the orphan girls from St. Margaret's Home down to Roanoke Rapids. At the family charity near Rokeby, the girls were being groomed to become servants—and even Archie recognized that there was not much future in that. Factory work at Roanoke Rapids would at least provide more freedom for the young women. And Archie believed that the chivalrous code of the South would provide a more secure life for them. He envisioned the St. Margaret orphans becoming skilled factory workers, and prime wife material, steeped as they were in the domestic arts. He could picture them nestled with their mill-hand husbands in their turtle-top homes, thanks to his beneficence. With that in mind, he had no compunction about siphoning $10,000 from the funds for St. Margaret's and investing it in the development of Roanoke Rapids. In his mind, the girls would soon be going there anyway. This was all part of his creative financing.

Archie had no doubt about the ultimate success of his mill town, and he bought three hundred acres of land adjoining the company property. A real estate boom would go hand in hand with the creation of a bustling, Lowell-like factory community of sixty thousand workers. He would follow in the steps of his forebear John Jacob Astor, who cannily invested his fur-trading money in empty stretches of Manhattan real estate and, in the process, made an immense fortune. In truth, Archie was less interested in the money itself than in the praise and honor that would come to him for establishing an idyllic mill town. He would become a kind of emperor in the wilderness, the father of a community whose members would hold him in the highest esteem. He could create his own order, his own world in this North Carolina backwater. He would be the Napoleon of the South.

All of this, of course, required large amounts of capital. The investment in Roanoke Rapids became a quicksand of interlocking companies, each one dependent on the success of the other. At Archie's insistence, the newly formed United Industrial Company, established to set up a textile mill and invest in others, bought half the stock of the Roanoke Rapids Power Company in 1893. The power company, which would supply hydroelectric power for the mills, was about to go under with the financial panic that gripped the country that year. Both companies were, in turn, counting on revenues yet to be generated by the Self-Threading Machine Company.

Archie needed additional capital to keep the whole enterprise rolling, and he set his sights on his younger brother Robert, a seemingly odd target, given Robert's scandalous history with Amélie. But in 1893 Robert turned twenty-one and he had a large inheritance coming to him. Archie had immediate plans for it, and managed to persuade Robert to jump onto the bandwagon and buy United Industrial stock. In addition, Robert agreed to lend the company $150,000 so that United Industrial could purchase the half-interest in the floundering Roanoke Rapids Power Company. This loan was secured by unrecorded mortgages on Astor real estate owned jointly by all the Chanler siblings. (Archie admitted in a later deposition that the need for secrecy about the mortgages—and the reason they were not officially recorded—was to make United Industrial appear more credit-worthy than it really was. This kind of semi-legal maneuvering was common with real estate empires like the one controlled by the Astors.) Archie assured Elizabeth that the only risk to the family was if there were a "bust up" of United Industrial, and "I needn't tell you how unlikely I think that contingency is." He asked Elizabeth to advise Alida—and even Margaret—about the scheme; but she should not, under any circumstance, mention it to Lewis, the straight-arrow lawyer, the only family member who worked for a living. Obviously he would not approve of such a tangled financial scheme. Thus it was that the fortunes of Roanoke Rapids became so entwined with the personal fortunes of the Chanler siblings.

Within a year, Robert needed money. He had married and was

in Paris, eager to sail for home. He wrote to Archie at his law firm, asking to draw on interest from the United Industrial mortgage. Furious that his brother might jeopardize the entire scheme, Archie wrote an angry letter to Robert, full of "chastisement." The Chanlers never backed down from fights with one another, and Robert rose to the occasion. He ordered his older brother to be "less overbearing or don't write, for the last letter I threw in the fire without finishing it." Robert denied the accusation that he was extravagant—he was no more so than his older brothers had been at his age—and he certainly did not deserve Archie's admonition to "put a knife to my throat to control myself." Robert went on angrily that he did not appreciate "such metaphors. . . . They remind me of a damnable gloom which is cast over my whole boyhood caused by ill health[,] a backward mind & the scoffs & rebukes of the older ones." And finally, Robert demanded that from that time on, any personal information that he sent to Archie's law firm should remain private. He did not appreciate news being shared with Winty, Lewis, or any other sibling; and if it happened again, Robert warned, "I shall return to America[,] take my affairs out of your hands and place them where none of my brothers have interest."

Further intrigue developed after Alida gained control of her inheritance in 1894. Archie put the arm on Alida and Elizabeth, both of whom had invested in United Industrial, and urged them to turn over the management of their New York properties—something that had always been done by the family lawyer, Henry Lewis Morris—to his own law firm. He and his law partners needed income and estate management would provide a good steady stream. Archie used guilt in trying to persuade his sisters: "Granted that Mr. Morris is an old & tried friend of you two—what am I? Does a brother give way to a more or less business-begotten friend?" And then he appealed to their own financial interests, as fellow investors in the Roanoke Rapids venture:

> *Now that Alida & you are my allies [&] have money placed in United Industrial it is of real importance to you both that my*

> *[law] office—that is Maxwell myself & my aides are as free from financial care & anxiety as possible in order . . . to look with a free mind after our mutual interests in U.I. [United Industrial]. Now I won't hide from you the fact that my personal expenses in running that office are . . . very heavy. I personally guarantee the salaries of everyone in that office from Maxwell to the office boy. If I hadn't had the courage to assume this grave responsibility the Firm would not be in existence, . . . [Winty] would not be a President [of United Industrial] & you & Alida stock holders in an undertaking which will ultimately surely make us all rich.*

He closed the letter by swearing his sisters to secrecy. They should not show the letter, or reveal its contents, to any other family member—especially Margaret, the most financially conservative among them.

By the end of 1894, dissension among the siblings was already simmering over Archie's industrial plan, and the discord would only grow worse. As uninterested as the Chanlers claimed to be about money, they all loved spending it. And having it. Over the next several years, when it became increasingly clear that Archie was leading the family down a financial rabbit hole, Winty (who, next to Archie, was the biggest investor in Roanoke Rapids) came to believe that his older brother had to be stopped.

Meanwhile, Archie and Amélie's marriage began to dissolve in a public way. Divorce seemed out of the question. Amid the gilded set, divorce was still considered taboo, and the penalty was complete social ostracism. It would mean disgrace for the Astor/Chanler family—and would add yet more scandal to Amélie's résumé. But the last pretense of a marriage ended when Archie purchased a new estate near Amélie in the spring of 1894, and moved his furniture out of Castle Hill. For much of the preceding two years, Archie had wandered from one hotel room and club to the next, with stops in between at his North Carolina wilderness. He spent Christmas of 1893 alone in Boston. He had been largely banished from Cas-

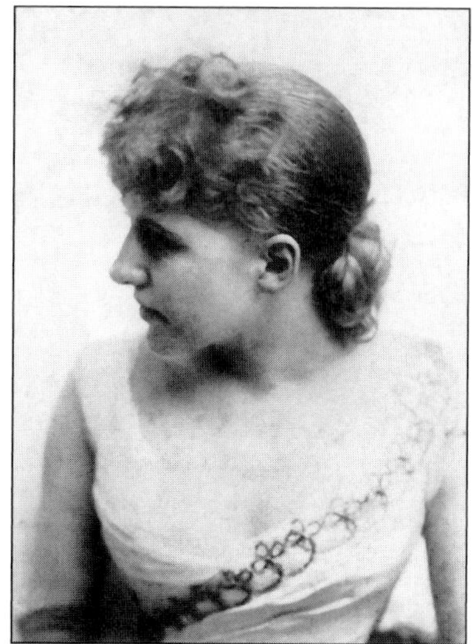

Archie and Amélie circa 1888, the year they were married.
(Left: *Rokeby Collection*. Right: *UVA Library*.)

Archie and his mother in an undated photo. *(Rokeby Collection)*

William B. Astor's octagonal library at Rokeby in the Hudson Valley.
(Library of Congress)

A Rives family portrait taken on the estate at Castle Hill in Virginia around 1880. Amélie stands between her grandmother and her aunt Ella. Her mother is on the far left, and her sister Gertrude sits on the ground. Absent are Amélie's father, Alfred, and her other sister, Landon. *(Valentine Richmond History Center)*

The Astor orphans assembled at Rokeby with cousin Mary Marshall, around 1884. *From left:* Willie, Alida, Archie, Elizabeth, Winty, Mary Marshall, Lewis, Margaret, and Robert. *(Rokeby Collection)*

The nineteenth-century manor house at Castle Hill as seen from the "lady's slipper" expanse of lawn. The view was taken in August 1925. *(Barclay Rives Collection)*

Archie in the "little salon" at the Hôtel de Pompadour, the estate in Fontainebleau, France, that he and Amélie rented in 1890. *(Rokeby Collection)*

Amélie poses in a Richmond photo studio with an umbrella that looks more like a scepter. *(Rokeby Collection)*

Archie and Amélie's guests are about to set off for a carriage ride through the forest at Fontainebleau in October 1890. Amélie sits in a chair to the far right, in front of their mid-eighteenth-century quarters. *(Special Collections, UVA Library)*

Amélie in Paris in the 1890s. *(Valentine Richmond History Center)*

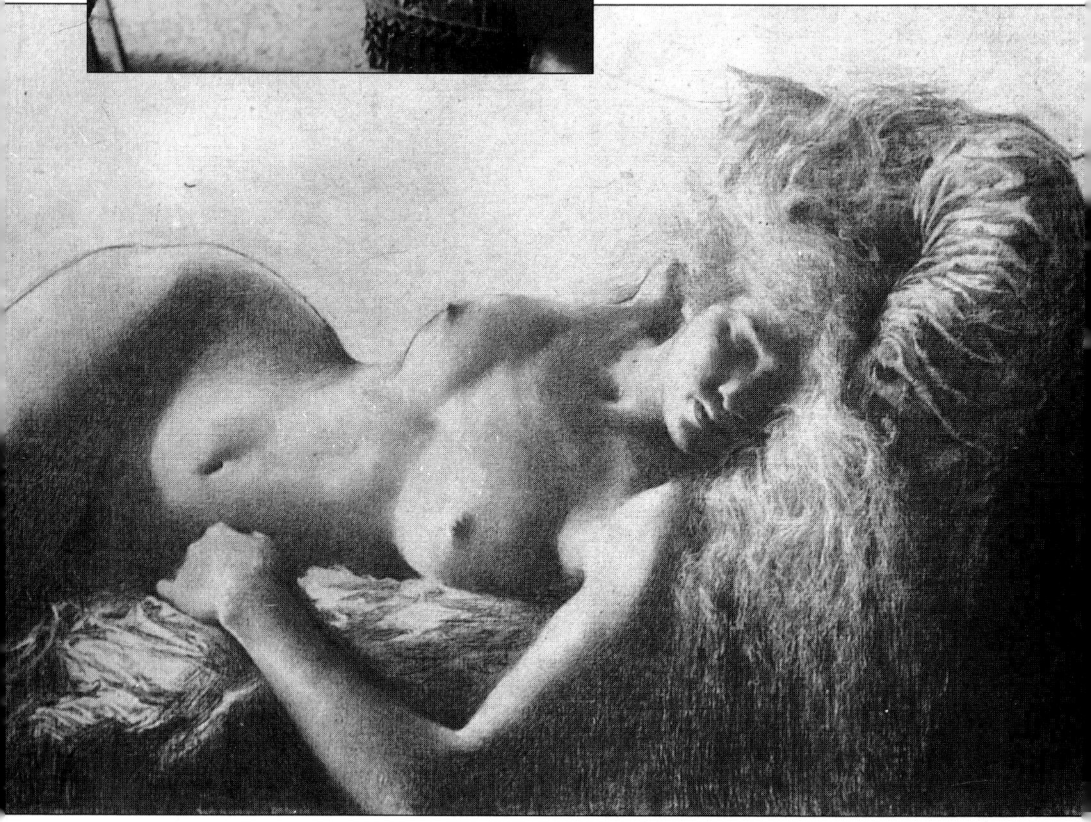

Amélie's self portrait, August 21, 1892. *(Special Collections, UVA Library)*

Lord Curzon, viceroy of India and paramour of Amélie. *(Library of Congress)*

Archie, armed and on horseback in Virginia, September 1912. *(Special Collections, UVA Library)*

Prince Troubetzkoy in fencing outfit. *(Bette Potts Collection)*

Prince Troubetzkoy, Amélie, and Lutie Pleasants enjoy a game of croquet at Castle Hill.
(Valentine Richmond History Center)

Amélie and the dog Caquin, photographed by the prince at Lago Maggiore.
(Eleanor Johnston Collection)

Archie, at left, admires the re-creation of the "lost city" of Pueblo Grande in Nevada, which he helped finance. With him in June 1925 is the governor of Nevada. While attending a Native American pageant at Pueblo Grande, Archie preferred being called "Sagebrush Jack." *(Library of Congress)*

Archie, visible in the wardrobe mirror, works amid the chaos of his bedroom at Merry Mills. He hired a local photographer to capture a psychic experiment involving the fall of a twelve-pound plaster bust from atop the wardrobe. *(Ella Scantling Morris Collection)*

Looking out toward the distant screen of boxwood from the front steps of Castle Hill. *From right to left:* the prince, Amélie, her sister Gertrude, and her grand-nephew Allen Potts. *(Welford Dunaway Taylor Collection)*

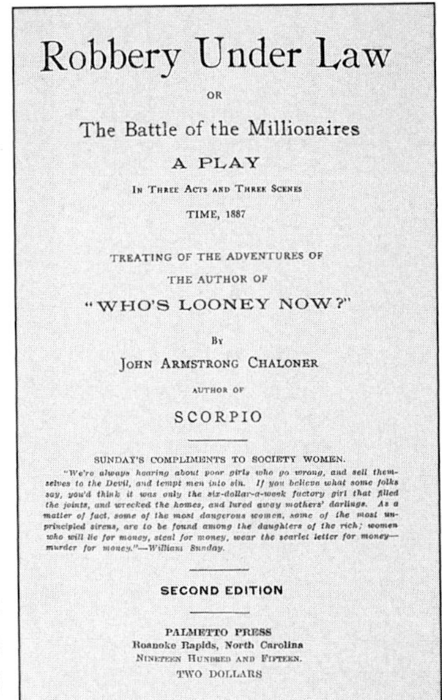

Robbery Under Law

OR

The Battle of the Millionaires

A PLAY

IN THREE ACTS AND THREE SCENES

TIME, 1887

TREATING OF THE ADVENTURES OF

THE AUTHOR OF

"WHO'S LOONEY NOW?"

BY

JOHN ARMSTRONG CHALONER

AUTHOR OF

SCORPIO

SUNDAY'S COMPLIMENTS TO SOCIETY WOMEN.

"We're always hearing about poor girls who go wrong, and sell themselves to the Devil, and tempt men into sin. If you believe what some folks say, you'd think it was only the six-dollar-a-week factory girl that filled the joints, and wrecked the homes, and lured away mothers' darlings. As a matter of fact, some of the most dangerous women, some of the most unprincipled sirens, are to be found among the daughters of the rich; women who will lie for money, steal for money, wear the scarlet letter for money—murder for money."—William Sunday.

SECOND EDITION

PALMETTO PRESS
Roanoke Rapids, North Carolina
NINETEEN HUNDRED AND FIFTEEN.
TWO DOLLARS

The title page for the play that re-created Archie's escape from Bloomingdale. *(Author's collection)* tle Hill, although the family still enjoyed the benefits of his largesse. It was clear that he could no longer even dream of living with Amélie. He decided to settle for the next best thing; he'd move nearby and keep an eye on his beloved. Archie bought an estate called Edgefield that was located within a short canter from Castle Hill. In addition, he purchased a neighboring tract of land that featured a still-operating pre-Revolutionary mill, a picturesque and historic prize that Archie wanted not so much to grind his corn, but for the redolent name, "Merrie Mill." He amended the name and christened his estate "Merrie-Mills" (which he soon changed to "The Merry Mills"), an ironic bit of nomenclature, considering what would unfold in the coming years.

Archie began renovations at the antebellum mansion (a rather modest place in contrast to the grandeur of Castle Hill), including the installation of a swimming pool, a decided novelty in that part of the world. Moving his furnishings out of Castle Hill caused some bruised feelings, though Amélie claimed she liked "Castle Hill . . . looking like its quaint, bare old self." Don't worry about me, she wrote Archie dramatically, "I shall be moving about a good deal and shall travel in a knapsack sort of way." That was hardly the case. Archie's manservant had already seen to a deluxe cabin for Amélie and her cousin, Eleanor Page. They were to leave shortly for France, with steamer trunks, not knapsacks.

Archie also traveled abroad that summer, but not with Amélie. He went to London on business, intent on selling international patent rights to the self-threading invention in order to raise more capital for his industrial empire. (He received a terrific offer of $100,000 for the British rights, but only if the mechanism could be fitted onto the Singer machine, a problem that had not yet been solved.) While in England, Archie fell ill, which made things a bit awkward for Amélie. She wanted to go to London for the social season. Among other old friends in town was George Curzon, engaged for over a year but still not married, so Amélie might spin another web around him.

Archie wrote to Amélie in Paris, suggesting that she put off the trip for the sake of propriety—and to avoid gossip. How would it look if she came to London and they stayed in separate quarters? It would lead to no end of whispering about their marriage. Amélie wrote back immediately that people "would talk much more, I assure you, if I broke engagements which I have up to the 10th of July, & left you ill in London, remaining myself in Paris!!!!" Not that she had any intention of nursing Archie back to health. She suggested that she spend one night at his hotel—in a different suite, with her maid Martha Jane and her cousin Eleanor—and then move on to the lodgings that she had already arranged. She ended the note by saying that she was going to have George Curzon stop by and check in on Archie. Curzon was doubtless the last person on earth Archie wanted to see.

Amélie had ensnared Archie, an eccentric millionaire, body and soul, and had bewitched countless others, including literary kingpins and the future viceroy of India. But that summer she found her prince. The account of that meeting has been told and retold with a number of variations, following the Virginia tradition that a story should never die for lack of nourishment. Amélie herself loved to recount the event, embellishing it no doubt with each retelling. She recalled that she met her prince at a private musicale in London. As usual, she created a stir as she entered. She looked stunning in a pale, rose-colored silk gown trimmed with bows made of lavender velvet. During a pause in the music, Oscar Wilde reportedly rushed over and introduced her to a tall, handsome man, a Russian prince, saying that they were the "two most beautiful people in London," and they should meet. Amélie claimed that she had foreseen it all in a dream—the musical gathering, the decor of the drawing room (down to the draperies), and even the handsome man himself.

His name was Prince Pierre Troubetzkoy, and he was an artist and an aristocrat. His father, a Russian prince and a friend of Tolstoy, had married an American opera singer and settled in an Italian villa on the shores of Lago Maggiore. There, Pierre and his two brothers were raised and took on the aura of Russian nobility. Pierre, with his rugged good looks—at six foot two, he towered over the tiny

Amélie—combined the physical appeal of the "savage Tartar" with the romance of his Old World Italian accent and villa. Amélie kept a picture of her prince from that summer of 1894. He is in fencing gear, his saber and mask in hand, looking every inch the swashbuckling star that he was.

Pierre asked the beautiful Amélie if he could paint her. She went day after day to his studio in London, and before long they were confiding in one another, sharing their life stories. One day he surprised her with a gift—an amethyst ring bearing the crest of the Romanovs. Within a month of meeting the prince, Amélie declared her independence from Archie: "Let us begin life over. Let us give each other our freedom," she wrote to her husband. And, as if to inspire him to a noble ambition, she went on:

> *How grand to show the world that a man & woman, both high-strung, both gifted, both unusual in regard to temperament & character, can remain staunch, loyal, devoted to one another, in spite of the accidental friction, which prevented their being happy as married people. . . . It seems to have come to me like an inspiration,—the idea, the sure feeling, of how much the whole world would "gain in grandeur & in moral height," were men & women to face such mistakes simply, generously, nobly & to say to each other—"I love you—I am your best friend as you are mine, but in this one way we make each other wretched."*

Amélie went off with her prince to his Italian villa in its storybook setting, on the edge of a magnificent lake at the foot of the Alps. Archie slunk back to Merry Mills, feeling anything but merry.

EIGHT

The X-Faculty

We can't analyze love because it is in the realm of the unconscious.

—Archie's notes from a psychology class at Columbia, 1883

Archie paced the hallways of Merry Mills, looking inward, thrown back upon himself to puzzle out what had gone wrong. He had never been so alone. Not since the death of his mother. How could he have lost Amélie? In his mind, Amélie and his mother were linked together inextricably. Hadn't Amélie taken a special interest in his dear mother? Hadn't she even felt her presence in a room? Archie sorted through the tangle of his life to try to make sense of it all.

Though he was born to privilege, to him the world had always seemed fraught with danger. Even as a young child, Archie had found that terror could lurk in the midst of the greatest festivity. He remembered the Christmas ball held at the White House when Andrew Johnson was president. His father, John Winthrop Chanler, was then serving as congressman from New York, and the whole family had been invited to the gala party. Archie was six years old, and his brother Winty five, and the two of them, caught in the swirl of the party, got separated from their parents. At their eye level, the whole world seemed reduced to a sea of crinoline. They thought they were lost forever. Terrified, they retreated to a corner, clutching each other in tears.

Archie recalled his mother lovingly; the memory of her was the one constant source of warmth and solace for him. He had even written a short story, a piece of fiction lifted directly from his own life, about his early days in Washington, D.C., in which she plays a central role. Mother and son ride together in a carriage in the afternoons, and she reads aloud to him fairy tales by Hans Christian Andersen or stories from the *Arabian Nights,* always careful to point out the moral of each story. He loves this closeness with his mother, and takes her advice to heart. She counsels the young boy to "never show the white feather," never show fear. Even in a fight, he must never reveal the terror in his heart. This need to control his emotions and hide his inner turmoil became the ruling obsession in Archie's life. He became, like the young boy in the story, "ashamed to show [the] secret inner chamber of himself."

The horror of his mother's death when he was thirteen still resonated with Archie. He had not even known she was ill. Shortly after her funeral, Archie had been sent back to boarding school. His widowed father, overwhelmed by his own loss and by the burden of caring for his motherless brood, seemed incapable of comforting his children. Archie was shattered by his mother's death. It was as if the sun had suddenly vanished, and the planets had been hurled out of their orbits. Thereafter he seemed to be sentenced to exile—first at his boarding school in Sing Sing, New York, and then at Rugby in England.

Archie recalled with a shudder that grim October day in 1877, just months after his arrival in England, when he was called into the headmaster's study by a servant. A cousin, looking pale and shaken, announced that Archie's father was dead. The funeral would be later that day in New York. His cousin advised Archie to be strong; that, as the eldest son, it was his duty to bear up under the strain. After a few more awkward moments, the cousin was gone and Archie was left behind in a new school, with no old friends or family, in a country not his own. He felt utterly abandoned. The Guardians in New

York—a well-meaning but rather Dickensian committee that made all major decisions concerning the Chanler orphans' upbringing—decreed that Archie had to stay in England for the next several years. To save money, they wouldn't let him even come home for a visit.

The code of behavior among the public-school boys in England was brutal. Any display of sentiment or emotion was considered a punishable offense. Marooned as he was in such a culture, it was small wonder that Archie tried at all costs to keep his innermost feelings tightly controlled. He developed his "Sphinx-faculty"—the ability to mask his "soft, tender heart"—that he would write about to Amélie's friend Julia Magruder in 1892. He had feared that his inscrutable personality, his inability to open up to his beloved and show his true heart, would be fatal for his marriage. His greatest fear had now been realized.

Amélie came back to the United States and told Archie that she wanted a divorce. She knew the public, and the Astor/Chanler clan, would be outraged, but she did not care. She wanted to put an end to a marriage that she described as nothing more than a sham, "a thing of name and words & dignified posing before the world." Archie and Amélie met in New York in February 1895, and the press took note. Amélie, just a shade over thirty, was reported as looking a bit fleshy compared to her willowy youth, but nonetheless still strikingly sensuous in her "walking dress [which] looks almost as if she had been melted into it." Archie, on the other hand, was a nervous wreck, chain-smoking and fidgeting, walking about compulsively. He caused a small scene while getting a shave. The barber, who counted royalty among his clientele, found Archie difficult. Midway through the shave, Archie leaped out of the chair, claiming he couldn't go on enduring such a brutal scraping of his cheeks without being sedated with chloroform. He left half-shaven.

What neither the press nor the barber knew was the source of Archie's distress. Amélie was about to set off for South Dakota to get a divorce. Archie would not contest it; he loved her too much and only wanted her to be happy. With his blessings—and the support of his law firm—Amélie headed west. It was relatively easy to get a divorce in South Dakota, but in order to do so, she had to establish residency there, which would take a number of months. (Not that she actually stayed in South Dakota the whole time. After setting up a residence, Amélie headed to California, which seemed much more to her taste.) Archie paid for it all, and sent along his valet. Writing from Monterey to "My own, only darling Brother," she turned on the charm and passed along one of her bills from Dr. J. Madison Taylor. ("He asks after you so cordially, all the time. Do write him a line.") She also had the nerve to ask Archie to hire yet another relative.

In October 1895 the divorce was announced, creating a huge stir in the press, in the Virginia countryside, in Manhattan drawing rooms, and at the Chanler estate on the Hudson. Archie's valet, back at Merry Mills, reported to his boss in North Carolina that a letter had arrived from Rokeby, "and that the place is worked up to the highest pitch over it, it is worse than if a cyclone had struck it and carried off all the buildings." For all its shock value, the press was not completely surprised by the turn of events. "If there is anything in the theory that a successful marriage rests upon a balancing of temperaments[,] the causes of this divorce are easy to see," one newspaper reported. On the one hand, Chanler "is a man of great force of character, a despiser of idlers, nervous, highly strung, bent upon accomplishing much in the world," while Amélie spends her time writing eccentric novels and poems of "frothing Swinburnean passion."

More frothing ensued four months later, when Amélie married the "brawny," thirty-two-year-old Prince Troubetzkoy at Castle Hill. It was a quiet ceremony with family (including her father this time) and a few friends. Amélie wore a white satin gown trimmed with violets and Russian sable; in a rather theatrical show of piety, she carried a large copy of the wedding vows in her hands.

Fortunately for Archie, he was not in the neighborhood. He had carefully removed himself to Roanoke Rapids, overseeing the construction of his industrial empire. The Chanlers in New York were outraged again, and none more so than Margaret, who had a positive horror of what she referred to as "plural marriage"—that is, remarrying while the first spouse was still alive. (Margaret upheld her commandment, "Thou shalt not have plural marriage," to the extreme, eventually banning from Rokeby the siblings who fell into that hated category.) The Chanlers, as noted previously, had a penchant for turning their backs on anyone—relatives included—who stepped beyond the pale. In the same way that Archie's poor, wayward great-uncle Henry Astor, who married against the wishes of his father, was virtually excised from the family genealogy, Amélie was now wiped clean from their collective memory banks. It was as if their sister-in-law had never existed.

Even the long, effusive letters between Amélie and Elizabeth came to an end. Amélie's final plea for understanding was contained in a twenty-seven-page letter to Elizabeth ("Beth, my Beth, <u>my</u> Beth, Oh, Darling") written on December 4, 1895; in it, she tried to prepare her only remaining ally for the worst. "X," as she called Pierre, would be coming over to marry her, and the "<u>monstrous</u>" press was going to have a field day. "The newspapers <u>will</u> be vulgar and, in this free & glorious republic of ours, every name is as a tennis-ball to toss back & forth."

And then Amélie had to broach an even more delicate subject: Archie's money. Apparently, Elizabeth had written Amélie and expressed concerns over her brother's finances. He was stretched thin indeed. The escalating cost of Roanoke Rapids and the self-threading company, the financial burden of his law firm and the art prize, and the cross-country divorce all added up. In addition, he was continuing to support Amélie and would continue to do so after she wed her handsome but penniless prince. Elizabeth was concerned for Archie—and probably mixed into that concern was some worry for herself and the other siblings who had a sizable financial stake in his success. His "reckless mortgages" were troublesome, and his generosity boundless. He was a soft touch for money, and almost everyone he came in contact with had his or her hand out. Amélie tried to reassure her ex-sister-in-law that *she* was not the cause of his profligacy. In fact, she had tried to talk some financial sense into him:

> *I made him promise me, solemnly, in his Dear Mother's sacred name, & on his word of honour as a gentleman, that he would never let his income get lower than $12,000 . . . a year. Now, darling, doesn't that comfort you a bit?*

Amélie admitted that she and Pierre were in fact going to be "poor," but they looked forward to being "bread-winners, wage-earners!":

> *Do you know darling, I believe that to contribute mutually, by one's separate endeavour to the maintenance of a home, be it only a cheery apartment in Kensington, is one of the solidest foundations for pure, wholesome married-happiness! . . . How it will make me write! With what zest, what ardour, what exultation!!*

In fact, the opposite occurred. Amélie had remained remarkably prolific during her marriage to Archie, even in the depths of her depression and drug addiction; but she endured a long fallow period after she married Pierre. For years, she produced virtually nothing. Her literary reputation and income rested primarily on her earliest work. None of her subsequent books ever reached the level of sales that her first novel, *The Quick or the Dead?*, had achieved. She continued to receive royalties on that book until at least the 1930s, but Amélie never made enough money to support the expense of Castle Hill and her own luxurious lifestyle. Nor did Pierre, who made only a modest income painting society figures.

When Amélie was first introduced to Pierre in London, he was a rising star. The year before they met, he had scored a great coup when he painted the irascible prime minister William Gladstone, who was then feverishly working to push the Home Rule bill through Parliament. Gladstone had little patience for formal sittings, but

Pierre managed to create a successful portrait, capturing "the face of an old lion, not toothless or broken down, which is the usual image, but full of dignity and force," according to one critic. That triumph, coupled with the prince's physical appeal, made him one of the most sought-after artists in London. Beautiful women from the highest rungs of British society flocked to this strapping young man who exercised with dumbbells between sittings. The prince exuded both beauty and hyper-masculinity, a heady and intoxicating combination. His physique so impressed the society reporter who covered the Amélie-Pierre nuptials that the wedding article noted the groom's measurements—over six feet tall and forty-eight inches around the chest—"a magnificent specimen of manhood."

Within weeks of their wedding, the couple departed for Italy, taking on pseudonyms while boarding the ship in New York, in a futile attempt to escape public scrutiny. A journalist unveiled them as "Mr. And Mrs. Stahl," which is how they appeared on the passenger list. The *New York Sun* also noted that Amélie nearly did not make the trip, as she was suffering from "nervous prostration." The stress of the wedding and the avalanche of adverse press she had been forced to endure since the divorce doubtless left her overwrought. Among other perceived atrocities, she dared to dispense with the name "Chanler" after her divorce and reverted to her maiden name. And, in a further, shocking display of independence, she continued to write as "Amélie Rives" after her remarriage.

The honeymooners went first to the Troubetzkoy villa in Italy, and then on to Paris and London, where the prince assumed he would continue to build his distinguished clientele, which was the only way he could ever hope to make a fortune. His own family certainly had none. Though they claimed blood ties to the Romanovs and princely titles, they lived in exile from Mother Russia. Pierre's father had been banished from the Russian court after falling in love with Pierre's mother, the charming American singer known as the "canary-bird of Lago Maggiore." The canary-bird in Italy was apparently much more pleasing than the wife in Russia he already had—a wealthy aristocrat who happened to be a close relative of the tsar.

The tsar summoned Pierre's father to return home to Russia at once, but he refused. The Troubetzkoys were thereafter banned from their homeland, and cut off from any family wealth. One newspaper reported that if they dared to return, it meant Siberia, or worse.

Archie and Amélie's marriage lasted less than eight years and had been fraught with problems from the start. But Archie would never get over her. On New Year's Day, 1896—well aware that Amélie was about to be remarried—Archie wrote of the nightmare he had endured for the previous two years, and of his fight to gain control over his life:

> With reservations & an eye fixed on the betterment of mankind this paints my point of view. "I am one whom the evil blows & buffets of the world have so incurred that I am reckless what I do to spite the world." After a 2 years fight & with God's help I've conquered Internal Calm Freedom! To <u>hold</u> this Kingdom of the Mind perpetual war against passions, impatiencies, brutalities & weaknesses, for perpetual vigilance is needed and must now conquer the outlying provinces of my Kingdom i.e. externals, manner, gesture. I must gain External . . . [control] that I have Internal Imperturbability. Must rise above hasty oaths & outbursts of unguarded rage at stupidity of waiters & other underlings. . . . The Serenest New Year of my Life. Serenity is the substitute for that childish word happiness. Happiness [is] impossible in this world to anyone of sympathies, because unhappiness of others kills his.

Archie realized that happiness was no longer within his reach. The hope of that was gone forever when he lost Amélie. Archie understood that he was totally alone. Even Stanford White, his friend and collaborator in Roanoke Rapids, recognized that deep loneliness in Archie, calling him at various times a "Hermit Crab and a Wild Eagle."

As 1896 opened, Archie should have been giddy. It was his

moment of triumph. He was then living in Roanoke Rapids, overseeing every aspect of his textile town. His knitting mill had opened just a few months before. The initial news was good—orders were pouring in and the hundred factory workers were scrambling to keep up. After years of arduous work—building and financing the town and mill, dealing with endless personnel issues and design details—the factory was finally in operation and the town was humming with activity. Another mill was even being constructed, which would mean an increased demand for water power provided by the Roanoke Rapids Power Company, in which Archie was then majority stockholder. Things looked bright for Archie, who later proclaimed that he had "nailed my colors to the mast of the R.R.P.Co"—and that he would "sink or swim with her." More factories would translate into a potential real-estate bonanza for Archie, as additional housing—on his land—would have to be built for the growing number of factory workers. As the town grew by leaps and bounds, he would duplicate the old Astor formula for printing money. Archie's investment—and that of his siblings and Stanford White—looked golden. And it had all been due to Archie's initial grand vision. His ambitious and noble scheme—creating a town in the wilderness—had become a reality.

But, for all the good news, Archie was still distracted by Amélie and his own inner confusion. His ex-wife remained in the news as a provocative siren. Though remarried and living abroad, she continued to attract prurient interest. The press showed renewed curiosity about the scandalous, divorced author who was now a princess. How exactly did she live, and how did she maintain that sensual allure? As to the latter question, even a newspaper in Milwaukee had an interest, reporting in March of 1896:

Beauty Rules of a Princess

> As a rule . . . the way of sleeping is responsible for ugliness or beauty, if the word of those who have studied looks can be weighed. Amélie Rives Chanler, now the Princess Troubetskoi, regards the way of sleeping as all important. Her method of

> sleeping her beauty sleep is to begin an hour before she goes to bed with a bath in cool cologne water, deepening to chilled water more highly perfumed than the first. . . . When sleeping the head rests upon a pillow of flowing hair, not twisted upon curlers or touched by hairpins. The pillow is a pine-needle one, with down underneath to make softness. The room in which the beautiful authoress sleeps is a cold one, made hot an hour before time to rise. Another cold bath in perfumed water, and the beauty sleep is over, and with most beneficial results, for no one is more beautiful than the newly-married princess.

Archie returned to Merry Mills in April 1896, after having spent most of the previous year in Roanoke Rapids. He had fortunately been away at his mill town—absorbed in work and removed from both the press and his family—when news of the divorce and remarriage broke. The time had come for him to try to re-create his life in Virginia. He could manage the North Carolina factory from afar and keep track of what was going on at Castle Hill down the road. He monitored news of Amélie and her prince abroad; he also kept up a healthy correspondence with Amélie's mother, who was concerned about the family's financial future—and even the furnishings that had been removed from Castle Hill. Early on, Archie resisted visiting Amélie's home, writing to his sister that "it would be trop bizarre even for me." But over the subsequent years he swallowed his pride, and there was a well-worn path between Merry Mills and Castle Hill.

Amélie took advantage of Archie's continued obsession with her. It was soon apparent that the prince would not be able to support her in the fashion to which she had become accustomed. He had no family fortune, and, though popular in London, he was clearly not going to become the next John Singer Sargent. By July of 1896, Amélie was writing to "My Dear Brother" Archie with humble apologies over her unpaid bills that were being directed to him. "My pride is so quivering," she wrote. In her best melodramatic fashion she announced that she was being forced to sell some of her jewels—but not, she assured him, the Louis XVII bow-knots with ruby and sapphire that he had given to her as a wedding present. She would never part with such treasures "given me by *you*, dear Archie!" No, she would part with "some of my *own* little brooches in order to pay my 'doctor's bills' which have been heavy."

In the same letter she brought up another delicate matter. Not long after the divorce had been finalized, Amélie had summarily fired her servant, Martha Jane, the woman who had served at Castle Hill since slavery time and whom Amélie had shown off in England and Europe, had sketched in Italy, and to whom she had professed undying devotion. There had been some sort of spectacular blow-up, some bit of "outrageous behavior" on "Mattie's" part, according to Amélie, and she wanted nothing more to do with her. End of story, until Amélie learned that Archie had taken Martha Jane into his own household. Amélie was nearly apoplectic as she tried to dissuade Archie from hiring her old servant. The stories Martha Jane could tell! This was one of the nightmares of upper-class life: discarded and bitter servants could unlock all kinds of secrets. Martha Jane was privy to lots of them. And Amélie needed to remain in Archie's good graces.

Amélie need not have worried. Archie remained so deeply devoted to his ex-wife that not even Martha Jane's whisperings would deter him. He could not deny his beloved Amélie anything—regardless of gossip or even of their marital status. In the midst of their divorce, he had transferred to Amélie one hundred shares of stock in his Self-Threading Sewing Machine Company, with the proviso that if she had not paid for the stock by his death, it would be a gift. This represented one-tenth of the entire stock. (Archie owned 737 shares, so between the two of them they owed more than eighty percent of the company.) Archie had such confidence in the self-threading invention and its eventual success that he wanted Amélie to partake in its riches.

> My respect, admiration, and affection for you . . . will remain among the highest inspirations of my life. . . . I consider you the greatest Genius—man or woman—that I have ever met, and . . . my interest in your happiness and success [will remain] . . . as intense as ever.

In response to Amélie's woeful financial predicament in the summer of 1896, Archie had nothing but good news about the stock she owned. In July the revamped self-threader had been successfully tested on a Singer sewing machine. Archie anticipated that large-scale production would begin shortly. (His prognosis turned out to be overly optimistic. It took another two years of refinements before the self-threader was commercially viable.) Archie had obtained new patents in both America and Europe, and needles for the attachment were currently being fashioned at the Roanoke Rapids machine shops. Archie announced proudly that after putting tens of thousands of dollars into the self-threading idea, it was all about to pay off. And it was all for her:

> Like the fighter in a tournament who has worsted all opponents and lays the prize at the feet of the Queen of Love and Beauty, I now lay the triumph of a four years fight at the feet of the woman whose heart I knew during all that time, beat in unison with my strokes. I now lay my victory at your, my dearest and greatest of sister's golden feet.

It was her birthday, and this triumphant news was his gift to her, the woman who remained his muse—even if she was married to someone else. Like Archie, Amélie believed in dreams and portents, and the year before she had had a "Golden Dream" about him. Archie had taken it as a prophecy of his future success. He now believed the dream was coming to fruition, and Amélie would take part in it. "For standing as you do on the shore of the vast sea of our S.T.

[Self-Threading] stock your feet will literally be golden—for they will be lapped and circled by waves of gold."

Archie predicted dizzying profits; his cable address was simply "Eldorado New York." More than thirteen million Singer machines were in existence, and he expected that at least two million of the owners would want the self-threading mechanism. And that was conservative, in his estimation, for he believed that the invention might eventually be "fitted on to all the sewing machines in the world." He planned to have salesmen go door to door to sell it. The sales force at that point, however, did not inspire much in the way of confidence. It consisted of the inventor himself, a man named Albert Legg, who was an old hand at sales, having previously hawked books and lightning rods. He intended to canvass neighborhoods in New York; and, Archie announced cheerfully, he would be joined by "Uncle Dick McMurdo," one of Amélie's relatives on the payroll—doubtless the incompetent one driving Archie's law partners to distraction. This would get him out of the office.

Archie translated what all this meant in dollars and cents. He expected that within the year Amélie would earn between $1,000 and $2,000 on her investment. After that there was no telling how high the stock would go, but he expected it to "jump upwards . . . like stock in a gold-mine in which new and rich leads are being discovered monthly." In addition, Archie planned to increase his monthly allotments to Amélie and her prince. He was currently paying them $300 per month, totaling $3,600 a year. He announced that for the fiscal year beginning 1897–98 he would pay them $4,600.

Amélie thanked her ex-husband profusely:

24th September 1896

My dear, dearest Archie,

. . . I told you that a long letter would soon follow, and I mean this to be the long letter— [&] want it to hold at least a hundredth part of the gratitude, love, admiration, respect— oh, Archie! I can't. My eyes are so full of tears that I can't write. I can't say what I want.

She complained bitterly about being penned up in an English country house with people who didn't even know "that there are such things as books, even <u>novels</u>!" and who can't hold a candle to Archie.

> *[They] are what you & I loathe so!— O, how they suffocate, depress, repress, shrivel me, these people! . . . I feel as though I were slowly dying, from the feet up, getting number & number every day, as poor Socrates did. . . . [In contrast] the thought of your grandeur, your nobility of character, your original fiery mind, your <u>genius</u> in fact, how it unnerves me—just the memory of what man can be, & what these English people <u>are</u>!*

This was the sort of praise that Archie craved. He needed to be needed, especially by Amélie. A letter like this one softened his heart anew, made him ever more bound to his princess. Knowing how to pull at his heartstrings, she went on to describe how desperately ill she had been, going into gory detail. In Milan her "grippe" had settled in her lungs and she had spat great gobs of blood. Then she had a painful and deep abscess on her thigh that had to be cut out "without any thing to deaden the pain, not even cocaine." In Paris she had taken to her bed with a bad knee. And then, of course, there had been a nervous attack: "my nerves revenged themselves on me for three or four months." And now Archie, once more the white knight, had come to her rescue. Amélie was relieved and touched by his kindness:

> *My Archie, before such kind greatness, such free, child-like generosity & highness as yours, one cannot help feeling that words are not only inadequate but almost profane.*

Archie continued to support the nearly penniless prince and his princess. And in the Virginia countryside this sometimes became the source of jokes. But Archie didn't care. He loved Amélie too much. One day a telegram came over the wires at the local railroad depot. It was from Pierre, who was off in some distant place, and read, "Our Amélie is ill—needs money." The message was read and reread by all the hangers-on at the station to great hilarity. "*Our* Amélie," they joked. But when the message was brought to Archie, he replied instantly, "It will be my pleasure—how much?"

Archie's generosity might have been a source of fun to the country folk in Virginia, but to the Chanlers, Archie's dealings with his ex-wife were irrational. In their estimation, Amélie was making a fool of Archie. To make matters worse, the press insulted the family name by continually identifying Archie as "the former husband of Amélie Rives."

In October 1896 the family began to close ranks against Archie when he committed a sin even graver than the Amélie embarrassment. Tradition required that Archie, as the eldest son, preside over the wedding of his sister Alida and give her away at the ceremony, for which the Chanler family would assemble at Rokeby along with august guests including Aunt Julia Ward Howe, members of the Guardians, and assorted Astors. In a letter, Winty expressed his trepidation at the notion of all the siblings being gathered under one roof.

> *Every Chanler is to have a large double bedroom to himself or herself and other people will sleep where they can. . . . I shall brew a Chanler Punch and then climb a tree. Archie says he will be there "drenched in calm"—ominous outlook!*

Ominous indeed. The event went as planned, down to the last gorgeous detail dreamed up by the wedding's artistic director, Stanford White. A special train from New York brought up two hundred of society's choicest members. Tapestries were draped across the exterior of Rokeby, Neapolitan minstrels strolled among the guests with their mandolins, and a wooden dance floor on the lawn featured a popular Hungarian orchestra. All was perfection except for one glaring problem. Archie was nowhere to be seen. He sent a telegram at the last moment claiming illness—pleurisy.

Alida, who had cried "into her strawberries" years before upon hearing that Archie had secretly wed Amélie, was inconsolable once more and wept for hours. She was certain that her brother Archie was dying, for nothing short of that could keep him from such a family event. (Not long after the wedding, however, he was well enough to make his annual trip to the New York Horse Show at Madison Square Garden. Not even the shame of having missed his sister's wedding could keep him from that event.) Winty handled the official wedding duties that day in a state of rage. "The man is daft!" he roared. Robert chimed in that Archie was "looney." Archie heard about this and smoldered. That a brother who had betrayed him over Amélie—and had suffered his own breakdown—should refer to him in such a way was loathsome. Archie filed away the insult and would get his revenge years later.

Whether Archie was truly ill that day is impossible to say, but he clearly had difficulty facing his family en masse. A rift had opened with his siblings when he secretly wed Amélie, and it had widened as his marriage collapsed. Archie had attended a reunion at Rokeby in June of 1895, when his divorce proceedings were under way. In the wake of seeing all his siblings, Archie wrote of how painful it had been—how "wounded & regretful" he felt over things they had said and done. With those feelings still raw, perhaps Archie just couldn't bear to face his family again, especially for a wedding, when his own marriage had ended so badly.

A permanent rupture with the family ensued a few months later. In December, Archie called a directors' meeting of the Roanoke Rapids Power Company in his room at the Kensington Hotel on Fifth Avenue and 15th Street. During the meeting he lay in bed in his nightclothes. (Winty claimed that Archie had taken to his bed during that time, and seldom left it until the end of the day. Archie insisted that he was ill.) A heated business argument broke out, with Archie and Winty taking opposite sides. Like the old days at Rokeby, where shouting matches and hand-to-hand combat were commonplace, the meeting descended into a pitched battle between the brothers. Winty later claimed that Archie would not let anyone else talk, including their Southern partners on the board, and that his older brother was "in a very violent frame of mind, intensely irritated and irritable, generally, with me."

Before long, the fight turned very bitter and personal. Winty was co-executor, along with brother Lewis, of their father's estate. That in itself was irksome to Winty, another example of Archie falling down on his familial duties. As the eldest son, Archie had been appointed the executor and, as a lawyer, seemed eminently suited for the task; nonetheless, he "never qualified"—never bothered to go to court to officially petition for the post. Thus Winty had gotten stuck serving as co-executor. This had become one of many touchy subjects between the brothers. In the middle of the business argument, Archie hinted that there was some malfeasance regarding the estate, and that he was going to have an auditor look over the books. That was the last straw for Winty. He leaped across the room, ready to slug it out with his pugilist brother. Archie scrambled out of bed in his nightclothes, ready to take on his brother; but first he bent down in search of his slippers. At that, Winty realized what a ludicrous situation it was, the two brothers about to fight like children, with an aghast audience of board members watching. Winty withdrew to the other side of the room, but the damage had been done. The next day Winty wrote to his brother, announcing he would no longer speak to him; henceforth he would communicate with him only in writing or through a third party. Archie agreed to the silence—and also notified his brother that he would be sending an accountant to check on the handling of their father's estate.

Both brothers recognized that their professional relationship had been compromised beyond repair. At risk was the operation of both the Roanoke Rapids Power Company and United Industrial, the company that ran the knitting mill. Archie owned the lion's share of United Industrial—$175,000 worth of stock, versus $50,000 controlled by Winty. Both brothers were directors of the company; in addition, Winty served as the salaried president for United Industrial. Archie now demanded that his brother resign both posts. Winty complied, happy not to have to deal with his brother anymore about company business. Archie reorganized the board and had himself elected president.

While consolidating additional power and responsibility, Archie knew that he was in desperate need of a rest. The long, grueling start-up of Roanoke Rapids and the final disintegration of his marriage had left him exhausted. Just at the moment his industrial empire seemed poised to blossom, his focus strayed. He became more and more interested in pursuing psychological studies—in mapping the landscape of his inner psyche—than in business. Stanford White, a limited partner in the development of Roanoke Rapids, had a financial stake in the enterprise, so he was concerned over the rocky state of affairs; as a friend, he was also worried about Archie's overwrought state. He understood that Archie needed a hiatus from work. Archie trusted White, whom he affectionately called "Fuzz Buzz," and he agreed to turn over power of attorney to him and to their mutual friend, Augustus Saint-Gaudens. Archie expected this would be a temporary situation; he planned to take at least two months off before returning to work. In the meantime, White would make decisions. White had no head for business. He spent much of his life in debt, and seemed the absolute worst person to entrust with financial decisions; but Archie needed a break, and this would only be for a limited time.

In despair over his failure with Amélie—with love itself—he became obsessed with trying to plumb the mysteries of his own inner psyche. He had long had an interest in psychology. He had studied psychology and philosophy for his master's degree at Columbia. But at that time it was just an abstract science to him; now, alone at Merry Mills, the study became concrete. He undertook himself as the subject of his research. At Columbia, Archie had been taught that love could not be analyzed, as it was in an unknowable realm—the realm of the unconscious. Archie now determined to explore that realm. He began a series of experiments, and eventually developed what he referred to as his "X-Faculty"—the ability to tap into his subconscious. It was the natural transformation of his "Sphinx-faculty"—the faculty that had crippled him emotionally and left him unable to live with Amélie. He would take the rigid control that had limited him, and turn it on its head; he would use that powerful capability to gain access to—rather than repress—his innermost being. Perhaps then he would understand himself.

At his Virginia estate one night, Archie idly began playing billiards by himself when he noticed that the balls had stopped in a configuration that mimicked the constellations. He broke the balls again, and the same pattern appeared. Once more he did it, with the same result. This seemed such a peculiar coincidence that Archie pulled an envelope and pencil from his pocket and in the shadowy gaslight tried to draw the pattern of the balls; but his hand failed to follow his will, and instead wrote the following command: "Get a planchette!"

Archie did as he was told and procured a planchette, an early form of Ouija board. Under his manipulation—but without any conscious control on his part—he began to receive a series of coherent messages. One of them directed him to invest in a certain stock. He did so, and in short order doubled his money. He continued his experiments and found that he could dispense with the planchette altogether. He began receiving messages that were transmitted directly to his hand. Holding a pencil lightly to a notebook, his hand seemed to take on a life of its own, writing page upon page unconsciously, a phenomenon referred to as "automatic writing." He also developed vocal automatism, described as "vocal utterances . . . unconnected with conscious cerebration." It was as if he were taking dictation from some otherworldly source. Archie rejected the notion that he was communicating with the Beyond. Quite the contrary, he believed he was tapping into his subconscious mind, and regarded the entire process as a scientific experiment, an opportunity to study firsthand the workings of the psyche.

The X-Faculty messages were not always coherent (though Archie maintained that the grammar was always correct) and on at least one occasion disaster ensued. Archie was commanded to pick up a handful of live coals from the fire and walk fifteen feet at right angles to a window. He should do this three times. The X-Faculty assured him he would not be harmed, but Archie badly blistered his hands. Despite that failure, there were other successes. The X-Faculty told Archie that he could transform the color of his eyes by standing at a window looking west, holding a mirror in one hand, and the valuable pearl stickpin that he wore in his scarf in the other. While staring into the mirror intently, Archie watched as the irises in both of his eyes changed color from the original light brown to gray, a change later certified by an oculist and verified, in court testimony, by Amélie. With this tangible evidence of the power of his X-Faculty, Archie was inclined to believe another one of his messages: that he had an "extraordinary destiny" ahead of him, that he would accomplish some great, albeit undefined, mission. Archie had harbored that belief for some time.

Archie's desire to plunge into psychic research might easily be written off as evidence of mental derangement, but in the late nineteenth century there was an enormous interest in the occult, and in parapsychology of all kinds. A wave of "spiritualism" swept the country—séances, trances, automatic writing, and other unexplained psychic phenomena blossomed in an attempt to touch the spirit world and commune with the dead. The impetus for this movement was in part a reaction to the rise of science and technology; it was an attempt to reconcile scientific rationalism with the spiritual impulse. As a new millennium loomed, many looked forward to the dawn of a "New Era" in the twentieth century.

Scientists and the medical community, including many prominent psychiatrists and psychologists, bristled at the very idea of spiritualism, condemning it as an impediment to progress and a danger to society. Other cutting-edge theorists and philosophers, however, viewed this explosion in occult activity as an opportunity. Such eminent figures as Freud, Jung, and William James visited mediums in an attempt to understand the spiritual or transcendent realms of the human psyche. Séances and other paranormal proceedings became their laboratory. The renowned Harvard psychologist and professor of philosophy William James made a case for studying "psychics" in his *Essays in Psychical Research.* Even if it meant having to weed out the charlatans among psychic practitioners, the end result was worth it, he claimed, for "in good mediums there is a residuum of knowledge displayed that can only be called super-normal: the medium taps some source of information not open to ordinary people." In James's view, the study of such psychic phenomena was critical.

> It throws open for us far more questions than it answers, questions about our subconscious constitution and its curious tendency to humbug, about the telepathic faculty, and about the possibility of an existent spirit world.

With that in mind, James helped found the American Society for Psychical Research in 1885.

Archie took on this mantle of science while examining his subconscious, and at the same time carefully distanced himself from those interested only in spiritualism. His was a scientific exploration; and in his case he was both the investigator and the subject of the investigation. A renowned expert in the field later marveled at Archie's self-control, at the way he could study his own paranormal activities with a clear and scientific detachment. As a man of science, Archie attempted to explore a whole new level of humanity—he wanted nothing less than to uncover the uncharted realms of consciousness—and he truly believed it was a noble undertaking.

Unfortunately, the Chanler family, or at least Winty, took a different view. When word of Archie's "experiments" reached New York, Winty huddled with Stanford White, who had temporarily stepped into Archie's positions as president and board director of the United Industrial Company. Winty's ouster as an officer in the company did not prevent Winty's wielding the primary influence in the entire operation at Roanoke Rapids. He was the largest shareholder after Archie, and once Archie had bowed out of the picture, Winty could reassert his control—even without formal title. Dealing with White about business matters, rather than with his troublesome and explosive brother, must have been a huge relief for Winty. Stanford White was a reasonable man—and he would also carry out Winty's wishes.

In addition to reports floating northward of Archie's weird experiments, Winty probably also got wind of a risky financial undertaking that Archie was then plotting. Archie claimed to be negotiating with the mayor of Marseille over a business proposition. The deal was as follows: Archie agreed to go to France and lay the roadway for horse-drawn vehicles that he had invented and patented worldwide (and for which he had garnered an award at the Chicago exposition). He would construct the roadway for one city block at his own expense; if it proved successful, Archie would be reimbursed for his costs and hired to repave much of Marseille. Archie believed that the roadway was well ahead of its time (he apparently did not think that the horseless carriage had much of a future), and he was eager to prove it. This need to take risks, to be out on a ledge at all times, was part of Archie's personality and characterized his business dealings.

The proposed French venture would be costly and complicated—the fact that it was taking place overseas added a whole new level of difficulty—and Archie would only be reimbursed for the paving if the mayor of Marseille deemed it a success. The cost did not seem to deter Archie in the least; he was about to form a company to take on this overseas venture when Winty managed to derail both Archie and his plans.

Winty never mentioned the Marseille project as a contributing factor to subsequent events, but it is hard to believe that it did not play a role, especially in light of the timing. Why otherwise did events unfold so quickly, at exactly the moment when Archie was formulating his French plan? And at a time when most of Archie's siblings were out of the country so they could not be consulted? It's not hard to imagine what would have happened if Archie had gone ahead with his speculative plan. Redirecting capital to the paving scheme could have caused the whole tenuous Roanoke Rapids / Self-Threading Company enterprise to collapse. Despite Archie's optimistic claims to Amélie in the previous summer, his textile empire was still very much in the formative stages. The factory at Roanoke Rapids had literally just opened, and the self-threading mechanism was in the final stages of being perfected and produced. As yet, no income was being generated. All looked promising but *only* if the directors of the companies acted prudently and directed all available capital to their fledgling enterprises. It would be the worst possible moment to divert monies to a potentially disastrous new venture that had no assurance of success or even of recouping initial costs.

Before the North Carolina venture, Winty had never worked a day in his life, and he was beginning to resent the fact that this supposedly "sure-thing" investment had turned into something of a quagmire and that it was taking up so much of his time. He preferred hunting to business affairs, and he wanted to get back to his pack of hounds. The whole North Carolina venture had proven much more complicated and costly than he had anticipated—owing in part to Archie's philanthropic and humanitarian instincts about housing his factory girls as agreeably and safely as possible. Now, at the moment when it looked as if there might be success on the horizon, Archie—in typically impetuous fashion—was embarking on a risky new venture. Winty had to be infuriated with his brother. He had put at least $50,000 of his own money into the venture, and siblings Elizabeth, Alida, and Robert had also invested substantial sums—and Archie seemed determined to blow it all. This surely was the action of an insane man. Thus Winty drew Stanford White into a plot to lure Archie to New York and have him placed somewhere he could be closely watched. Events moved swiftly.

In late February 1897, Stanford White sent a telegram to Archie asking if he could drop by Merry Mills and bring along a friend. White's presence in the area would not have aroused Archie's suspicions because White was shuttling back and forth to Charlottesville, overseeing reconstruction of the Rotunda, the capstone building at the University of Virginia, which had been destroyed by fire. White had recently sent what Archie considered an "abusive letter" (Archie was so touchy at that point, that anything could have set him off, even a piece of good-hearted advice); so he fired a telegram back to the architect saying that he was too ill to see him. To Archie's surprise, White turned up anyway, appearing at his doorstep with a Dr. Eugene Fuller in tow. White managed to sweet-talk Archie into accompanying them to New York for a "plunge in the metropolitan whirl." As they boarded the train for New York, another interested party witnessed the scene—Winty was also on board, carefully keeping his distance in a separate part of the train. Winty had never been to Merry Mills, and he was on such bad terms with Archie that there was not a prayer that he would be able to lure his brother to New York. En route north, Archie spoke excitedly about the development of his X-Faculty and his automatic writing. The doctor took particular interest, and questioned Archie closely.

Archie checked into the Kensington Hotel in New York, and shortly thereafter he received a message from his X-Faculty. He was told that he would soon have the power to enter into a "Napoleonic trance," and that in doing so, he would represent the death of Napoleon Bonaparte and that his face would take on a strong resemblance to that of the dead emperor. The sculptor Augustus Saint-Gaudens came by in the evening and found his friend in bed. At that moment Archie got word from his X-Faculty that it was time to enter the trance. He asked Saint-Gaudens if he would witness the event and give him a scientific account of what transpired. Saint-Gaudens thought that a bit of psychic adventure sounded like fun. At the direction of the X-Faculty, Archie took a small shaving mirror and stared into it as he held it over his head. Archie described what happened next:

> After a minute or two of complete passivity and rigidity, for the first time in my life I experienced the entrance to a trance. It is excessively interesting as an experience. The first symptoms I had of the entering therein were slow, deep breaths, utterly involuntary on my part; these gradually increased in force and frequency until they resembled what I

> imagine are death gasps, by which I mean a man dying and gasping for breath. . . . These gasps continued in frequency and force to increase, and my mouth to distend, and remain open, stretched open to its fullest extent. This continued for . . . [perhaps] ten minutes . . . [until] my hands slowly placed the mirror on the bed, my eyes closed, and the Napoleonic death-trance, so-called by my "X-Faculty," had begun. Of course I cannot judge, having my eyes shut, of the resemblance of my features and face under the above described circumstances to those of Napoleon Bonaparte in death; all I know is from the remarks of the persons who have witnessed this Napoleonic death-trance.

Saint-Gaudens was so unnerved that he asked Archie to stop, and made him promise never to enter into a trance again in his presence. A few days later, Stanford White and Dr. Eugene Fuller witnessed Archie falling once again into the Napoleonic trance. White was genuinely terrified, feeling as if he were truly in the presence of death. "It is exactly like Napoleon's death-mask," he whispered to Dr. Fuller. "I have the photograph of it at home."

Dr. Fuller returned once more—unannounced—with another doctor whom Fuller introduced as an oculist, who said he wanted to examine Archie's eyes as he had heard about their change in color. In fact, the "oculist" was a prominent neurologist, Dr. Moses Starr. He was also an official "medical examiner in lunacy," and in that capacity he could declare a person legally insane. The two doctors grilled Archie about his Napoleonic trance, and he talked freely about the experience. In Dr. Starr's account, Archie said he could see his name carved in the mantel and his initials in a picture of the Sphinx. During their talk Archie frequently lapsed into trances during which he spoke French. According to Starr, Archie stated that his eyes had changed color, that the shape of his nose and ears had been changed so that he resembled Napoleon, and that he would "lead a holy war in Europe" foretold in the Book of Revelations. Archie would insist that these odd pronouncements came from his subconscious and that he was engaged in scientific research. Dr. Starr stated that Archie believed he was in communication with a spirit and on that basis he officially certified "that he is insane and a proper subject for custody and treatment in some institution for the insane."

As Archie lay in bed reading in his hotel room the following night, the door opened unexpectedly. It was Dr. Starr—who revealed himself as an examiner in lunacy—accompanied by another doctor and two other assistants. Starr said they had come to take him away and grabbed Archie by his left wrist. With his right hand, Archie managed to get hold of a loaded revolver—a relic of his adventures out West—that he always carried while traveling and had stashed under his pillow. Archie leveled the gun "straight at the middle button of Dr. Starr's waistcoat" (he had come in evening clothes, not expecting a tussle), instantly persuading the doctor to release Archie's wrist. Having gained control, Archie turned conciliatory: "I will sit up and discuss the matter with you if you promise not to try any rough tactics." But Starr was not inclined to enter a discussion with an armed man and left.

More determined than ever to commit Archie to an institution, Winty contacted the police commissioner in New York, his old pal from the Porcellian Club at Harvard, Theodore Roosevelt. Winty used to prowl the streets of New York with the commissioner. On the afternoon of March 13, 1897, two plainclothes detectives from police headquarters were dispatched to the Kensington Hotel. They came with a court order for Archie's commitment to an insane asylum, a warrant for his arrest—and strict instructions from Roosevelt that they show Archie every possible courtesy.

When confronted by the detectives, Archie decided "to let these scoundrels have all the rope they want and see if they won't hang themselves." He got out of bed, dressed with the help of his valet, and accompanied the officers in a closed carriage to Grand Central Station. As they rode uptown, Archie chatted amiably, certain that there had been a mistake, and that the entire situation would soon be resolved. After pulling up to the station, one of the detectives left to purchase train tickets. The other officer waited impatiently for his partner to reappear; after a while, he went in to look for him—leaving Archie, the supposed homicidal lunatic, completely alone. Archie took the opportunity to stroll across the street and purchase cigars, so that they could all enjoy a good smoke en route to their destination.

Archie and the detectives then took the twenty-mile train trip to White Plains, a tranquil farm village in Westchester County; from there they took a carriage to a hilltop on the outskirts of town. Archie peered through the window as they turned in at a gateway and made their way through a campuslike setting. Atop the hill was a series of redbrick buildings that had just been completed a few years before. Lacking only the patina of age, and perhaps some ivy on the walls, the place looked like a small New England college. The carriage stopped at the central building, a handsome four-story structure topped by a clock tower, and Archie got out. This would be his new home: the institution for the insane run by the New York Hospital, a place commonly known as Bloomingdale Asylum.

NINE

Four Years Behind the Bars of Bloomingdale

Oppression was the rod that struck the rock
And loosed the fiery floodgates of my tongue. . . .

—Sonnet written by Archie at Bloomingdale

The "Certificate of Lunacy," the legal document that condemned Archie to Bloomingdale for an indefinite stay, has a quaintness about it—almost an innocence—that is jarring. The New York Supreme Court justice who ordered Archie into the asylum bore the whimsical name Henry A. Gildersleeve. (In reality, Gildersleeve was a battle-hardened veteran of the Union army who had fought at Gettysburg and joined Sherman in his vicious "march to the sea.") The questions on the bureaucratic form required by the State Commission in Lunacy were answered in dark ink, with a neat, legible handwriting. The responses were straightforward and concise, and give no hint of the gravity of the consequences that were to ensue once the certificate was signed by the judge. On its face, the document seems to carry no more weight than the less-than-stellar report cards that Archie routinely got at school.

Two official medical examiners interviewed Archie—Doctors Starr and Fuller—and provided the information on the form, which described Archie as being a white male, thirty-four years old, a lawyer by profession. His personal habits were "Cleanly," though his general physical health was described as "Poor . . . Anaemic . . . emaciating." The document noted that he abstained from tobacco, liquor, opium and other drugs, but that he was considered "dangerous" as he was "Violent[,] excited—is armed, threatens people." In answer to questions about the source of his insanity the consulting doctors noted "family anxiety . . . [and] General nervous hereditary influences," and specifically mentioned his paternal aunt who suffered from mental illness.

When Archie later had the chance to see his commitment form, he referred to it as that "amalgam of avarice, malice and mendacity." He vigorously denied two of the most critical assertions on the official papers: first, that he had been previously confined in a mental institution near Paris, presumably during his marriage to Amélie (his ex-wife also refuted that claim), and, second, the location of his legal residence. The document stated that Archie legally resided in New York, at the Kensington Hotel. Archie protested that he was *not* a resident of New York; that he had been a long-standing citizen of Virginia, and that he had been lured to New York for the sole purpose of incarcerating him there under the laws of that state. According to Archie, that single fact made the entire commitment proceedings illegal. But Judge Gildersleeve never heard Archie's side of the story and declared him insane without ever having set eyes on him. The judge dispensed with the usual procedure of examining the "alleged insane person," basing that exemption on the following:

> *The patient is in such a state of excitement and is so easily made dangerous to himself and to others by . . . criticism of or opposition to his delusions that a personal service would be attended by great danger.*
>
> *Signed. H. A. Gildersleeve*

That opinion of Archie's "state of excitement" had obviously been rendered by the doctors and by the original petitioners in the case—Archie's brothers Winty and Lewis, and a cousin from Boston, Arthur Carey. According to the Certificate of Lunacy, Archie's nervous attack had begun in November 1896; but Arthur Carey had not seen Archie for several years and had never been to Merry Mills, so he had no idea of his cousin's recent mental condition. (Nonetheless, Arthur took a keen interest in Archie's sanity for a very practical reason: he had entrusted $25,000 of his deceased brother Harry's estate to Archie for the art prize.) Likewise, Lewis had seen nothing of Archie for some time. Not long after Alida's wedding in October, Lewis retired from his criminal law practice in New York and moved his family to England. Winty hastily summoned Lewis to New York in the wake of Archie's threat in December to have their father's estate audited. While in New York, Lewis heard tales from Winty about their eldest brother's odd behavior; but it's doubtful that Lewis even saw Archie before setting off once more for England. The other family members were scattered to the four winds—Robert in France, Margaret and Elizabeth in England about to embark for India, Willie on the high seas. The commitment proceedings had obviously not been talked over and thought through by the assembled family.

Clearly, Winty was the ringleader. He was the one who had orchestrated the plot to spirit Archie off to New York. He was the one who gathered Lewis and Arthur Carey to the cause. Though Stanford White had helped entice Archie to New York, he refused to join in the official petition to have Archie committed. Since White held Archie's power of attorney, Winty pressed the architect to join in the proceedings, but White declined, not wanting to turn his back on his old friend. Interestingly enough, a half-dozen letters that Stanford White wrote to Archie's law firm in February and March of 1897—the precise time period when Archie was being lured to New York and committed to Bloomingdale—are all missing from White's carefully collected letterbooks at Columbia University's Avery Library. Several of the letters were clearly torn out, and subsequently marked as "void" in the index. Others are just missing, with no official acknowledgment of the fact. When or why these letters were removed—and by whom—is unknown. They perhaps contained information embarrassing to White or to Archie's law partners or to the Chanlers. The loss of the letters is one more bit of evidence that there was a great deal of guilt and regret over Archie's forced incarceration—and that there might also have been some things that had to be covered up.

Once Archie had been placed behind the bars of Bloomingdale, it was almost as if he ceased to exist. The siblings continued to write newsy letters to one another, full of reports of the wandering band of brothers and sisters—this one in Paris, that one in Calcutta, another one gun-running in Cuba—but Archie seemed to vanish. He was almost never mentioned. The siblings exchanged year upon year of letters and never made the slightest reference to their poor brother stuck in an insane asylum—no reports on his condition, no concern expressed over his health. Like Uncle Henry Astor and Amélie, Archie was practically edited out of the family. Margaret never told her children that they had an Uncle Archie until he reappeared like a ghost at Rokeby more than twenty years later.

Amélie was frantic when she heard the news about Archie. What would she and the prince do for money? Amélie didn't dare write to any of the sisters; instead she wrote several letters to Stanford White, who held power of attorney for Archie as well as for her when it came to matters dealing with the share of Chanler property she still controlled. (Cannily, Amélie had never given up her dower rights, a sore point with the siblings.) Amélie asked after her ex-spouse—"I never thought I should have to turn to others for tidings of Archie"—and she complained bitterly of being cut off so thoroughly by the Chanlers that they had not even told her of Alida's engagement and marriage! Amélie needed leverage with the family, and White was her best bet: not only was he her legal representative, but he had always been enchanted with her. White attempted to broker a peace between Elizabeth, the most forgiving of the sisters, and Amélie. But Elizabeth would not relent. Her heart had been broken for her brother Archie when she had seen Amélie and the prince in Italy.

> I told Stanford of my terrible days on Lago Maggiore, watching Troubetzkoy & Amélie make love to each other, & that I knew then that never would I be near them after that— He then understood my having withdrawn from Amélie—almost blessed me for severing my instincts so trenchantly from my worshipping love of her. [He] said "Forgive them Elizabeth. They are in love"— "I do forgive them" I answered, "but I cannot ever see them again." "You are right" he said, "and I'll make Amélie understand."

White advised Elizabeth not to write to Amélie—none of the siblings should communicate with her—"but let things sleep." Amélie understood only too well that she had lost her place at the Astor/Chanler table. That same month she had a nervous breakdown and was committed to a sanatorium in Philadelphia, presumably under the care of Dr. J. Madison Taylor.

It was feared that news of Archie might also unbalance Robert, as he had suffered the earlier breakdown over Amélie and, as everyone knew, he was notoriously odd. At one point Winty called Robert " 'quite weird' . . . but loveable in spite of his ridiculous personal vanity & other eccentricities." At the time of Archie's commitment, Robert was married and living in Paris. His wife, Julia, assumed that the Chanlers would be worried about their younger brother—"you must have thought of him almost immediately"—and wrote from the Champs Elysées. She reassured the siblings that Robert's mental health was fine, and that they were both being vigilant about it. As for the news about Archie, she admitted that it had been a "great shock" to both her and Robert, but, in the end the situation might not be so bad after all:

> On thinking it over, it does not seem so very dreadful, you see I know several people who had the same thing happen to some of their family, & they seem quite resigned to the idea; besides he himself is probably perfectly unconscious, & not at all unhappy.

Unfortunately, Archie was perfectly conscious and furious over the turn of events. He considered himself completely sane, and he believed that his commitment was part of a conspiracy among his siblings to take over his property in North Carolina and to gain control of his estate. He became convinced that it was his money that they were after. What else could prompt such an action by them?

When Elizabeth returned from India the following month and heard the full report of what had transpired, she rushed to visit Archie in Bloomingdale. She was the first sibling to do so. Archie ranted on and on to her about the family's greedy motives. He was certain that dear, sweet Elizabeth was not part of the cabal. But when she tried to persuade him that there was no such conspiracy—Chanlers would *never* haggle about money, she argued—Archie turned angry. He pointed to the bars at the window and asked if that indeed was an indication of their concern and brotherly love. She tried to soothe him, gently telling him that the bars were only there to keep him from running away. Her casual manner in speaking about something that Archie considered a personal atrocity was more than he could bear. He suddenly believed that Bessie, too, was part of the plot. Archie became agitated, and demanded that Elizabeth leave and never come back. He didn't need her sympathy, but he predicted that his brothers would need it "by the time I get through with them." Elizabeth never returned to Bloomingdale.

It took some nine months before another family member managed to visit the asylum in White Plains. Willie stopped by to see Archie in January or early February of 1898, just before departing for another round of adventure—this time to aid insurgents fighting the Spanish-led government in Cuba. Archie was suspicious at first, certain that Willie had been sent as a family spy. He and Willie were hardly on good terms. They had not seen each other for more than a year because they'd had a titanic argument. The incident occurred in December 1896, probably in the wake of Archie's infamous boardroom battle at the Kensington Hotel. The two brothers chanced to meet on a southbound train when Archie was heading back to Merry Mills, and Willie was en route to a Southern farm where he was breeding racehorses. Willie's horses were doing well on the New York race circuit, but there had been insinuations in the press about cheating involving one of his recent winners, a horse named Salvacea. Archie became incensed that Willie's integrity had been impugned, and that his younger brother had neither demanded an apology nor sued the paper. The family honor was at stake. Willie laughed the matter off, and broadly hinted that he had been guilty after all. Archie got furious, and the two men nearly came to blows on the train. They had not communicated since.

Thus Archie was caught completely off guard when Willie's card was delivered to his rooms at Bloomingdale, indicating that his younger brother had arrived for a visit. They spent nearly two hours amiably discussing Willie's budding political career and all manner of other conversational gambits, carefully skirting any mention of their blow-up on the train or of the unfortunate business about Archie's being confined in Bloomingdale. But as Willie got up to leave, Archie issued a word of warning for his turncoat brothers Winty and Lewis and cousin Arthur Carey, who had committed him. It was inevitable, he said, that the "majesty of the law" would take its course, and the three men would end up in Sing Sing for their perjury. With that in mind, Archie suggested that "the said three gentlemen with their wives and children emigrate without delay to the Argentine Confederation, as [he] understood that extradition did not go there." Willie's visit was the last one made by a family member. Archie sat in Bloomingdale for nearly four years, and not one of his siblings ever tried to see him again.

Archie became convinced that the only reason he was not being rescued from Bloomingdale was the unfortunate timing of the Spanish-American War; it had distracted the country from his personal plight. He told his doctor that as soon as the war ended, the people would rise up, especially those in the South, to rectify this gross miscarriage of justice.

His own family was certainly obsessed with the political situation in Cuba. Willie took up the Cuban revolutionary cause wholeheartedly, and smuggled guns and other war supplies to the rebels.

He reveled in the cloak-and-dagger danger as he eluded Spanish gunboats, became a colonel in the Cuban army, and was finally commissioned an officer in the U.S. Volunteers. Theodore Roosevelt got all the headlines for his famous charge up San Juan Hill, but Willie, who was caught in furious fighting himself, managed to poke a little fun at his friend just before the attack. As Roosevelt sat atop his horse, scouting troop movements, and bullets began to fly close by, he turned to withdraw. Willie, nearby, yelled to him: "Don't move, Teddy! That's a bully place to be photographed!" Willie knew a little something about calling attention to himself. Years later he virtually took singlehanded credit for instigating the Spanish-American War, boasting that he was the one who had engineered the destruction of the *Maine.* At the least, he got his other family members interested in the war. Winty joined in the adventure, getting his arm shot in the process and muttering memorably to a rescuer, "This is no place for a married man." Lewis and Robert waited too long, and regretted missing the action. Alida's husband, Temple Emmet, looked dashing in his uniform, but never quite made it into battle. While in Tampa with troops awaiting shipment to Cuba, he was recalled by his wife, who had come to her senses about the risks involved. According to family lore, Alida drove into the army camp in a buggy and called her husband out of the ranks, announcing in loud tones, "You must come home, Temple. I find that this war is dangerous." Margaret had better luck. As a nursing volunteer for the Red Cross, she never made it to Cuba (the women were turned back and not allowed entry), but went on to Puerto Rico, where she nursed wounded soldiers.

Archie fought his own solitary battle within "that living Hell, a madhouse cell," while his siblings concerned themselves with matters of international war and peace. In their defense, Archie's brothers and sisters believed that he was being well cared for. The asylum was brand-new, staffed by well-known alienists (the term used for psychiatrists at that time), and run according to the enlightened nineteenth-century principle of "moral treatment" of the mentally ill. There were no more chains or brutal beatings or attempts to terrify patients (one German asylum used snake-filled dungeons), as had been the accepted eighteenth-century mode of therapy. In Archie's era there was a firm belief in the curative power of tranquil surroundings and humane living conditions. A pastoral retreat in the country was considered the most advantageous environment for the mentally ill—thus the New York Hospital had recently moved the asylum from the former hamlet of Bloomingdale in upper Manhattan, where life had become increasingly hectic. (Columbia University purchased the site from the hospital. One building still survives from the lunatic asylum—it is the oldest building on campus.)

The grounds at the White Plains asylum covered several hundred acres.* The prestigious landscape firm founded by Frederick Law Olmsted created portions of the lush, campuslike environment. Its winding pathways, open vistas, and handsome plantings were not only aesthetically pleasing, but were considered part of the treatment. Doctors encouraged a regular regimen of "bodily exercise," though Archie complained bitterly of a "total deprivation of horseback exercise." The main building had a gymnasium, and there was also a separate "Recreation Pavilion" on the grounds. A bowling alley offered diversion, and a large greenhouse on the front lawn encouraged patients to take an interest in horticulture. Part of the acreage included a working farm that supplied all the produce needed for the hospital. Patients gardened, and tended to the chickens and cows that supplied the asylum with eggs and milk. It was a totally self-contained world, and on the surface it looked quite homey and pleasant.

Archie lived in a spacious suite with two rooms and a private bathroom in the Macy Villa, the plushest quarters available for male patients "who could pay a good price." It cost $100 per week for his room, board, doctors, and round-the-clock care by two alternating attendants. This money was paid out of Archie's financial accounts now under the control of the court; the legally declared lunatic had

---

*The campus is still being used for the treatment of the mentally ill. It is currently known as the New York Hospital–Cornell Medical Center, Westchester Division.

no say in the matter. In contrast to Archie's princely payments, the other patients paid an average of $12.98 per week. The exorbitant cost rankled Archie to no end—that he was being kept against his will in this place, and then charged more than $5,000 per year for the privilege. His quarters didn't even feel very grand to him; he described it as "solitary confinement, in a two-roomed cell."

He was one of about 315 patients at Bloomingdale—roughly half men and half women—who lived on separate sides of the campus; they ranged in age from sixteen to sixty. Though a handful were paupers unable to pay for treatment, the vast majority of the clientele were well-to-do members of high society. Archie referred bitterly to Bloomingdale as the "Bastille of the Four Hundred," that inner circle of New York society so designated by his great-aunt Caroline Astor. Bloomingdale's governing board sounded like the roster of an upper-crust Manhattan club, and included a Schuyler, a Beekman, several Kings, and the eminent lawyer Joseph Hodges Choate. Tea was served to the inmates every afternoon from a sterling silver tea service engraved with the monogram *B.A.* for Bloomingdale Asylum. Archie described how Bloomingdale was a useful tool for the Four Hundred: troublesome adolescents who defied their parents could be hidden from view, and white-collar criminals could dodge prison and avoid besmirching their family names. The thief who lived across from Archie spent his time strumming his guitar and singing (Archie said he had only a "fairish" voice) "instead of making shoes at Sing Sing." After three months that man was released. According to Archie, there were other patients, like himself, who had been railroaded. There was a woman at Bloomingdale who had been declared insane only because she objected to her husband's patronage of whorehouses. He was a doctor, so he arranged for several of his fellow physicians to pronounce his wife insane. She was released only after agreeing never to bring up her husband's philandering again.

Exactly what kind of treatment Archie received is unknown. There are apparently no medical documents concerning his stay at

Bloomingdale that survive, a not-uncommon reality of nineteenth-century psychiatric record-keeping in asylums. Doctors of that era often did not keep a detailed account of day-to-day treatment; and if they did, such records were considered their personal property, which they could keep or destroy as they pleased. Archie's case became a cause célèbre, so the alienists at Bloomingdale might have been quite happy to make his records quietly disappear. Archie had little to say about the treatment. He claimed that the doctors did not really have much contact with him, that they only saw him for about five to ten minutes a day, and that they spent most of that time trying to convince Archie that he was insane. These alienists were, in Archie's estimation, "as smooth spoken and deceptive in their manner as any set of confidence men you ever encountered."

Archie spent all of his time in the company of "keepers"—mainly burly Irish attendants—who watched over him twenty-four hours a day and reported what he said and did. Archie claimed the keepers thought he was perfectly sane, though he did have a serious run-in with at least one of them—his favorite attendant, a six-foot-tall, strapping athlete of two hundred pounds who had been assigned to Archie upon his arrival in March 1897. Archie enjoyed his company, and the two of them played the card game picquet every night. But in July of 1898 the keeper, who liked to take a drink, went on a bender (perhaps he had played one too many hands of picquet) and did not appear for work the next day. Archie could not abide such dereliction of duty, and he confronted his attendant the next day. In short order the "warm-hearted honest Irishman" had his hands around Archie's throat. The keeper had several inches and about thirty pounds on his patient, so Archie called for help through the barred window. ("I may say that I have a rather powerful voice, and a windpipe, which experience proved, a keeper could not compress," Archie later wrote proudly.) None of the other attendants bothered to respond to his screams (perhaps they too had endured Archie's hauteur and sarcasm); as soon as the keeper yelled for help, however, the cavalry arrived. Archie celebrated his pitched battle in a lyric:

Within this cell I for my life have fought.
Wrestl'd and struggl'd for it hand to hand.
My keeper's fingers round my throat were caught,
With deadly hate he pressed my strong weasand . . .
By fortune and by strength I won the day.
Now knows he well that choking me "don't pay."

Archie wrote four hundred sonnets while in Bloomingdale—proof in itself of his sanity, according to the wordsmith. He contended that even the doctors agreed that he was a master poet and that he had "greater command over the Shakespearian form of sonnet than anyone but Shakespeare." Though he had failed as a novelist years earlier, Archie claimed that he "assiduously cultivated the pen" inside Bloomingdale, a natural outgrowth of his newfound psychic gift for "automatic writing"—and his being incarcerated with "three authors of world-note." Archie does not mention who those three authors were, but among the inmates was at least one journalist who had been at Bloomingdale for some months, being treated for morphine addiction. As the newspaperman prepared to leave the asylum, Archie saw an opportunity; he would send out an SOS and try to get legal help to extricate himself from his "living tomb." He gave the newspaperman a lengthy letter he had written (when later published, it ran to thirty-four pages), and asked him to forward it to the Commonwealth's Attorney in Charlottesville, Virginia. Archie had penned the letter outlining his predicament some months before, but had no way of sending it as his mail was being carefully censored by the doctors. It was virtually impossible for him to communicate with the outside world about his situation; but if he could entrust the letter to the journalist, he would outsmart the asylum authorities. Archie was certain that the lawyer in Charlottesville, Micajah Woods, would jump immediately to his aid, in light of the fact that a citizen of Virginia was being victimized and virtually held captive by New York law. In addition, Woods was a personal friend, and Archie had dined at his house.

In vivid detail, Archie described the horror of life in an insane asylum—even one that purported to treat its residents with kid-gloves. He was living among violent patients, some of whom had to be carted off in straitjackets. To protect himself from potentially homicidal inmates, Archie pushed a table against his door at night. On several occasions when he had failed to do so, he discovered intruders; one night he found a "gigantic maniac," over six feet tall and wearing only a nightshirt, wandering in his quarters. Archie had to drive the man out.

Living amid such chaos, having to endure the screams of fellow patients, would cause anyone to "go stark raving mad," in Archie's words. The food was nearly inedible, and Archie became convinced that it was poisoned with "ptomaines." After a certain point he insisted that his bread come from New York City, as he hated—and distrusted—the locally made product. Though he was not permitted to carry any money, Archie could order whatever luxuries he wanted and have them put on his tab—but it was small consolation.

Archie's impassioned plea for justice did not have the desired result. The Virginia lawyer did nothing. But the journalist scored a huge coup. He raced back to the newsroom and reported that one of the heirs to the Astor fortune, the famous Archie Chanler, was in a madhouse. The Chanlers had spread word that Archie was abroad for an extended stay; but on the morning of October 14, 1897, members of New York society picked up the *Times* and were startled to read the headlines:

MR. CHANLER NEEDS REST

Cause of the Well-Known New York Clubman's Commitment to Bloomingdale.

SOME QUEER HALLUCINATIONS

The Former Husband of Amélie Rives Breaks Down Mentally and Is Placed in an Asylum by His Nearest Friends.

The article described how Archie had been "quietly" committed to Bloomingdale, and that the cover story of his being abroad had been disseminated only to preserve his privacy. His law partner Harry Philip, interviewed for the article, insisted that Archie himself did not want anyone to know his whereabouts, "and for that reason has taken extra precaution to maintain his seclusion." Archie must have bristled when he read that sentence, for he was desperate to have his plight known. He was incarcerated against his will and, thanks to the blanket of silence maintained by the asylum and his family and friends, no one was even aware of it! Philip claimed that Archie was not insane, but just "overtaxed" and exhausted by the Roanoke Rapids business; he categorically ruled out the emotional stress of his breakup with Amélie as a cause. The article then raked over the whole story of Archie's marriage to the famous author of *The Quick or the Dead?*—their troubled relationship, their divorce, and then Amélie's subsequent marriage to the prince.

The public loved all the salacious details and the family quaked. Willie, the only male Chanler in town, handled questions posed by a reporter for the *Tribune.* "My brother has been in the asylum for a few months, [it had actually been seven long months] but is improving, and we hope for his complete recovery," Willie diplomatically told the journalist. "He has a splendid constitution, and there is every reason to expect that with rest he will cease to suffer from the nervous exhaustion which has been his trouble." Circling the wagons, Willie urged his sisters *not* to "volunteer information about the case," and surely *not* to veer from the party line that he had just spouted to the press. The *Times* article did admit that Archie himself expressed a "strong objection to his incarceration," insisting that he had been committed illegally to the New York institution, as he was a citizen of Virginia. As for his "alleged hallucinations," the paper stated that Archie believed he was the reincarnation of Napoleon, and that he kept in his rooms at Bloomingdale two pictures of the emperor; he also had a miniature roulette wheel there, and said that he had devised a system to beat the house at Monte Carlo. Archie objected to the paper's description of both of his supposed "hallucinations," but he had no forum. Only his brother and his law partner had been interviewed.

Humiliated at his seemingly hopeless plight, Archie resigned from all his New York clubs—the Knickerbocker, Union, Manhattan, Metropolitan, Century, University, Racquet, Calumet, Lambs, Players, Democratic, and St. Anthony, as well as the Sons of the American Revolution and the Alumni Association of Columbia College. He remained a member of the French Club—perhaps it was an oversight, or maybe it was in homage to Napoleon. He bristled at the New York blue-bloods whom he blamed for his incarceration, and his allegiance to the South intensified. In Virginia Archie was still a beloved figure. He retained his membership in the Keswick Hunt Club (organized for the purpose of "Social Intercourse and Fox and Drag Hunting"), a club he helped found not long before he was lured to New York by Stanford White. Archie's money had doubtless made the club possible; some of the other members had contributed hound puppies in lieu of cash. The alleged madman's contribution was not forgotten: when the club's charter was formally registered with the local county court in March 1898, John Armstrong Chanler was listed as president—a full year after he had been committed to an asylum.

Despite being a member of the New York bar, with his own law firm—and a partner who vehemently maintained in the press that Archie was sane—he turned to a Virginia lawyer to help spring him from Bloomingdale. Archie believed that the crux of his case was based on his Virginia citizenship. In his appeal to the Charlottesville attorney Micajah Woods, Archie advised a habeas corpus action in a federal court. With the power of the Astor family against him, Archie did not believe he would ever be able to get a fair hearing in a New York court—and he regarded New York law on commitment proceedings as patently unjust. He was outraged that he had been incarcerated without even being given the chance to prove he was sane.

> It seems fair that you should be allowed to confront your accuser—a common murderer has that privilege—and be

> heard in defense . . . before being summarily arrested like a malefactor, as I have been, and put behind bars without a trial for an indefinite period, perchance for life.

The loophole of New York State law through which the judge could dispense with having the accused lunatic brought before him (such as happened with Judge Gildersleeve) opened the way to all manner of corruption, according to Archie:

> In other words a citizen of the State of New York can be condemned and imprisoned without a hearing. All that is required to deprive a citizen of the "Empire State" of his liberty, is, one or two false witnesses, two dishonest doctors, and a judge who can swallow conflicting sworn statements without a qualm. No defence is allowed to the accused.
>
> This is truly the "Empire State." I sometimes wonder, as I look through the bars of my cell, how such things can be, outside the Russian Empire State.

Archie threatened to sue everyone—his family, the hospital, and anyone else he believed was a party to his incarceration. On Saturday, December 4, 1897, Winty huddled with his brother Willie, Archie's valet, and the supervising doctor at Bloomingdale. There seemed to be no discussion of Archie's health at the meeting; rather they conferred about the legal repercussions that might ensue now that Archie had successfully contacted a lawyer. Earlier that day, Winty and Stanford White had forced Archie's law partner, Maxwell, to resign from the board of the Roanoke Rapids Power Company. With Archie in Bloomingdale, Winty and White had been able to run the North Carolina enterprise without interference. In fact, on March 23, 1897, only ten days after Archie was committed, Stanford White wrote a rather upbeat note about business prospects to Elizabeth Chanler—even advising the holdout sister, Margaret, to take stock in the textile empire that Archie had founded. White wrote from the

Players Club on Gramercy Park to the sisters, who were in England about to depart for India.

> *My beloved Elizabeth . . .*
>
> *I wish I were with you in your old Heathen palaces. . . . Everything is going along in the usual sixty mile an hour gait with me. . . . I have been seeing a lot of Wintie lately. He is a brick & of the good old sort. I am getting into self threader—Roanoke Rapids & all sorts of things—tell Margaret she will have to take some stock in it. Dear old Archie (as you will probably have heard when you get this) has been sick in mind & body. He is getting all right in body & well in mind I hope before long—Bless his heart. . . . Bring me home a pretty little Indian girl. Give her (Margaret I mean) my love—& lots . . . to thyself—& mighty glad we all will be to see you*
>
> *affectionately Stanford*

The cheerful tone of White's note was in stark contrast to "Dear old Archie's" situation. Similarly, Archie's brothers and sisters did their best not to think about him. That changed, however, when Archie managed to break through the wall of silence and retain a lawyer. Winty—as the prime target of Archie's anger—was especially worried. The doctor at Bloomingdale assured Winty that "though A. had sent his case to a lawyer he at present did not intend to press his suit but keep quiet, get cured & discharged & then send us all to jail." That seemed small consolation. At the advice of the doctor and the family estate lawyer, Henry Lewis Morris, Winty immediately hired another attorney just in case Archie should suddenly bring suit against the family. He retained Egerton Winthrop Jr. (the polo-fancying cousin Archie had once used to spread news of his engagement to Amélie) and his blue-blood partners at the New York law firm of Jay & Candler to represent the Chanlers' interests.

Before leaving town—and he seemed very eager to do that—Winty went to see Dr. Starr, who had committed Archie, and asked him to report on Archie's progress. He wanted the assessment in two days. Winty feared that by remaining in the city he would inevitably get drawn deeper into the problem. "I can put everything in Egerton's hands & go away," he wrote to his wife. Winty pointed out the advantage of his being scarce: if Archie's lawyers absolutely insisted, he could be sent for; but if he left New York, he might not be forced to appear. Archie's Southern lawyer never took up the cudgel against the Chanlers. In fact, he did nothing. He might not have been eager to face down the Astor interests on their home court. He might also have had his own doubts about Archie's state of mind.

It was the Chanler family's lawyers who made the first move. On June 12, 1899, the firm of Jay & Candler successfully petitioned the New York Supreme Court to declare Archie incompetent and hand over the management of his affairs to a "Committee." The petition was taken up in a Manhattan courtroom before a jury in the late afternoon. The official record notes that there was "no appearance on the part of the alleged lunatic." Archie had been in bed for three weeks with pain in his spine, and refused to go. The superintendent of Bloomingdale, Dr. Samuel Lyon, discounted the pain, saying it was delusional. Archie, naturally, disagreed, but the jury did not hear his version of events.

In truth, Archie probably could have gone to the hearing. He was in pain, but he was in even greater fear of the proceedings. An emissary from the Chanler family had visited Archie and advised him to attend the hearing, saying it was his only hope of ever getting out of the asylum. But Archie was certain that in a New York courtroom, the Astor/Chanler interests and the "plutocrats" who ran Bloomingdale would surely triumph. As a lawyer, he also knew that the outcome of the proceedings could seal his fate forever. He could not see the advantage of attending; by not going he at least had the basis for a later appeal. Archie argued that "examination at the hands of a distinguished and honest man is the last thing I would avoid," but these "Star Chamber" proceedings were another matter entirely.

Doctors Carlos MacDonald and Austin Flint, prominent alienists from New York who had been hired by the Chanler family's lawyers to examine Archie and render a verdict on his sanity, took the stand. They had only visited the patient twice in Bloomingdale, but both agreed that he was insane. In fact, Dr. MacDonald pronounced that Archie suffered from a textbook case of paranoia. "It is the most striking case of paranoia that I have ever seen in my life. . . . It presents all the essential and diagnostic signs of that disease—delusion, grandeur, exaltation, conspiracy and change of personality." The disease was considered incurable; the only recourse, a lifetime of incarceration.

The hearing had something of a kangaroo-court atmosphere. There were no witnesses on Archie's behalf. Stanford White, who held Archie's power of attorney, did not attend. By this time White wished he had never taken on legal responsibility for his old friend; it was turning into a nightmare. "I am in a perfect hell of a mess over Archie's affairs & my own," White had written to Augustus Saint-Gaudens the previous winter. When the hearing in June took place, White wanted no part of witnessing Archie's demise. During his testimony Winty was asked why the famous architect was not present in the courtroom. "Because he was . . . [Archie's] friend," Winty replied, "and the only person in whom he had absolute confidence; he did not want to appear in these proceedings; it is a matter of delicacy with him." Proceedings began at 4:00 p.m., an unusually late starting time—and a guarantee that jury members would be eager for a fast conclusion so they could get home for dinner. After all the witnesses had given testimony and the trial seemed to be at an end, the Chanler lawyers cannily introduced the possibility of adjourning until a later date when Archie could be produced. The jurors, naturally enough, did not want to prolong their civic duty. It all seemed so cut-and-dried, they did not see the point of extending the proceedings. The jurors said they wanted to render the verdict immediately, and that they had no need to see Archie. They concurred with the testimony of Dr. Flint:

> It seems to me his case is so plain and distinct that it is practically unnecessary; and if it should be necessary to use

> force to bring him down here against his will[,] I think it will be detrimental to him. Those are my views, although I quite agree with the principle that a lunatic ought to be produced in Court if he can.

It took the jury little time to pronounce Archie incurably insane and unable to manage his own affairs. His estate would be taken over for him, and all financial matters removed from his control. Archie's fortune was thenceforth out of reach. And he was sentenced to a lifetime behind the bars of Bloomingdale.

If Archie indeed suffered from paranoia, then the selection of the Committee to oversee his affairs was guaranteed to make him even more paranoid. The Committee consisted of one person, Prescott Hall Butler—a wealthy New York lawyer and brother-in-law of Stanford White, Archie's betrayer. Worse, Butler was a partner with Joseph Choate in the white-shoe law firm of Evarts, Choate & Beaman. How convenient, Archie thought, for Choate was also on the board of governors of Bloomingdale. The hospital was making a pretty penny from Archie, so it was naturally to the board's advantage to keep him on as a long-term paying resident. "Did you ever see a prettier bunco game?" Archie wrote.

> P. H. Butler quietly skins me to the tune of five thousand dollars per annum ($5000), that's what I'm made to pay against my will, not counting extras. . . . Prescott Hall Butler rakes off five thousand per annum from my annual stack of income chips and drops it into the "kitty" of the concern his partner is a director of, and [for] which his . . . firm is the legal counsel. How is that for high? Is it rich enough for your sporting blood, or isn't it. Prescott Hall Butler would be a fool, would have no eye for business, did he not hold me here for life. At a low risk, I am good for twenty years yet. That means a cool hundred thousand, not counting extras. Those extras, by the way, are made out by the concern for which his firm is legal counsel, and of which he is the Auditor! It smells like a bit of a "con" game to me.

Archie brooded over the injustice. He demanded that he speak face to face with his Committee. Prescott Hall Butler came to Archie's rooms that summer for their one and only meeting. Butler stayed for about an hour, during which time Archie talked eagerly about business plans. The previous summer, while Archie was in Bloomingdale, the inventor Albert Legg had finally perfected his self-threading mechanism so that it could fit onto a Singer sewing machine. At long last, it was time to cash in. Archie had begged Stanford White, who had power of attorney, to begin filling the four thousand orders that dated back to the Chicago world's fair in 1893. For years Archie's Self-Threading Company had continued to get letters about the orders. Two thousand mechanisms had already been produced, but White refused to sell them; instead he warehoused them in an "ordinary dwelling house," an uninsured one. (A few years later the house burned to the ground, along with some $20,000 worth of the self-threaders.) Archie further claimed that an American millionaire industrialist had approached Legg and proposed buying world patent rights, including U.S. rights, for $2.5 million. White never pursued the possibility. Archie begged Butler to follow up on the offer.

Butler was unmoved by Archie's excitement over the self-threading invention. The Committee said he didn't believe in investing in patents; he'd done it once and lost money. He was a conservative man and was not interested in risky investments. Archie was apoplectic. All his years of struggle were for naught. The time had finally come to market the self-threader. The company could now fill the orders they already had. And Archie believed that new business could be easily drummed up by hiring agents who'd work on commission only, no salaries. The international patent rights could be sold for a hefty sum. But Butler refused to listen to Archie's pleas. He left Archie's quarters at Bloomingdale and, despite repeated requests, never returned. Archie became convinced that his business was being intentionally sabotaged; it was, he believed, an "assassination." After all, if his industrial scheme were successful, it would prove that he was sane.

Archie was determined to find a way out of Bloomingdale. He had already been given the run of the grounds at the asylum—he was permitted to wander freely by himself for an hour or so, a license granted because, in the words of Dr. Lyon, the hospital superintendent, "he is a very honorable man" and he promised not to attempt an escape. In the summer of 1899, facing lifetime incarceration in the asylum, Archie asked for the additional privilege of walking beyond the gates of Bloomingdale without a keeper. For more than two years at the hospital his conduct had been "so exemplary and docile" that the superintendent agreed. Archie set a plan in motion.

Despite a painful back, Archie trained himself to walk farther and farther from the asylum every day. He incrementally quickened his pace, as he was only permitted off the grounds for a few hours at a time. By January of 1900 he could cover twelve miles in three hours. He chose a post office six miles from the asylum—far enough away not to arouse suspicion—and began sending and receiving mail under an alias. In this way he circumvented one of the most rigid rules of the asylum: that no communication could be sent or received without first being scrutinized by hospital authorities. He continued to write to his attorney Micajah Woods in Charlottesville, but his entreaties were ignored. In March he finally received a letter from Woods saying that Archie was better off seeking help from "some prominent friend of yours in New York." Archie wrote a series of letters to two New York lawyers, but months rolled by and he got no response. Archie later wrote that "by the middle of October, 1900, [my] . . . patience began to wear." He came to believe that he personified the old adage, "Give a dog a bad name and hang him"; for in the court of public opinion he was a convicted madman who should be avoided at all costs. In November, Archie tried a third attorney, a man "whom he had known intimately in the past"—probably his law partner Maxwell, who had been forced off the board of the Roanoke Rapids Power Company by Winty. Archie persuaded the lawyer to meet with him surreptitiously at a distance from the asylum. The conference was friendly enough, but despite Archie's pleas, the attorney would not take on the case. Archie asked if he might borrow ten dollars. His old cohort doubtless felt sorry for the convicted lunatic—a millionaire and scion of the Astor clan who literally did not have a dollar in his pocket—and gave him the money. Archie escaped the next day.

He slipped through the gates of Bloomingdale on Thanksgiving Eve (the same day his great-grandfather, William B. Astor, had died twenty-five years before) and made his way to the White Plains station, where he boarded a train for New York. At Grand Central, Archie sent a telegram to Dr. J. Madison Taylor, Silas Weir Mitchell's chief clinician and the Philadelphia doctor who had treated Amélie for a number of years. Over time Archie had gotten to know and trust Taylor, so in his hour of need he turned to him. Archie wrote the telegram under a pseudonym—he identified himself as John Childe, and said that he was a lawyer representing John Armstrong Chanler, and that he would like to meet with him that evening in Philadelphia.

Archie emerged onto the sidewalks of New York. It had been nearly four years since he had seen the city, though he had closely followed the ins and outs of life in Gotham from Bloomingdale. Every day he had read cover to cover the five daily newspapers he subscribed to—the *World,* the *Sun,* the *Journal,* the *Herald,* and the *Tribune* (notably absent was the preferred newspaper of plutocrats, the *Times*). He "blue-pencilled" the articles he read, underlined passages, and commented on what he considered lies. He saved every one of the papers he had received—they stood in stacks around his room; the doctors pointed to this as yet another manifestation of his illness. Archie, however, considered it research. He could follow the vicissitudes of the marketplace, as well as the comings and goings of his own family. His siblings turned up regularly in the social notes, and the vast wealth of the Astors was fodder for the populist press. On New Year's Day in 1899 he opened the Sunday edition of the *World* and found visual evidence of his family's legacy. Illustrations of block after block of Manhattan real estate, including all of the individual buildings therein—grand hotels and churches and tenements and mansions, all cheek by jowl—ran across an entire two-page spread in the magazine section. The Astors owned all of it. It was a stunning display of "wealth accumulated by one family that taxes human credulity—a princely domain in New York City." As for the sheer amount of real estate involved:

> It would line a thoroughfare seven miles long—a brisk walk of two hours would not traverse it, passing $15,000 worth of property every step. . . . In itself this property would cover the area of a big city. It is hard for the human mind to grasp the immensity of such a landed fortune. It surpasses the dream of avarice and runs into the hazy infinitude of nine figures.

But Archie's inheritance would not help him now. In fact, it was a hindrance. The whole power and might of the Astor/Chanler family were arrayed against him. He was a fugitive not only from the asylum, but from the law that had placed him there, and from his own family. Thus he hid his face as he passed over the Astor property en route to the docks and the Jersey City ferry. In New Jersey he boarded a train for Philadelphia, where he went directly to see Dr. Taylor. Archie introduced himself as the attorney John Childe. At first Dr. Taylor did not recognize his old acquaintance, who had shaved off his mustache and had aged since he'd last seen him six years before; but, after conversing a few minutes, the doctor suddenly realized with whom he was speaking. Archie admitted the deception and begged the doctor to help him. He wanted to be placed under scientific observation for six months; he wanted to be proven sane in the court of science—and then overturn the legal ruling against him. As a certified incompetent, Archie had no rights whatsoever. He was a fugitive from the law, subject to arrest.

Dr. Taylor sympathized with Archie's plight and took him in. He placed him in a private sanatorium on Chestnut Street and observed him closely on an almost daily basis for a little over six months.

Archie was free to leave at any time, but did not. He submitted to the probing questions and critical gaze of Dr. Taylor until early June, when the sanatorium closed for the summer. The neurologist declared Archie perfectly sane and capable of managing his own affairs. He then turned Archie over to the care of a Dr. Darlington, who ran a "private retreat for nervous patients" at his house in the country outside of Philadelphia. Archie stayed there for about a month and a half for further observation, taking meals and conversing with the physician's family during that time. Dr. Darlington concurred with Dr. Taylor's assessment.

In the meantime, Archie's family and the officials at Bloomingdale were baffled. When he escaped the asylum, Archie could not resist taking a parting shot (metaphorically) at the superintendent, Dr. Lyon, who had testified against him in the 1899 hearing. Archie penned a brief note to his nemesis—"My dear Doctor," the letter began,

> *You have always said I am insane. You have always said that I believe I am the reincarnation of Napoleon Bonaparte. As a learned and sincere man, you, therefore, will not be surprised when I take French leave.*
>
> *Yours, with regret that we must part,*
> *J. A. Chanler*

"French leave" indeed. Archie had assumed the eighteenth-century French custom of leaving without saying good-bye to the host. In military parlance, taking French leave simply means going AWOL; but in typical fashion, Archie had departed with a gesture of erudition and sarcasm.

Neither the asylum authorities nor the Chanler family wanted news of the escape to leak. For days the guards from Bloomingdale scoured the grounds and the surrounding woods and countryside, in search of Archie. When they came up empty, Archie's brother Lewis finally went to the police. The press, of course, loved it. On December 5, 1900, headlines in the *New York Herald* screamed:

CHANLER ESCAPES
Amelia Rives' First Husband
IS OUT OF ASYLUM
Search Fails to Find Wealthy Demented Man Who Left
Bloomingdale Institution . . .
Former Wife, Princess Troubetzkoy, Also Insane.

The article included an image of Archie, and an even larger one of Amélie. Once more, Archie's troubles were trumped by the siren. Their unhappy marriage and divorce were cited as contributing factors in Archie's "hopelessly insane" condition. Reporters for both the *Herald* and the *Times* also alluded to Amélie's insanity, the *Herald* noting that she was being "cared for by attendants at Castle Hill near Charlottesville, Va.," and the *Times* mentioning that since remarrying she had "shown evidence of mental trouble, having fled from her home, to be found later wandering in the Virginia mountains."

As for Archie's whereabouts, no one had a clue. The authorities feared suicide and dredged several ponds in search of his body. Whenever a dead vagrant's body turned up, rumor would run rampant that it was the young eccentric millionaire. Stories spread that he had been seen in Washington, Virginia, and Europe. On Christmas Day, much of the Chanler family—minus Archie, of course—gathered around the dining table at Rokeby and raised their glasses in a toast: "To all who have been here; to all who are here; to all who would like to be here." Presumably Archie was in their thoughts, regardless of where he might be. Winty, in Europe, was convinced that Archie was alive and well. After a visit from his brother Lewis, he wrote confidently to his wife:

> *Archie is in Paris, we have every reason to suppose. He is all right and money has reached him. . . . When Archie left Bloomingdale, Lewis says every man he met was sure that Archie was after*

him particularly. Alice [Lewis's wife] made Lewis carry a pistol. Mrs. Morris [wife of Henry Lewis Morris, the family estate attorney] wouldn't let Mr. Morris leave the house, and once actually shut him up in a closet when there came a ring at the door late at night. Stanford White was sure that Archie had only left in order to kill him and so on. It is all very sad of course, but the Good God sends laughter in order to save us from madness.

Winty's information about Archie was, of course, completely wrong. And where that money actually went remains a mystery.

Generations of Chanlers have also wondered how Archie managed his escape so perfectly. Someone must have helped him, perhaps met him beyond the grounds of Bloomingdale and shuttled him away. Over the years, several candidates have been proposed, including Archie's valet, Hartnett, or even George Galvin, the loyal manservant to Willie. Galvin would have been acting under Willie's orders. Despite his feud with Archie, Willie had not been a party to the original commitment petition, and he had been the only brother to visit him in Bloomingdale. The sheer adventure of busting his brother out of an asylum sounded like something Willie would love. Several family members came to believe that theory; but others objected strenuously. It seems plausible that Willie would orchestrate such an event, except for one salient fact: he never boasted about it. If Willie had pulled off such a heist, he surely would have bragged about it endlessly; in fact, he would have taken pleasure in pointing it out to his siblings. There was no end of competitiveness among them; and Willie, especially, couldn't resist taking credit for extraordinary acts of rebelliousness. This was, after all, the man who claimed to have blown up the *Maine.* He probably *wished* he had rescued Archie, but it's doubtful that he did.

Archie was adamant that no one from the outside had helped in his escape, that he'd managed to vanish on his own. Yet there remains a lingering suspicion about that assertion, and a play that Archie wrote in 1914, titled *Robbery Under Law or The Battle of the Millionaires,* points to an intriguing possibility. Over the years, all of Archie's "fictional" works were based entirely on his own life. Not just based on them, but mirror reflections of them. He was his own best subject, and his poetry, stories, novels, and plays inevitably re-created personal events. In his prologue to *Robbery Under Law,* Archie described the play as a "photographic exposition of cold, hard, every-day facts."

In almost every detail and character the play is autobiographical. The main character, Hugh Stutfield, bears the same name that Archie used years earlier in his novel that hashed over his real-life struggles with Amélie. In this play Stutfield and Archie have a virtually identical story: both are millionaires orphaned by parents who die of pneumonia; both are educated at Rugby and Columbia, and study psychology at the latter school; both initiate a system of art scholarships based on Napoleon Bonaparte's Prix de Rome; both invest heavily in a self-threading patent that was invented by the "genius . . . Albert Wedge" in the play, and by Albert Legg in reality; both own extensive real estate and water power rights on the Roanoke River in North Carolina, as well as valuable Manhattan property and choice acreage along the Hudson. In a slight twist of fact, Stutfield's estate in Virginia is named "Rokeby." Amélie also appears in the play as "Viola Cairston," daughter of an ex-Confederate officer, and a woman in love with Stutfield. That was, of course, one bit of wishful thinking on Archie's part. By the time he wrote the play in 1914, Archie had legally changed his name from Chanler to "Chaloner," and had disavowed all of his siblings. Thus it comes as little surprise that in the play his arch enemies are not siblings (since he no longer had any), but a cousin who is after his fortune, and "a millionaire man-about-town" (based on Stanford White) who is after his beloved Viola. The two fiends hire a pair of doctors who declare Stutfield insane after they observe him entering into a trance at the Kensington Hotel. Archie's own experience at the Kensington is recounted detail by detail, down to the "distinguished New York sculptor" in the mold of Augustus Saint-Gaudens who has a role in the drama. After pulling a pistol on the doctors, Stutfield ends up in an insane asylum named "Fairdale." Life inside the asylum at Fairdale duplicates Archie's horrific experience at Bloomingdale, including a burly Irish keeper who specializes in attacking and squeezing the throats of patients. Stutfield, like Archie, determines that he must escape.

Whom does he recruit to help him? It is the most unlikely suspect of all—the rather meek, dreamy inventor of the self-threader, Alfred Wedge, who has been coming regularly to see Stutfield in the asylum, and who is totally dependent on him for his financial support. Stutfield reminds Wedge that he will continue to act as his patron, and promises to support the inventor handsomely for the rest of his life if he will only help him escape the asylum. In real life, Archie had supported and encouraged Legg since 1892. Archie's "Committee," Prescott Hall Butler, planned to pull the plug on the entire self-threading operation. Butler had no intention of ever marketing the mechanism, and he had made that clear to Archie. Legg's entire livelihood depended on his invention, and on the Self-Threading Company's continued existence. At Archie's behest, Legg would surely have come from his farm in Allendale, New Jersey, to visit his patron at Bloomingdale. Archie would have explained what was about to happen if he did *not* get out of the asylum. He must have promised to support Legg once he was freed from Bloomingdale, for Legg remained on Archie's payroll for years thereafter, even while Archie had little money of his own, mired as he was in a decades-long legal battle to have his fortune restored.

Several years after the escape, Legg visited Merry Mills, and Archie promised the inventor $100 a month, a substantial sum at the time for a man whose early promise was surely on the decline. Apparently Archie was Legg's only source of income. The inventor drank heavily, and deserted his wife for a stenographer who worked for Philip, Archie's old law partner. Legg's abandoned wife, homeless and penniless, turned to Archie for help in 1903: "Mr Legg has always claimed that you were ready and willing to assist him, this is why I write to you for you have been very good to him." Archie, quite old-fashioned in his way, disapproved of Legg's philandering, and promised the spurned wife that "I will see that you are comfortably provided for, the rest of your life," even offering to sign a paper to the effect that he would be responsible for her expenses. He also remained committed to paying the dissolute Legg. His actions reveal Archie's deep generosity to those in need, but it may also indicate a gratitude to Legg for services beyond the call of duty. It might be that Archie had some outside help in escaping from Bloomingdale after all.

The larger question, however, remains why Archie's siblings had him thrown into the insane asylum. The Chanlers prided themselves on their eccentricity; it was practically a badge of honor among them. In fact, a number of them were so decidedly odd that they, too, might easily have been considered insane. Why pick on Archie? There was indeed a history of mental illness in the Astor/Chanler family, but the treatment provided for those who suffered was of a gentler sort. In the past, family members had never been thrown into an asylum for life and left to molder. John Jacob Astor's son received private care in his own mansion. Archie's aunt Sarah, though a decided embarrassment and worry to the Chanlers, had been cared for at home by relatives. When brother Robert had his breakdown, he was sent off to a farm in Wales, not to a hospital. Robert's behavior was erratic and highly unusual his entire life. Winty wrote in jest of how Lewis couldn't even stand to be in the same room with his younger brother: "The sight & society of Bob give Lewis a series of nervous shocks which culminate in reserved hysterics." Archie, on the other hand, "sees reason to believe that Bob has an artistic future—*et ça suffit pour lui* [and for him that is enough]. They get on like birds in different nests admirably." It's ironic that Archie took a generous view of his brother's peculiarities. Both Archie and Robert seemed to walk a fine line between eccentricity and madness. Yet why was it that Archie, and not Robert, was institutionalized against his will? Even old Uncle Henry Astor, the family black sheep who was disowned and virtually disinherited for his outré behavior, did not suffer the indignity that Archie endured.

If more evidence were needed to prove how differently Archie was treated from other members of his family, it is only necessary to recount the strange psychological history of John Jay ("Jack") Chapman, the brilliant but deeply troubled literary critic and political gadfly who married Elizabeth in 1898. Chapman had all the right credentials for the Chanler family: Harvard, Porcellian Club, a line of wealthy and prominent ancestors. His grandmother, Maria Weston Chapman, was a famous abolitionist, and Jack fostered his own intense brand of reform politics. He and Theodore Roosevelt had a bitter falling-out, and the future president famously described Chapman as being "on the lunatic fringe." Emotionally he was on the fringe as well. He lived amid his own psychic storms. While at Harvard he actually burned off his own arm—put it into the fire and held it there until it was destroyed—as an act of penance and remorse after having beaten another student over a misunderstanding. He was prone to breakdowns throughout his life. At the exact same time that Archie was being observed in Philadelphia and declared sane, his brother-in-law Jack was undergoing a complete mental and physical breakdown. Confined to a dark room in the tower at Rokeby, he lay in the fetal position and suffered from hallucinations. A nurse had to feed, clothe, and bathe him. He remained in that state for nearly a year, until he began to crawl like a baby. Throughout that time, his illness was tolerated; *he* was not sent to Bloomingdale. In fact, Jack's continued mental instability, and that of the entire Chanler brood, was described humorously in a letter that Winty wrote to his wife, Daisy, in 1901.

> *It seems that Jack Chapman has delusions, in fact he is mad, but so far perfectly harmless. . . . Lewis does not want it mentioned, so you may say he has nervous prostration. Lewis says that Elizabeth and Alida are so raddled with Christian Science that they are as good as mad anyway and don't seem to mind Jack's condition. . . . "Tis a mad world, my masters". . . .*
>
> *Willy keeps away from Rokeby because Jack Chapman occupies his room. Margaret keeps away from Christian Science, and is*

the only untainted sister. Alida is lean as a shadow dreaming all day. She turns from beans as a diet to beef and makes [her husband] Temple do the same. On beans Temple is lean and hungry, on beef he is stout and happy. He never complains but sneaks a chop on the sly when Alida is not looking. At Rokeby Maggie Crockwell [the cook] chops up meat and puts it under his beans. Alida wrote an article called "Mind," or to a paper called "Mind" or both. Lewis read it and changing "Mind" to "Wind" sent it back to her. She had him—Lewis—treated by a man called Patterson who is a professional Mental Science healer, who is mad too, and thinks that the Christian Science people have focused their brains on him and taken his power for their own use. Well this Patterson at Alida's instigation worked on Lewis and then sent him a bill for $15 for "Mental Treatment." Lewis . . . was in a blue funk lest the bill should turn up at the office and the people there would think him mad too. I suggested that he send Patterson a mental check.

Margaret first suspected Jack because he ran round the room on all fours. Elizabeth said it only meant he had a pain in his stomach. So he was examined by a doctor for appendicitis and pronounced sound as a bell physically. They tried Mental and Christian Science on him at a distance and he made them stop because it started all his works going inside him. This is all pure motley. . . . It is God's mercy that they have taken this line instead of another. Forty years ago they would probably have joined the Mormon Church.

Despite all the peculiar goings-on at Rokeby, it was Archie who got singled out for his eccentric behavior. The family later claimed that Archie had been committed because he was a menace to himself and others in Virginia; but the reality was that none of his siblings had ever even been down to Merry Mills. They had no idea of what his behavior was like there. They claimed that Archie's neighbors had complained, but that seems hard to believe. Archie was a beloved figure in the hunt country in Virginia; in fact, half the people in his neighborhood were on his payroll. They depended on Archie, and tolerated his eccentricities with amusement. As for the one incident in which Archie carried hot coals in his hands—even he later admitted he should not have followed that particular instruction from his X-Faculty. The certificate of lunacy cited eyewitness reports by the valet, Hartnett, that Archie had secluded himself and had developed delusions. In rebuttal, Archie claimed that Hartnett had visited him at Bloomingdale and told him, "I didn't describe no gradual development of no delusion for I didn't see none."

The reality of whether Archie did or did not suffer from mental illness seemed less important to the family, to Winty in particular, than the fact that Archie was being increasingly difficult to deal with over the Roanoke Rapids enterprise. In addition, Winty harbored a long-term resentment over Archie's failure to carry out his familial duties, duties that then fell upon Winty. Some of that failure revolved around money. As eldest son, Archie had inherited $100,000 from their father's estate, an "unconditional gift" bestowed "with the hope and wish that my said son shall invest the said sum . . . and use the income . . . in maintaining and keeping up the said country seat at Rokeby." This sum was on top of the regular inheritance payments that Archie and his brothers received. What had happened to that $100,000 endowment? Archie certainly had *not* invested that money for Rokeby. In fact, he had little to do with the family estate, and was certainly not spending any money to maintain it. Archie had apparently spent the $100,000, perhaps on Roanoke Rapids or the self-threader. Winty believed that it had been frittered away on Amélie and the extravagant life that she and her entourage had enjoyed in Europe. Despite his supposed indifference to money, Winty could not abide this continued pattern of fiscal recklessness, especially as it was rippling out to the rest of the family.

All of these financial factors seemed to weigh more heavily in the decision to incarcerate Archie than whether he was a danger to himself or others, or whether he was suffering from mental torment. Winty could no longer tolerate his brother as a business partner. Jack Chapman could suffer incapacitating delusions and be kept in the Rokeby tower for a year without bothering the family. But Archie's erratic behavior might be very costly. Winty had invested a great deal of time and money on the Roanoke Rapids project, as had his siblings, and he was not about to stand by and let the whole operation come to ruin because of Archie's wild schemes. Winty had to admire the energy and vision that Archie had brought to creating a town in the North Carolina wilderness. (In fact, Roanoke Rapids would eventually become a thriving textile center, and city leaders remained ever grateful to Archie; the middle school in town is still named after him.) But Winty did want to put a stop to Archie's frenetic, and increasingly risky, business plans such as the paving enterprise in Marseille. The only way to prevent Archie from undermining the foundation of their textile operation was to remove him entirely from management. Archie's family certainly did not want to *steal* Archie's estate, as he came to believe when they put him in Bloomingdale—but they *did* want to put him out of harm's way for all of their sakes.

The family was perplexed about Archie's whereabouts as 1901 progressed, but when his dead body didn't turn up, they began to look on the bright side. Even before he got the misinformation about Archie's being safe in Paris, Winty was already upbeat about his brother's situation. He also didn't seem to think Archie was that ill, after all.

> Where is Archie? The fact that nothing has been heard of him is a good sign—He is with friends who take care of him. I consider that apart from our total ignorance of his whereabouts, his escape is a good thing for him & for all of us. His money is rolling up for him. His affairs will be straightened out. So that when he turns up, as he is sure to do, there will be enough to keep him well wherever he wants to be. Poor old boy—There are lots of madder men than he at large.

TEN

Who's Looney Now?

. . . yet time serves wherein you may redeem
Your banish'd honours and restore yourselves
Into the good thoughts of the world again,
Revenge the jeering and disdain'd contempt. . . .

—Shakespeare, *King Henry IV,* Part I

The shadows of his failure with Amélie and his nightmare in Bloomingdale hung over Archie. He had lost everything: his beloved, his fortune, and his good name. He was determined to avenge his disgrace, regain control of his property, and have himself declared sane in a court of law. While his siblings assumed he would eventually turn up in a familiar haunt like Paris, Archie managed to surprise them once again. Traveling incognito, he headed south to a far-from-fashionable locale: he went to Lynchburg, Virginia, an industrial town on the James River noted for its tobacco warehouses and not much else. Under the assumed name of "John Chilton," he registered at the Arlington Hotel and stayed there for two months. The proprietor of the hotel assumed "Chilton" was in town on business; he had no suspicion of Archie's real identity, nor did he have the impression that his guest was mentally unhinged. The hotelier dined with Archie frequently, and even allowed the kind stranger to take his children to a matinee in the park. Archie meanwhile was conferring with a lawyer in Lynchburg and plotting his return to Merry Mills.

On the morning of September 21, 1901, there was another cloudburst for the Astor/Chanler family in New York. A headline on the front page of the *Times* read, "John Armstrong Chanler Reappears in Virginia." The press greeted his reemergence with glee, the supposed madman and ex-husband of Amélie Rives who had been "lost for nearly a year" having arrived in Charlottesville the day before. He was, the reporter wrote, "the picture of vigorous physical health." In addition, Archie had a fistful of endorsements of his mental health by some of the leading neurologists and psychologists of the day. Archie announced to the *Times* that he was about to publish a short treatise on experimental psychology titled "The X-Faculty." The Chanlers braced themselves.

Cary Ruffin Randolph, a co-founder of the Keswick Hunt Club and recent Master of the Foxhounds, was delighted to have old Archie back for the hunting season. On Archie's behalf, Randolph filed a petition with the county court to rule on his friend's state of mind in order to "determine whether a Committee of his person and estate should be appointed" for his property in Virginia. Within weeks, Archie's sanity went formally and very publicly on trial in the Albemarle County courthouse in Charlottesville.

In contrast to the one-sided proceedings against Archie in New York, the Virginia trial was practically a celebration of his genius. After hearing Archie's opening testimony, the opposing lawyer didn't even bother to hang around and listen to the rest of the witnesses: "I did not do anything for I knew I'd get beaten," he later admitted. Witness after witness—neighbors, business associates, and the doctors who had observed the alleged madman in Philadelphia—testified on Archie's behalf. Was Archie insane? They all said no. Perhaps he was eccentric and "a little in advance of the ordinary man," as one august professor at the University of Virginia (and a cousin of Amélie's) testified, but he was certainly sane. Major Emry, a partner in the Roanoke Rapids Power Company, testified that he and Archie had shared quarters together in North Carolina for about a year and a half when the town was being established, and he'd found the plaintiff neither reckless nor extravagant as a manager. Others testified to his business acumen: "I have bought horses for him and he was a good judge," the former farm manager at Castle Hill stated. "I would not care to trade with him unless I had my eyes open pretty well."

Affidavits from a parade of experts were introduced. Dr. Horatio Wood, Professor of Nervous Diseases at the University of Pennsylvania, had examined Archie in five interviews in Philadelphia and found him "certainly mentally peculiar," but sane. Dr. Joseph Jastrow, professor of psychology at the University of Wisconsin and the expert in charge of the psychological section at the Columbian Exposition in 1893, weighed in with his considered opinion about Archie's automatic writings: they were "expressions of his normal mentality" and not indicative of illness. Jastrow buttressed his argument by citing other experts who believed that "automatic writing" could be done by perfectly healthy individuals who happened to be "gifted with sensitive nervous organizations." Such seemed to be the case with Archie, in Jastrow's estimation.

Finally, a statement was introduced from William James, longtime professor at Harvard and author of the definitive text in the overlapping fields of psychology and philosophy, the twelve-hundred-page masterpiece titled *The Principles of Psychology.* James had a particular intellectual interest in the psychic phenomena that Archie had been pursuing; he also had a personal interest in the high-society madman, for he was part of the same social set. Members of the James family had gathered around the living room of Archie's great-aunt Julia Ward Howe in Newport; and William's brother Henry James, the novelist, had been awed by Amélie when she and Archie stormed London about a decade earlier. William James's opinion carried particularly heavy weight, and he came down forcefully on Archie's side, maintaining that Archie's "inner conversation with his X-Faculty" was an example of the subconscious part of his personality "making irruptions into the conscious part." He believed that Archie possessed a "strongly 'mediumistic' or 'psychic' temperament," and that he used that gift to further scientific inquiry. James marveled at the way Archie "set to work systematically . . . to explore" rare manifestations of "mental automatism." He continued:

> In this attempt he seems to me to deserve nothing but praise. . . . The most injudicious act of which he is accused is the experiment with fire. As described, its motivation was rational and its results interesting and but moderately harmful. It seems to me a monstrous claim to say that a man may not make experiments, even as extreme as that, upon his own person without putting his legal freedom in jeopardy. . . . Psychology would be more advanced, were there more subjects of automatism ready to explore carefully their eccentric faculty.

Furthermore, James made clear his disdain for the so-called "specialists in insanity" at asylums. In his professional opinion, these alienists were "ignorant" when dealing with people like Archie who had a psychic temperament. They made the mistake of assuming that such behavior was "delusional insanity" rather than the manifestation of a paranormal gift. James argued that if the doctors at Bloomingdale were correct and Archie did suffer from classic "Paranoia," then his delusional illness would have prevented his being able to distinguish between psychological states and to discern movement from one to the next. "In Mr. Chanler's case," he noted, "there appears to have been complete alternation . . . between the primary and the 'X' consciousness." In addition, in reading through Archie's own writings, James found "no sign whatever of delusions." In summation, William James was clear:

> [M]y opinion of Mr. Chanler is that he is intellectually sound. No evidence to show his dangerousness to others or his inability to manage his property has been shown me. In default of such evidence, further treatment of him as a lunatic would seem a crime.

Archie had been vindicated. The preeminent authority in the country had declared him sane, and at the conclusion of the November 6, 1901, proceedings the Virginia court did likewise, stating categorically that Archie was a "sane man, capable of taking care of his person and estate." Archie's court victory, however, made him the occupant of the nation's largest cell. Though legally sane in Virginia, he could not step across its borders, as he remained legally a lunatic in every other state, subject to arrest.

A small army of journalists descended on Albemarle County in the hope of interviewing the "strong, combative, yet gentle" Chanler. He turned them all away on the advice of his attorneys. He and his legal team expected that they would shortly "carry his battle for legal mental freedom right into the Empire State," and be victorious. Publicity at the moment might be harmful to his interests, but he couldn't resist granting an interview to a charming young female journalist. When the reporter met Archie, he was dressed in riding gear, "cloaked, booted and spurred. In one hand he held his gloves, which he hastily threw on the table . . . and with the other hand impatiently tapped his riding whip against his foot." He was the very image of "a man who knows how to command himself, as well as other people." She found his "mental equipment" formidable, and detected his striking resemblance to Napoleon, a likeness he encouraged by his grooming: "a lock of heavy dark hair drops over his forehead in the Napoleonic way and his clean shaven lips are set in a thin, firm, unwavering line." The reporter noted his strong physique as well as the "impulsive, erratic movements of the highly strung nervous organism." The journalist wrote sympathetically that Archie had been victimized by his own psychological investigations, delving into "mysteries which men have known little about. . . . Like other men ahead of their time he has paid the penalty for it in persecution." Archie consented to a photograph, the first taken since his escape from Bloomingdale, posed on his horse.

As the countryside welcomed Archie home, feelings began to run against his ex-wife. Some local women took inspiration from Amélie's routine flouting of conventions—she gave them hope that their own lives might not be as restricted in the future—but the general consensus was that she was, in local parlance, a "caution." Her flirtatiousness and capriciousness were the stuff of local legend, and her divorce had sent shock waves through the community. "A divorce was a thing an Albemarle woman never even thought of as a remote possibility," the *New York World* had reported. "So when it was announced . . . Albemarle County's first families almost took to their beds. . . . All through the South death is looked upon as the only aristocratic and respectable form of divorce." Divorce was bad enough; at the ensuing news of Amélie's remarriage, the countryside "simply sat with its mouth ajar."

Cynics speculated that the lurid publicity surrounding Amélie would enhance her career. Willa Cather thought as much: "So Amélie Rives is married again and to a Russian Prince. Princess Troubetzkoy, that will look well under the title of her next sensational novel." But, save for a novel set in the Middle Ages that she had written years earlier, Amélie did not publish a book for nearly a decade after marrying Pierre. The couple wrestled with serious financial problems largely because Archie's generous allowance had ceased after his commitment to Bloomingdale. Amélie's medical bills mounted: she had returned to Castle Hill as a semi-invalid after her breakdown and commitment to the Philadelphia sanatorium in May 1897.

In desperate need to jump-start her stalled career, Amélie permitted a reporter for the *New York Journal Sunday* to interview her at home in July 1897. She described her working mode as if she were some kind of elfin creature in a magical world:

> Do you know when and where I do most of my serious work? . . . It is in the open field. I take a rug, drag it along after me. I find a field of oats. If in the Spring the sheaves seem nodding a welcome. If it be midsummer, when the shocks are standing, sentinel-like, I run through them all and select the biggest for my guard, throw myself down in the midst of it and write—write tirelessly, from noon till dusk.

Amélie gave the interview to tout a book she had begun to write several weeks before; though not yet finished, she assured the journalist that the novel would be her "greatest effort . . . more startling than 'The Quick or the Dead.' " It was to be a meditation on marriage, and the danger of sexual passion and lust. Her noble characters, clearly stand-ins for herself and the prince, fall madly in love but decide to have a kind of chaste marriage based on principles espoused by Tolstoy in "The Kreutzer Sonata." The main character in Tolstoy's controversial 1890 story is a married man so deranged by jealousy that he brutally murders his wife. With that as backdrop, Tolstoy called for a higher form of marriage in which abstinence rather than sexual passion ruled. Amélie's lofty characters cope with the struggle between their own passionate urges and Tolstoy's radical call for chastity. The Amélie and Pierre characters marry and make "the 'Kreutzer Sonata' the family Bible"; they determine "to pursue the Tolstoi doctrine after marriage, and . . . free themselves from sin." The novel was never published.

The interviewer doubtless found it hard to conceive of Amélie as a sexless wife, for as she earnestly outlined her plot to him, she lay on a divan, dressed alluringly in a "graceful, flowing, silken negligee, which revealed the perfection of her velvety white arms and soft full throat." The reporter noted that "clematis vines and Japanese ivy threw fantastic shadows athwart her recumbent form." Lying there, the siren incarnate, she seemed hardly the spokesperson for chaste love. But perhaps that was just the sort of union she yearned for with the prince, after her tempestuous years of "perfume and flame" with Archie: a marriage based on companionship, deep friendship, and mutual respect. She believed that a "wife-friend," rather than a "wife-chattel" or "wife-vassal," was the ideal status for a woman in marriage. Not that she would entirely dispense with passion, as she noted in a later article in the *New York Times*:

> The married man and woman must be partners, friends . . . I don't mean platonic friendship, of course. Love is the foundation. But in addition to being lovers, husband and wife should also be comrades and share existence in a spirit of camaraderie.

If that "spirit of camaraderie" did not exist, she contended that the marriage contract should be just as easy to put aside as any other civil contract. As Amélie puffed on a cigarette, the iconoclast spoke forcefully against staying in an unhappy marriage and becoming imprisoned like a bird in a cage. Amélie, for one, would never cage her pets. "Freedom," she insisted, "is the all-desirable thing—the sensation of wings." This was rather revolutionary talk at the time, and she went on to describe her own marriage to her "painter-Prince" as the embodiment of a marriage based on friendship, shared intellectual and creative interests, and freedom. She believed firmly that a married woman should have "an occupation for the mind" and independence; those traits would, in fact, help strengthen the marriage bond "by doing away with monotony and by keeping husband and wife somewhat apart."

For much of their marriage, particularly in the early years, Amélie and Pierre lived separately; he maintained a studio in New York or Washington, while she remained at Castle Hill. There were whispers about this; perhaps Amélie discussed their relationship so openly in order to defuse the gossip. She maintained that a marriage remained fresh and interesting only if husband and wife did not see each other constantly. Amélie used the metaphor of having a bouquet of fresh violets in her room: When they are first brought in, "their fragrance is compelling, delightful, a thing which makes itself felt"; but if she stayed with the flowers too long she could no longer smell them. "Marriage is like that. If you are too much together the aroma loses strength and may vanish altogether."

When Pierre opened a studio in Washington in 1898, Amélie stayed behind at Castle Hill, saying she was too weak to leave the estate. Though Washington was just a few hours away by train, the prince generally returned to Castle Hill only twice a month. He was enjoying the adulation of Washington's high society: "He is the lion of the hour," the press exclaimed in February 1898; "He is beyond the threshold of a career both brilliant and swift. His studio in the Corcoran building is the rendezvous of Washington's smart set." Beautiful young women and hostesses were eager to be painted by the "tall, clean limbed athletic looking fellow" who was said to be the third strongest man in America. His slightly accented English and touch of a lisp lent him an intriguing aura. While at work he wore a linen blouse and carried a palette in his left hand, the very image of the bohemian artist at work. His studio was sparsely furnished, and standing up along the walls were some of his favorite sketches and paintings of Italy and Virginia. One painting depicted the lawn at Castle Hill with the mountains in the distance; Amélie stood in the foreground with her golden hair, a red shawl thrown over her shoulders. The mystery of Amélie and their unconventional marriage only added to the prince's appeal.

While Pierre quickly became a leading social and artistic presence in Washington, Amélie's health deteriorated. The symptoms were never specified: perhaps she was being plagued by her blinding headaches, or her recurrent "grippe," or her harrowing emotional demons. She did not return to the sanatorium in Philadelphia; doubtless she couldn't afford it without Archie's money. Amélie sank into a deep depression and became something of a recluse, retreating to her locked bedroom, refusing to see visitors and sometimes even her own husband when he came down from Washington. A newspaper article called her a "wreck of her former self . . . a voluntary prisoner in the little white bedroom in the west wing of the famous old colonial mansion in Albemarle County . . . [with] only a faithful old colored woman attending her." At night Amélie would emerge and wander through the house, dressed all in white.

Archie assumed that his victory in Virginia would soon be followed by vindication up north, but months turned into years as Archie and a small army of lawyers fought one legal skirmish after another. As the years dragged on, Archie's case seemed to rival that of the fictional Jarndyce and Jarndyce in Charles Dickens's *Bleak House*—and in the process of trying to prove his sanity, he became unhinged. His paranoia grew, along with increasingly bizarre behavior. He exhibited symptoms that seem to indicate a bipolar disorder: wild mood swings that ranged from euphoric grandiosity (such as seeing himself as Napoleon-like), to bitter anger, to depressive "Sphinx-like" feelings. As can be the case with this illness, a high level of intellectual functioning and creativity accompanied Archie's intense bursts of manic energy. Genetic factors play a role in bipolar disorders, and mental illness clearly ran through both the Astor and Chanler clans. Archie and his siblings prided themselves on being thrill-seekers—a manic propensity that runs strongly in families. Archie's symptoms waxed and waned, but they grew decidedly worse during periods of high emotional stress. Being forcibly incarcerated in an insane asylum certainly fed his feelings of rage and paranoia; and during the grueling years he spent trying to prove his sanity, he careened from one self-aggrandizing cause and outrageous endeavor to the next. If there is indeed a fine line between eccentricity and madness, Archie surely crossed it. Certainly, the cruel manner in which he was lured to Bloomingdale and cast aside by his family contributed to his disintegration. Archie's bitterness is palpable in this blast at his siblings:

> There can be no slightest doubt as to the deadly, cold-blooded, malevolent, animosity of plaintiff's family, male and female, towards plaintiff. . . . One would think that the least brothers who had had the heartlessness to have plaintiff confined for life as a hopeless lunatic and incompetent without a hearing or an opportunity to be heard, that the least brothers worthy the name could do, upon hearing of plaintiff's escape from gaol and approaching trial to test plaintiff's sanity and competency in Virginia, would be to be present at said trial and . . . present plaintiff with the glad hand of brotherhood and propose to plaintiff to let bye-gones be bye-gones—and let it go at that.

Instead the family had totally ignored the Virginia hearings. This further enraged Archie and tempted him to bring the battle to their turf in New York, but he was caught in a catch-22: he was guilty of contempt of court for escaping the asylum; the only way to clear that charge would require going back to New York; but if he went there he would be subject to immediate arrest. He feared that his family and the authorities, given another crack at him, would find a stouter cell: "It's an easy matter to hire alienists in Gotham to swear in any direction . . . to run me in [the asylum] this time for life."

Archie was also barred from visiting his industrial town in North Carolina. He did, however, have a spy in place, a machinist named F. H. Treacy. Like almost everyone else in Roanoke Rapids, Treacy admired Archie, applauded his generosity, and looked upon him as a savior. He had, after all, created the town and given its citizens work and housing. Archie had lived among the workers and managers while the town was being built and everyone loved his flamboyant style; he brought a touch of glamour and the Astor aura to an otherwise humdrum factory existence. Once the mill was up and running, Archie continued his hands-on approach, following the day-to-day operations of the factory from Merry Mills and making frequent trips back and forth to North Carolina until his incarceration.

When Winty and Stanford White took over the reins at Roanoke Rapids, their absentee-management style did not win them much in the way of local support. Despite their initial enthusiasm for the town's business prospects, Winty and White had no interest in personally managing a knitting factory, and when profits did not roll in immediately, they began to lose interest. The knitting mill failed altogether around 1901. According to local lore, the end came about when the paymaster who arrived once a month from New York failed to show up. He had absconded to Europe with the workers' wages. The factory then shut down and the whole empire began to crumble. Whether the failure was due mainly to economic conditions or the neglect of the new management is not clear. Treacy, for one, was not terribly impressed by the diligence of the New Yorkers, referring to the "7 years siesta" that had overtaken the business as soon as Archie was put in Bloomingdale.

Desperate for money, Archie swallowed his pride and contacted several chums from the Union Club in New York. Among his targets was the well-known racehorse breeder Herman Duryea. Since Duryea was a sporting man, Archie thought he might be willing to take a chance on his old friend. He wrote to him at the Union Club on August 20, 1904:

Dear Hermie

I am going to make you laugh. I am about to propose to touch you on my note of hand @ 6% for $500 for about a year or until I win my law suit now on in New York to recover my property from the hands of my alleged committee of my person and estate who has his clamps on all my New York property. I need not say that I am not on speaking terms with any of my family for certain reasons or I should not be forced thus to bush-whack for supplies to keep body and soul together. In any event, old man, I count on your keeping the said laugh to yourself and not giving it away to <u>any body</u>. This is strictly confidential.

very truly yours,
Jno. Arm. Chan.

P.S. I might add that I'm bound to win said suit. J.A.C.

The idea of Archie having to *ask* for money seemed improbable even to him; he was used to giving it away. In fact, when Archie received a "wind-fall" ten days later, he couldn't give it away fast enough. He instantly sent $150 to a woman in Washington, D.C., a perfect stranger who had been writing letters to him asking for a handout. Archie was besieged with begging letters. A carpenter who had worked at Roanoke Rapids claimed to have stomach hemorrhages and sought Archie's financial help in opening a store. A psychic researcher in New York wanted to set up an institute of experimental psychology and was looking for $25,000. A woman who had known Archie as a child and had hit upon hard times in Brooklyn wrote pathetically of her poor son who suffered with acute rheumatism and could not walk.

Archie understood only too well the power that his money wielded; he could, in effect, buy people's loyalty and, he hoped, their respect. Having lost everything—his wife, command of his industrial empire, and his gold-plated inheritance—Archie knew that his only leverage lay in the promise of his economic future. He made it clear that once he regained his New York property, he would be handing out money freely, and this endowed him with a great deal of power in his financially depressed neighborhood in Virginia. Thus he was able to keep around him a virtual army of retainers, all of whom expected to get their share of the pie once Archie was vindicated in New York. What Archie called his "glad gold hand" of philanthropy was restrained by the allowance granted him by his Committee. He repeatedly had to petition the courts to have his annual payments increased; and they rose from $10,000 to $13,000 to $25,000, but still fell short of the exorbitant bills he was generating with his legal defense. Whenever he got his allowance from the Committee, everybody was paid; but soon enough the money would run out, and there would be a long trough before the next flush time. During those dry spells Archie would inevitably raise the stakes, promising even larger salaries in the future. At a public meeting he arranged in Richmond, Archie promised that once he was able to get his income "out of the hands on the New York thieves holding same," he would build the city a public meeting hall and buy Christmas presents for all its poor children.

Amélie, a hardheaded realist when it came to money, began to despair that Archie was ever going to restart the $3,600 annual payments she had been promised when they divorced. (She didn't even try to hold him to the $4,600 future payments he'd pledged in the summer of 1896.) In 1911, Amélie filed suit against Archie's estate in New York, claiming that Archie had promised her $3,600 a year in lieu of alimony, and that he had borrowed $20,000 from her literary earnings. Archie sputtered when he read that. Twenty thousand dollars? "She never let me have $20," he fumed. The court ruled in Amélie's favor, directing Archie's Committee to take the money out of his estate. The *New York Times* reported that his property generated $39,000 a year in income, a figure that Archie disputed. He maintained that he earned closer to $50,000, and accused his Committee, T. T. Sherman, of low-balling the figure and skimming a hefty rake-off for himself and his law firm. After all he had done for Amélie, after his undying devotion to her, Archie felt betrayed. "It shows that Princess Sapphira is down & out," Archie wrote bitterly, comparing his ex-spouse to the biblical Sapphira, the beautiful but mendacious wife who lied about money and was struck dead. Despite his initial bluster, Archie did not contest the court ruling, and conceded that he would not object to the $3,600 allowance. Perhaps he just couldn't bring himself to be vindictive toward Amélie.

His eccentricities grew more pronounced. He lived by night, starting his "day" at 6:00 p.m. He typically went to bed at 4:00 a.m. and slept twelve hours. On awakening he had "an ice cold bath in a bright clean bath room" and then a leisurely dressing process, all of which took about two hours. He adopted one radical diet after the next. In one letter he reported that he was eating only bread, "the staff of life"; in another he announced that he had pulled himself out of a depression, out of the "Valley of the Shadow of Death," within twenty-four hours by consuming "Brownie's 'Pullman' bread ('Mother's' bread) 16 pieces thereof & 35 fresh mushrooms, & 3 large pieces of perfect apple pie and a quart & a half of plain ice water." For a time he ate nothing but salsify and tapioca pudding, and his weight fell below 154, his pre-Bloomingdale weight, which he considered about perfect. He grew so concerned over his emaciated state that he called two University of Virginia doctors at eleven o'clock one night and demanded that they see him the next day.

Archie became a veritable one-man publishing industry: legal briefs, pamphlets on psychology, broadsides on political issues, advertisements for his own public appearances and speeches. Bound in a distinctive purple cloth, perhaps a royal touch, he self-published collections of plays, sonnets, essays, and missives dictated by his X-Faculty—all basically tirades against his family and the injustice of his forced incarceration and lunacy law in general. The printing expenses were astronomical, but Archie considered it all part of his legal campaign. A few of the titles give a hint of his seething anger: *Four Years Behind the Bars of "Bloomingdale" or The Bankruptcy of Law in New York,* and *Robbery Under Law or The Battle of the Millionaires.* A volume entitled *Scorpio No. 1* included a collection of sonnets, several of which take direct aim at his siblings. A whip with seven lashes was etched into the cover of the book, and lest anyone fail to comprehend the depth of his feelings against his seven brothers and sisters, he titled two poems about them, "The Heart Is Deceitful Above All Things and Desperately Wicked" and "The Love of Money Is the Root of All Evil." In 1908 he took, perhaps, the ultimate revenge: he legally renounced his family by changing his name from Chanler to Chaloner, what Archie considered to be the ancient form of the name. He declared to the newspapers that he wanted to slough off "the modernized form of my name . . . and leave this crime-stained patronymic for the Chanler family to hold."

The back pages of Archie's tomes were filled with reprints of newspaper articles about him and his case—at least ones the alleged lunatic deemed flattering; likewise reviews to his taste. He sent copies of his books to every conceivable publication in Britain and the United States, in both major cities and tiny hamlets. How he even found some of these publications is astounding: the *Monmouthshire Evening Post,* the *Bridport News,* the *Dorset, Devon and Somerset Advertiser,* the *North-eastern Reporter* from St. Paul, Minnesota, and the *Oklahoma Law Journal.* He bought out the entire runs of his books (thus he was beloved by his printer) and then claimed they were bestsellers. He personally inscribed the books with messages written in blue pencil—his preferred writing instrument, particularly when taking dictation from his X-Faculty—and gave them away to everyone he knew, and even to people he didn't know. Ample supplies of his "bestsellers" eventually found their way to local secondhand bookstores.

Amid his legal rants were samples of his psychic power. He published a pamphlet-length work titled "Hell: Per a Spirit-Message Therefrom (Alleged). . . . A Study in Graphic-Automatism," which was the verbatim message he received from the spirit of a deceased friend, a fellow member of the Manhattan Club and former noncommissioned officer in the Confederate navy. The spirit took over Archie's hand and dictated an accounting of the Beyond that gave a detailed picture of hell. His friend claimed that he did not suffer very much there "largely because I had my share of hell while on earth in being a New Yorker of social standing, but no money," and he described the Hall of Audience in hell as being like a sumptuous palace made entirely out of jewels: enormous rubies the size of building bricks were interspersed with diamonds and sapphires. The room itself was beyond human comprehension, being miles long and wide and high. Satan—who, oddly enough, bore an exact resemblance to Napoleon Bonaparte—sat there atop a fiery throne. Archie took this dictation from the spirit in the summer of 1912 and immediately rushed to the press with it, while claiming that he did not believe a damned word of it; he was convinced that it was an invention of his subconscious, his X-Faculty. The press, of course, had a field day. "HELL'S NOT HALF BAD OLD PLACE, YOU KNOW," one headline read.

Beginning with his ill-fated marriage to Amélie, Archie had become a long-running public melodrama, his life punctuated by sudden bursts of sensational news. In March 1909 he shot a man in the dining room of Merry Mills. The victim was a local mechanic named John Gillard, an ex-Australian bushwhacker, a brutal, strong man who regularly terrorized his wife and five children. Archie had told the wife that if she ever needed protection, she should come to Merry Mills. She did so one night, with her husband in pursuit. Gillard burst into the house, found his wife cowering in the dining room, and began to beat her with heavy fireplace tongs until Archie interceded. As was his custom, Archie carried a small revolver in his dressing gown, and he pulled it out. A struggle ensued, and Gillard was shot and killed. Reporters from Richmond raced to the scene early the next morning, only to find Archie in the dining room, enjoying his breakfast of roast duck and vanilla ice cream while dressed in leather pajamas. The room was in complete disarray: a woman's hat in one corner, hairpins strewn about, and the fireplace tongs, bent and bloody, lying on the floor. Nearby was the corpse. Archie had spent the entire night in the room with the dead body, as he wanted to test his nerve. When one of the reporters expressed sympathy to Archie for having had to endure such a tragedy, he immediately responded, "Sorry for *me*? *I'm* all right!" Pointing to the dead man he said, "*There's* the man to be sorry for!"

A coroner's jury quickly absolved Archie of any guilt. He testified that he had followed his duty as a Christian gentleman. Gillard's wife confirmed the long-term abuse she had suffered at the hands of her husband. Archie's trusted farm manager, Ernle Money, had been present during the struggle, as had another of Archie's employees, an African-American farm laborer named John Grady; both men confirmed Archie's story, and the case was closed. But, interestingly enough, an entirely different version of events became common knowledge among members of the black community who worked at Merry Mills and other local estates. They insisted that it was John Grady, and not Archie, who had killed Gillard. Archie had ordered Grady to do it, and then had taken the blame. Archie knew that a black man accused of killing a white man in Virginia didn't stand a chance of acquittal; he'd face the end of a rope. On the other hand, Archie was confident that he'd be acquitted. This alternative version of Archie handing off his gun to his rugged farm worker and letting him grapple with the enraged Gillard fits in neatly with Archie's psychology. He had a grandiose notion of himself as lord of the manor, and ordering one of his vassals to kill an enemy, and then gallantly taking responsibility for it in order to shield his minion from danger, sounds just like something that Archie would do. It would feed into his swashbuckling, heroic, and paternalistic image of himself. Faced with two stories, it's impossible to know exactly what transpired; but either scenario fit in with his romantic code of chivalry.

Word of the sensational killing by an heir to the Astor fortune spread abroad. Schoolboys at Eton read the news of the eccentric American; among them was Archie's nephew, Lewis's son, who took refuge in the peculiar spelling of his uncle's last name and disavowed any relation to the shooter. Archie, on the other hand, took total ownership of the deed. He paid for the widow and children to return to relatives in England, and also for Gillard's funeral; his own team of horses brought the body to the church. Archie's victim was buried in the churchyard at Grace Episcopal, though at a discreet distance from the other graves set aside for the local gentry. Archie arranged for a tombstone that read simply "John Gillard Died March 15, 1909 Aged 45 years." He was dissuaded from the original epitaph he wanted to use, the more sporting, "He died game." In his dining room, in the spot where Gillard fell, Archie installed a six-pointed star made of copper to memorialize his chivalrous act.

Newspaper accounts of the shooting alarmed the Chanlers; but this time concern for Archie outweighed their usual fixation on the family's public image. Elizabeth and Robert rushed to Virginia two days after the incident and checked into a hotel in Charlottesville. The town was abuzz with news and speculation; Gillard's funeral was that day. Archie remained sequestered at Merry Mills and did not attend the funeral service, but he was surprised to learn that his siblings were nearby and offering a helping hand. He received a note from Robert.

Dear Archie:

I congratulate you on the magnificent courage you have shown. We are proud of you. Elizabeth and I came to help you if needed, but the compliment paid you by the jury relieves you of any need of it. Can I see you? Please allow me the pleasure.

Affectionately,
Robert

Archie sent back a one-line reply: "I regret it, but it will be impossible to see you." Archie shared the notes with the press, as if to prove his toughness, his unwillingness to compromise with his family until he had reached his stated goal of "redress and mental vindication." Robert and Elizabeth left the next day for New York.

The Chanlers were famous for bitter feuds that lasted for

decades. Archie shared that pig-headed trait. He'd hold on to his anger until *he* had won. But the shooting and aftermath took its toll on him. Several weeks after the events, the *New York Times* reported that Archie had suffered a nervous breakdown and, on doctor's orders, had left Merry Mills to recuperate at the home of an old business associate. The rest, however, did little to diminish the rage that Archie felt toward his family over their betrayal. In the summer of 1909 he sat down and wrote in his own hand a document that began, "To whom it may concern." In it he spelled out precisely what he wanted done in the event of his death or serious accident. The instructions basically revolved around the banning of any and all members of his family.

> I hereby order: (1) My agent Ernle S. Money Esq is to assume full control of this place. He is to permit no member of the Chanler family, male or female, near or remote, to enter these grounds. He is to call on a Magistrate or Sheriff . . . to make said order efficient if necessary. (2) Only in the event of my death are said parties to be allowed to see me, & then only in my coffin, when my neighbors view me. The said parties are to be put off the premises . . . immediately after the said view, for good.

Archie wanted vindication and justice—and revenge against his family—and in 1910 he saw his chance. His brother Robert, divorced from his first wife, had fallen madly in love with the beautiful but scandalous Italian opera diva Lina Cavalieri. He followed her to Europe and begged her to marry him. She consented, but only after he had signed away his fortune to her in a prenuptial agreement. After marrying Robert, Lina promptly took up with her former lover, the Russian Prince Dolgorouki. The cuckolded Robert was handed a measly allowance by his wife and told that if he needed more, he could sell his paintings. Humiliated, he quietly disappeared from Paris—but the press picked up the story. For weeks, one salacious detail after the next emerged of how Robert had been fleeced by the onetime naked dancer for the Folies Bergère. The *New York World* reported the titillating news in September 1910:

> Robert Winthrop Chanler, who last June was a millionaire, is now a pensioner on $20 a month allowed him by his wife, Lina Cavalieri. His dream of love has been shattered. . . . Cavalieri has Chanler's entire fortune, and he is in America, penniless.

Oh, the delicious irony for Archie, the alleged madman, to read about the deranged judgment of his brother—the same brother who had once called him "looney"! Archie knew exactly how to play the media. He had a keen sense of dramatic timing and a clever way with words. Gleefully, Archie dashed off to his brother—and the press—a three-word cable: "Who's looney now?" The phrase swept the country. It inspired a cartoon strip, a comedic film, and a series of illustrated trading cards showing various social faux pas under the headline "Who's Looney Now." It became *the* favorite punchline of the day, and a staple in sermons, political speeches, and editorials. Robert would never get over the infamy of the insult; and Archie reveled in the notoriety. Ever after, he was known as the originator of the most famous phrase in America.

Indifferent to appearing foolish, and determined to keep his case in the public eye, Archie manipulated the press as much as the press exploited him. In bizarre fashion, his love-hate relationship with the press led to his final, long-sought vindication. After the shooting of Gillard at Merry Mills, Archie brought a libel suit against the *New York Evening Post* for an article referring sarcastically to him as "the latest prominent assassin [who] had the rare foresight to have himself declared insane before he shot his man." Archie sued for $100,000 in damages. The case had been delayed for years, but finally a date was set for New York's Federal District Court in May 1919. To ensure Archie's appearance in court, the judge handed down a writ of prohibition that prevented the police from arresting the escaped lunatic. Archie left for New York almost immediately. Reporters met the exile at the train, and trailed after him as he dramatically reacquainted himself with the town of his birth. It had been twenty-two years, nearly a generation, since he'd had a chance to walk the streets of New York without fear of arrest. The city had been transformed in his absence. "Where are all the horses?" he asked incredulously. He declared the recently opened Automat restaurant "like a miracle of the Arabian Nights!" Archie was agog at the grand new buildings, which surpassed the architecture of "Rome in the height of its splendor"; and he rode a New York subway for the first time and deemed it "delightful," as the trains had plenty of fresh air. The press couldn't get enough of this colorful Rip Van Winkle.

The courtroom was full of reporters, but his own family was conspicuously absent. The lawyer for the *Post,* William Wherry, tried to portray Archie as insane, and quizzed him on the stand about his X-Faculty and his automatic writing. Archie parried the questions deftly, putting the attorney on the defensive. When asked if he had indeed written poetry and books unconsciously, Archie said he had never written an unconscious word; he corrected Wherry and told him that the proper term was "*sub*-conscious." In interrogating the self-published author, the lawyer displayed a thorough knowledge of Archie's texts. "You have been mightily well coached in this case, Brother Wherry," Archie said, to the amusement of the jury. "I ought to give you a fee myself." The jury found for Archie after deliberating for less than an hour; they declared that they had no doubt of his sanity, and awarded him $30,000 in damages. The judge immediately halved the award, and Archie's creditors—including the lawyers who had just represented him—lined up for payment. The entire libel award was gone instantly. But Archie had won something more important: the key to unlocking his fortune.

With this judgment in hand, the game was virtually over. A jury in New York had said that Archie was sane; another New York court would surely follow suit. Archie's family knew there was no point in resisting; they'd have to surrender. But what were their brother's conditions? Archie's sister-in-law Beatrice, an actress married to Willie, reached out as an intermediary. Archie had never met Beatrice before (she and Willie had married during Archie's long Virginia exile), or her two teenaged sons, and he was delighted to do so. From his hotel room at the Brevoort House, Archie wrote his demand: if the family dropped their opposition to his taking control of his property, he promised never to "raise pen or tongue again against any Chanler, male or female." Elizabeth, eager to embrace her tormented brother, took up her own pen to relieve Archie of his decades-long burden, and formally wrote on behalf of all of the siblings on June 9, 1919:

Dearest Archie:

I know that I speak for all your brothers and sisters when I tell you that they will do nothing to obstruct any steps that you may take to recover complete control of your rights and property, nor do anything to interfere with your personal freedom.

Indeed, it has been for many years their wish that you should be reestablished in your personal freedom and property rights.

Your affectionate sister,
Elizabeth

The siblings agreed, though Winty and Margaret did so with objections, Winty claiming that Archie was "mad as a hatter," and Margaret fearful that such a letter would open the floodgates for lawsuits against individual family members and advisers. Part of the problem for the Chanlers was that Archie's lawyers were not members of their own club. Heaven forbid, they were Jewish, and one family counselor strenuously advised Archie to jettison them and find a proper "gentleman" to represent his interests. After all, how could the white-shoe Astor lawyers deal with such "sharks and sheisters"? Since the family property was all interconnected, there would be interminable problems if Archie's lawyers were held in "perpetual suspicion" by the family counselors. Thus, even the final capitulation by the Chanlers was effected somewhat grudgingly, with more concern about legal niceties than about Archie's emotional well-being.

Nonetheless, a weight was lifted from Archie. He wrote back to his sister Elizabeth, thanking her and her husband for championing his cause: "I deeply appreciate the affectionate interest you have shown in my heart's desire." After all his years of bluster and bombast, his response was one of humility and simple relief. The Chanler siblings' letter was formally entered into the legal record. The last hurdle had been cleared and the New York Supreme Court rendered its ruling in July: "I declare the petitioner to be sane and competent to manage himself, his property, and his affairs, and to go forth and mingle with his fellow men, freed from the incubus which he has borne these many years." In his moment of triumph, not a single sibling was there to witness his "mental vindication." In an instant, however, Archie set aside his animosity toward his family. He immediately cabled congratulations to each one of his brothers and sisters and offered an end to past hostilities. That night he went to Elizabeth's home on West 82nd Street for a long-overdue reunion with her.

The next day Archie summoned the press to his quarters at the Brevoort Hotel and declared that he intended to spend the next seven years of his life fighting the "lunacy trust" in the United States and Europe; it would, he said, take five years to reform the United States and two years to "clean up Europe." His million-and-a-half-dollar fortune would provide the "war chest fund" for the campaign. On a lighter note, he offered his opinions on modern life in New York: the manners of New Yorkers had vastly improved over the years "except, of course, in the subway," and he declared the telephone service "the worst out of Hell." All of these pronouncements were given considerable play in the newspapers, under the headline "Who's Looney Now?"

Archie had to catch up on his own family: there were in-laws and nieces and nephews he'd never met. Archie adored meeting an entire new generation of Chanlers, many of them already young adults. He returned to Rokeby for a visit. Margaret and her family now owned the place outright. This was supposed to have been Archie's patrimony. Emerging from the corner room after lunch, the previously unknown "Uncle Archie" delighted his young niece and nephew. He read aloud to the family, motored about in his pink and blue automobile, and lavished affection on all of them. In subsequent visits he captivated his nieces and nephews with his supposedly outlandish eating habits. As the children watched in wide-eyed wonder, Archie would consume a full serving of grass clippings, and nothing else, as his dinner. He amazed the children and gave them a story of "crazy" Uncle Archie that they would tell and retell into their old age. Having played his little trick, later in the evening Archie would surreptitiously lower a basket from his bedroom window and have a servant send up a chicken dinner.

With his own siblings—his bitterest enemies for all those tortured years—Archie was remarkably forgiving; though there were limits to his tolerance. Winty's wife, Daisy, ever the literary snob, could not resist criticizing Archie's poetry, even as the reconciliation was just under way. "I was never more surprised in my surprising existence than to hear you tell me my verse needed polishing!" he retorted. "Truly a prophet is never without honour save in his own house!" Elizabeth tried to soothe her "dreadfully excitable" brother Archie. "His sweetness always wins out," she wrote to her son, though he "needs a lot of praying over." She feared that Robert would unsettle the hard-won peace, for he was determined to confront Archie about changing his name back to Chanler from Chaloner.

Archie was fifty-seven years old by the time he reacquainted himself with his own family. He'd missed decades of family holidays, weddings, births, and deaths. His sister Elizabeth's stepson, Victor Emmanuel Chapman, had been killed during World War I, the first American aviator to die; he had become a nationally known figure. Archie had never even met him. His own brothers and sisters, the tight-knit clan of "Astor orphans," were like strangers to him now. Elizabeth described a heartbreaking scene in which Archie did not even recognize his brother Lewis, the man who had signed the commitment papers for Bloomingdale. It happened at a glittering dinner at the Colony Club in New York celebrating the upcoming nuptials of Alida's oldest daughter, who had been born the year Archie was locked away. Elizabeth wrote to her son of the affair:

> *The dinner was a charming occasion,—very stately & well mannered, but with a strong undertow of deep feeling & happiness. Uncle Archie more than rivalled the bride as star-of-the-evening. He looked so dear, so sad, so noble, so lovely as he sat there at table,—except when one of his brothers would start talking to him, & then his face lit up with an angelic sort of happiness. He sat next [to] Uncle Lewis, whom he had not seen before in 20 years. They were both alone in the room together before other people arrived without know[ing] who the other was. They fell into each other's arms, figuratively speaking, when they discovered their identity, & Uncle L. devoted himself to Uncle A. all the evening.*

Archie's victory was complete.

Epilogue

An elderly local woman recalled how, as a young girl in the 1930s, she and her mother would occasionally visit Archie at Merry Mills. They'd pass through the dusty entrance hall and stairway crowded with statues and busts en route to the bedroom upstairs, where the master of the house had secluded himself. The pair would be ushered into the bedchamber by the farm manager, who closed the door behind them and locked it. The little girl hated the sound of the key turning in the lock. It still terrified her decades later. The room was a shambles: books and manuscripts piled everywhere, and messages from Archie's X-Faculty littering the floor. Sheets of galvanized iron fortified the window shutters as a hindrance to the burglars the reclusive occupant dreaded. Archie lay in bed, the walls covered with his handwritten scrawl: "JOHN ARMSTRONG CHALONER," over and over again. It was like a scene out of hell.

Incongruously, from outside of the house came the sounds of laughter. Archie had turned his estate into a veritable community center for all the local farmers and gentry to enjoy, young and old, black and white. On hot summer afternoons, picnickers spread out on the grounds and then went for a swim in Archie's delightfully cold, spring-fed pool. Canal-like, it stretched one hundred feet long and twenty-five feet wide. All the children in the countryside learned how to swim there. From his room Archie could look out upon the scene of hilarity below; as time went on, he rarely emerged from his darkened room. Sometimes he could be seen peering out through the window.

In the evenings there were dances with live music and movies. Archie transformed a cow barn into a theater for three hundred people, where he regularly showed silent movies, double features, along with agricultural films on subjects such as treating hog cholera or raising chickens. A player piano, manned by the farm manager's son, accompanied the silent films. There were snacks available. There had never been such entertainment offered in the countryside before, and farm folk walked and rode great distances to get to Merry Mills; long lines formed to get into the theater. A quarter of the movie house was set aside for blacks, this in an era of strict segregation, Archie's sentiment being, if you don't like it, don't come. They came.

The Fourth of July was the grandest event of all, the neighborhood children anticipating it more than Christmas. Flyers advertised the event for miles around; special trains and jitneys were set up to deliver celebrants to Merry Mills. It was estimated that more than ten thousand people attended the 1923 Fourth of July party. The all-day and evening festivities included baseball, running races, jousting matches on horseback, and a greased-pole climb. There were bands and fireworks, movies and dancing, and airplane rides from Archie's private airfield. Archie deputized and armed his farm manager, and if any of the guests got out of hand they were imprisoned overnight in a one-room log jailhouse or "calaboose," as Archie called it.

In the Virginia countryside, Archie was treated as a beloved, albeit eccentric, uncle by the local farmers and workers. He kept as many as 250 of them on his payroll, lent them money, and paid their medical bills. He bought his neighbors automobiles, and taught the local women how to protect themselves: he gave them pistols and shooting lessons, setting up teddy bears for target practice. These people were his family now.

After his reconciliation with his brothers and sisters, he had turned away from them again—not in anger, but in exhaustion. They required too much work, too much emotional turmoil. The habitual competitiveness and combativeness among all the siblings reared up before long. Archie didn't want to be second-guessed about his causes. He traveled across the country, railing against the lunacy laws and promoting his "Movies for the Farmers" campaign to keep farmers on the land by making rural life less dull and isolated. His family rolled their eyes as he rented the Cort Theater in New York for a series of free lectures on "Advanced Experimental Psychology and the Occult" in 1921. "There is a fairyland in every one's head," Archie announced, and he was eager to share his inner reality with the public. His performances consisted of messages he was receiving from the spirit world: Shakespeare dictated two new scenes for "Hamlet," P. T. Barnum admitted his deceptions on earth, and his great-aunt Julia Ward Howe revealed that in Paradise she was stark naked, though blessed with Godiva-like tresses.

In the wake of his legal victory, Archie's eccentricities grew even more pronounced. Once declared sane, this brilliant man, who had built an industrial empire only to have it stripped away, who had lost his wife, his friends, and his family, seemed to sink into the madness that the world had wished on him. In Los Angeles he channeled George Washington and Abraham Lincoln, and at the same time announced that he was producing a film based on his life in Bloomingdale. He would, of course, star in it himself. His encounters with the press grew more and more bizarre, and embarrassed reporters began to ignore him.

By the 1930s Archie had withdrawn to his Virginia estate, and eventually secluded himself in his bedroom, where he spent much of his time writing furiously. He ran through his entire fortune and had to borrow from his once-hated brothers and sisters to fend off creditors. Servants and farmhands weren't paid for years, but they stayed on anyhow in the vain hope that once Archie died, he'd leave behind a fortune for them. Caring neighbors and friends became alarmed over Archie's state. His family had long despaired of visiting their deranged brother, so they had seen neither Merry Mills nor the condition Archie was in. A member of the local gentry wrote to Elizabeth saying that Archie was "left in squalor. I found him once locked in the house, in his semi-helpless condition without food for 24 hrs." In December 1932, Margaret decided to visit, and she was stunned at what she found:

> There were inscriptions on the wall. Dates when the devil had come out etc. The house was distressing in its disorder and shabbiness. He was by that time borrowing large sums from us. . . . I made the mistake of asking "Archie, do you think there will be a second World War?" Instantly he drew his knees up, and clasping them said "A [hell] of a war and I am in charge. I have my platoon drilling out there now." He mentioned some huge number of men. But he added with his beautiful smile "They drill with weapons which can not hurt anyone. The Lord has put it all in my hands. In this war there will be no suffering."

By that time Archie was lost in his own dream world. He thought of himself as a kind of Napoleon in exile, awaiting some international event that he would take charge of. An engraving of Napoleon hung above the mantle in the library, and busts of the leader were scattered about the house. Archie prized photos of himself in which he looked like the emperor. Exile had been the theme of both of their lives: Napoleon to his island prison, Archie to his darkened bedroom.

Archie hired a photographer to document his universe at Merry Mills: his swimming pool and movie theater, his dance pavilion and calaboose, his parrots and books, his billiards table and study, and his bedroom where he remained locked away, taking dictation from his subconscious and performing psychic feats. Archie directed the photographer to set up his large-format camera and shoot directly into the mirror in his bedroom, convinced that he would capture some occult phenomena on the glass-plate negative. One photograph shows the room itself, and it is the perfect image of Archie's mental confusion: the writing on the walls, the piles on the floor, the bedclothes in a jumble. Archie is visible in the mirror's reflection. He is seen from the back, seated on the edge of his bed, his head bent down as if he is hard at work on some secret task, some weighty interior mission.

In the spring of 1935, Archie was hospitalized with cancer, the same disease that vanquished Napoleon. Elizabeth came down and kept a "sorrowful vigil" for the last several months of her brother's life. When word reached Castle Hill of Archie's condition, Amélie wrote a note "from my heart," to her ex-husband.

> *I have thought of you so constantly for a long time, and night and morning since your illness I have remembered you in my prayers. . . . Anything that I could do to please you I would do so gladly. I am sending you a charming photograph that I have kept all these years.*

It was a photo of Archie as a handsome young college student. Archie wrote back to thank her, ending the message, "With long life, health, and happiness for the Prince and yourself." It was the last note he would attempt to write in his own hand. He died on June 1, 1935, at the age of seventy-two, leaving part of his estate to Amélie.

Despite Archie's handwritten instructions that he be interred beside his pool at Merry Mills, the family arranged for burial in the churchyard at Grace Church. None of his siblings came. Archie's thirty-one-year-old nephew, William Astor Chanler Jr., served as an emissary from the family. He later recalled the funeral oration, the rector recounting the parish's deep debt to his deceased uncle. It was thanks to Archie that the beautiful stone church stood at all. An earlier structure had burned to the ground in 1895. Conveniently—and perhaps suspiciously—Archie had just purchased an insurance policy for the church at his own expense. "Mr. Chaloner was the friend of every poor resident of the community and never refused to help the needy," Reverend Robinson intoned. "This neighborhood will never forget him." The interment was, in nephew Willie's words, "awe-inspiring. . . . The choir of negresses, dressed in the colorful skirts & headdresses of the slave era, delivered a moving & beautiful number of spirituals in memorable voice." Two years later the family still had not bothered to put up a stone marking Archie's grave. The minister wrote to Margaret to try to shame the family into doing something: "I do not like to think of so wonderful a man lying in a nameless grave. . . . Everyone here who knew him loved him." He offered to take up a collection in order to put up a simple marker. The family belatedly commissioned a stone with the epitaph, "Blessed is the man who considereth the poor and needy."

For generations, the Chanler family has debated the meaning of poor Uncle Archie. Was he railroaded by his own flesh and blood and unjustly forced into a madhouse, his life ruined in the process? Or was he hopelessly insane, and his commitment an act of mercy? A screaming debate broke out at a family Thanksgiving dinner thirty years after his death. For many of his relatives, Archie remained the conscience of the family. He was considered the most generous, the one most devoted to those in need, the visionary industrialist, the art patron, even, it was said, the handsomest. One contemporary of Archie's pronounced with finality, "He was the best of them."

Archie's siblings, particularly Margaret, blamed Amélie for touching off his troubles. Margaret admitted that for a brief time the pair exuded a golden aura. "The atmosphere was affectionate and very witty," she wrote in retrospect. "Both he and Amélie could have been stars in improvised comedy." Margaret acknowledged that even she had been taken in by the magnetic Amélie:

> Her talents were numerous. She painted as well as she wrote. She sang charmingly, composing words and music. When one of her devastating "Headaches" was not blotting everything out, her mind showed wide reading, clever selection

> and memory. In a museum she was unconscious of others, a vital pilgrim moving from one thing to another like a sibyl.

But before long the idyll ended and, to Margaret, it became clear that Amélie was using her besotted brother.

> I suppose Amélie Rives was tempted by the Prince Charming who asked to rescue her from the dream-world of Castle Hill. She had visited the New York Rives and thought she would enjoy all my brother could give her. What she really wanted was to be surrounded by her women relatives and friends from home. They sailed together; her mother, . . . a friend, a coloured maid, for France, only my brother speaking french. He loved her people. He lavished upon them his great enjoyment of generosity.

Even in his final derangement, Margaret had to admit that there was a touching nobility about Archie:

> After he was alone, and never loved another woman, Archie lived in a mystical world of his own making in which he was very important. The only part of his nature which never suffered . . . from the tragedy of his wrong marriage, was his generosity. He loved to give and wanted nothing for himself.

Archie's choice of Amélie as spouse was disastrous, but also indicative of his manic craving for danger, for his need to take chances and live on the edge. Though Archie probably suffered from a bipolar disorder, his mental state certainly did not warrant the drastic step of lifetime incarceration in an institution, cut off from friends, family, and the outside world—"one of the cruelest outrages ever perpetrated by any man's family," according to a sympathetic acquaintance. The supposed cure, and his siblings' indifference to his plight over decades, surely worsened Archie's condition. With the extensive press coverage of his case, Archie himself became a public symbol of the murky nature of psychiatry in that era, and his tragic story helped spur reform: in 1906 a U.S. congressman solicited Archie's expert advice when St. Elizabeth's Hospital in Washington was being investigated.

Archie never got over Amélie. Found amid his possessions after he died was a miniature photo of Amélie dressed as the main character in *The Quick or the Dead?*. She had inscribed the photo in February 1889, "For: My Boy from his Amy." His bequest to her, generous as it was intended to be, came to naught. He was so deeply in debt that Merry Mills and everything in it had to be auctioned off. When the house was opened for the sale, Amélie's letters to Archie were strewn about the floor. He had obviously kept them close to hand in his last days. The letters were gathered up and delivered to Amélie by a friend. She later had them burned, along with all her other correspondence.

Only a few miles from Merry Mills, Amélie lived with her prince in genteel poverty. The prince and Amélie and her unmarried sister Landon, who lived grumpily with them, were forced to open the house to tourists. At the entrance to the estate they set up a table with leaflets and charged admission. One of Amélie's cousins lived for a time at Castle Hill, serving as a hostess for the tourists. She later recalled that

> she rarely saw [Amélie], even though it was her home! Cousin Amélie stayed in her room, writing and resting. Her meals were sent in by tray, and when she did come downstairs, she was always en negligee—beautifully. . . .
>
> They were very poor after Mr. Chaloner died, and opened Castle Hill to be shown to visitors—at a fee. . . . The meals were very sparse, and Pierre would forage for salad greens in the fields and on the lawn (cress, dandelions etc). One day, Lloyd, the butler, came up to my sister and said "Miss Anne, there ain't going to be any lunch today: the Prince couldn't find no weeds."

A decayed elegance enfolded Castle Hill in a kind of romantic cocoon. The French drawing room remained a virtual museum piece from a century earlier, the grass-green silk draperies now in tatters, the only addition to the room a signed photo from George Curzon. Captured in her youth by some of the most famous photographers of the late nineteenth and early twentieth centuries, Amélie now avoided the camera's gaze. She did not age well, which was the worst kind of crisis for a woman as vain as she, whose very identity was bound up in her physical allure. At times she tried to hide behind too much makeup, while at other times she just took to her bed, claiming illness. Nonetheless, Amélie still had a powerful magnetic presence, and as a respected member of the Southern literary establishment she held court at Castle Hill for a parade of prominent admirers, including H. L. Mencken, Sherwood Anderson, and William Faulkner. A young Katharine Hepburn arrived one day and was greeted cordially by the barefoot prince, who asked, "And what do you do, Miss Hepburn?" She, in turn, mistook him for the gardener. The master of the house, known as "Mister Prince" to the servants, loved wandering about the grounds and playing croquet without shoes and socks so that he could enjoy the feel of the grass; but he wore full white-tie evening attire at dinner every night.

Pierre kept a small studio in Washington, as they depended on the modest income from his portraiture; but since times were tough, he had to give up a grander place in New York. On August 24, 1936, the day after Amélie's seventy-third birthday, the prince died suddenly of a heart attack. Amélie was devastated and took to her bed. Sequestered in her room, she could not even bear to look out the window and watch as the coffin was lifted onto a farm wagon, covered with pine boughs, and drawn to the small family burial ground just beyond the ancient ring of boxwood by a team of white horses. There the prince was buried near Amélie's grandparents.

Amélie briefly considered taking her own life. A revolver that had been given to the prince by Alfred du Pont came to hand, as did enough sleeping pills "to put three or four or even five people to sleep forever," but Amélie resisted the urge. She became a recluse, but took delight in reaching out to a few chosen young people who possessed literary flair. Among them was Louis Auchincloss, who would go on to become a distinguished novelist of New York life. He was then studying law at the University of Virginia, having turned his back on his dream of becoming a writer after his first novel was rejected by Scribner's. Amélie helped rekindle his literary ambition, for which he remained ever grateful to her.

Auchincloss vividly recounted his first encounter with Amélie and Castle Hill, an afternoon tea in the fall of 1938. He turned onto the estate grounds, drove up the winding road leading to the house, and entered the driveway.

> I could hardly believe the boxwood that lined the narrow driveway. It towered over my Pontiac, thirty feet high, and scratched against the door on both sides as I drove slowly through it. I later learned that a tree surgeon had warned the Princess that it would die unless treated for a price beyond her means, and she retorted: "It was planted by a gardener who worked for George II. I think it will last my time—and yours!"

The princess was right; the boxwood has survived to this day, no thanks to Landon, who, when they had no money at all, resorted to selling pieces of it.

Like a siren of yore, Amélie entranced Auchincloss. Though she was ravaged by age and illness, he could still see the beauty that had once captivated the world, and he was mesmerized by her tales of a nearly vanished society. He came back again and again to her antiquated manor house with no central heating or electricity and only the barest concession to indoor plumbing, to listen to her stories of gilded life in the 1890s: the endless and pompous dinner parties, the literary conversations with Henry James and Oscar Wilde, her own morphine addiction. Her stories were, according to Auchincloss, "halfway between a startling truth and a tale in True Romances."

Amélie looked back upon her life with the prince with the greatest contentment. They had formed a true partnership of heart and mind—while spending enough time apart that, in Amélie's metaphor, they continued to smell the violets. After years of creative silence, Amélie produced two well-received novels in the 1910s and then re-created herself as a successful playwright in New York in the late 1910s and 1920s. Continuing to act the part of the Gilded Age temptress, despite being middle-aged, she appeared after one curtain call in a negligee. Amélie was initially taken to be an easy mark by Broadway sharpies, but she quickly proved otherwise. She tangled with agents and theatrical lawyers and an egotistical actor/producer over money and writing credit, and she managed to get the best of all of them. Over the course of a decade, five of her plays were produced on Broadway; one of them, a comedy called *The Fear Market,* was turned into a silent film in 1920. She and the prince lived high atop the artistic and theatrical world in New York, rubbing shoulders with the likes of Ethel and John Barrymore ("Mad love, Jack," he signed one letter), the famous Russian designer Leon Bakst, and the art photographer Alfred Stieglitz.

But the limelight faded along with Amélie's looks. In her final years she retreated almost entirely to the sanctuary of her boudoir, lying in bed beneath a gold valance that bore the Troubetzkoy coronet. Sympathetic friends, including Louis Auchincloss, helped support the impoverished princess and her sister. From afar, Auchincloss paid for Amelie's subscription to the *New York Times,* arranged to have several good bottles of French brandy shipped to her at Christmastime in 1942, and sent the occasional check. Amélie refused to sell her beloved but ramshackle Castle Hill. "But where would I live?" she'd ask dramatically. "In some horrid, vulgar little apartment in Charlottesville? What would be the point of that? I should never be able to breathe away from Castle Hill. It is the only life I have left."

The onetime siren who outraged Virginia society had, by the 1940s, been grudgingly embraced as one of their own. Children in the Old Dominion learned about Amélie in their history books; she was proudly touted as one of the first women writers in Virginia.

One local woman recalled that as a child she visited regularly at a nearby Rives estate where Amélie's cousins lived. She would ride on horseback over to Castle Hill, hoping to get a glimpse of the famous Amélie; but she never did. She imagined her as the beautiful young author who had broken new ground and earned her place among the pantheon of Virginia heroes.

Amélie lay in her darkened bedroom, afflicted with rheumatic fever, her sight and hearing both gone. By the end of 1944 she was brought to a nursing home in Charlottesville, a skeletal creature weighing only eighty-eight pounds. One day her wedding ring slipped off her emaciated finger and got lost amid the bedclothes. She had few visitors, but one cousin recalled that during her final illness "she insisted upon keeping her face covered with a chiffon scarf, because she wanted no one to see that she had lost her beauty." Finally she lapsed into a coma, died on June 15, 1945, and was buried next to the prince at Castle Hill, under a tombstone with an inscription she had chosen herself: "Love is strong as death." Two years later, Castle Hill was sold and its contents dispersed at auction. A reporter covering the sale for a Richmond newspaper recalled people scooping up parasols and other items from a bygone day.

NOTES

Quotations from primary sources retain their original spelling, punctuation, and grammatical construction.

Introduction

3 *Passion is perfume and flame*: Clark, *Innocence Abroad,* 79.

3 *showing off . . . shut up*: Thomas, *A Pride of Lions,* 35.

4 *Do you think if I drank a whole cupful*: Hurrell, "Some Days with Amélie Rives," 532.

4 *sensual rot*: Thomas, *A Pride of Lions,* 72.

4 *a sizzling vessel*: Chaloner, *A Brief for the Defence,* 182.

Chapter 1. The Education of an Astor, or A Name That Rings Like Bullion

6 *Landlord of New York*: Sinclair, *The Astors,* 17.

6 *hard dreary looking*: Homberger, *Mrs. Astor's New York,* 242.

6 *More's the pity*: Sinclair, *Dynasty,* 20.

7 *FURS AND PIANOS*: *Harper's New Monthly Magazine,* February 1865, 314.

8 *Why, Mr. Astor*: Ibid., 317.

8 *like unto bullion*: Melville, "Bartleby the Scrivener," www.bartleby.com/129/.

8 *peas with a knife*: Homberger, *Mrs. Astor's New York,* 243–44.

9 *I used to know him*: Ibid., 244.

9 *monarch of the counting-room*: *Harper's New Monthly Magazine,* February 1865, 308; *The roll-book*: Ibid., 320.

9 *now and then*: Ibid., 319.

10 *self-invented money-making machine*: Wecter, *The Saga of American Society,* 115.

10 *Astor . . . estate*: Porter, *John Jacob Astor,* vol. 2, 1267, 1268, 1276–77, 1091–92; *Harper's New Monthly Magazine,* February 1865, 322.

10 *hoarding wealth*: Sinclair, *Dynasty*, 149.

11 *In a fitting touch*: *New York Herald*, November 25, 1875, 3.

12 *Eager to become*: Stein, ed., "La Bergerie / Rokeby," the $50,000 figure comes from *Deed Book*, Dutchess County Courthouse, Poughkeepsie, recorded July 12, 1836, Book 59, p. 537.

13 *imbecile*: *New York Herald*, November 25, 1875, 3; Sinclair, 92–93.

13 *He was practically taught*: *New York Herald*, November 25, 1875, 3.

14 *thousands of buildings*: Sinclair, *Dynasty*, 167; *a very good and trusted*: Gates, *The Astor Family*, 54.

14 *Of the late William B.*: *Harper's Weekly*, January 15, 1876, 43.

14 *$40 or $50 million*: Homberger, *Mrs. Astor's New York*, 246; Wecter, *The Saga of American Society*, 115.

14 *one hundred millions*: *New York Times*, November 25, 1875, 1.

14 *A contemporary*: *New York Herald*, November 25, 1875, 3.

15 *thinks twice*: Nevins, ed., *The Diary of Philip Hone*, 690.

15 *clink of gold*: Elliott, *Uncle Sam Ward*, 159.

15 *city of Sin and Science*: Ibid., 47.

15 *wore handsome rings*: Homberger, *Mrs. Astor's New York*, 100.

15 *Everything here is greed*: Ibid., 99.

16 *your mind . . . lost day*: Elliott, *Uncle Sam Ward*, 160.

16 *magician*: Chanler, "Memoirs of Rokeby," 16–17; Sinclair, *Dynasty*, 137; O'Connor, *The Astors*, 72–73.

16 *the most cheerful . . . Arabian nights*: Elliott, *Uncle Sam Ward*, 169; Sinclair, *Dynasty*, 137; Brandt, *An American Aristocracy*, 192, signing marriage agreement.

16 *I love . . . fever*: Elliott, *Uncle Sam Ward*, 164; O'Connor, *The Astors*, 72; Howe, *Reminiscences*, 65, diamond star on forehead.

16–17 *Death robbed my house . . . raise the little boy*: Elliott, *Uncle Sam Ward*, 286–87; Emily gives birth February 16, dies February 18, infant dies February 22.

17 *torture . . . I woke up*: Aldrich, unpublished typescript on mourning, Rokeby Collection; discussion of mourning for Emily—Gates, *The Astor Family*, 62, and Sinclair, *Dynasty*, 138; general discussion of mourning practices at the time—*The Delineator*, October 1908, 612, 615.

17 *society dictated*: Aldrich, unpublished typescript on mourning, Rokeby Collection; *The Delineator*, October 1908, 612, 615.

18 *a sort of outwitting*: O'Connor, *The Astors*, 73.

18 *Sam . . . has probably*: Ibid.; Elliott, *Uncle Sam Ward*, 390–91.

18–19 *Knowing the power . . . social improprieties*: Chanler, "Memoirs of Rokeby," Rokeby Collection, 19; discussion of banning relatives from Rokeby, interview with Bronson Winthrop Chanler.

19 *rearrange the furniture*: Thomas, *A Pride of Lions*, 61–63, discussion of Daisy's arrival at Rokeby. Archie's brother, Winthrop Astor Chanler, was nicknamed Winty, but the spelling varied over the course of his lifetime. As a child he was known as Wintie, but as an adult he referred to himself as Winty. I have followed his own preferred spelling in the course of the text, except in direct quotations that spell his name in the alternative fashion.

19 *En route, Howe*: Chanler, "Memoirs of Rokeby," 19–20.

19 *In the immediate aftermath . . . rankled William B.*: Thomas, *A Pride of Lions*, 12–13, discussion of Ward's loss of his daughter; O'Connor, *The Astors*, 73, threat of losing Bond street property; Elliott, *Uncle Sam Ward*, 410, 419, 423, discussion of Ward's finances, and experience in San Francisco.

20 *inherited Astor land*: Homberger, *Mrs. Astor's New York*, 102; Elliot, *Uncle Sam Ward*, 434.

20 *King of the Lobby*: Elliott, *Uncle Sam Ward*, 445; 440–55, 459, discussion of Ward's international dealings and charm.

20 *Sam Ward could strut*: Patterson, *The First Four Hundred*, 72.

21 *the means of information . . . Bohemianism*: Dartmouth, Rauner Special Collections Library, The Papers of Augustus Saint-Gaudens, May 20, 1898, letter from Joseph H. Choate to Augustus Saint-Gaudens.

21 *[she] had been taught*: Elliott, *Uncle Sam Ward*, 480.

22 *unremitting shadow*: Aldrich, *Family Vista*, 4.

23 *silk-stockinged . . . true-blue*: Moody, *The Astor Place Riot*, 2.

23 *den of the Aristocracy*: Ibid., 8.

23–24 *Police and militia . . . turned away*: Ibid., 12, 158–159; Jackson, ed., *The Encyclopedia of New York City*, 1007.

26 *God's brightest inspiration*: Thomas, *A Pride of Lions*, 20.

27 *to see how very quietly*: Aldrich, *Family Vista*, 1. On William B.'s funeral, *New York Herald*, November 28, 1875, 6; *New York Times*, November 28, 1875, 12.

27–28 *is as familiar*: *New York Herald*, November 25, 1875, 3.

28 *the most fashionable*: Wecter, *The Saga of American Society*, 209.

28 *This is mixed*: Ibid., 210.

28 *Brown's Brigade*: Amory, *Who Killed Society?*, 117; also Wecter, *The Saga of*

American Society, 210, and Homberger, *Mrs. Astor's New York,* 118, for discussion of Brown.

29 *beadle-faced*: Amory, *Who Killed Society?,* 115; discussion of his weight, Homberger, *Mrs. Astor's New York,* 116.

29 *Archie was separated*: *New York Herald,* November 28, 1875, 6.

30 *Noticeably absent*: Thomas, *A Pride of Lions,* 80; "Memoirs of Rokeby," back pages. As children the Chanler siblings only saw their uncle once or twice, though he was remembered darkly whenever inappropriate behavior or an untoward marriage loomed. In the final decade of Uncle Henry's life, Margaret Chanler Aldrich took her own children to visit the wayward relative, though she did not include him in the official family genealogy, the "Background Outline Pedigree," she compiled in the back of her unpublished memoir. John Winthrop Aldrich annotation.

31 *My son Henry . . . his issue*: Sinclair, *Dynasty,* 144.

31 *Money counts*: Gates, *The Astor Family,* 133; Thomas, *A Pride of Lions,* 80; and Porter, *John Jacob Astor,* vol. 1, 1266, discussion of Henry Astor's financial situation.

31 *become unworthy*: Porter, *John Jacob Astor,* 1266.

32 *the red-eyed hound*: Sinclair, *Dynasty,* 145.

32 *the last cookie*: Gates, *The Astor Family,* 135.

33 *representatives of all*: *New York Times,* November 28, 1875.

34 *dearest boys . . . leg a little way*: Margaret Ward Chanler to JAC, December 1, 1875, Rokeby Collection.

34–35 *private equipages . . . heaped upon it*: *New York Herald,* December 17, 1875, 5.

35 *Yesterday morning . . . self-restraint*: *New York Times,* December 17, 1875, 4. That "self-restraint" would be a trait noticeably absent in her brood.

35 *goods, chattels*: December 28, 1875, legal notice to John Armstrong Chanler, Rokeby Collection.

36 *Tell Archie to bring down*: John Winthrop Chanler to Winthrop Astor Chanler, March 10, 1876, Rokeby Collection.

36 *Special Guardian*: Last Will and Testament and Codicils of William B. Astor, submitted November 29, 1875, County of New York Surrogate's Court, p. 10, Rokeby Collection.

36 *modest*: *New York Herald,* November 25, 1875, 3.

36 *In the mean time . . . your affairs*: John Winthrop Chanler to Winthrop Astor Chanler, March 10, 1876, Rokeby Collection.

36– *write often . . . & thin ice*: John Winthrop Chanler to JAC, postmarked
37 January 14, 1876, Rokeby Collection.

37 *I received . . . play ground*: JAC to John Winthrop Chanler, January 10, 1877, Rokeby Collection.

37 *King Death*: John Winthrop Chanler poem, dated September 19, 1877, Newport, Rhode Island, Rokeby Collection.

39 *checkered with light . . . dismal winter*: John Winthrop Chanler to Winthrop Astor Chanler, Jun 24, 1876, Rokeby Collection.

39 *black despair*: John Winthrop Chanler, "Sonnet No. 3," written September 19, 1877, Newport, Rhode Island, Rokeby Collection.

40 *We like our . . . ventillater*: JAC to John Winthrop Chanler, September 12, 1876, Rokeby Collection. Rev. Gibson to John Winthrop Chanler, August 23, 1876, Rokeby Collection, about room switch.

40 *our room leaked*: Winthrop Astor Chanler to John Winthrop Chanler, January 7, 1877, Rokeby Collection. JAC to John Winthrop Chanler, December 10, 1876, Rokeby Collection, about the frozen pitcher of water.

40 *Did you see us*: Winthrop Astor Chanler to John Winthrop Chanler, May 28, [1876], Rokeby Collection.

41 *Don't stop her*: Aldrich, *Family Vista,* 11.

41 *share and share alike*: Last Will and Testament of Margaret Astor Chanler, submitted December 18, 1875, County of New York Surrogate's Court, p. 376, Rokeby Collection.

41 *went forth . . . Palestine*: John Winthrop Chanler to JAC and Winthrop Astor Chanler, November 19, 1876, Rokeby Collection.

41 *three Pirates*: John Winthrop Chanler to JAC and Winthrop Astor Chanler, October 1, 1876, Rokeby Collection.

41 *wasp-haunted*: Margaret Chanler Aldrich, "Rokeby and Environs," Rokeby room-by-room descriptions; "The Tower," unpublished typescript, Rokeby Collection.

42 *superannuated*: Minutes of meetings held by Guardians, April 29, 1879, entry, Rokeby Collection. This leather-bound notebook details the education, care, and expenses of the Chanler orphans. It reads like something out of Dickens, with a decided emphasis on keeping costs down.

42 *mysteries of swagger*: Memoir of Rugby written by JAC, July and August 1880, transcription, p. 54, Rokeby Collection. Archie wrote on the opening page of his two-volume memoir: "The object of this book is to give people, this side of the Atlantic, an idea of what 'Rugby' of today is as opposed to the Rugby of 'Tom Brown'; for my friends are continually asking me, how I

liked Rugby and 'was it any thing like Tom Brown's account of it.' " Rugby was familiar to every schoolboy in the mid-to-late-nineteenth century as the setting of the wildly popular 1857 novel *Tom Brown's School Days*.

42–43 *What was swagger*: Memoir of Rugby written by JAC, July and August 1880, Rokeby Collection. Transcription, 50–51.

43 *culture of "manliness."*: Honey, *Tom Brown's Universe*, 223.

44 *In the first letter*: JAC to John Winthrop Chanler, April 29, 1877, Rokeby Collection.

44 *I saw dear*: JAC to John Winthrop Chanler, May 2, 1877, Rokeby Collection.

44–45 *dear Papa was dead . . . From your loving Archie*: JAC to Chanler siblings, October 28, 1877, Rokeby Collection.

46 *a copy of Dear*: JAC to Mary Marshall, November 25, 1877, Rokeby Collection.

46 *As the eldest son*: Last Will and Testament of John Winthrop Chanler submitted to County of New York Surrogate's Court, November 1, 1876, p. 64, Rokeby Collection.

46 *unconditional . . . as a memorial*: Ibid., 64, 66–67. See Thomas, *A Pride of Lions*, 32–33, for discussion of will.

47 *Gives a great deal*: Rugby School report from June 23 to July 20, 1878, Rokeby Collection.

47 *titled swells*: JAC to Mary Marshall, June 7, 1885, Rokeby Collection.

48 *know his own mind*: Ada Patterson, "The Strange Case of John Armstrong Chaloner," 12.

Chapter 2. The Marriage Mart

49 *the very Holy of Holies*: Lehr, *"King Lehr" and the Gilded Age*, 112.

50 *a kind of elixir vitae . . . fogs are proverbially*: Gannon, *Newport Mansions: The Gilded Age*, 22.

50 *hospital of the Carolinas*: Ibid., 3.

51 *the Newport season should entirely evaporate*: Ward, *Reminiscences*, 40.

51 *furnished the champagne with his witticisms*: Elliott, *This Was My Newport*, 112.

52 *at the social pretenders and their vulgarities*: Aldrich, *Family Vista*, 43–44.

52 *handsome two story house*: *Newport Mercury*, January 4, 1873.

52 *almost on the extreme verge of the cliff*: Mason, *Newport and Its Cottages*, 83.

53–54 *It is a most singular house . . . a black in Oriental costume*: Elliott, 203.

54 *He never stifled an impulse*: O'Connor, *The Golden Summers,* 93.

55 *as imperative for a social aspirants's claims*: Lucey, *I Dwell in Possibility,* 178.

56 *"melancholy" place*: O'Connor, *The Golden Summers,* 280; Lucey, *I Dwell in Possibility,* 189.

56 *had not a friend in the wide world*: Thomas, *The Astor Orphans,* 1999, 64–65; Sinclair, *Dynasty,* 198–99, 205–6.

57 *Here Lies One Who Laughed*: Chanler, ed., *Winthrop Chanler's Letters,* ix.

58 *The brothers quarreled*: Chanler, *Roman Spring,* 186–87.

58 *thrifty German taste for* Ersatz: Ibid., 183.

59 *dreadful little 'home parlour'*: Ibid., 184.

59 *smothered the little creature*: Thomas, *A Pride of Lions,* 1971, 63.

59 *rose and fled*: Chanler, *Roman Spring,* 190.

60 *Avoid Newport like the plague*: Lehr, *"King Lehr" and the Gilded Age,* 112.

60 *a sizzling vessel*: Chaloner, *A Brief for the Defence,* 182.

61 *The girls left us*: Matilda Rives to Judith Page Rives, August 16 (no year given), Rives Family Papers, #2313, Box 7, Folder: Misc. Corresp., Special Collections, UVA Library.

61 *large costly houses*: Matilda Rives to Judith Page Rives, September 26 [1880], Rives Family Papers, #2313, Box 7, Folder: Misc. Corresp., Special Collections, UVA Library.

62 *The display of diamonds*: *Newport Mercury,* August 27, 1887.

62 *akin to fairy land*: *Newport Daily Season,* September 17, 1887; *New York Times,* June 10, 1888.

63 *Dined out*: JAC to Margaret Livingston Chanler, September 1887, Rokeby Collection.

Chapter 3. Behind the Boxwood, or The Wind Down My Chimney

65 *his ardors*: Chanler, *Roman Spring,* 211.

66 *I am as sure that*: AR to Thomas Nelson Page, March 4, 1884, Papers of Thomas Nelson Page, #7581, Special Collections, UVA Library.

66 *quite as perfect*: AR to Page, March 4, 1884 (Henry James), December 25, 1885 (Shakespeare), Papers of Thomas Nelson Page, #7581, Special Collections, UVA Library.

66 *I have been very near to death*: AR to Page, March 4 [1884], Papers of Thomas Nelson Page, #7581, Special Collections, UVA Library.

66 *neuralgia of the brain*: AR to Page, October 3, 1884, Papers of Thomas Nelson Page, #7581, Special Collections, UVA Library.

66 *At present I am 'maladive'*: AR to Page, March 16, 1884, Papers of Thomas Nelson Page, #7581, Special Collections, UVA Library.

67 *Don't think I neglect*: AR to Page, n.d. [1884], Papers of Thomas Nelson Page, #7581, Special Collections, UVA Library.

67 *susceptible*: AR to Page, March 4, 1884, Papers of Thomas Nelson Page, #7581, Special Collections, UVA Library.

67 *what one would look for from the pen of a girl . . . Methinks an author*: AR to Page, July 20, 1884, Papers of Thomas Nelson Page, #7581, Special Collections, UVA Library.

68 *To be called a good, true woman*: AR to Page, March 4, 1884, Papers of Thomas Nelson Page, #7581, Special Collections, UVA Library.

68 *if 'Lorna Doone' had never been written*: AR to Page, October 26, 1885, Papers of Thomas Nelson Page, #7581, Special Collections, UVA Library.

69 *TOM! You villain!*: AR to Page, October 10, 1885, Papers of Thomas Nelson Page, #7581, Special Collections, UVA Library.

69 *here's for a long talk with you*: AR to Page, March 16 [1884?], Papers of Thomas Nelson Page, #7581, Special Collections, UVA Library.

70 *You must be sure*: AR to Thomas Bailey Aldrich, November 23, 1885, Thomas Bailey Aldrich Papers, bMS Am 1429, Houghton Library, Harvard.

71 *You know I have not been much in the world*: AR to Aldrich, December 6, 1885, Thomas Bailey Aldrich Papers, bMS Am 1429, Houghton Library, Harvard.

71 *I hope you will not think me a very wild and uncivilized being*: AR to Aldrich, December 31, 1885, Thomas Bailey Aldrich Papers, bMS Am 1429, Houghton Library, Harvard.

73 *Hedges of Box*: Amélie Rives, *As the Wind Blew,* 211.

77 *Calling cards*: Papers of the Rives Family, #2532, Box 2, Folder: ca. 1828–1854, "Calling cards," Special Collections, UVA Library.

78 *trifle*: John Hammond Moore, "Amélie Louise Rives and the Charge of the Light Brigade," 92.

78 *I cannot express to you*: Judith Page Rives to [Her Children] William Cabell Rives Jr. and Amélie Louise Rives Sigourney, Papers of the Rives, Sears and Rhinelander families, #10596, Box 2, Folder: 1873–1874, Special Collections, UVA Library.

79 *Go! Go! Please go! . . . very charming but very imperious Lady*: Massie and Christian, eds., *Homes and Gardens in Old Virginia,* 199.

80 *an air of civilized taste and ancient leisure*: Chanler, *Roman Spring*, 210.

81 *We are a different race*: Papers of John Armstrong Chaloner, #38-394a–b, Box 2, folder: 1910 "Misc. Items—Confederate newspaper, p. 1," Special Collections, UVA Library.

81 *I have seen the pavements*: Sowle, "Trials of a Virginia Unionist," 14.

81 *He seemed to be good-natured . . . nothing but jokes & stories*: William Cabell Rives to WCR Jr., February 24, 1861, Papers of William C. Rives, Library of Congress.

82 *a rail splitter might have been deemed*: Judith Page Walker Rives, Autobiography, Rives Family Papers, #2313, Box IV, p. 60, Special Collections, UVA Library.

82 *You know I never had any faith*: Judith Page Walker Rives to William Cabell Rives Jr., Rives Family Papers, #2313, March 19, 1867, Special Collections, UVA Library.

82 *It has been said*: Interview with Barclay Rives.

83 *My family was happy in godparents*: Auchincloss, *A Writer's Capital*, 135.

84 *She was never sent to school*: *Harper's New Monthly Magazine*, n.d. [Fall 1888?] Papers of the Rives Family, #2532, Box 2, Scrapbook of Amélie Rives, Special Collections, UVA Library.

85 *childish effusions*: AR, "Notes for a biographical sketch of Amélie Rives Troubetzkoy," July 18, 1934, typescript p. 2, Papers of the Rives Family, #2532, Box 1, Special Collections, UVA Library.

85 *was fond of shutting herself up*: *New York Times*, June 10, 1888.

86 *Married love is like champagne*: AR, handwritten autobiography, April 1, 1925, p. VII, Papers of the Rives Family, #2532, Box 1, Special Collections, UVA Library.

86 *sad, unsatisfied life*: AR to Page, [ca. 1884], Papers of Thomas Nelson Page, #7581, Special Collections, UVA Library.

86 *Alfred's movements are so erratic . . . cheerful and bears it bravely*: Judith Page Walker Rives to Grace Sears Rives, March 12, 1869, Papers of the Rives, Sears and Rhinelander families, #10596, Box 1, Folder: 1860–1869, Special Collections, UVA Library.

87 *There is nothing left to pay House servants*: 1875 accounting, Rives Family Papers #2313, Box 4, Folder: 1875, "Receipts, Statements," Special Collections, UVA Library.

87–88 *Napoleon ascribes his success . . . to become a millionaire*: William Cabell Rives Jr. to Ella Rives, July 17, 1875, Rives Family Papers #2313, Box 4, 1875, Folder: "Misc. Corresp.," Special Collections, UVA Library.

88 *Every year the same parting . . . How I hate this southern town*: AR's Journal, November 7 and 11, 1879, Papers of the Rives Family #2532, Box 2, Special Collections, UVA Library.

89 *I am so very tired*: Alfred Rives to Sadie, August 20, 1885, Papers of the Rives family #2532, Box 1, Folder: "1830–1886 Corresp.," Special Collections, UVA Library.

89 *New York magnates*: Alfred Rives to Sadie, August 26, 1885 [two letters with same date], Papers of the Rives family #2532, Box 1, Folder: "1830–1886 Corresp.," Special Collections, UVA Library.

90 *This is the worst place I ever was in*: JAC to Robert Chanler, March 8, 1886, Rokeby Collection.

Chapter 4. Armida's Garden

93 *Curling brown hair*: *Lippincott's Monthly Magazine,* April 1888, 446.

93 *kissed her dress*: Mixon, "New Woman, Old Family," 128, 135. Though the "prurience" of Amélie's novel may seem quaint today, she was a pioneering writer of her time—the literary historian Wayne Mixon writes that *The Quick or the Dead?* "depicted passion much more explicitly" than Kate Chopin did in *The Awakening,* which came out more than ten years later.

94 *Jock! kiss* me!: *Lippincott's Monthly Magazine,* April 1888, 511.

94 *those who call me impure . . . foulness*: Amélie Rives, *The Quick or the Dead?* Philadelphia: J. B. Lippincott, 1889, iii–vii.

94 *Women secretly read*: At the Woman's Club in Richmond, Virginia—a grand old institution with a magnificent nineteenth-century Italianate mansion to match its fine lineage—a member told me that her grandmother had grown up in the countryside near Castle Hill, and that Amélie had been an inspiration to her and to other women who dreamed of a more unconventional life.

95 *haunted chamber . . . an inoffensive creature*: Hurrell, "Some Days with Amélie Rives," *Lippincott's Monthly Magazine,* April 1888, 533–35.

95 *Beastly*: Thomas, *A Pride of Lions,* 72.

96 *dreadful*: Margaret Terry Chanler to her mother, May 12, 1888, Winthrop and Margaret Terry Chanler Papers, Bms Am 1595, Houghton Library, Harvard.

96 *the life of the party . . . exquisitely refined person*: Margaret Terry Chanler to her mother, May 12, 1888, Winthrop and Margaret Terry Chanler Papers, Bms Am 1595, Houghton Library, Harvard.

96–97 *the effect was dazzling . . . perhaps a genius*: Chanler, *Roman Spring,* 210–11.

97 *this . . . is strictly private*: Margaret Terry Chanler to her mother, May 12, 1888, Winthrop and Margaret Terry Chanler Papers, Bms Am 1595, Houghton Library, Harvard.

97 *The Quicker the Better*: *Town Topics*, May 3, 1888, 13.

97–98 *Be Quick and Be Dead*: Longest, *Three Virginia Writers*, 151–52.

98 *He was the proudest and happiest man*: Walter Wellman, "Amélie Rives Chanler," *Chicago Times-Herald*, n.d., Amélie Rives file, Valentine Richmond History Center.

98 *Just engaged Amélie Rives . . . shadiest young authoress of the day*: Elizabeth Chanler Chapman to Chanler Chapman [1928?], Rokeby Collection.

99 *"The news . . . burst like a thunderclap . . . Make the best of it I imagine"*: JAC to Elizabeth Chanler, June 14 and 24, 1888, Rokeby Collection.

99 *literally speechless with astonishment*: JAC to Elizabeth Chanler, June 14 and 24, 1888, Rokeby Collection.

100 *He has no interest whatever*: Ibid.

102 *there being no malaria . . . take down the jam*: Margaret Livingston Chanler to Elizabeth Chanler, June 17, 1888, Rokeby Collection.

103 *for her brain has been much excited*: Margaret Livingston Chanler to Elizabeth Chanler, June 10, 1888, Rokeby Collection.

103 *The engagement of Mr. Armstrong Chanler*: "Society Topics of the Week," *New York Times*, June 10, 1888.

104 *In Boston . . . they are now laying odds . . . the Astor name from intellectual nothingness*: *Town Topics*, June 14, 1888, 4.

105 *fine, well knit figure . . . with half long sleeves*: *New York Herald*, June 15, 1888.

105 *radiantly joyful*: Margaret Livingston Chanler to Elizabeth Chanler, June 17, 1888, Rokeby Collection.

105 *bounteous dinner*: *New York Times*, June 15, 1888.

106 *supported in her ordeal*: *Town Topics*, June 21, 1888, 1.

106 *tears rolled down her cheeks*: Thomas, *A Pride of Lions*, 85–86.

106 *If ever two people deserved*: Ibid., 84.

107 *You do not seem to realize*: Ibid., 85–86.

107 *Dear Brog*: Ibid., 86.

107 *I shall want an apology*: Ibid., 86.

Chapter 5. The Bride Stripped Bare

108 *The woman soul leads us*: AR to Elizabeth Chanler, June [17] 1892, Rokeby Collection.

108 *dear, dear Sister*: AR to Margaret Livingston Chanler, June 30, 1888, Rokeby Collection; Thomas, *A Pride of Lions*, 87–88.

109 *My darling Sister of Charity*: AR to Margaret Livingston Chanler, July 15, 1888, Rokeby Collection.

109 *Oh! Margaret, pray for me*: AR to Margaret Livingston Chanler, July 2, 1888, Rokeby Collection.

110 *Margaret, tell me as though you were my own*: AR to Margaret Livingston Chanler [ca. summer 1888], Rokeby Collection.

110 *There is a type of cold blonde*: from Elizabeth Chanler Chapman to her son Chanler Chapman, June 1, 1924, Rokeby Collection.

111 *impulse to break into raptures*: Walter Wellman to JAC, March 6, 1889, Chaloner Papers, Box 1, folder 1876–91, William R. Perkins Library, Duke University.

111–12 *moods of genius . . . radiant sunshine took their place*: Newspaper clipping, no date or source, Amélie Rives file, Valentine Richmond History Center.

112 *We are all waiting . . . till we drop*: Winthrop Chanler to Margaret Livingston Chanler, August 22, 1888, Rokeby Collection.

112 *It was curious to see*: Margaret Terry Chanler to her father, July 2, 1888, Margaret (Terry) Chanler Letters 1888 *44M-383, bMS Am 1595 (449–53), Houghton Library, Harvard.

113 *treachery*: AR to Margaret Livingston Chanler, July 15, 1888, Rokeby Collection.

113 *The Chanlers are like turkeys*: Margaret Terry Chanler, *Autumn in the Valley*, 12.

113 *It was quite a Baronial scene*: Winthrop Chanler to his father-in-law, July 4, 1888, Winthrop Chanler Letters, 1888–1985, bMS Am 1595 (744–53), Houghton Library, Harvard.

114 *egad*: Lehr, *"King Lehr" and the Gilded Age*, 124–25.

114–15 *cargo of sumptuous furnishings*: *Town Topics*, June 14, 1888, 5.

115 *the handsomest house I ever was in*: JAC to Margaret Livingston Chanler, October 1, 1888, Rokeby Collection.

115 *one of the grandest fêtes*: *Newport Mercury*, Aug 25, 1888, 1.

115 *Miss Amélie Rives Chanler was the centre*: *Stafford* (Kansas) *Democrat*, September 24, 1888.

115 *Tolerably*: *Newport Daily Observer*, September 17, 1888.

116 *Amélie Rives Chandler*: *Shreveport Times*, August 21, 1888.

116 *being known through life*: "A Chat with Amélie Rives," *New York World*, September 25, 1888.

116 *chatted by the column*: *St. Louis Republic*, September 30, 1888.

117 *A Complete Failure*: *Boston Herald*, October 2, 1888.

117 *My brother J. Armstrong Amélie Rives*: French, *Some Letter from "Chan,"* 8.

117 *Amélie has arrived*: Thomas, *A Pride of Lions*, 90.

118 *You don't know how delighted*: JAC to Margaret Livingston Chanler, October 1, 1888, Rokeby Collection.

119 *a drawing room their battleground*: Untitled manuscript, Chaloner Papers, Box 24, dated October 20, 1888, William R. Perkins Library, Duke.

123 *Many years later she told a friend*: Interview with Louis Auchincloss.

123 *sisterly . . . maidenhood*: Rives, *Barbara Dering*, 42ff, 139.

123 *old Archie I used to know*: AR to Margaret Livingston Chanler, November 18, 1888, Rokeby Collection.

124 *Dearest, sweet Margaret*: AR to Margaret Livingston Chanler, November 15, 1888, Rokeby Collection.

125 *Thanks so much for your sweet letter*: JAC to Margaret Livingston Chanler, December 1, 1888, Rokeby Collection.

126 *O Margaret I can scarcely believe it all*: AR to Margaret Livingston Chanler, Feb 15, 1889, Rokeby Collection.

126 *Dearest Bess*: JAC to Elizabeth Chanler, March 4, 1889, Rokeby Collection.

127 *the most useful man*: Auchincloss, *The Vanderbilt Era*, 73, 78.

128 *awe-inspiring*: Ibid., 127.

128 The *happy American here*: Abdy, *The Souls*, 160, 162.

129 *Wild and rank*: Aïdé, " 'The Quick or the Dead?' and 'Virginia of Virginia,' " *Nineteenth Century Magazine* 25 (February 1889): 228; *monstrous deal of talk*: "The American Widow—New Style," *The Saturday Review of Politics, Literature, Science, and Art* 66 (November 17, 1888): 570.

129 *For Amélie Rives, from her sincere admirer*: Taylor, "A 'Soul' Remembers Oscar Wilde," 43.

129 *It would mean a different future . . . I'll promise you that!*: Clark, *Innocence Abroad*, 80–81.

130 *more pagan than soulful*: Abdy and Gere, *The Souls*, 11.

131 *most aristocratic cult*: *The World*, July 16, 1890, 22.

131 *the insidious dry rot*: Gilmour, *Curzon: Imperial Statesman*, 101.

131 *a British gladiator*: Asquith, *An Autobiography*, vol. 2, 35.

132 *I shall always remember*: Abdy and Gere, *The Souls*, 61.

132 *an expression of enamelled self-assurance . . . honourably and categorically mentioned*: Asquith, *An Autobiography*, 14, 23, 16.

133 *is not always responsible*: AR to Margaret Livingston Chanler, August 27, 1889, Rokeby Collection.

133 *above poetic prose*: JAC to Margaret Livingston Chanler, August 28, 1889, Rokeby Collection.

134 *The fluttering draperies*: AR to Margaret Livingston Chanler, December 1, 1889, Rokeby Collection.

134 *The only cheerful thing*: AR to Margaret Livingston Chanler, December 30, 1889, Rokeby Collection.

134–35 *Your voice has so little timbre*: JAC to Margaret Livingston Chanler, December 2, 1889, Rokeby Collection.

135 *cold & patronizing tone . . . regarding serious 'roughing it'*: JAC to William Astor Chanler, December 15, 1889, Chaloner Papers, William R. Perkins Library, Duke University.

135 *flippant*: William Chanler to JAC, Jan 20, 1890, Chaloner Papers, William R. Perkins Library, Duke University.

135 *I was delighted with your letter*: JAC to William Astor Chanler, January 23, 1890, Chaloner Papers, William R. Perkins Library, Duke University.

136 *half-financed and half-starved*: Aldrich, *Family Vista*, 52.

136 *At noon there was a recess*: Rives, "Notes for a Biographical Sketch," Papers of the Rives Family, #2532, Box 1, July 1934, p. 5, Special Collections, UVA Library.

136 *What a strange Country*: AR to Elizabeth Chanler, Good Friday night, 1890, Rokeby Collection.

136 *jilted*: *New York Times*, March 25, 1890.

136 *She probably now has a better idea*: *Pittsburgh Gazette*, March 21, 1890.

137 *immense old trees*: Julia Magruder, "The House of Madame de Pompadour," *Once a Week*, undated, 157–58, Amélie Rives, Papers, 1830–1940, #2495, Special Collections, University of Virginia (UVA) Library.

138 *la place d'honneur*: photograph, Manuscripts of Amélie Rives, # 2495, Box 9, Special Collections, UVA Library.

138 *Inlaid with porcelain . . . never sweeter trysting-places*: Julia Magruder, "The House of Pompadour," *Once a Week*, undated, pp. 159–60, Amélie Rives, Papers, 1830–1940, #2495, Special Collections, University of Virginia Library.

138 *painting and book scribbling . . . I want to do*: AR to Margaret Livingston Chanler, July 16, 1890, Rokeby Collection.

138 *Give dearest Bobbems*: AR to Margaret Livingston Chanler, Good Friday night, 1890, Rokeby Collection.

138 *en pleine aire*: AR's legal deposition circa 1907, Box 14, p. 8, Chaloner Papers, William R. Perkins Library, Duke University.

138 *in a state of dirt*: AR to Margaret Livingston Chanler, July 16, 1890, Rokeby Collection.

138–39 *In a secluded corner . . . corn-shucking songs*: Julia Magruder, "The House of Pompadour," *Once a Week*, undated, pp. 160–62, Amélie Rives, Papers, 1830–1940, #2495, Special Collections, University of Virginia Library.

139 *the story of a young Virginian*: AR to Mr. Collier, November 18, 1890, Papers of Amélie Rives, #7208-b, Special Collections, UVA Library.

140 *with its violet gray mist . . . Page*: Amélie Rives, *According to Saint John*, 189, 238, 270.

140 *Next came a delicious languor*: Ibid., 347–48.

141 *In her later years Amélie spoke openly*: Interview with Louis Auchincloss.

141 *It's such anguish*: AR to Elizabeth Chanler, August 31, 1890, Rokeby Collection.

141 *I had not the slightest idea*: Margaret Chanler Aldrich, "John Armstrong Chanler," typed memoir, p. 1, Rokeby Collection.

142 *showed character and originality*: Ronaldshay, *The Life of Lord Curzon*, vol. 1, 172.

142 *tried to drag out my wings*: AR to Elizabeth Chanler, October 15, 1892, Rokeby Collection.

142 *No more bold* ***Chanler***: Amélie Rives file, Valentine Richmond History Center.

Chapter 6. In the Valley of the Shadow of Soul Death

144 *In the valley of the shadow*: Chapter title from letter, JAC to Julia Magruder, June 3, 1892, Chaloner Papers, William R. Perkins Library, Duke University.

145 *support some young riffraff*: Thomas, *A Pride of Lions*, 119.

145 *As for your art scheme*: W. Sigourney Otis to JAC, December 24, 1891, Chaloner Papers, William R. Perkins Library, Duke University.

146 *an added feather in his cap . . . the village*: JAC to Bishop Potter, April 6, 1891, Archives of the Episcopal Diocese of New York.

146 *Amélie's friend Julia Magruder recommended*: Julia Magruder to Elizabeth Chanler, April 2, 1891; Margaret Chanler to Elizabeth Chanler, March 12, 1892; Winty Chanler to Elizabeth Chanler, March 16, 1892, Rokeby Collection. The scandal at St. Margaret's revolved around the newly hired "Southern Siren" distributing racy photos of herself and inflaming all of Red Hook with her brazen "antics." The matron was hustled out of town and summarily fired by Archie. Winty could barely contain his glee over Archie's acute embarrassment about the entire affair.

148 *Like a cameo*: Robert Chanler to Elizabeth Chanler, November 6, 1891, Rokeby Collection.

148 *He should not see Amélie . . . as I did to Archie*: Daisy White to Elizabeth Chanler, June 27, 1891, Rokeby Collection.

149 *O dear me the pictures*: Thomas, *A Pride of Lions,* 135.

149 *hallucination*: JAC to Elizabeth Chanler, July 10, 1891, Rokeby Collection.

149 *she was the one who helped me*: Hervey White, autobiography.

150–51 *Our passage to Newport . . . get in with the boys once more*: JAC to Elizabeth Chanler, July 10, 1891, Rokeby Collection.

151 *go directly to Castle Hill*: Clipping, *Herald,* July 31, 1891, Papers of the Rives Family, #2532, Box 2, newspaper clippings, Special Collections, UVA Library.

152 *the old colored woman*: *Richmond Dispatch,* August 25, 1891.

152 *Welcome Home*: JAC to Elizabeth, August 27, 1891, Rokeby Collection.

153 *It is fully as hysterical*: *St. Paul* (Minnesota) *Pioneer Press,* October 18, 1891.

153 *The volcanic sensuousness*: *Nashville Appeal-Avalanche,* October 26, 1891.

153 *The young ladies of Virginia*: *Spirit of the Times,* October 31, 1891.

154 *A Voice from the Night*: January 17, 1892, Amélie Rives manuscript, Rokeby Collection.

154 *Amélie [is] so sick*: Lutie Pleasants to Elizabeth Chanler, January 15, 1892, Rokeby Collection.

154–57 *gruesome, uncanny period . . . until my meeting with Penelope*: JAC to Julia Magruder, June 3, 1892, Chaloner Papers, William R. Perkins Library, Duke University.

158 *One of the strangest things about Amélie*: Margaret Livingston Chanler to Elizabeth Chanler, June 17, 1888, Rokeby Collection.

158 *Sphinx-faculty . . . 'Mother, comfort me'*: JAC to Julia Magruder, June 3, 1892, Chaloner Papers, William R. Perkins Library, Duke University.

159–60 *aesthetic distress . . . sanguineously red*: Curzon diary, August 14–16, 1892, pp. 4–13, British Library, India Office.

160 *40 hours of happiness*: Curzon to Sadie Rives, August 24, 1892, Barclay Rives Collection.

160 *in the liberty . . . under the soft sky with my sweetheart!*: Curzon diary, August 21–23, 1892, p. 13, British Library, India Office.

161 *tastefully & artistically furnished*: Curzon diary, August 24, 1892, p. 15, British Library, India Office. The Players Club was founded by Edwin Booth, who lived and died there. Over the years, snobbish, careful distinctions were drawn among the three clubs in the city associated with the theater: "The Lambs comprised actors who wanted to be gentlemen; the Players, gentlemen who wanted to be actors; and the Friars, neither who wanted to be both." John Winthrop Aldrich annotation.

162 *I think constantly*: Curzon to Sadie Rives, August 24, 1892, Barclay Rives Collection.

163 *There's something monstrous . . . has outlived despair*: Amélie Rives, *Barbara Dering,* 211, 138, 45, 74, 284, 285.

163 *Innocence Versus Ignorance*: Amélie Rives, "Innocence Versus Ignorance," *The North American Review,* September 1892, 287–90.

164 *My Elizabeth, my treasure*: AR to Elizabeth Chanler, January 24, 1893, Rokeby Collection.

164 *a shadow of her former self*: Thomas, *A Pride of Lions,* 120.

165 *Woman is altogether*: Nisbet, *The People's Select Cyclopedia,* 118–19.

165–66 *nervous women . . . Two months were spent in bed*: Mitchell, *Fat and Blood,* 8, 41–42, 94, 77–79, 94.

166 *hysterical girl is . . . a vampire*: "Silas Weir Mitchell," whonamedit.com.

166 *childlike acquiescence*: Mitchell, *Fat and Blood,* 91.

166 *never to touch pen*: Gilman, "Why I Wrote 'The Yellow Wallpaper,'" *The Forerunner,* October 1913, 271.

167 *Socialites flocked to Mitchell*: Interview with Louis Auchincloss. He recalled that his own grandmother endured the cure, and whenever he and his family went to visit her in the country, it was always "Shush! Be quiet! She's resting!"

167 *no top or bottom to his arrogance*: E-mail from Dr. Nancy Cervetti, Avila University, September 8, 2005.

167 *crowd my canvas a little more*: Edith Wharton to Silas Weir Mitchell, November 5 [no year], YCAL, MSS 42, Series VIII, Box 61, Folder 1790, Beinecke Library, Yale University.

168 *Archie arrives today*: Thomas, *A Pride of Lions*, 121.

168 *Amélie is with Weir Mitchell*: Winthrop Chanler to Elizabeth Chanler, May 14, 1893, Rokeby Collection.

168 *self-imposed rest cure*: Chanler, *Four Years*, 96.

Chapter 7. Master of the Universe

169 *My darling Archie*: AR to JAC, May 23, 1893, Chaloner Papers, William R. Perkins Library, Duke University.

170 *The Evelyn is one absolutely safe boat*: AR to JAC, June 12, 1893, Chaloner Papers, William R. Perkins Library, Duke University.

170 *malicious talk*: AR to JAC, June 12, 1893, the "Leddems & Annums affair," Chaloner Papers, William R. Perkins Library, Duke University; AR to Elizabeth Chanler, December 4, 1895, Rokeby Collection.

171 *Dearest Elizabeth*: JAC to Elizabeth Chanler, November 22, 1893, Chaloner Papers, William R. Perkins Library, Duke University.

171 *He swam on a wave*: Mooney, *Evelyn Nesbit and Stanford White*, 162.

172 *Pie Girl Dinner*: Baker, *Stanny*, 250.

172 *Do take care of Archie*: AR to Stanford White, August 6, 1892, Stanford White File, Correspondents—Chanler, Amélie Rives, New-York Historical Society.

172 *You old rascal you*: White to JAC, March 18, 1895, Chaloner Papers, William R. Perkins Library, Duke University.

172–73 *pure . . . dead after all*: Winthrop Chanler to Elizabeth Chanler, March 16, 1892, Rokeby Collection.

174 *won the highest award*: JAC to AR, August 20, 1896, Chaloner Papers, William R. Perkins Library, Duke University.

174 *the future is golden with promise*: JAC to Elizabeth Chanler, December 23, 1893, Rokeby Collection.

174 *brilliant hopes*: Alfred Landon Rives to Landon Rives, April 29, 1893, Virginia Historical Society.

174 *River of Death*: Braswell, *The Roanoke Canal*, 2.

175 *boot-licking*: JAC to W. G. Maxwell, June 3, 1896, Papers of John Armstrong Chaloner, #38-394-a, Box 1, folder 1881–1909 Correspondence, Special Collections, UVA Library.

175 *The air round me*: Margaret Terry Chanler, ed., *Winthrop Chanler's Letters,* 15.

175 *up to de limit*: Winthrop Chanler to Elizabeth Chanler, March 9, 1894, Chaloner Papers, William R. Perkins Library, Duke University.

175 *busy laying the foundation*: Winthrop Chanler to Elizabeth Chanler, May 14, 1893, Rokeby Collection.

176 *first rate, very handsome*: Winthrop Chanler to JAC, March 9, 1894, Chaloner Papers, William R. Perkins Library, Duke University.

176 *It is the handsomest mill*: Leland M. Roth, "Three Industrial Towns by McKim, Mead & White," *Journal of the Society of Architectural Historians,* December 1979, 330.

178 *bust up*: JAC to Elizabeth Chanler, November 3, 1893, Rokeby Collection.

179 *chastisement . . . my brothers have interest*: Robert Chanler to JAC, March 22, 1894, Chaloner Papers, William R. Perkins Library, Duke University.

179 *Granted that Mr. Morris*: JAC to Elizabeth Chanler, n.d. [ca. 1894], Rokeby Collection.

181 *Merry Mills*: Lay, *The Architecture of Jefferson Country,* 10.

181 *Castle Hill . . . looking like its quaint*: AR to JAC, June 5, 1894, Chaloner Papers, William R. Perkins Library, Duke.

182 *would talk much more*: AR to JAC, July 3, 1894, Chaloner Papers, William R. Perkins Library, Duke University.

182 *two most beautiful people*: Moore, "Amélie Rives: A Personal Reminiscence," *The Magazine of Albemarle County History, 1984,* 95.

183 *savage Tartar*: Borgmeyer, "The Art of Prince Pierre Troubetzkoy," *Fine Arts Journal,* December 1911, 335. His brother Paul, a sculptor, won even more renown as an artist than Pierre. Paul was awarded the grand prize at the Paris Exposition of 1900, and his roster of subjects included Auguste Rodin, George Bernard Shaw, and a young Franklin Delano Roosevelt.

183 *Let us begin life*: AR to JAC, August 10, 1894, Chaloner Papers, William R. Perkins Library, Duke University.

Chapter 8. The X-Faculty

185 *never show . . . chamber of himself*: "Wolf Knorditore" by JAC, Chaloner Papers, Box 24, pp. 5, 9, William R. Perkins Library, Duke University.

186 *a thing of name*: AR to Elizabeth Chanler, December 4, 1895, Rokeby Collection.

186 *walking dress*: Unidentified New York newspaper, February 15, 1895, Papers of the Rives Family, #2532, Box 2, Special Collections, UVA Library.

187 *My own, only . . . a line*: AR to JAC, April 24, 1895, Chaloner Papers, William R. Perkins Library, Duke University.

187 *and that the place*: Charles Hartnett to JAC, October 14, 1895, Chaloner Papers, William R. Perkins Library, Duke University.

187 *If there is anything . . . Swinburnean passion*: Unidentified newspaper clipping, 1895, Chaloner Papers, William R. Perkins Library, Duke University.

187 *brawny*: John Chartres, "Amélie Rives's Princely Spouse," *Leslie's Weekly*, December 31, 1896, Chaloner Papers, William R. Perkins Library, Duke University.

187 *It was a quiet ceremony*: "Amélie Rives Weds Again," *New York World*, February 19, 1896; "Is a Princess Now," *Richmond Dispatch*, February 19, 1896.

188 *Beth, my . . . back & forth*: AR to Elizabeth Chanler, December 4, 1895, Rokeby Collection.

188 *reckless mortgages*: AR to Elizabeth Chanler, December 4, 1895, Rokeby Collection.

189 *I made him . . . what exultation!!*: AR to Elizabeth Chanler, December 4, 1895, Rokeby Collection.

189 *the face of*: Borgmeyer, "The Art of Prince Pierre Troubetzkoy," *Fine Arts Journal*, December 1911, 335.

190 *a magnificent specimen*: "Is a Princess Now," *Richmond Dispatch*, February 19, 1896. Pierre's imposing size was made clear to me when visiting with W. D. Taylor, a literary scholar in Richmond with a particular interest in Amélie. Included in his collection of "Rivesiana" is one of the prince's custom-made English shirts. Taylor held up the immense shirt and its length and width dwarfed him.

190 *Mr. And Mrs. Stahl . . . nervous prostration*: "Princess Troubetzkoi Sails," *New York Sun*, March 1, 1896, Papers of the Rives Family, #2532, Box 2, Special Collections, UVA Library.

190 *canary-bird of Lago Maggiore*: "Troubetskoi's Romance," *San Francisco Call*, n.d., Papers of the Rives Family, #2532, Box 2, Special Collections, UVA Library.

191 *With reservations*: January 1, 1896, diary excerpt, Letters 1894–1900, Chaloner Papers, William R. Perkins Library, Duke.

191 *Hermit Crab*: JAC to AR, August 20, 1896, Chaloner Papers, William R. Perkins Library, Duke University.

192 *nailed my colors*: Chanler, *Four Years,* 19.

192 *Beauty Rules*: *Milwaukee Sentinel,* March 29, 1896.

193 *it would be trop*: JAC to Elizabeth, April 17, 1896, Rokeby Collection.

193–94 *My Dear Brother . . . outrageous behavior*: AR to JAC, July 12, 1896, Chaloner Papers, William R. Perkins Library, Duke University.

195 *My respect*: JAC to AR, Aug 20, 1896, p. 1, Chaloner Papers, William R. Perkins Library, Duke University.

195 *Like the fighter*: JAC to AR, Aug 20, 1896, p. 5, Chaloner Papers, William R. Perkins Library, Duke University.

195–96 *Golden Dream . . . waves of gold*: JAC to AR, Aug 20, 1896, p. 5, Chaloner Papers, William R. Perkins Library, Duke University.

196 *Eldorado . . . in the world*: JAC to AR, Aug 20, 1896, pp. 18, 7, Chaloner Papers, William R. Perkins Library, Duke University.

196 *Uncle Dick McMurdo*: JAC to AR, Aug 20, 1896, pp. 3–4, Chaloner Papers, William R. Perkins Library, Duke University.

196 *jump upwards*: JAC to AR, Aug 20, 1896, p. 6, Chaloner Papers, William R. Perkins Library, Duke University.

196–97 *24th September 1896 . . . almost profane*: AR to JAC, September 24, 1896, Chaloner Papers, William R. Perkins Library, Duke University.

197–98 *Our Amélie . . . how much?*: Chanler, *Four Years,* 74; interview with Barclay Rives.

198 *the former husband*: Thomas, *A Pride of Lions,* 194.

198 *Every Chanler*: Winthrop Astor Chanler to Margaret Terry Chanler, September 18, 1896, Chanler, *Winthrop Chanler's Letters,* 60.

199 *The man is . . . "looney."*: Thomas, *A Pride of Lions,* 196. Archie may have missed the event, but he gave Alida the best of her wedding presents: a museum-quality, eighteenth-century solid silver tankard that was a prized possession. It was sold at Sotheby's after Alida's death in 1969. John Winthrop Aldrich annotation.

199 *wounded & regretful*: "June 3rd 1895 Extract after . . . Family Reunion at Rokeby," Papers of John Armstrong Chaloner, #38-394-A, Box 1, Special Collections, UVA Library.

200 *in a very violent . . . never qualified*: Winthrop Astor Chanler's 1905 legal deposition, p. 23, Chaloner Papers, William R. Perkins Library, Duke University.

201 *Fuzz Buzz*: JAC to Stanford White, December 26, 1893, Stanford White Papers, New-York Historical Society. For discussion of turning over power of

attorney to White, JAC to Micajah Woods, July 3, 1897; Chanler, *Four Years,* 4.

202 *Get a planchette!*: Bryan, "Johnny Jackanapes," *The Virginia Magazine of History and Biography,* January 1965, 6.

202 *vocal utterances*: Chanler, *Four Years,* 68.

203 *Archie was commanded*: "John Armstrong Chaloner Controlled by Fourth Dimension," *New York Herald,* October 28, 1906.

203 *extraordinary destiny*: Ibid.

204 *in good mediums . . . spirit world*: James, *Essays in Psychical Research,* 367–68.

205 *In addition to reports floating*: "1907 Feb 20 A Ms 'Answer to Deposition' by Chaloner," 43–44 on the roadway plan, Papers of John Armstrong Chaloner, #38-394-A, Box 2, Special Collections, UVA Library.

207 *plunge in the metropolitan*: Chanler, *Four Years,* 4.

207 *After a minute or two*: Ibid., 70–71.

208 *It is exactly like*: Ibid., 71.

208 *medical examiner in lunacy*: May 5, 1899, deposition by M. Allen Starr, M.D., Papers of John Armstrong Chaloner, #38-394, Special Collections, UVA Library, p. 93.

208 *lead a holy war . . . for the insane*: Ibid., 94.

209 *straight at the middle button*: Thomas, *A Pride of Lions,* 208.

209 *his old pal*: Winty and Roosevelt were not at Harvard together, but became friends through their membership in the ultra-elite Porcellian Club. They both loved adventure and shared an interest in big-game hunting—the pair helped found the Boone and Crockett Club.

209 *to let these scoundrels have*: Ibid., 208.

210 *Bloomingdale Asylum*: New York Hospital–Cornell Medical Center, "The Beginning."

Chapter 9. Four Years Behind the Bars of Bloomingdale

211 *Certificate of Lunacy*: "Petition in the Matter of an Application for the Commitment of John Armstrong Chanler," p. 5, Box 16, folder 1893–1903, Chaloner Papers, William R. Perkins Library, Duke University.

212 *amalgam of avarice*: Chanler, *Four Years,* 25.

212 *alleged insane person*: "Petition in the Matter. . . ," p. 4, Box 16, folder 1893–1903, Chaloner Papers, William R. Perkins Library, Duke University.

213 *void*: Stanford White Correspondence, October 19, 1896–March 20, 1897,

letters #363 and 364 "void"; letters # 414, 415, 377 and 395 missing, Avery Library, Columbia University.

214–15 *I never thought . . . but let things sleep*: White to Elizabeth Chanler, quoting letter from AR, with additional annotation by EC, May 1897, Rokeby Collection.

215 *'quite weird'*: Winthrop Chanler to Elizabeth Chanler, May 14, 1893, Rokeby Collection.

215 *you must have thought of him . . . not at all unhappy*: Julia Chanler to Elizabeth Chanler, undated [1897], Rokeby Collection.

216 *by the time I get through with them*: Thomas, *A Pride of Lions,* 214.

217 *majesty of the law*: Chanler, *Four Years,* 129.

218 *Don't move, Teddy!*: Thomas, *A Pride of Lions,* 258.

218 *This is no place for a married man*: Ibid., 256.

218 *You must come home, Temple*: Ibid., 253.

218 *that living Hell*: Chanler, *Four Years,* 64.

219 *bodily exercise*: New York Hospital–Cornell Medical Center, "The Beginning," 5.

219 *total deprivation*: Chanler, *Four Years,* 10.

219 *who could pay a good price*: New York Hospital–Cornell Medical Center, "The Beginning," 5.

220 *solitary confinement*: Chanler, *Four Years,* 9.

220 *Bastille of the Four Hundred*: Ibid., 242–43.

220 B.A. *for Bloomingdale Asylum*: New York Hospital–Cornell Medical Center, "The Beginning," 5.

220 *instead of making shoes at Sing Sing*: Chanler, *Four Years,* 244.

221 *as smooth spoken*: Ibid., 31.

221 *warm-hearted honest Irishman*: Ibid., 143.

221 *I may say that I have a rather powerful voice*: Ibid., 144.

222 *Within this cell*: Ibid., 174.

222 *greater command over the Shakespearian form*: Ibid., 168.

222 *assiduously cultivated the pen*: Ibid., 20, 40.

222 *living tomb*: Ibid., 259.

223 *gigantic maniac*: Ibid., 147.

223 MR. CHANLER NEEDS REST: *New York Times,* October 14, 1897.

224 *My brother has been in the asylum*: Thomas, *A Pride of Lions*, 233–34.

225 *The alleged madman's contribution*: Barclay Rives, *The 100 Year History of the Keswick Hunt Club*, 6.

225–26 *It seems fair . . . outside the Russian Empire State*: Chanler, *Four Years*, 27–28.

227 *My beloved Elizabeth*: White to Elizabeth Chanler, March 23, 1897, Rokeby Collection.

227–28 *though A. had sent his case . . . I can put everything in Egerton's hands*: Winthrop Chanler to Margaret Terry Chanler, December 5, 1897, Winthrop Chanler letters, bMS Am 1595 (764–73), Houghton Library, Harvard University.

228 *no appearance on the part of the alleged lunatic*: New York Supreme Court proceedings, June 12, 1899, p. 157, Papers of John Armstrong Chaloner, #38-394, Special Collections, UVA Library.

228 *plutocrats*: JAC to "First New York Lawyer," March 26, 1900, p. 7, Box 14, Chaloner Papers, William R. Perkins Library, Duke.

228–29 *examination at the hands of a distinguished . . . conspiracy and change of personality*: Chanler, *Four Years*, 33, 201, 199.

229 *I am in a perfect hell*: White to Augustus Saint-Gaudens, January 30, 1899, MC 4, 20:44, Augustus Saint-Gaudens Collection, Rauner Special Collections Library, Dartmouth University.

229 *Because he was [Archie's] friend*: Chanler, *Four Years*, 214.

229–30 *It seems to me his case is so plain*: Ibid., 218–19.

230 *P. H. Butler quietly skins me*: JAC to "First New York Lawyer," March 26, 1900, Box 14, Chaloner Papers, William R. Perkins Library, Duke University.

231 *ordinary dwelling house*: "1907 February 20 A Ms. 'Answer to Deposition' by Chaloner," Box 2, Papers of John Armstrong Chaloner, #38-394-a, Special Collections, UVA Library.

231 *assassination*: JAC to Streusand of Kaplan, Kosman & Streusand, June 1, 1919, handwritten ultimatum, Papers of John Armstrong Chaloner, #38-394, Box 1, "1919–3 Tablets Containing Notes & Copies of Letters & Wires"; #38-394-a, Box 2, "1907 February 20 A Ms. 'Answer to Deposition' by Chaloner," Special Collections, UVA Library.

232 *he is a very honorable man*: Testimony by Dr. Samuel Lyon, 1899 New York Supreme Court Proceedings, p. 189, Papers of John Armstrong Chaloner, #38-394, Special Collections, UVA Library.

232 *so exemplary and docile*: Chanler, *Four Years*, 37.

232 *some prominent friend . . . in the past*: Ibid., 38, 42–43, 47; Thomas, *The Astor Orphans*, 150.

234 *wealth accumulated by one family*: Baker and Brentano, *The World on Sunday*, 20–21.

235 *My dear Doctor*: Thomas, *A Pride of Lions*, 287.

236 CHANLER ESCAPES . . . *wandering in the Virginia mountains*: *New York Herald*, December 5, 1900; *New York Times*, December 5, 1900.

236 *To all who have been here*: Thomas, *The Astor Orphans*, 151, 284; Chanler, *Four Years*, 8–9.

236–37 *Archie is in Paris*: Winthrop Chanler to Margaret Terry Chanler, n.d. [1901], private collection.

238 *photographic exposition of cold, hard, every-day facts*: Chaloner, *Robbery Under Law*, ii.

238 *genius . . . a millionaire man-about-town*: Ibid., 1.

239 *Mr Legg has always claimed*: Mrs. Legg to JAC, December 4, 1903, Papers of John Armstrong Chaloner, #38-394-e, Special Collections, UVA Library.

239 *I will see that you are comfortably provided for*: JAC to Mrs. Legg, December 23, 1903, Papers of John Armstrong Chaloner, #38-394-e, Special Collections, UVA Library.

240 *The sight & society of Bob*: Winthrop Chanler to Elizabeth Chanler, May 14, 1893, Rokeby Collection.

241 *on the lunatic fringe*: Thomas, *A Pride of Lions*, 271.

241 *It seems that Jack Chapman has delusions*: Winthrop Chanler to Margaret Terry Chanler, n.d. [1901], Bronson Winthrop Chanler collection. In April 1901 Elizabeth Chanler Chapman gave birth to a son while her husband, Jack Chapman, was secluded at Rokeby, incapacitated by mental illness. She named him Chanler Armstrong Chapman after his missing uncle Archie. He, too, spent time in a mental hospital. John Winthrop Aldrich annotation.

243 *I didn't describe no gradual development*: Chanler, *Four Years*, 23; Margaret Chanler Aldrich, "John Armstrong Chanler," biographical sketch, pp. 1–2, Rokeby Collection.

243 *unconditional gift*: Last Will and Testament of John Winthrop Chanler, pp. 64, 67, New York County Surrogate's Court, Rokeby Collection.

244 *Where is Archie?*: Winthrop Chanler to unidentified sibling, n.d. [spring 1891], Rokeby Collection.

Chapter 10. Who's Looney Now?

245 *John Chilton*: Chanler, *Four Years,* 58–60.

246 *John Armstrong . . . X Faculty*: "John Armstrong Chanler Reappears in Virginia," *New York Times,* September 21, 1901.

246 *determine whether a Committee*: Chanler, *Four Years,* 44.

246 *I did not do anything*: Ibid., 49.

246 *a little in advance*: Ibid., 56. Dr. James Morris Page, professor and future Dean of the University of Virginia.

247 *I have bought horses*: Chanler, *Four Years,* 63.

247 *certainly mentally peculiar*: Ibid., 67.

247 *expressions of his normal*: Ibid., 77.

247 *gifted with sensitive*: Ibid., 78–79.

247–48 *inner conversation . . . their eccentric faculty*: Ibid., 83–84.

248 *specialists in insanity . . . would seem a crime*: Ibid., 84.

249 *sane man, capable*: Ibid., 104.

249 *strong, combative . . . in persecution*: *The Sunday North American* [undated, 1901], Chaloner Papers, William R. Perkins Library, Duke University.

249–50 *caution . . . its mouth ajar*: *The World,* February 23, 1896, Papers of the Rives family, #2532, Box 2, Special Collections, UVA Library.

250 *So Amélie Rives is*: Taylor, *Amélie Rives (Princess Troubetzkoy),* 72.

250 *Amélie's medical bills mounted*: "More Startling Than 'The Quick or The Dead,' " *New York Journal Sunday,* July 18, 1897, Papers of the Rives family, #2532, Box 2, Special Collections, UVA Library.

250–51 *Do you know when . . . recumbent form*: Ibid.

251 *wife-friend . . . may vanish altogether*: "Princess Troubetzkoy Discusses 'Saner' Feminism," *New York Times,* April 19, 1914.

252–53 *He is the lion . . . athletic looking fellow*: "Prince Troubetzkoy a Painter," *New York Journal,* February 27, 1898.

253 *wreck of her former*: "Amélie Rives Career," Amélie Rives file, undated newspaper clipping, ca. 1898, Valentine Richmond History Center.

254 *There can be no slightest doubt*: Chanler, *Four Years,* 34.

255 *It's an easy matter to hire*: JAC to Julien Isaacs, Esq., Pine Street, New York, 1903, Papers of John Armstrong Chaloner, #38-394, Special Collections, UVA Library.

255 *7 years siesta*: F. H. Treacy to JAC, October 30, 1904, Papers of John Armstrong Chaloner, #38-394-e, Special Collections, UVA Library.

256 *Dear Hermie*: JAC to Herman Duryea, August 20, 1904, Papers of John Armstrong Chaloner, #38-394A, Box 1, Special Collections, UVA Library.

257 *glad gold hand*: JAC to Mrs. Bella Kilbourne Bourgiat, July 17, 1904, Papers of John Armstrong Chaloner, #38-394A, Box 1, Special Collections, UVA Library.

257 *out of the hands*: January 4, 1914, "Rex Lecture," handwritten notes by JAC, Papers of John Armstrong Chaloner, #38-394-a, Box 1, Special Collections, UVA Library.

257 *She never let me have $20*: JAC to Rose Wilmer Page, March 20, 1911, Papers of John Armstrong Chaloner, #38-394-e, Special Collections, UVA, Library.

258 *It shows that Princess*: JAC to Rose Wilmer Page [undated, 1911], Papers of John Armstrong Chaloner, #38-394-e, Special Collections, UVA Library.

258 *an ice cold bath*: JAC to Rose Wilmer Page, April 3, 1911, Papers of John Armstrong Chaloner, #38-394-e, Special Collections, UVA Library.

258 *the staff of life*: JAC to Rose Wilmer Page [April 1911], Papers of John Armstrong Chaloner, #38-394-e, Special Collections, UVA Library.

258 *Valley of the Shadow . . . plain ice water*: JAC to Rose Wilmer Page, April 14, 1911, Papers of John Armstrong Chaloner, #38-394-e, Special Collections, UVA Library.

259 *The Heart is Deceitful . . . Evil*: Chaloner, *Scorpio No. 1*, 56–57.

259 *the modernized form*: Unidentified newspaper, June 2, 1908, Chaloner Papers, William R. Perkins Library, Duke University.

259 Monmouthshire Evening Post: Chaloner, *Scorpio No. 1*, 24–25; Chaloner, *Robbery Under Law*, 291–92.

260 *largely because I had*: Chaloner, "Hell: Per a Spirit-Message Therefrom (Alleged)," *Scorpio No. 1*, 28.

260 *HELL'S NOT HALF BAD*: *Portland* [Oregon] *Telegram*, August 5, 1912, "Hell: Per a Spirit-Message Therefrom (Alleged)," *Scorpio No. 1*, 90.

261 *Sorry for* me?: Bryan, "Johnny Jackanapes," 10; *New York Times*, March 17, 1909.

262 *John Gillard Died . . . game*: Barclay Rives, *A History of Grace Church*, 56; Thomas, *The Astor Orphans*, 188; *New York Times*, March 18, 1909.

262 *Dear Archie . . . impossible to see you*: *New York Times*, March 18, 1909.

262 *redress and mental vindication*: JAC to Hon. Thomas M. Hill, June 19, 1904,

Papers of John Armstrong Chaloner, #38-394-a, Box 1, Special Collections, UVA Library.

263 To whom it may concern: JAC, "Rules to be followed in the contingency of my illness or accident," July 21, 1909, Papers of John Armstrong Chaloner, #38-394-e, Special Collections, UVA Library.

264 *Robert Winthrop Chanler*: Thomas, *The Astor Orphans*, 191.

264 *Who's looney now?*: Winthrop Astor Chanler to John Jay Chapman, September 17, 1910, Rokeby Collection. The letter notes that Archie sent the telegram to the *New York World*.

264 *the latest prominent assassin*: *New York Times*, May 17, 1919.

265 *Where are all the horses . . . Arabian Nights!*: Thomas, *The Astor Orphans*, 233–34.

265 *Rome in the height . . . delightful*: Columbia University Archives, John Armstrong Chaloner file, newspaper clippings, [undated] 1919.

265 *You have been mightily*: *New York Times*, May 21, 1919.

266 *raise pen or tongue*: JAC to Beatrice Ashley Chanler, June 5, 1919, Rokeby Collection.

266 *Dearest Archie*: Papers of John Armstrong Chaloner, #38-394-a, Box 1, Correspondence file, 1919 typescript, Special Collections, UVA Library.

266 *mad as a hatter*: Winthrop Astor Chanler to Elizabeth Chanler Chapman, June 6 [1919], Rokeby Collection. On Margaret's fear of lawsuits: Margaret Chanler Aldrich to Elizabeth Chanler Chapman, "Saturday" [June 1919], Rokeby Collection.

266 *sharks and sheisters*: Margaret Chanler Aldrich to Elizabeth Chanler Chapman, "Saturday" [June 1919], Rokeby Collection.

266 *perpetual suspicion*: Howard Taylor to Beatrice Ashley Chanler, July 31, 1919, Rokeby Collection.

267 *I deeply appreciate*: JAC to Elizabeth Chanler Chapman, June 12, 1919, Rokeby Collection.

267 *I Declare the petitioner*: New York Supreme Court, Judge Ford Decision, July 26, 1919.

267 *lunacy trust . . . war chest fund*: "Chaloner to War on 'Lunacy Trust,' " *New York Times*, July 28, 1919; "Chaloner Has $1,635.195," *New York Times*, August 13, 1919.

267 *except, of course . . . Looney Now?*: Thomas, *The Astor Orphans*, 239.

267–68 *Archie had to catch up on his own family*: Archie gave Orlot Farm, south of Rokeby on the Hudson, to Bronson Winthrop ("Bim") Chanler, grandson of Lewis Stuyvesant Chanler, when Bim was a toddler "so there will always be a Chanler of the name on family land in the Hudson Valley." To protect the property during Bim's minority, Archie gave Lewis's sons a life interest in the land. John Winthrop Aldrich annotation.

268 *I was never more surprised*: JAC to Margaret Terry Chanler, May 6, 1919, Papers of John Armstrong Chaloner, #38-394, Box 1, Special Collections, UVA Library.

268 *dreadfully excitable . . . praying over*: Elizabeth Chanler Chapman to Chanler Chapman, October 11, 1920, Rokeby Collection.

269 *The dinner was a charming occasion*: Elizabeth Chanler Chapman to Chanler Chapman, February 12, 1920, Rokeby Collection.

Epilogue

270 *JOHN ARMSTRONG CHALONER*: Rufus Holsinger photo, Special Collections, UVA Library; interview with Anne Rafferty Barnes; Barclay Rives, "John Armstrong Chaloner: Albemarle Fantastic," 49.

272 *Advanced Experimental Psychology and the Occult*: *New York Times*, April 2, 1921, 18.

272 *There is a fairyland in every one's head*: *New York Times*, January 31, 1921.

273 *left in squalor*: Mary Minor Lewis to Elizabeth Chanler Chapman, October 22, 1935, Rokeby Collection.

273 *There were inscriptions on the wall*: Margaret Chanler Aldrich, "John Armstrong Chanler," 2–3, Rokeby Collection.

274 *sorrowful vigil*: Maud Howe Elliot to Elizabeth Chanler Chapman, [1935], Rokeby Collection.

274 *I have thought of you so constantly*: Thomas, *The Astor Orphans*, 303–4.

274 *With long life, health, and happiness*: JAC to Princess Troubetzkoy, April 20, 1935, Rokeby Collection.

274–75 *Mr. Chaloner was the friend of every poor resident*: Barclay Rives, *History of Grace Church*, 57.

275 *awe-inspiring*: William Aston Chanler Jr. to Henry Wiencek, April 22, 1988, author's collection.

275 *I do not like to think of so wonderful a man*: Rev. Robinson to Margaret Chanler Aldrich, July 5, 1937, Rokeby Collection.

275 *Blessed is the man who considereth the poor and needy*: Grace Episcopal churchyard, Albemarle County. Archie is buried on the other side of the churchyard from John Gillard, the man he claimed to have killed.

275 *He was the best of them*: Interview with Bronson Chanler.

275–76 *Her talents were numerous . . . After he was alone*: Margaret Chanler Aldrich, "John Armstrong Chanler," p. 4, Rokeby Collection.

276 *one of the cruelest outrages ever perpetrated*: Watt, *Is the Liar In?*, 63.

277 *For: My Boy from his Amy*: photograph from Ella Scantling Morris Collection.

277 *she rarely saw [Amélie]*: Constance Page to Elizabeth Langhorne, March 7, 1990, Rives Family Papers, #2532, folder: "1874–1900 Amélie Rives," Special Collections, UVA Library.

278 *And what do you do, Miss Hepburn?*: Taylor, *Amélie Rives*, 73.

278 *Mister Prince*: Moore, "Amélie Rives: A Personal Reminiscence," 73.

278 *to put three or four*: AR to Ellen Glasgow, August 25, 1937, Ellen Glasgow Papers, 1880–1963, #5060, Special Collections, UVA Library.

279 *I could hardly believe the boxwood*: Auchincloss, *A Writer's Capital*, 133.

279 *The princess was right*: Amélie may not have touched the precious boxwood, but she was forced to sell a family treasure, an original letter from Robert E. Lee. A copy of the letter is in the Rives Family Papers at the University of Virginia, with a note written across the top: "The original had to be sold in a hard time." Papers of the Rives Family, #2532, Box 1.

279 *Like a siren of yore*: Interview with Louis Auchincloss. Archie's sister Alida stopped briefly at Castle Hill to see the widow Troubetzkoy, and had a less generous assessment, saying that Amélie had lost her luster, as she did not have the "ageless bone structure" required of long-lasting beauty. Longest, *Amélie Rives Troubetzkoy*, 44.

279 *halfway between a startling truth and a tale in True Romances*: Auchincloss, *A Writer's Capital*, 137, Special Collections, UVA Library.

280 *Mad love, Jack*: Langford, *Ingenue Among the Lions*, 12.

280 *But where would I live?*: Auchincloss, *A Writer's Capital*, 138.

281 *she insisted upon keeping her face covered*: Constance Page to Elizabeth Langhorne, March 7, 1990, Papers of the Rives family compiled by Elizabeth Langhorne, #1096-d, Special Collections, UVA Library.

281 *Love is strong as death*: Taylor, *Amélie Rives (Princess Troubetzkoy)* 110; Interview with Barclay Rives. There are two family cemeteries at Castle Hill. The larger, older one is farther from the house. Amélie and the prince decided to be buried in the plot closer to the ring of boxwood, where only Senator William Cabell Rives and his wife, Judith Page Rives, had been interred.

BIBLIOGRAPHY

Abdy, Jane, and Charlotte Gere. *The Souls*. London: Sidgwick & Jackson, 1984.

Aïdé, Hamilton. " 'The Quick or the Dead?' and 'Virginia of Virginia.' " *Nineteenth Century Magazine* 25 (February 1889): 228.

Aldrich, Margaret Chanler. *Family Vista*. New York: The William-Frederick Press, 1958.

———. "John Armstrong Chanler." Typescript, undated. Rokeby Collection.

———. "Rokeby and Environs." Typescript, undated. Rokeby Collection.

"The American Widow—New Style." *The Saturday Review of Politics, Literature, Science, and Art* 66 (November 17, 1888): 570.

Amory, Cleveland. *Who Killed Society?* New York: Harper & Brothers, 1960.

Asquith, Margot. Countess of Oxford and Asquith. *Margot Asquith: An Autobiography*. 2 vols. New York: George H. Doran Company, 1920.

Auchincloss, Louis. *A Writer's Capital*. Minneapolis, University of Minnesota Press, 1974.

———. *The Vanderbilt Era: Profiles of a Gilded Age*. New York: Charles Scribner's Sons, 1989.

Baker, Nicholson, and Margaret Brentano. *The World on Sunday: Graphic Art in Joseph Pulitzer's Newspaper (1898–1911)*. New York, Boston: Bullfinch Press, 2005.

Baker, Paul R. *Stanny: The Gilded Life of Stanford White*. New York: Free Press, 1989.

Barrett, Richmond. *Good Old Summer Days: Newport, Narragansett Pier, Saratoga, Long Branch, Bar Harbor*. New York and London: D. Appleton-Century, 1941.

Beam, Alex. *Gracefully Insane: The Rise and Fall of America's Premier Mental Hospital*. New York: Public Affairs, 2001.

Beaux, Cecilia. *Background with Figures*. Boston and New York: Houghton Mifflin and Company, 1930.

Borgmeyer, Charles L. "The Art of Prince Pierre Troubetzkoy," part 1. *Fine Arts Journal* 25, no. 6 (December 1911): 323–35.

———. "The Art of Prince Pierre Troubetzkoy," part 2. *Fine Arts Journal* 26, no. 1 (January 1912): 1–21.

———. "The Art of Prince Pierre Troubetzkoy," part 3. *Fine Arts Journal* 26, no. 2 (February 1912): 67–83.

Brandt, Clare. *An American Aristocracy: The Livingstons.* Garden City, NY: Doubleday, 1986.

Braswell, Peggy Jo Cobb. *The Roanoke Canal: A History of the Old Navigation and Water Power Canal of Halifax County, North Carolina.* Roanoke Rapids, NC: Roanoke Canal Commission, Inc., 1987.

Brown, Alexander. *The Cabells and Their Kin: A Memorial Volume of History, Biography, and Genealogy.* Richmond, VA: Garrett and Massie, 1939.

Bryan, J., III. "Johnny Jackanapes, The Merry-Andrew of The Merry Mills." *The Virginia Magazine of History and Biography* 73, no. 1 (January 1965): 2–21.

Cable, Mary. *Top Drawer: American High Society from the Gilded Age to the Roaring Twenties.* New York: Atheneum, 1984.

Castle Hill Grounds Tour Hand Book. Undated. Private Collection.

Cervetti, Nancy. "S. Weir Mitchell Representing 'A Hell of Pain': From Civil War to Rest Cure." *Arizona Quarterly* 59, no. 3 (Autumn 2003): 69–96.

Chaloner, John Armstrong:

The X-Faculty; or, The Pythagorean Triangle of Psychology. Roanoke Rapids, NC: Palmetto Press [ca. 1911].

Scorpio No. 1. Roanoke Rapids, NC: Palmetto Press, 1913.

The Swan-Song of "Who's Looney Now?" Roanoke Rapids, NC: Palmetto Press, 1914.

Robbery Under Law; or, The Battle of the Millionaires. Roanoke Rapids, NC: Palmetto Press, 1915.

Movies for the Farmers in Rural Public Schools. Roanoke Rapids, NC: Palmetto Press, 1922.

Brief for the Defence of the Unequivocal Divinity of the Founder of Christianity as the Son of Jehovah. New York: Palmetto Press, 1924.

Hell, Per a Spirit-Message Therefrom (Alleged) and The Infernal Comedy. New York: Palmetto Press, 1924.

Chanler, Margaret Livingston. "Memoirs of Rokeby." Typescript, May 1900. Rokeby Collection.

Chanler, Margaret Terry, ed. *Winthrop Chanler's Letters.* New York: Privately printed, 1951.

Chanler, Mrs. Winthrop. *Roman Spring.* Boston: Little, Brown, 1935.

———. *Autumn in the Valley.* Boston: Little, Brown, 1936.

Chanler, John Armstrong. *Four Years Behind the Bars of "Bloomingdale"; or, The Bankruptcy of Law in New York.* Roanoke Rapids, NC: Palmetto Press, 1906.

———. *The Lunacy Law of the World: Being That of Each of the Forty-Eight States and Territories of the United States, With an Examination Thereof and Leading Cases Thereon; Together With That of the Six Great Powers of Europe—Great Britain, France, Italy, Germany, Austria-Hungary, and Russia.* Roanoke Rapids, NC: Palmetto Press, 1906.

Chartres, John. "Amélie Rives's Princely Spouse." *Leslie's Weekly,* December 31, 1896.

Childs, James Rives. *Reliques of the Rives (Ryves).* Lynchburg, VA: J. P. Bell, 1929.

Churchill, Allen. *The Upper Crust: An Informal History of New York's Highest Society.* Englewood Cliffs, NJ: Prentice-Hall, 1970.

———. *The Splendor Seekers: An Informal Glimpse of America's Multimillionaire Spenders—Members of the $50,000,000 Club.* New York: Grosset & Dunlap, 1974.

Clark, Emily. *Innocence Abroad.* New York: Alfred A. Knopf, 1931.

Crowley, Richard, and John Winthrop Aldrich. "St. Margaret's Home, Red Hook, New York." *Dutchess County Historical Society Yearbook* 78 (1993): 37–45.

Deed Book. Dutchess County Courthouse, Poughkeepsie, New York.

De Leon, T. C. *The Rock or the Rye. An Understudy. After "The Quick or the Dead."* Mobile, AL: The Gossip Printing Company, 1888.

Elliott, Maud Howe. *Uncle Sam Ward and His Circle.* New York: Macmillan, 1938.

———. *This Was My Newport.* Cambridge, MA: University Press, Inc., 1944.

Flournoy, Théodore. *From India to the Planet Mars: A Case of Multiple Personality with Imaginary Languages.* Princeton, NJ: Princeton University Press, 1994.

French, Amos Tuck, ed. *Some Letters from "Chan," 1886–1926: For a Chosen Few.* Chester, NH: Privately printed, 1939.

Gannon, Thomas. *Newport Mansions: The Gilded Age.* Little Compton, RI: Foremost Publishers, 1982.

Gates, John D. *The Astor Family.* Garden City, NY: Doubleday, 1981.

Gilman, Charlotte Perkins. "Why I Wrote 'The Yellow Wallpaper.' " *The Forerunner,* IV, no. 10 (October 1913): 271.

Gilmour, David, *Curzon: Imperial Statesman.* New York: Farrar, Straus and Giroux, 2003.

Greenleaf, Margaret. "Castle Hill, Virginia: The Country Home of the Prince and Princess Troubetzkoy." *Country Life in America,* October 1914, 41–43.

Haber, Carole. "Who's Looney Now?: The Insanity Case of John Armstrong Chaloner." *Bulletin of the History of Medicine* 60 (1986): 177–93.

Hamilton, Walter. *The Aesthetic Movement in England.* London: Reeves & Turner, 1882.

Hayden, Laura Endicott. "Judith Page Walker Rives." *The Magazine of Albemarle County History* 52 (1994): 65–85.

Homberger, Eric. *Mrs. Astor's New York: Money and Social Power in a Gilded Age.* New Haven, CT: Yale University Press, 2002.

Honey, John Raymond de Symons. *Tom Brown's Universe: The Development of the Victorian Public School.* London: Millington, 1977.

Howe, Julia Ward. *Reminiscences, 1819–1899.* Boston and New York: Houghton, Mifflin and Company, 1900.

Hughes, Thomas. *Tom Brown's School-Days.* New York and London: Harper & Brothers, 1911.

Hurrell, J. D. "Some Days with Amélie Rives." *Lippincott's Monthly Magazine* 41 (April 1888): 532.

Ingram, Roderick R. "John Armstrong Chaloner's 'Movies for the Farmers.' " *The Magazine of Albemarle County History* 53 (1995): 58–69.

Insley, Rebecca H. "An Interview with Mrs. Astor." *The Delineator,* October 1908, 548–50, 638–39.

Jackson, Kenneth, ed. *The Encyclopedia of New York City.* New Haven, CT: Yale University Press; New York: New-York Historical Society, c1995.

James, William. *The Principles of Psychology.* 2 vols. Cambridge, MA: Harvard University Press, 1981.

———. *Essays in Psychical Research.* Cambridge, MA: Harvard University Press, 1986.

Kern, Dick, ed. *A History of Roanoke Rapids, N.C., 1890–1969.* Roanoke Rapids, NC: Herald Printing Company, Inc., 1969.

Keyes, Donald D., with additional essays by Linda Crocker Simmons, Estill Curtis Pennington, and William Nathaniel Banks. *George Cooke, 1793–1849.* Athens: Georgia Museum of Art, University of Georgia, 1991.

Lamb, G. F. *The Happiest Days.* London: Michael Joseph Ltd., 1959.

Lambert, Angela. *Unquiet Souls: A Social History of the Illustrious, Irreverent Intimate Group of British Aristocrats Known as "The Souls."* New York: Harper, 1984.

Langford, Gerald, ed. *Ingenue Among the Lions: The Letters of Emily Clark to Joseph Hergesheimer.* Austin: University of Texas Press, 1965.

Langhorne, Elizabeth. *The Golden Age of Albemarle: A Portrait Show, 1800–1860, The University of Virginia Art Museum, November 4–December 16, 1984.* Charlottesville: The University of Virginia Art Museum and the Albemarle County Historical Society, 1984.

Lay, K. Edward. *The Architecture of Jefferson Country: Charlottesville and Albemarle County, Virginia.* Charlottesville and London: University Press of Virginia, 2000.

Lay, K. Edward, and Martha Tuzson Stockton. "Castle Hill: The Walker Family Estate." *The Magazine of Albemarle County History* 52 (1994): 39–64.

Lehr, Elizabeth Drexel. *"King Lehr" and the Gilded Age.* Philadelphia and London: J. B. Lippincott, 1935.

Longest, George Calvin. "Amélie Rives Troubetzkoy: A Biography." Ph.D. thesis, University of Georgia, 1969.

———. *Three Virginia Writers: Mary Johnston, Thomas Nelson Page, and Amélie Rives Troubetzkoy: A Reference Guide.* Boston: G. K. Hall, 1978.

Lovering, Joseph P. *S. Weir Mitchell.* New York: Twayne Publishers, 1971.

Lucey, Donna M. *I Dwell in Possibility: Women Build a Nation, 1600–1920.* Washington, DC: National Geographic, 2001.

Mason, George C. *Newport and Its Cottages.* Boston: J. R. Osgood & Co., 1875.

Massie, Suzanne Williams, and Francis Archer Christian, eds. *Homes and Gardens in Old Virginia.* Richmond, VA: J. W. Ferguson, 1930.

McAllister, Ward. *Society As I Have Found It.* New York: Cassell Publishing Company, 1890.

Mead, Edward C. *Historic Homes of the South-West Mountains, Virginia.* Philadelphia and London: J. B. Lippincott, 1899.

Meade, Julian R. *I Live in Virginia.* New York and Toronto: Longmans, Green and Co., 1935.

Melville, Herman. "Bartleby the Scrivener." www.bartleby.com/129/.

Mitchell, S. Weir. *Fat and Blood: And How to Make Them.* Philadelphia: J. B. Lippincott, 1877.

"Silas Weir Mitchell." whonamedit.com.

Mixon, Wayne. "New Woman, Old Family: Passion, Gender, and Place in the Virginia Fiction of Amélie Rives." In *The Adaptable South: Essays in Honor of George Brown Tindall.* Edited by Elizabeth Jacoway, Dan T. Carter, Lester C. Lamon, and Robert C. McMath Jr., Baton Rouge: Louisiana State University Press, 1991.

Moody, Richard. *The Astor Place Riot.* Bloomington: Indiana University Press, 1958.

Mooney, Michael Macdonald. *Evelyn Nesbit and Stanford White: Love and Death in the Gilded Age.* New York: William Morrow and Company, 1976.

Moore, John Hammond. "Amelie Louise Rives and the Charge of the Light Brigade." *Virginia Magazine of History and Biography* 75, no. 1 (January 1967): 89–96.

Moore, Virginia. "Amélie Rives: A Personal Reminiscence." *The Magazine of Albemarle County History* 42 (1984): 91–105.

Morris, Lloyd R. *Incredible New York: High Life and Low Life of the Last Hundred Years.* New York: Random House, 1951.

Mosley, Leonard Oswald. *Curzon: The End of an Epoch.* London: Longmans, 1960.

Mount, Charles Merrill. *John Singer Sargent: A Biography.* New York: W. W. Norton & Company. New York, ca. 1955 (Kraus Reprint Co., 1969).

Nevins, Allan, ed. *The Diary of Philip Hone, 1828–1851.* New York: Dodd, Mead & Company, 1936.

Newman, John W. " 'Castle Hill,' The Home of Dr. Thomas Walker." *Kentucky Progress Magazine* 4, no. 8 (April 1932): 23, 32–33.

New York Hospital–Cornell Medical Center, Westchester Division, "The Beginning: Early History of Psychiatric Services at The New York Hospital." *Briefings: Centennial Edition,* 1994.

Nicolson, Nigel. *Mary Curzon.* New York: Harper & Row, 1977.

Nisbet, Charles. *The People's Select Cyclopedia.* London: Hodder and Stoughton, 1897.

O'Connor, Harvey. *The Astors.* New York: Alfred A. Knopf, 1941.

O'Connor, Richard. *The Golden Summers: An Antic History of Newport.* New York: Putnam, 1974.

Olson, Stanley. *John Singer Sargent: His Portrait.* London: Macmillan, 1986.

Oltmans, Thomas F., and Robert E. Emery. *Abnormal Psychology.* Upper Saddle River, NJ: Prentice-Hall, 2001.

Ormond, Richard, and Elaine Kilmurray. *John Singer Sargent: The Early Portraits.* New Haven, CT: Published for the Paul Mellon Centre for Studies in British Art by Yale University Press, 1998.

———. *John Singer Sargent: Portraits of the 1890s.* New Haven, CT: Published for the Paul Mellon Centre for Studies in British Art by Yale University Press, 2002.

[Parton, James]. "John Jacob Astor." *Harper's New Monthly Magazine* 30, no. 177 (February 1865): 308–23.

Patterson, Ada. "The Strange Case of John Armstrong Chaloner." *Human Life,* (November 1908): 12, 20.

Patterson, Jerry E. *Fifth Avenue: The Best Address.* New York: Rizzoli, 1998.

———. *The First Four Hundred: Mrs. Astor's New York in the Gilded Age.* New York: Rizzoli, 2000.

Porter, Kenneth Wiggins. *John Jacob Astor: Business Man.* 2 vols. Cambridge, MA: Harvard University Press, 1931.

Rein, David M. *S. Weir Mitchell as a Psychiatric Novelist.* New York: International Universities Press, 1952.

Reynolds, William W. "Merchant and Investor: Additional Chapters on the Career of Dr. Thomas Walker." *The Magazine of Albemarle County History* 52 (1994): 1–21.

Rittenhouse, Anne. "Little Matters of Good Taste: The Proper Observance of Mourning—What Different Members of the Family Should Wear." *The Delineator,* October 1908, 612, 615.

Rives, Amélie (Princess Troubetzkoy):

"Inja." *Harper's New Monthly Magazine* 76, no. 451 (December 1887). *A Brother to Dragons, and Other Old-Time Tales.* New York: Harper & Brothers, 1888.

Herod and Mariamne. A Tragedy. Philadelphia: J. B. Lippincott, 1888.

"The Quick or the Dead? A Study." *Lippincott's Monthly Magazine* 41, no. 244 (April 1888).

Virginia of Virginia, a Story. New York: Harper [1888].

The Quick or the Dead? A Study. Philadelphia: J. B. Lippincott, 1889.

The Witness of the Sun. Philadelphia: J. B. Lippincott, 1889.

According to Saint John. New York: J. W. Lovell, 1891.

Barbara Dering: A Sequel to the Quick or the Dead? Philadelphia: J. B. Lippincott, 1892.

"Innocence Versus Ignorance." *The North American Review* 160, no. 430 (September 1892): 287–92.

Athelwold. New York: Harper and Brothers, 1893.

Virginia of Virginia. New York and London: Harper & Brothers, 1901.

Shadows of Flames: A Novel. New York: Frederick A. Stokes Company, 1915.

World's End. New York: Grosset & Dunlap, 1916.

As the Wind Blew. New York: Frederick A. Stokes Company, 1920.

Rives, Barclay. "John Armstrong Chaloner: Albemarle Fantastic." *Albemarle* no. 15 (April–May 1990): 45–49.

———. "The Good Old Days at Keswick Horse Show." *Albemarle* no. 27 (April–May 1992): 35, 51–53.

———. *A History of Grace Church, Cismont, Walker's Parish*. Keswick, VA: Grace Church, Cismont, 1993.

———. *The 100 Year History of the Keswick Hunt Club*. Keswick, VA: Barclay Rives, 1996.

———. "Gertrude Potts Master by Heredity." *In & Around Horse Country* (December 1998–January 1999): 4–6.

Rives, Judith Page Walker. "By a Lady of Virginia." *Tales and Souvenirs of a Residence in Europe*. Philadelphia: Lea & Blanchard, 1842.

———. "The Autobiography of Mrs. William Cabell Rives." Unpublished typescript, Rives family papers, compiled by Elizabeth Langhorne, #10596-d, Special Collections, University of Virginia Library.

Robinson, Robert B., III, ed. *Roanoke Rapids: The First Hundred Years, 1897–1997*. Lawrenceville, VA: Brunswick Publishing Corporation, 1997.

Ronaldshay, Earl of. *The Life of Lord Curzon*. 3 vols. New York: Boni and Liveright, 1928.

Roth, Leland M. "Three Industrial Towns by McKim, Mead & White." *Journal of the Society of Architectural Historians* 38, no. 4 (December 1979): 317–47.

———. *McKim, Mead & White: Architects*. New York: Harper & Row, 1983.

Rugby School Register. Vol III. From May 1874 to May 1904. Revised and annotated by Rev. A. T. Michell. Rugby: Printed for subscribers by A. J. Lawrence, 1901.

Simon, Brian, and Ian Bradley, eds. *The Victorian Public School: Studies in the Development of an Educational Institution: A Symposium*. Dublin: Gill and Macmillan, 1975.

Sinclair, David. *Dynasty: The Astors and Their Times*. London: J. M. Dent & Sons Ltd., 1983.

Skeen, C. Edward. *John Armstrong, Jr., 1758–1843: A Biography*. Syracuse, NY: Syracuse University Press, 1981.

Slater, Kitty. "Castle Hill." *Spur Magazine*, July 1967, 42–46.

Sowle, Patrick. "Trials of a Virginia Unionist." *Virginia Magazine of History and Biography* 80, no. 1 (January 1972): 3–20.

Stein, Susan, ed. "La Bergerie / Rokeby." *Historic American Buildings Survey.* HABS No. NY-5623, National Park Service, Department of the Interior, 1981.

Taylor, Welford Dunaway. "Amélie Rives: A Virginia Princess." *Virginia Cavalcade* (Spring 1963): 11–17.

———. "A 'Soul' Remembers Oscar Wilde." *English Literature in Transition* 14, no. 1 (1971): 43–48.

———. *Amélie Rives (Princess Troubetzkoy).* New York: Twayne Publishers, 1973.

Thomas, Hugh. *Cuba: The Pursuit of Freedom.* New York: Harper & Row, 1971.

Thomas, Lately. *Sam Ward: King of the Lobby.* Boston: Houghton Mifflin and Company, 1965.

———. *A Pride of Lions: The Astor Orphans.* New York: William Morrow, 1971.

———. *The Astor Orphans: A Pride of Lions.* Albany, NY: Washington Park Press Ltd., 1999.

Van Urk, John Blan. *The Story of American Foxhunting from Challenge to Full Cry.* New York: The Derrydale Press, [c1940].

"Wakehurst." www.salve.edu / virtualtour / buildings / wakehurst.html.

Watt, George W. *Is the Liar In? Experiences of a Philadelphia Lawyer.* Clearwater, FL: 1948.

Wecter, Dixon. *The Saga of American Society: A Record of Social Aspiration, 1607–1937.* New York: Charles Scribner's Sons, 1970.

White, Hervey. "Autobiography." www.woodstocknation.org/ chanler.htm.

Willensky, Elliot, and Norval White, eds. *AIA Guide to New York City.* San Diego: Harcourt Brace Jovanovich, 1988.

"William B. Astor." *Harper's Weekly* 19, no. 990 (December 18, 1875): 1028.

Wilson, Derek A. *The Astors, 1763–1992: Landscape with Millionaires.* New York: St. Martin's Press, 1993.

SOURCES

Newspapers:

Boston Herald

Chicago Times-Herald

Colon Telegram, The (Panama)

Confederacy and Solid South, The

Daily Progress, The (Charlottesville, Virginia)

Milwaukee Sentinel, The

Nashville Appeal-Avalanche

New York Herald

New York Journal

New York Journal Sunday

New York Sun

New York Times

Newport Daily Observer

Newport Daily Season

Newport Mercury

Pittsburgh Gazette

Richmond Dispatch

Richmond News Leader

Roanoke News

San Francisco Call

Shreveport Times

Spirit of the Times

St. Louis Republic

St. Paul (Minnesota) *Pioneer Press*

Stafford (Kansas) *Democrat*

Sunday North American

Town Topics

World, The

Private Collections:

Margaret Chanler Aldrich Papers and the Elizabeth Chanler Chapman and John Jay Chapman Papers, courtesy Rokeby.

Chanler Papers, courtesy Bronson Winthrop Chanler.

Rives Family Papers, courtesy Barclay Rives.

Rives research, courtesy Welford Dunaway Taylor.

Amélie Rives letters, courtesy Louis Auchincloss.

Rives photos and memorabilia, courtesy Bette Potts.

Merry Mills photos, courtesy Ella Scantling Morris.

"Who's looney now" ephemera, courtesy Jeff Looney.

Amélie Rives photo, courtesy Eleanor Johnston.

Manuscript Collections:

University of Virginia Library, Special Collections:

Amélie Rives, Papers, 1830–1940, Accession #2495 and 2495-a.

Papers of Amélie Rives Troubetzkoy, 1931–1941, #9418.

Papers of Amélie Rives [manuscript], 1920–1938, #2411.

Amélie Rives, Papers, 1887–1936, #214.

Amélie Rives Troubetzkoy Collection, #214-d, 214-e.

Amélie Rives Chanler Troubetzkoy Papers, 1887–1920, #8925.

Amélie Rives, Papers, 1886–1941, in the Clifton Waller Barrett Library, #7208 [a–d].

Rives Family Papers, 1791–1908, #2313.

Papers of the Rives family, (1777) 1822–1945, #2532.

Letters of the Rives family, 1832–1882, #10596-c.

Rives Family Papers Compiled by Elizabeth Langhorne, 1839–1990, #10596-d.

Papers of the Rives, Sears and Rhinelander families, #10596.

John Armstrong Chaloner, Papers, 1881–1933, #38-394 [a–d].

Papers of John Armstrong Chaloner, 1897–1921, Accession #38-394-e.

William Cabell Rives Papers, 1824–1842, #11375.

William Cabell Rives Papers, 1861–1865, #38-348.

Papers of Thomas Nelson Page, #7581.

Papers of Louis Auchincloss, #9121-g.

Holsinger's Studio photographic negatives, #9862.

Ellen Glasgow Papers, 1880–1963, #5060.

Duke University, William R. Perkins Library, John Armstrong Chaloner Papers.

Harvard University, Houghton Library:

Winthrop and Margaret Terry Chanler Papers, bMS AM 1595.

Beatrice Ashley Chanler Papers, Bms AM 1311.

Thomas Bailey Aldrich Papers, Bms AM 1429.

Dartmouth College, Rauner Special Collections Library, The Papers of Augustus Saint-Gaudens.

Yale University, Beinecke Library:

Edith Wharton Papers, YCAL MSS 42.

Alfred Stieglitz/Georgia O'Keeffe Archive, YCAL MSS 85.

ZA Letter file.

Columbia University:

University Archives–Columbiana Library.

Avery Library, Stanford White Papers.

Archives of the Episcopal Diocese of New York.

New-York Historical Society, Stanford White file.

Virginia Historical Society, Rives Family Papers.

Valentine Richmond History Center.

Albemarle County Historical Society Collection.

College of Physicians of Philadelphia Library, Silas Weir Mitchell papers.

North Carolina State Archives.

Halifax County Library, Halifax, North Carolina.

British Library, Oriental and India Office Collections, Curzon Travel Diary, OIOC: MSS Eur F111/105.

Library of Congress:

Historic American Buildings Survey.

Papers of William C. Rives.

ACKNOWLEDGMENTS

This book would not have been possible without the extraordinary generosity and help of a number of people. I am first and foremost grateful to Archie's grandnephew, John Winthrop ("Wint") Aldrich, of New York and Rokeby. The undisputed family historian, he opened to me the rich treasure trove of manuscripts at Rokeby that make up the Margaret Chanler Aldrich Papers and the Elizabeth Chanler Chapman and John Jay Chapman Papers. He rummaged through forgotten corners of the estate to track down box upon box of family letters, and then carefully sorted through them to find material dealing with Archie and Amélie. He also kindly invited me to Rokeby, where I was able to breathe in the Chanler/Astor atmosphere with its heady mix of memory, faded grandeur, and intense pride. Family ghosts seemed to hover over the vast household, and I had my own encounter with one while sleeping on Mrs. William B. Astor's horsehair-stuffed mattress. Wint proved to be the perfect tour guide: erudite and knowledgeable about every bibelot and architectural detail in the house, and with an endless store of anecdotes about his distinguished and eccentric forebears. I am also indebted to Wint's brother Richard Aldrich and his wife, Ania, who welcomed me to Rokeby and shared their knowledge of the Chanler orphans and life on the estate during that era. In addition, Bronson ("Bim") and Evelyn Chanler at nearby Orlot kindly offered their hospitality, family papers, and stories of Archie. Other family members who provided me with useful information included Mrs. William Astor Chanler Jr., William Astor Chanler III, Peter White, Dr. William B. Carey, and Benjamin La Farge. I would also be remiss if I did not pay tribute to the deceased Lately Thomas, who wrote two magnificent volumes about the Chanler clan. I have made extensive use of his books, as well as his research notebooks.

In the Virginia countryside I had the great fortune to be guided by Amélie's distant cousin, Barclay Rives, who kindly shared his extensive family research, including original letters and photographs, fielded endless queries, and showed me around the grounds at Castle Hill. He and Sara Lee Barnes of Cloverfields farm introduced me to old-timers in the area who had personal memories of the Gilded Age couple. (Sara Lee even fixed meals to go along with the conversations.) Sara Lee's mother, Anne Rafferty Barnes, vividly recalled "Cousin Amélie," as well as visiting Archie in his cell-like bedroom. She also remembered Archie's ill-fitting false teeth, which riveted her attention as he savored chicken dinners—eating even the bones—at Cloverfields.

One of the high points of my research was having lunch with Louis Auchincloss at the Colony Club on Park Avenue in New York. He regaled me with stories of "The Princess," as he referred fondly to Amélie, and lent me original letters she had written to him in the late 1930s. After lunch, he pointed out the deep Chanler connection to the club: the portrait of Archie's sister Margaret, who was one of the founding members, and the ceiling of the members-only dining room that had been painted by Archie's brother Robert.

Judy Simpson-Kicq and Michel Kicq, the current owners of Archie's old estate, Merry Mills (now reverted to its earlier name, Merrie Mill), kindly gave me a tour of the house and grounds. The farm manager, Kim Radcliffe, lent me a useful book from Archie's era about the local estates, and a resident in one of the outbuildings, Larry Tharpe, offered stories that he had heard. Ella Scantling Morris, whose father had managed Merry Mills for Archie, recalled the estate during the 1920s and 1930s, shared her early photos, and showed me the Victrola that Archie had given her as a child. Two generations of the Chapman family—including Alexander, who was born at Castle Hill in 1910 and baptized at Merry Mills, and his wife, Elizabeth, who opened the gates for Archie when he was on horseback—offered critical insights into life on the local estates. Others with vivid stories of Archie and Amélie included Lyndell Dowell, Lee Gildea, Molly Cassell, and Sylvia Costen, who covered the sale at Castle Hill as a Richmond newspaper reporter.

I am exceedingly grateful to George and Lynn Worthington, who patiently allowed me to read and copy their collection of Archie's original correspondence. These letters proved pivotal in understanding Archie's personality and motivations, and my discovery of them was one of the great serendipitous moments in my research. While attending a church picnic at the old Merry Mills estate, I happened to overhear Worthington say that at a yard sale in the 1940s he had purchased a steamer trunk for $1. The trunk had belonged to Archie and inside it was a large cache of original letters. After introducing myself to Worthington, he kindly invited me to his farm and showed me the letters. (They are now part of the Chaloner collection at the Special Collections Library at the University of Virginia.)

Welford Dunaway Taylor, distinguished writer and retired James A. Bostwick Professor of English at the University of Richmond, selflessly lent me his many years' worth of research on Amélie. In 1971 he published a groundbreaking work on Amélie's literary career. "W.D." offered his unstinting encouragement, advice, and friendship during the project, all of which I treasured. Bette Potts, whose husband had been raised by Amélie's sister Gertrude, shared stories of life at Castle Hill and showed me her collection of paintings by Prince Troubetzkoy, as well as photographs and an opium pipe that belonged to Amélie. Bette's daughter, Jane Potts, also enthusiastically recounted stories from her father, and her own tales as a tour guide at Castle Hill.

Literary scholar George C. Longest, who wrote his dissertation on Amélie, discussed his research with me. Eleanor Johnston, whose stepfather had been a great friend of Amélie's, allowed me to use one of her photos, and Jeff Looney shared his collection of "Who's Looney Now?" cartoons.

In sorting through the tangle of Archie and Amélie's psychology, I was helped immeasurably by a number of experts. Dr. Irv

Gottesman, the renowned psychiatric geneticist from the University of Minnesota, carefully considered the possibilities regarding Archie's mental condition. Dr. Nancy Docherty from Kent State University generously read through a thick packet of Archie's writings and offered her opinion on his psychological state as evidenced by his use of language. Dr. Sy Rabinowitz, retired professor from the University of Virginia, read sections of the manuscript and offered fascinating insights into Amélie's character. Paul Lombardo, director of the Program in Law and Medicine at the Center for Biomedical Ethics at the University of Virginia, advised me on late nineteenth-century psychiatric record-keeping.

For an extended period, my home away from home was the Special Collections Library at the University of Virginia. The entire staff was extraordinarily helpful and efficient, but I must heap particular praise on the director of the library, Michael Plunkett, and the reference coordinators, Regina Rush and Margaret Hrabe. The Valentine Richmond History Center, a wonderful repository of Virginia history (one local described it to me as "the attic for Richmond's old families"), let me go backstage to look at Rives family material, including gowns, hats, and swords. Special thanks are in order for the costume curator, Suzanne Savery, and the photo archivist, Meghan Glass. Margaret O'Bryant at the Albemarle County Historical Society provided a helping hand when I was trying to pin down George Curzon's visit to Castle Hill. Other research librarians who proved to be especially helpful included Marilyn Pettit, director of the University Archives–Columbiana Library at Columbia University, and Thomas Ford at Harvard's Houghton Library.

I am deeply indebted to my dear friend Jane Colihan, who offered much-needed encouragement and photo assistance from afar and tracked down obscure publications in New York. Nathaniel Roberts in London tackled the Curzon papers at the British Library for me, and Christina D'Amico in Newport combed through original newspapers to gather research about that resort's gilded society. Thanks as well go to Catherine Zipf, professor at Salve Regina University. Sona Johnston, senior curator of painting and sculpture at the

Baltimore Museum of Art and expert on the nineteenth-century expatriate artist Theodore Robinson, scanned the artist's diaries for references to his friend Archie. She also tracked down Archie's old address in Paris and sent me a photo of the neighborhood as it appears today. Roberta Y. Arminio, director of research at the Ossining Historical Society provided in-depth information on St. John's School during Archie's matriculation there; and P. Hatfield, college archivist at Eton, fielded questions about Winty's academic career in England.

Lloyd Andrews spent an entire day showing me the sights and explaining the history of Archie's industrial creation, Roanoke Rapids, in North Carolina. Jim Kern, retired newspaper editor there, also provided helpful information. In my attempt to track down Archie's medical records at the old Bloomingdale Asylum, I am very grateful to Dr. Roger Christenfeld and Brad Edmondson. Marcia Miller, director of the library at the current psychiatric hospital in White Plains, provided me with research on the early days at Bloomingdale.

Neighbors and friends pitched in as well and deserve thanks: John and Margo Thompson weighed in on grammatical niceties, and their son Evan helped me distinguish a saber from a foil; Merle Aus offered animal lore; and Tom Whitehead provided much food for thought. Henry Stow Lovejoy III advised me on the legality of Archie's business dealings, and Annie Becker uncovered court records. Felicity and Guy Blundon inadvertently triggered the book by inviting me for an afternoon of beagling, during which I had my engaging conversation with Aggie Rives.

My insightful and long-suffering agent, Howard Morhaim, helped shape and launch the project, and Shaye Areheart remained patient as the research lengthened. My editor, Julia Pastore, deftly sharpened and improved the text, and was good humored in the face of ferocious deadline pressure. Hearty thanks go to Kate Kennedy, Jim Walsh, and Linnea Knollmueller, and to the designers Jennifer O'Connor and Elina Nudelman.

Finally, I must pay tribute to my two Henrys, husband and son, both brilliant writers who offered encouragement and love throughout the project. It was Henry Sr. who first stumbled onto Castle Hill when it was still a house museum in the 1980s. He pursued the story for a time, but put it aside and urged me to take it on. I demurred until after we had moved to Charlottesville and I had my fateful afternoon following a pack of hounds. Henry's early research was critical, as he had been able to contact sources who have since died. When I grew tangled in the difficult task of merging two biographies into one, Henry helped prune "my imaginative shrubs," as Amélie would say. Henry is my inspiration. I am ever in awe of his brilliance, talent, and high moral character. I dedicate this book to him with all my love.

INDEX

ABOUT THE AUTHOR

Donna M. Lucey is an award-winning writer and photo editor whose previous books include *Photographing Montana 1894–1928: The Life and Work of Evelyn Cameron* and *I Dwell in Possibility: Women Build a Nation 1600–1920.* She lives with her husband and son in Charlottesville, Virginia, where the story of Archie and Amélie is part of local lore.